Enhancing Literacy for All Students

S. Jay Kuder

Rowan University

Cindi Hasit

Rowan University

Merrill
Prentice Hall

Upper Saddle River, New Jersey
Columbus, Ohio

Library of Congress Cataloging in Publication Data

Kuder, S. Jay.
　　Enhancing literacy for all students/S. Jay Kuder, Cindi Hasit
　　　　p. cm.
　　Includes bibliographical references and index.
　　ISBN 0-13-011307-7 (alk. paper)
　　　　1. Language arts. 2. Language arts—Ability testing. 3. Literacy—Evaluation. I. Hasit, Cindi.
　　II. Title

LB1576.K85 2002
428.4—dc21　　　　　　　　　　　　　　　　　　　　　　　　　　2001054691

Vice President and Publisher: Jeffery W. Johnston
Executive Editor: Ann Castel Davis
Editorial Assistant: Keli Gemrich
Production Editor: Sheryl Glicker Langner
Production Coordination: UG/GGS Information Services, Inc.
Design Coordinator: Diane C. Lorenzo
Cover Designer: Linda Sorrels-Smith
Cover photo: Corbis Stock Market
Production Manager: Laura Messerly
Director of Marketing: Kevin Flanagan
Marketing Manager: Amy June
Marketing Coordinator: Barbara Koontz

This book was set in Palatino by UG/GGS Information Services, Inc. It was printed and bound by R.R. Donnelley & Sons Company. The cover was printed by Phoenix Color Corporation.

Photo Credits: p. 2, 26, 275 by Tom Watson/Merrill; p. 21 by Laima Druskis/PH College; p. 46 by Julie Peters/Merrill; p. 58, 172, 208 by Anthony Magnacca/Merrill; p. 82, 109, 219, 294, 301 by Anne Vega/Merrill; p. 96, 128, 158, 184, 234, 248, 264 by Scott Cunningham/Merrill; p. 320 by Dan Floss/Merrill; p. 331 by Barbara Schwartz/Merrill.

Pearson Education Ltd., *London*
Pearson Education Australia Pty. Limited, *Sydney*
Pearson Education Singapore, Pte. Ltd.
Pearson Education North Asia Ltd., *Hong Kong*
Pearson Education Canada, Ltd., *Toronto*
Pearson Educación de Mexico, S.A. de C.V
Pearson Education{md}Japan, *Tokyo*
Pearson Education Malaysia, Pte. Ltd.
Pearson Education, *Upper Saddle River, New Jersey*

Merrill
Prentice Hall

10 9 8 7 6 5 4 3 2 1
ISBN: 0-13-011307-7

Dedicated to

Julia, Emily, and Suzanne

and to

Eric, Arie, and Michele

because sometimes it takes three
to make a whole

About the Authors

■■ S. Jay Kuder, Ed.D.

S. Jay Kuder holds a doctoral degree in applied psycholinguistics from Boston University, where he studied with Dr. Paula Menyuk. His research interests continue to be in the field of language and reading development and disorders. Dr. Kuder is currently the Interim Dean of the Graduate School at Rowan University. He was formerly the chairperson of the Department of Special Educational Services/Instruction at Rowan.

Dr. Kuder is the author of a textbook entitled *Teaching Students with Language and Communication Disabilities*, published by Allyn and Bacon. His current research focuses on the literacy skills of children with mental retardation.

He is a member of the Council for Exceptional Children and the American Speech, Language, and Hearing Association and is a fellow of the American Association on Mental Retardation, where he has held various positions in the Communication Disorders subdivision.

■■ Cindi Hasit, Ph.D.

Cindi Hasit holds a doctoral degree in Language in Education and Educational Leadership from the University of Pennsylvania, where she studied with Dr. Morton Botel. Her research interests continue to be in the field of reading diabilities and appropriate assessments and instruction for at-risk learners. Dr. Hasit is currently the chairperson of the Department of Reading at Rowan University, and was Director of the Rowan University Reading Clinic.

Dr. Hasit is the author of several articles on reading development. Her current research focuses on classroom assessment of literacy behaviors.

She is a member of the International Reading Association, the College Reading Assocation, the National Council of Teachers of English, and the Association for Supervision and Curriculum Development.

Preface

Literacy—the development of skills in language, reading, and writing—is essential for success in school and in life after school. Therefore, it is critically important that all children acquire essential literacy skills. For this to occur, teachers and other education professionals must be aware of the latest developments in research on literacy. More importantly, they must be able to translate this research into useful instructional activities. It is our hope that this book will enable teachers and other educational professionals to do just that.

▮▮ EMERGENT LITERACY AND DIVERSITY

Two contemporary developments in the field of education prompted us to develop this book. One is the new perspectives offered by the emergent literacy model as a way to understand literacy development. The emergent literacy model recognizes the interrelationship of language, reading, and writing skills; the essential contribution of the home environment to the development of literacy skills; and the acceptance of a child's skills as the place to begin instruction rather than waiting for the development of prerequisite skills.

The second development is the movement toward diversity in the classroom. By diversity we mean not only racial and ethnic diversity but also the inclusion of children with diverse learning abilities as well as children who speak English as their second language. Many of these children experience significant difficulty acquiring literacy skills. In the past, such children may have been placed in specialized programs for children with special needs or in bilingual or English as a Second Language class. Today, most children with literacy difficulties, including some children with significant learning problems, are being educated in regular education classrooms. However, it has been our experience that few teachers feel adequately prepared to teach children with literacy difficulties in regular eduation classrooms.

We see these two developments, the emergent literacy model and classroom diversity, as complementary. The emergent literacy model suggests that literacy instruction begins at the point where the child is developmentally. There is no need to wait for the development of prerequisite skills. This model suggests that it is possible for children with diverse learning and language skills to participate together in classroom literacy activities. Each child will benefit from participating, but in different ways.

▌▌TEXT ORGANIZATION AND SPECIAL FEATURES

We have designed this text to be a comprehensive treatment of literacy development across the age and ability range. Content spans the developmental sequence from early childhood through high school. Throughout this book there is special emphasis on the modification of instruction so that children with special needs can participate in literacy activities in regular education classrooms. In addition, there are chapters devoted to the specialized techniques that may be required for children with significant literacy development difficulties and for children with severe disabilities. This latter population, though often served by special education professionals, is increasingly found in regular education classrooms.

We recognize that technology is becoming an increasingly important part of the instructional techniques used in schools. Therefore, we have included computer-based and web-based methods and materials throughout the text. In addition, each chapter contains a brief listing of websites that can be accessed for additional information.

Each chapter begins with a graphic organizer that presents an overview of the chapter content and ends with a set of questions that we call "linkages." These questions have been designed to help readers reflect on the chapter content and extend their learning rather than just recapitulate chapter content. Most chapters include case studies and/or classroom examples that we hope will facilitate the application of research to the classroom.

We hope you will find this text to be both informative and ueful. Our goal is to help you become a better-informed and more-effective education professional, ready to work with children with diverse skills and to collaborate with your peers.

▌▌ACKNOWLEDGMENTS

Any book reflects a lifetime of experience, not just the months and years specifically devoted to producing the text itself. Therefore, we would like to acknowledge some of those who have influenced our thoughts and development during the years, including:

The schoolchildren and their teachers with whom we have worked during the years who have challenged (and sometimes frustrated) us, but who have served as our inspiration and motivation for this project. We would like to especially acknowledge those teachers who allowed us into their classrooms, including Barbara Colton, Sharon Green, Zehava Halpern, and the fifth-grade teachers at the Johnson School in Cherry Hill, New Jersey.

To our university students, whose curiosity and questions have helped us to understand what they need from a textbook and how we might be able to meet that need.

To our mentors, Drs. Paula Menyuk and Diane Bryen for S. Jay Kuder and Drs. Morton Botel, J. Wesley Schneyer, and Jane Sullivan for Cindi Hasit. They provided the intellectual challenges and opportunities that helped guide us toward our career goals.

To the staff at Merrill, especially Ann Davis, who was always ready to offer encouragement and helpful suggestions, and to the reviewers who offered constructive criticism that helped strengthen this book. They include:

Kathleen Briseno, College of DuPage; Jim Burns, The College of St. Rose; Sheila Dunn, D'Youville College; Ann L. Lee, Bloomsburg University of Pennsylvania; Maurice Miller, Indiana State University; and Roberta Strosnider, Hood College.

Finally, but most importantly, we acknowledge our families, who have been supportive throughout this project. They often had to put up with our long hours away from home and our obsessions with this project. We thank them for their understanding and love. A special thank you to our spouses, Lucy Kuder and Yakir Hasit.

Discover the Companion Website Accompanying This Book

▌▌The Prentice Hall Companion Website: A Virtual Learning Environment

Technology is a constantly growing and changing aspect of our field that is creating a need for content and resources. To address this emerging need, Prentice Hall has developed an online learning environment for students and professors alike—Companion Websites—to support our textbooks.

In creating a Companion Website, our goal is to build on and enhance what the textbook already offers. For this reason, the content for each user-friendly website is organized by topic and provides the professor and student with a variety of meaningful resources. Common features of a Companion Website include:

▌▌For the Professor—

Every Companion Website integrates **Syllabus Manager**™, an online syllabus creation and management utility.

- **Syllabus Manager**™ provides you, the instructor, with an easy, step-by-step process to create and revise syllabi, with direct links into Companion Website and other online content without having to learn HTML.
- Students may log on to your syllabus during any study session. All they need to know is the web address for the Companion Website and the password you've assigned to your syllabus.
- After you have created a syllabus using **Syllabus Manager**™, students may enter the syllabus for their course section from any point in the Companion Website.
- Clicking on a date, the student is shown the list of activities for the assignment. The activities for each assignment are linked directly to actual content, saving time for students.

- Adding assignments consists of clicking on the desired due date, then filling in the details of the assignment—name of the assignment, instructions, and whether or not it is a one-time or repeating assignment.
- In addition, links to other activities can be created easily. If the activity is online, a URL can be entered in the space provided, and it will be linked automatically in the final syllabus.
- Your completed syllabus is hosted on our servers, allowing convenient updates from any computer on the Internet. Changes you make to your syllabus are immediately available to your students at their next logon.

▮▮ For the Student—

- **Topic Overviews**—outline key concepts in topic areas
- **Characteristics**—general information about each topic/disability covered on this website
- **Read About It**—a list of links to pertinent articles found on the Internet that cover each topic
- **Teaching Ideas**—links to articles that offer suggestions, ideas, and strategies for teaching students with disabilities
- **Web Links**—a wide range of websites that provide useful and current information related to each topic area
- **Resources**—a wide array of different resources for many of the pertinent topics and issues surrounding special education
- **Electronic Bluebook**—send homework or essays directly to your instructor's e-mail with this paperless form
- **Message Board**—serves as a virtual bulletin board to post—or respond to—questions or comments to/from a national audience
- **Chat**—real-time chat with anyone who is using the text anywhere in the country—ideal for discussion and study groups, class projects, etc.

To take advantage of these and other resources, please visit the *Enhancing Literacy for All Students* Companion Website at

www.prenhall.com/kuder

Contents

CHAPTER 3   Assessment   58

CHAPTER 4   Enhancing Emergent Literacy   96

NOTE: Every effort has been made to provide accurate and current Internet information in this book. However, the Internet and information posted on it are constantly changing, so it is inevitable that some of the Internet addresses listed in this textbook will change.

C H A P T E R

Foundations of Literacy

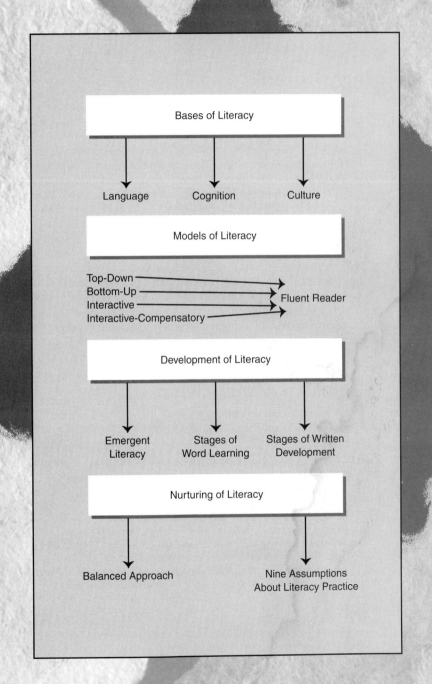

Bases of Literacy

Language　　　Cognition　　　Culture

Models of Literacy

Top-Down ─────────────▶
Bottom-Up ─────────────▶
Interactive ─────────────▶　Fluent Reader
Interactive-Compensatory ─────▶

Development of Literacy

Emergent　　　Stages of　　　Stages of Written
Literacy　　　Word Learning　　Development

Nurturing of Literacy

Balanced Approach　　　　　Nine Assumptions
　　　　　　　　　　　　　About Literacy Practice

Books are to be called for and supplied on the assumption that the process of reading is not a half-sleep; but in the highest sense an exercise, a gymnastic struggle; that the reader is to do something for himself.

Walt Whitman

▮▮ IN THE BEGINNING

The title of this book is *Enhancing Literacy for All Students*. Before delving into literacy development, we need to consider the term *what we mean by all students*. Picture yourself as a teacher in your first class. Consider the classroom filled with students eagerly attending to your words. Look closely at your students. Do they all look alike? Are their backgrounds the same? Are their abilities the same? The answer to all three questions is "probably not." Schools are now very diverse. Children come from different cultures, have different family structures, and may have widely differing abilities. Some students will be receiving special services. At times they may leave the classroom to receive these services. At other times, support personnel will be working with you in your classroom to help these children succeed. Your responsibility as a teacher is quite different from what it was 25 years ago. You need to develop instructional strategies that meet the needs of children with varying backgrounds and abilities. You will be collaborating more with other professionals than teachers did in the past. As you develop your understanding of literacy development, you need to always consider the ways in which you will deliver instruction to accommodate all the members of your classroom community. Literacy is for all students regardless of their cultural heritage, ethnic background, learning ability, or age.

Thinking About Literacy

Pat R. is a Language Arts Coordinator for a suburban school district. In frustration one day, she described the evolution of the reading program for her district. Listen to her words.

A few years ago we switched over from the traditional reading program to a literature-based one. Teachers used many trade books, and children were developing a great love of reading, but similar to many school districts which first introduced literature-based reading, some teachers interpreted this to mean no explicit phonics instruction. We saw reading scores actually decrease for some of our at-risk first graders. So this year we introduced a stand-alone phonics program, which we used in conjunction with the literature—We tested the children at the end of the year—I might add with great expectations—but I found that some of the at-risk children were still having trouble. They knew more sounds, but had so much trouble putting the sounds together that they forgot the beginning of the word by the time they sounded it all out! They still couldn't read a sentence. Now what?

As you read the preceding example, a great deal of it may have sounded familiar to you. Newspapers, television, and radio have been full of articles and programs about the "correct" way to teach reading. You may have already formed some opinions about this yourself. As you continue reading through this text, think about your initial beliefs about reading. Consider how your new knowledge will help to strengthen some of your beliefs and modify others (Box 1.1).

Now let's return to Pat's comments. Pat has considerable knowledge of literacy development and continually upgrades her knowledge through reading professional literature, attending conferences, and observing teachers and students. Her cogent comments remind us that reading is a complex mental activity. It extends beyond the act of mapping sounds to letters, but also involves using our knowledge of sound-letter correspondences to access words and extract meaning from print. Reading is a communicative act. Before we begin to respond to Pat's concern we need to develop a greater understanding of literacy and its development.

▍Box 1.1

Before you read any further in this chapter, jot down your memories of reading both in and out of school. When you think about learning to read, do you associate it with a particular person, event, or time in your life? Is it a positive or negative memory? After you complete your reflection, compare notes with a classmate. What did you find? Did you have the exact same memories? Were there similarities? How could people with different experiences still become literate? Think about this as you continue reading the chapter: What are the differences and what are the common experiences with literacy that all good readers have had?

As we begin our exploration of literacy development there are four major questions that we want to consider:

1. What is literacy and what does the reader bring to literacy development?
2. What are the characteristics of the mature, fluent reader/writer?
3. How does literacy develop in the young child?
4. What instructional practices have been shown to be effective in helping all children develop their literacy potential?

We will begin to answer these questions in this first chapter as we provide an overview of the reading process and literacy development. As we continue through the book we will address these questions in broader and deeper ways.

▍▍THE DEFINITION AND THE BASIS OF LITERACY

The Random House Dictionary of the English Language defines literacy as "the state of being literate, esp. the ability to read and write." The definition of literacy has been further extended to include the processes of reading, writing, speaking, listening, visualizing, and viewing. It is important to note that all these processes are connected and dependent on one another.

The dictionary definition, however, does not provide much actual information about literacy, for what does it mean to have the ability to read and write? A close examination of the reading process may provide more insight into literacy.

Reading is a complex, cognitive process, linguistic act, and social activity (Bloom & Green, 1984). It is an interaction between reader and text that, if completed successfully, results in the reader bringing meaning to the text and then obtaining new meaning from the text (Rosenblatt, 1969, 1978). The reader is not a passive vessel, waiting to have the knowledge from the text "poured in," but rather the reader must enter the reading act prepared to make sense of the text from his or her own perspective. The reader must be actively involved by using prior experiences, thought processes, attitudes, emotions, and interests to affect an understanding of the text. Although there are some common understandings when readers read, interpretations of reading will also vary from the unique perspective of the reader. One cannot, then, discuss the reading act without first examining the reader and what the reader brings to literacy development.

The Child as Language Learner—Language Development

Our understanding of the child as a language learner has undergone a tremendous transformation since the late 1950s. Prevailing theory of language acquisition at that time was based on the principles of behaviorism. According to behaviorist theory, language production resulted from operant conditioning, in which appropriate forms were rewarded and inappropriate ones punished, and from imitation. If the imitation appeared similar to the model, the child's utterances were rewarded, thus increasing the likelihood it would occur again. If the child's utterance was judged unsatisfactory, it was ignored. Children were viewed as passive recipients in language development (Piper, 1998).

From observations of children as they develop language conducted by researchers such as Lois Bloom (1970) and Roger Brown (1973) and changes in our theoretical understanding of language (e.g., Chomsky, 1957), it is now believed that language is not acquired merely through imitation and discrete teaching with the child as recipient, but that the child is a very active participant in discovering the rules of language and applying them in a more and more precise manner (Chomsky, 1968; Rice, 1996; Ruddell & Ruddell, 1994). Young language learners often produce forms that they have never heard, as in "carry you me" when they want someone to pick them up. In order for children to learn to speak, they must first be in a language environment. Studies of children who were raised with limited or no interaction with other people, sometimes known as feral children, have found that language as we know it does not develop without linguistic feedback (deVilliers & deVilliers, 1978).

Studies of children who are severely hearing impaired support the argument that language input is critical to language learning. These studies found that these children appear to babble like the hearing child for the first few months, but the babbling then decreases. Some degree of residual hearing is required for language to develop naturally (deVilliers & deVilliers, 1978). Humans appear to have a unique ability to use their language environment to discover the rules of their native language and to build theories using limited amounts of data and to build theories from which they can generate appropriate language (Chomsky, 1968; Menyuk, 1991). Although their earliest attempts are imperfect, most children develop language proficiency without explicit teaching. In observing language development, one must distinguish between receptive language, or the individual's ability to understand language, and language production, which involves speech. Although there is an interaction between the two, language competence may develop earlier than language production. It is not uncommon for parents of young children to exclaim that their child may not be talking, but understand everything that is said to them!

Stages of Language Development

In studying the language of young children, Roger Brown (1973) and colleagues described various stages of language development. Stages were described by mean length of utterance (MLU) (Box 1.2).

▌ Box 1.2

In his book entitled *A First Language* (1973), the Harvard University psychologist Roger Brown described the results of a remarkable effort by him and several of his talented students to document the early language development of three children—Adam, Eve, and Sarah. Brown developed a measure of syntactic development called mean length of utterance (MLU), which he used to describe the stages of language they observed. These stages provide a brief overview of the early development of the structural (syntactic) element of language:

- **Stage I (MLU = 1.0–2.0; Age = 12–26 months):** At this stage recognizable words begin to emerge, often following a period of wordlike utterances (pseudowords).
- **Stage II (MLU = 2.0–2.5; Age = 27–30 months):** The emergence of grammatical morphemes (prefixes, suffixes, prepositions, etc.) is the major development of this stage.
- **Stage III (MLU = 2.5–3.0; Age = 31–34 months):** At this stage, the major sentence types, such as negation, imperatives, and questions, begin to emerge and develop.
- **Stage IV (MLU = 3.0–3.75; Age = 35–40 months):** Stage IV marks the emergence of complex sentence types such as conjunctions and embedded sentences—sentences in which two or more clauses (a group of words with a subject and predicate) are joined together.
- **Stage V (MLU = 3.75–4.5; Age = 41–46 months):** At this stage, children continue to develop and refine the structures that emerged in earlier stages.

Although language development (and the ages at which various forms emerge) may vary somewhat from child to child, it generally occurs in the following sequence:

Birth to Age One: The earliest vocalizations are crying and "vegetative" sounds such as burping. Gradually, cooing sounds and babbling emerge. By about six months most babies show the intent to communicate, refusing things they do not want and pointing to items they seek. By the end of this period, most children are using true words, sometimes in combinations with other words or with wordlike utterances.

One to Two: Children begin to put words together into longer utterances. They match words with semantic intention, learning to say "No milk," for example, if they do not want milk. This period of language development is sometimes known as the "telegraphic" stage, as children typically drop out "functional" words such as "the" and "is" (e.g., "Kitty go.")

Two to Three: One of the major accomplishments of this period is the emergence of "grammatical morphemes," or word suffixes and prefixes. During this period, children typically acquire hundreds of new words, and their utterances become more fully formed.

Three to Four: During this stage of early language development, children begin to use a variety of sentence types (questions and negation as well as declarative utterances) and begin to use complex language forms such as conjunctions and embedded sentences.

Four to Five: By age five, the young child's language has taken on most of the features of adult language. They have acquired most of the grammatical rules of the language, have learned to match their language to objects and ideas (semantics), and have learned at least the basic rules for using language in social situations (pragmatics).

Components of Language

In their language development, children learn the phonological, morphological, syntactic, semantic, and pragmatic components of language. The different components interact in the child's attempts to obtain and produce meaning (Table 1.1).

Phonological

The phonological component comprises the appropriate sounds (phonemes) and sequencing of sounds in a particular language. Although many sounds are shared by languages, not all sounds exist in every language. English speakers, for example, have difficulty pronouncing the guttural *h* from German because it doesn't exist in English. In addition, language learners must learn the appropriate sequencing of sounds for their language. In English only a limited number of consonants may be combined and in only certain positions within a word. *Bk* is never combined within a single syllable. Similarly, *ng* may only be combined after a vowel, as in *ring* or *hanger*. In Vietnamese, in contrast, *Ng* may be placed in the beginning of the word as in the name, *Ngo*.

Morphological

The morphological component is the structure of words. A morpheme is the smallest unit of meaning within a word. It includes base words and the addition of word segments to denote changes in meaning, as in adding *s* to nouns to indicate plurals. Prefixes and suffixes, such as *un*important*ly* are other examples of morphemes. Language learning involves learning the different morphemes and using them appropriately (e.g., one adds *s* to *boy* to indicate plural, but one does not add *s* to *child* to indicate more than one).

Syntactic

The syntactic component is the grammar of the language or the appropriate order for strings of words. English speakers recognize that *"Lenup rikked the strop fleg"* is a possible sentence whereas *"Rikked because fleg"* is not. Why? This is because there are syntactic rules that govern the order of words in sentences. Children's developing syntax is often perplexing to the adult listener. Children may use terms such as *goed* or *runned.* The invention of these terms is evidence of the child's understanding of the basic syntactic structures of the language and of themselves as active hypothesis-developers (Wells, 1986). By kindergarten and first grade the majority of children are able to comprehend and produce expanded and elaborate sentences through the use of words, phrases, and clauses. Syntactic development continues well into and through elementary school (Ruddell & Ruddell, 1994).

Semantic

The semantic component is the meaning of language—the understanding of individual words and more complex units. Although *"Lenup rikked the strop fleg"* may be syntactically correct, it does not convey any meaning to the reader. Studies of the first words of children find that their meaning is consistent across children and languages. The language that develops first is that which is most important or interesting to children (Wells, 1986).

Pragmatic

The pragmatic component is the use of language. It comprises the social rules for communication. These include the rules for using language as, for example, greetings, turn-taking, and terms of address, as well as the rules surrounding the use of language, as in distance between speakers and use of hands while speaking. Speakers who share language and the uses of it belong to a speech community.

Despite the obvious complexity of the rules of language, most children appear to learn language quite effortlessly. In sum:

1. For most children language is learned without any explicit teaching. If you think back to your early days as a language learner or consider a young child you

TABLE 1.1 Definition of Language Elements

Element	Definition
Phonology	The sound system of language. Includes the rules that govern the combination and pronunciation of phonemes (the smallest unit of sound in a language).
Morphology	The rules that determine how sounds can be put together to make words. It includes rules for adding word prefixes and endings.
Syntax	The rules that govern how words are put together to make sentences. Includes phrase structure rules that describe how the major sentence elements (noun, verbs, adjectives, etc.) can be combined and the rules for moving elements around (transformational rules).
Semantics	Rules that govern which words can meaningfully go together.
Pragmatics	The rules that govern the use of language for communication. Includes the rules that govern communicative functions (or speech acts) and conversational rules.

know in the process of learning to speak, you see that children do not wait for instruction before attempting their own utterances. They learn by constructing their theories, making attempts at language, and receiving feedback. The feedback they receive is generally in the form of praise for their attempt and then modeling of the correct form rather than direct error correction. Thus, when Arie first asked for *muk*, his mother did not say, "No it's milk, now repeat it after me the correct way," but instead expressed her delight at this attempt and then told Arie, "Here's your milk."

2. Some children do not develop language spontaneously. About 3% of the general population has a language disability separate from general sensory or cognitive disabilities (Leske, 1981). If not addressed during the preschool years, these children are greatly at risk for reading difficulties. In approximately 40% of these children, the language-learning difficulties may be secondary to other disabilities such as hearing loss, limited intellectual ability, or atypical social/emotional functioning (Dublinske, 1981). For the remainder of the children, the language-learning disability is primary. These children do not have general intellectual disabilities; rather, they appear to have problems with "online linguistic processing" (Rice, 1996). A critical point to remember, however, is that even when children have difficulty acquiring language independently, language can be taught. As we will show in later chapters in this text, there are a number of procedures for teaching language. Although early intervention leads to greater success, it may be necessary to make adjustments throughout the school years as well.

3. Children use their knowledge of oral language to help them develop literacy. Their understanding of appropriate sounds, syntax, and semantics, as well as their ability to build theories about linguistic rules and generalize them appropriately with limited information, are all applied to written language as children come in contact with written materials.

The Child as Meaning Maker—Cognitive Development

In 1923 Jean Piaget, a Swiss psychologist, observed young children in their attempts to make sense of the world. From his observations Piaget developed his theory of human learning that continues to have great impact on our view of cognitive development and its effect on reading. Contrary to the prevailing belief that children were "tabulae rasae" (blank slates) waiting for knowledge to be poured into them, Piaget believed that children were actively involved in making their own meaning in the world (1996). Through experimentation with their world, children developed concepts about the world and their place in it. Central to Piaget's theory was the concept of schema. Schemata (plural of *schema*) are the organizational structures in the brain that allow us to store our existing knowledge and to add new knowledge. Through the process of adaptation learners either assimilate new knowledge into their existing schema or change their schema to accommodate the new knowledge. Young children may refer to all animals as dogs. At first they may define dogs as something that is black and shaggy, similar to their own dog. As they hear other breeds also referred to as dog, they assimilate that information and add it to their "dog schema." They may also define anything that crawls on all fours as dog. This overgeneralization leads to situations where they may chase cats, calling *doggie,* or even people, as Talia, a young learner, did when she saw 10-month-old Michele crawling on the carpet. As they gather more information about dogs and the differences among animals—and people—their schema changes to accommodate this new information. They now develop a schema for *animal,* with *dog* being defined as a certain type of animal.

The learner is, thus, an active participant in the learning process, receiving new knowledge, evaluating it according to previous knowledge, and then either adding it to existing schema or modifying schema as needed to assimilate the knowledge. As we will discuss later in the text, this has profound implications for reading instruction.

The Child as a Social Being—Cultural Influences

The pragmatic component of language is the use of language in social contexts. As should be apparent by now through the discussions of language and cognition, environment plays a critical role in human development. Children develop language for a purpose—to communicate to those around them. As their language develops, they learn different structures to communicate their intent. In describing the language development of children, Halliday (1969) defines seven models of language use:

- Instrumental: the simplest model and one of the first to evolve. Its purpose is to accomplish something, in its earliest stages, satisfaction of material needs, e.g., "I want."
- Regulatory: Its purpose is to regulate the behavior of others; e.g., "sit down."
- Interactional: Use of language in the interaction between self and others. Its purpose is to define and consolidate the group, include, exclude, or confer status.
- Personal: Awareness of language as a form of individuality and as a direct expression of feelings and attitudes.
- Heuristic: Language as a means of learning (e.g., question). When learning to read and write children need to learn the "language about language."
- Imaginative: Linguistic make-believe—may be rhythmic sequences of rhyming syllables (e.g., using a rhyme before or after someone's name when calling them; ill Bill or Hannah banana). Children's linguistic play reinforces this model.
- Representational: Means of expressing propositions.

The different models of language use are used with different frequencies as a child matures and to various degrees in different cultural groups. There may be, at times, a mismatch between the type of language used in school and found in some of the early reading texts and the language that the child has been exposed to in the home. In a landmark study, Shirley Brice Heath (1983) studied the language patterns of two *similar socioeconomic status* communities in the Piedmont section of the Carolinas: Trackton, a minority-culture community and Roadville, a nonminority-culture community. In her study she found that there were differences in the ways that parents spoke to young children, particularly in the types of questions that they asked them. In the Trackton community parents asked questions in order to obtain information, not to see whether a child knew something. Children's language was intended to extend the existing conversation. Children might be asked, for example, if they had seen someone, or what someone was doing. Questions were used to provide parents with information that they did not previously have. In Roadville, however, parents often questioned children to allow them to demonstrate their knowledge, as when parents point to their noses and ask the child, "What that is?" This type of questioning is more comparable to the types of questions that teachers ask in school, where they often question children to assess their knowledge. The children in the Trackton culture, not accustomed to this language use, may not understand the purpose of the question and, thus, not exhibit their knowledge. Teachers need to be aware of these language differences in order to differentiate between children's lack of knowledge and their unfamiliarity with the language structure. By understanding the child's culture and language development within that culture, the school can help the child bridge new school knowledge with home knowledge.

Teachers should be aware, not only of the oral language used in the home, but also of the absence or presence of a "literate environment." There is solid research (Durkin, 1966) about the positive effects of a literate environment on the child's literacy achievement. (See Chapters 4 and 11 for more detailed information.) Children who have been exposed to reading materials, have been read to, and have had opportunities to experiment with reading and writing before attending school generally find it easier to acquire reading skills. However, in our understanding of language development, teachers need to expand their concept of a literate environment. In some cultures, literacy may be embedded in activities (e.g., shopping lists, manuals). It may not be used for recreational purposes, but rather to extend knowledge in various ways (Moll, 1994). If one reflects on Piaget's schema theory, one sees that teachers' awareness of and willingness to utilize the different types of literacy present in diverse cultures can have an impact on the child's success with early literacy instruction.

MODELS OF READING—THE CHARACTERISTICS OF LITERACY

Various theorists have attempted to study the fluent reader and develop models of the reading process. An understanding of the strategies used by fluent readers leads to more informed decision making about reading instruction.

Although the models have been modified with the addition of newer research, they still are generally classified as "top-down," "bottom-up," and "interactive." Stanovich has also added a fourth model of the struggling reader, the "interactive compensatory" model.

Top-Down Model

Psycholinguistic theorists such as Kenneth Goodman (1967) have extended our understanding of language acquisition and learning to develop a model of literacy development. In the top-down model, the process of reading is analogous to the process of language acquisition. The fluent reader uses knowledge of the phonological, morphological, syntactic, and semantic elements of language to hypothesize about the text. Goodman postulates that the phonological element becomes less important as the reader matures, to the degree that it is rarely used by the fluent reader. The syntactic and semantic elements narrow one's choices so that one only needs to use a limited amount of phonological data to confirm one's expectations. To illustrate, look at the following sentence: "The father wrote a _____ to his son at college." From our knowledge of syntax we know that the blank space must be a noun. Further, it must be a noun that begins with a consonant. From our knowledge of semantics, we know that the blank must be something that is written, and from our prior knowledge about the situation we know that it will probably be something short and personal. This limits our possibilities to *note, letter, check, message, postcard,* and a few others. E-mail has been eliminated through syntax. If we then read the message and see "The father wrote a le_____ to his son at college," we need not analyze the word any further, as *letter* has been confirmed. Goodman differentiates between immediate word recognition, where a familiar word is recognized without analysis—such as the word *book* and mediated word recognition. Mediated word recognition is reserved for unfamiliar words, such as *strephosymbolia,* which is not a part of our vocabulary and thus requires some analysis of the parts. In Goodman's view the learner is an active participant who generates new knowledge through exposure to reading and writing and builds theories through contact with reading and writing materials. In place of instruction in the discrete elements of reading, instruction should center on encouraging the reader to make better hypotheses. Thus, in the top-down model, the reader's prior knowledge is of primary importance, not the elements of the text (Goodman, 1967).

Some psycholinguists accept the top-down model of the fluent reader, but differ in their views of instruction for the developing reader. They believe that developing readers need instruction in decoding print to maximize efficiency; mere exposure to reading and writing is not sufficient (Rozin & Gleitman, 1977).

Bottom-Up Model

In contrast to the top-down model, according to the bottom-up model the text is of primary importance. In the bottom-up model children learn to decode words and systematically move to larger and larger units from letter to syllable to word to phrase and onward in comprehension (Figure 1.1). A seminal work describing this model is "Toward a Theory of Automatic Information Process in Reading" by LaBerge and Samuels (1974). In the original model, the serial nature of the task was stressed. However, in revisiting the model, Samuels (1994) states that the beginning reader switches alternately from decoding to comprehension. Three major concepts form the core of this model. They are:

1. Alertness—the active attempt to come in contact with a source of information
2. Selectivity—the decision to switch attention as necessary
3. Limited capacity—the belief that an individual can only concentrate on one task at a time

Given this selectivity, Samuels postulates that it becomes important for the fluent reader to become automatic in decoding abilities in order to attend primarily to comprehending the text. The concept of *automaticity,* which is the automatic recognition of words so that decoding requires little attention, thus freeing the reader to focus on meaning, is a very important concept for instruction, particularly with children with reading disabilities.

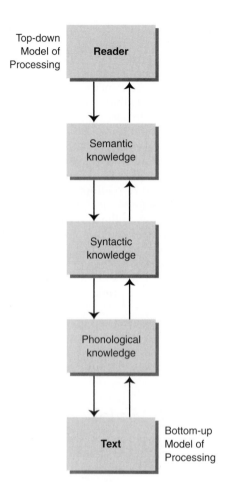

FIGURE 1.1

Models of Reading

Interactive Models

Interactive models share certain features with both the top-down and bottom-up models (Figure 1.2). The major difference is in the concept of parallel processing, rather than strict serial processing. In parallel processing, the reader engages in a number of tasks simultaneously, whereas in serial processing, the reader engages in each task sequentially. In the interactive models word recognition is necessary for comprehension to occur. The reader moves through a series of stages in which word recognition and comprehension interact with one another.

Interactive models have three major points, the first of which is that even in the adult fluent reader some attention is given to word recognition. The second point is that the role of context is not as great as once thought. Studies have failed to support the idea that good readers rely more on context for word recognition than poorer readers.

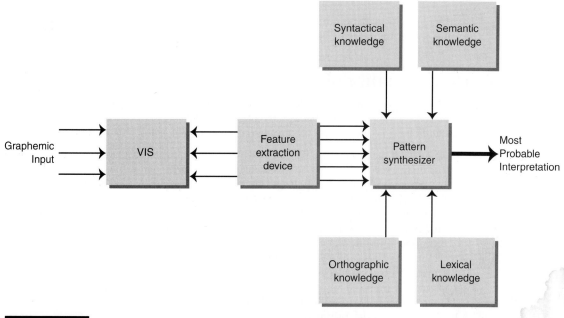

An Example of the Interactive Model of Reading
Source: From D. Rumelhart (1985). Toward an Interactive Model of Reading. In H. Singer, R. B. Ruddell, and
M. R. Ruddell (Eds.), *Theoretical models and processes of reading* (3rd ed., p. 736). Newark, DE: International Reading
Association. Copyright 1985 by the International Reading Association. Reprinted by permission of the International
Reading Association.

On the contrary, adult fluent readers appear to use less context whereas novice readers
do use context (Stanovich, 1993–1994, 1996). The final point is that phonological coding is important to word recognition in reading acquisition. In other words, knowledge
and use of sound–letter relationships is a necessary component of early reading development. The fluent reader, in these models, does not proceed sequentially from word
recognition to context, but uses various types of knowledge (e.g., phonological, syntactic, semantic, pragmatic, schematic, and discourse) in parallel to obtain meaning
from text.

Interactive-Compensatory Model

Stanovich (1980) presents a fourth model, with particular implications for disabled
readers. In this model the reading process is comprised of both top-down and bottom-
up processing, similar to the interactive models. The disabled reader, however, does
not use both efficiently, but rather selects the type of processing that is most comfortable. Thus, a disabled reader who has difficulty with decoding will strongly emphasize context in reading, giving little attention to the visual and phonological cues from
the text. Conversely, a reader with higher-order thinking difficulties will attend almost

exclusively to phonological data. This model suggests that instruction for disabled readers should include attention to strengthening the use of contextual clues as well as improving the use of phonological cues.

Commonality of Models—The Fluent Reader

At this point you may be wondering whether there is any agreement about the nature of the reading act. Despite some very explicit differences, however, one can see that there are certain concepts on which there is clear agreement.

- The fluent reader is actively involved; look back at the quote at the beginning of the chapter by Whitman. This is an accurate description of the reading act. The fluent reader does not approach the task passively, but expects to be actively involved in the process. While reading, the reader uses prior knowledge, forms questions, and makes predictions about the reading. The fluent reader is aware that reading must make sense and, thus, uses different strategies to gain meaning from the text. The fluent reader also interacts with the text on different levels. There is the cognitive level, or as Rosenblatt refers to it (1978) the efferent level, in which the reader focuses on the meaning of the text, and also the affective level, in which the reader is interacting on an emotional level. The fluent reader involves the whole self in the reading process.
- The fluent reader brings different types of knowledge to the reading act. Although differences exist in the weighting of the different types of knowledge and the sequence of use, there is common agreement that one must bring different types of knowledge to the reading act. The fluent reader integrates the different areas and uses them efficiently.
- The fluent reader comes to the reading act with a linguistic, cognitive, and cultural foundation. Language development, cognitive development, and cultural influences all affect reading acquisition. Variations exist among children, but before entering school, all children have a fund of knowledge that, if accessed appropriately, can facilitate the acquisition of literacy.
- The fluent reader understands that reading is a communicative act. The fluent reader focuses on the meaning of the text, expects to obtain meaning, and uses compensatory strategies when comprehension fails. By decoding text automatically, the fluent reader is able to attend to the meaning of the text.

As teachers, we can focus on the commonalities within the different models, and also recognize that the different models can help us understand differences among learners.

▪▪ THE DEVELOPMENT OF LITERACY

How does literacy develop in the child? In previous discussions in this chapter, we have seen that the foundations for literacy develop from birth, that the language and cognitive development of the preschool years have an impact on literacy. The presence of a literate environment also contributes to literacy development. Let us examine the child's developing knowledge of print.

Emergent Literacy vs. Reading Readiness

For many years educators talked about the concept of reading readiness. It was assumed that children needed certain prerequisite competencies before learning to read. In the early part of this century, reading readiness was defined as the attainment of a mental age of approximately six and a half. Gates and colleagues (1939), however, refuted this notion, replacing it with a model that placed emphasis on the acquisition of certain skills, such as color recognition, letter recognition, and sequencing ability. It was believed that children needed to acquire these particular skills before they could enter into formal reading instruction. The concept of reading readiness appears to say that there is a point when a child is not ready to read and a point when a child is ready to read. Although this concept may have worked for normally developing children, it had the effect of delaying or denying reading instruction to children who lacked reading readiness skills.

In more recent years reading readiness has been replaced with the concept of emergent literacy. In contrast to reading readiness, the concept of emergent literacy presumes that along with cognitive and language development, literacy development also begins in the preschool years. Further, literacy is an ongoing process. There is no one point at which a child is ready to learn to read, but rather, with exposure to diverse types of printed material, the child develops many literacy competencies from a very early age. Thus, "reading instruction" begins much before school age and is not dependent on the acquisition of prior competencies. Further, literacy competence may continue to develop throughout life as literacy demands increase and shift. With the advent of new technologies, for example, many people have had to learn new ways of interacting with print.

This conceptual shift from reading readiness to emergent literacy has had major implications for children with special needs because it has allowed many of them the access to literacy that had been denied previously.

Aspects of Emergent Literacy

From the first time a child holds a book or a pencil, sees an adult reading or writing, or looks at the signs for a favorite restaurant, he or she is learning something about literacy. As the child grows and develops so does his or her knowledge of literacy. As there is no finite point for beginning literacy, there is no finite point at which one can say that one is fully literate. As literacy demands change, our literacy development continues.

In her discussion of early reading, Mason (1984) describes three knowledge strands that develop when the young child first begins to encounter print:

- Concepts about print: As children begin to develop literacy, they need to understand that meaning is shared by both speech and print. They learn about word consistency, that *boy* is always boy, not sometimes Jeff or Sam. Young children at first may substitute synonyms or brand names for words. They may see a sign for hamburger and call it by their favorite fast-food restaurant. They also need to learn the concept of word, that in printed form it is bounded by white space. Word concept develops through the preschool years. Michele, listening to the tape for *Alice in Wonderland*, asked about "Allison"; the word boundary was not clear to her. Word concept is not always established by the time a child enters formal schooling.

- Form and structure of print: As children are exposed to printed material, they learn about letters and sounds. They need to learn the critical features of letters—that size does not matter, nor thickness or color, but line and curve do. Unlike objects, position in space may change a letter. To clarify this concept, a chair may be upside down, but it is still a chair. However, if one takes the letter *p* and turns it upside down, it becomes a *b* or if one rotates it right to left, it becomes a *q*. This understanding of letters continues to develop through the primary grades. It is not uncommon for first- and second-grade students to have difficulty with letter reversals and discrimination between certain letters.

  Children also begin to develop an awareness of the sounds in words. A term that you will encounter frequently throughout the book is *phonemic awareness*. Phonemic awareness is the understanding that words are made up of different sounds. Simple phonemic awareness is the ability to match or identify beginning sounds of words, tell how many sounds are within a word (e.g., cat has three sounds), and segment words into their sounds (Yopp, 1988). Phonemic awareness does not develop naturally in all children; the lack of it is considered to be one of the primary causes of reading disability in later years (Adams, 1990; Lyon, 1998; Snow, Burns, & Griffin, 1998). Fortunately, it can be taught.

- Conventions of print: The third major strand of emergent literacy is the conventions of print, or "book" knowledge. This area comprises learning where the front of the book, the back of the book, the top of the page, and bottom of the page are; how to turn pages; and reading from left to right in English. Children generally learn these from watching others reading and interacting with books.

Stages of Word Learning

As children begin to learn words, both prior to and during school years, there are developmental stages of word learning that have been identified. By recognizing these developmental stages and identifying children's stages, teachers can plan more appropriate literacy instruction (Ehri, 1996).

Logographic/Selective Cue Stage

At this stage children tend to look at words as wholes; they are not fully cognizant of the parts or letters in the words. They focus on the word as a picture and may use any clue within the word to help them remember it. For example, children may remember the length of the word, or the presence of "high" letters such as *l* or *t*. There is no systematic attempt at decoding the word at this stage.

Rudimentary Alphabetic Stage

At this stage children are becoming aware that words consist of letters and sounds. They begin to include letter cues in their attempts to recognize words. They are not consistent in their ability to do so, however, only partially using letter cues present within the word.

Alphabetic Stage

At this stage children have developed greater proficiency with letter–sound correspondences. They apply them consistently and in an orderly sequence in attempting to read unfamiliar words.

Orthographic Stage

Children have mastered the alphabetic system. They use their knowledge to generalize from known words to unknown words. Their reading is characterized by accuracy, but may still contain a number of self-corrections, as the children need to decode many words rather than recognizing them on sight.

Automatic Stage

This is the stage of the fluent reader. Reading is smooth and with expression. Most words are identified immediately with little attention being given to decoding of words. At this stage the reader's main attention is reserved for comprehension.

Writing Development: Stages of Spelling Development

Parallel to reading development, spelling and writing ability also appears to develop through predictable stages. These stages are often referred to as invented spelling, developmental spelling, or temporary spelling. The stages of spelling development begin during the early childhood years when children first begin to put pencil—or crayon—to paper and attempt to communicate through their scribbles. The stages represent characteristics of spelling strategies and may continue through high school (Bear & Barone, 1998; Gillet & Temple, 2000).

Prephonemic Stage

As children become more aware of print, they realize that meaning is conveyed through words and that words are made up of letters. Thus, at this early stage of spelling development, children abandon scribbles for letters. Not having a sense of phonemic awareness or sound–letter correspondence, however, their spelling usually has no relation to the word they're trying to convey, mainly consisting of random strings of letters.

Early Phonemic/Semiphonemic Stage

Children at this stage are beginning to acquire phonemic awareness (Henderson & Templeton, 1986). In their attempts they will often represent one or more of the sounds within the word. They may choose the initial sound as in writing *b* for *boy* or may represent the most salient sound in the word for them, as when Michele wrote *I   v u* for *I love you*. At the beginning of this stage, sounds are not represented completely and although the child may be able to read back her own writing, it is very difficult for an adult to do so. As the child moves through this stage toward the letter–name stage, more of the sounds within the word are represented.

Letter–Name Stage

At this stage children represent many of the sounds within the word. When in doubt, children at this stage appear to choose the letter whose name is closest to the sound they wish to represent. For example, they may write *breg* for *bring*, as the letter name *e* most closely represents the sound of short *i*. They often do not represent *m* or *n* before consonants and may write a syllable without a vowel.

Transitional and Derivational Stages

The child's spelling at this stage shows evidence of the child's understanding of phonic elements within words. At the early stage of transitional spelling, the child has generally mastered short vowel sounds within a single syllable. All sounds within the word are represented. Spellers have difficulty with long vowels, many prefixes and suffixes, and consonant doubling rules. As they progress through the transitional to the derivational stage, children's control of many of the letter features and combinations increases. They often, however, do not appear to use knowledge of similar morphemes to aid in their spelling.

■■ THE NURTURING OF LITERACY DEVELOPMENT: A BALANCED APPROACH TO LITERACY

As you have been reading about the foundations of literacy, characteristics of the fluent reader, and the development of literacy, you may have been wondering how all this information impacts on teaching. Perhaps a look at Sharon G.'s reading lesson will give a clearer picture of the relationship between the theory and the classroom.

Sharon G. teaches second grade in an ethnically diverse elementary school in a large urban area. She has 30 children in her class, 2 of whom receive special education services. The story that the class is reading is called "The Lost Button" from the book, *Frog and Toad Are Friends*.

Sharon begins the lesson on Monday by pairing up the children and having them talk to one another about a time that they lost something. She then brings them back to the large group for a group share. After the children have shared their experiences, they then write in their journals about the time when they lost something. As they are writing, Sharon circulates around the room, providing assistance as necessary. Jeffrey is at the early phonemic–semiphonemic stage of spelling, and his journal consists mainly of initial consonants. Sharon helps him listen for other sounds in the word and then writes his message on the left-hand side of his notebook so that he can read it back. Carla cannot get started with her writing. She is not sure even of initial sounds and is reluctant to put anything on paper. At this point in the year, Sharon has Carla dictate her story, which Sharon writes on the the left-hand side of the page. Carla then copies this into her journal. As Carla's reading and writing begin to develop, she will start to write letters on her own.

The next day, Sharon reads the story aloud to the class. As she reads, she shows the pictures, asks children for predictions, and links the story to the students' experiences. For the first reading Sharon reads the story completely through herself, dramatizing it through voice inflection and expression. She then reads the story a second time, this time having the children participate by reading certain lines and words with her, repeating certain lines, or reading them by themselves. During this reading Sharon will point out key words to the children. They will then divide into groups of four or five to begin reading the story with each other. During this time and the independent reading later in the week, Sharon will work with some children who need particular help with decoding. They will be receiving more intensive instruction.

In working with "The Lost Button," Sharon decides to focus on compound words. She begins her lesson by explaining what a compound word is and how it helps us to read "big" words. She provides examples for the students, showing them how the compound words consist of two smaller words. She then provides some compound words and asks the class to tell her which words they consist of. Next, Sharon divides them into groups (different groups from the previous day). They are given sentence strips (8 × 3) with compound words on them. They have to cut them apart and then form new compound words.

At subsequent times during the week, children engage in independent reading. Sharon has created color-coded cartons for her books and has divided them according to approximate reading level. Students choose books from the appropriate carton for their independent reading.

Sharon's lesson illustrated certain assumptions that we can make about effective literacy practice for all children.

> *Assumption One:* Children must be exposed to oral as well as written language during instruction. They should have many opportunities to speak and listen and to read and write. They should interact with one another, providing the opportunity to use their language and to listen to others. They should be placed in social situations that encourage the use of language for all students.
>
> *Assumption Two:* Children should be encouraged to activate their prior knowledge about a subject before being asked to read. They should have

Giving children many opportunities to interact with print facilitates literacy development.

opportunities to share their knowledge to enhance others' and to expand on their own. By activating prior knowledge, one is encouraging children to become active readers, continuously making decisions about their reading.

Assumption Three: Children can enter into the literacy act before they are proficient in reading and writing. Even before they are actual readers, they should listen to stories and books. They can begin to "write" before they actually see themselves as readers and writers. Good teachers encourage students to explore literacy and support them in their attempts. They are aware of their students' abilities and needs and provide experiences that not only allow them to feel successful, but also to grow in their literacy.

Assumption Four: Teachers should provide various amounts of support to children when introducing them to a story. They should begin by providing a great deal of support and then lessening that support and allowing children to assume more independence. In the preceding lesson, this was illustrated by beginning the story with a read-aloud, continuing with a shared reading, and then allowing the children to read in groups.

Assumption Five: Children should be given choices of reading material. In viewing the reading act as a transaction between reader and text, the uniqueness of the reader is seen as an integral component of reading. Self-selection of books enables children to read books that are of particular interest to them and that engage them. Teachers, however, can guide choices by providing a variety of material to allow children to read successfully. Instructional time should be provided for self-selected reading to ensure that all children have an opportunity to participate.

Assumption Six: Children must have many opportunities to explore literacy and have various interactions with print. As one sees from the models of reading, reading is an interaction of various types of knowledge. As children work with print in different contexts, they have an opportunity to use their knowledge and increase the efficacy of their strategies. In conjunction with this assumption, reading instruction should never be confined to addressing only one area of reading. Developing readers must receive support in developing decoding, discourse, syntactic, semantic, and pragmatic knowledge to become more effective readers. The intensity of the instruction for individual children may vary as necessary. Reading programs should encompass reading within meaningful contexts with attention to response and strategy, opportunities to write, word study, and self-selected reading.

Assumption Seven: Reading material for children should be at an appropriate level for them. In selecting instructional materials, one should be careful to choose materials that are within a student's zone of proximal development (Vygotsky, 1978), which is the range in which it is not too difficult for a person to learn, but neither is it too easy so that the child is not challenged to make any progress. Appropriate-level books should be readily available to children and should be organized to make selection easier.

Assumption Eight: Given the social nature of reading, children should have various interactions with language and print in varying social situations. Grouping should not remain static, nor solely based on one criterion. Groups can be established by need, interest, proximity, and many other bases. Children should be encouraged to contribute their own unique knowledge and abilities in various grouping patterns. Instruction should attend to helping children interact with one another and learning to work cooperatively to reach a goal.

Assumption Nine: Literacy instruction should focus on helping all learners develop the characteristics of fluent readers and writers. By providing appropriate instruction and support for learners, teachers can enhance all students' literacy development, thus helping them reach the goal of literacy.

▮▮ SUMMARY

Many new concepts were introduced in this chapter. The underlying concept is that in looking at reading in inclusive classrooms, one must look at both the reading act and the reader. Readers bring linguistic, cognitive, and social knowledge to the reading act. Their language, ways of thinking, and culture affect their view of and competency with reading. The fluent reader engages in various strategies and applies knowledge of text, language, print, and his or her environment to reading as necessary to obtain meaning. The concept of emergent literacy, in which the continuum of literacy knowledge and the developmental stages in reading and writing provide us with information about the learners, helps us to design instruction appropriately.

The complexity of the reading process and the reader support the belief that literacy instruction must provide a variety of experiences for children in supportive social situations. Based on our understanding of the nature of literacy and learners, we posit nine assumptions about literacy instruction. Good instruction should (1) expose children to oral and written language experiences, (2) develop and activate schema prior to reading, (3) allow children to enter into the literacy act at different stages, (4) provide different amounts of support as children read and write, (5) provide children with choices in their reading, (6) give children many opportunities to explore literacy, (7) provide reading material at an appropriate level for all children, (8) create different social situations for literacy interactions, and (9) focus on helping all learners become fluent readers and writers. As you read through the following chapters in this book, you will encounter more in-depth discussion of these ideas and the application of specific classroom techniques to enhance literacy development for all learners.

▮▮ Linkages

In the text
1. Determine the connections between the bases of literacy and the assumptions about literacy. How do the classroom assumptions consider the similarities and differences among learners in language, cognitive, and cultural bases?
2. Before continuing to the next section, think back to your early reading instruction. What model appeared to be the prevailing one for your instruction? Provide some examples.

Outside the text
1. Interview a teacher about the literacy program in his or her classroom. Determine how the teacher is addressing the assumptions about literacy presented in Chapter 1. What modifications could you consider making in your own classroom to address diverse needs of learners?

▰▰▰ ▪▪▪ On the Web

International Reading Association: Contains links to classroom activities, research, etc.
www.reading.org
Center for the Improvement of Early Reading Achievement
www.ciera.org/ciera/links

National Reading Panel: Has links to other research organizations.
www.nationalreadingpanel.org
LDOnline: Produced by WETA, a Washington, DC PBS station—links to many teacher resources.
www.ldonline.org
Learning First Alliance: An alliance of major educational organizations—provides research and
practical suggestions for teaching literacy and subjects.
www.learningfirst.org

▰▰▰ ▪▪▪ References

Adams, M. J. (1990). *Beginning to read: Thinking and learning about print.* Cambridge, MA: MIT Press.

Bear, D. R., & Barone, D. (1998). *Developing literacy: An integrated approach to assessment and instruction.* Boston: Houghton Mifflin.

Bloom, D., & Green, J. (1984). Directions in the sociolinguistic study of reading. In P. D. Pearson (Ed.), *Handbook of reading research* (pp. 395–422). New York: Longman.

Bloom, L. M. (1970). *Language development: Form and function in emerging grammars.* Cambridge, MA: MIT Press.

Brown, R. (1973). *A first language: The early stages.* Cambridge, MA: Harvard University Press.

Chomsky, N. (1957). *Syntactic structures.* The Hague: Mouton.

Chomsky, N. (1968). Language and the mind. *Psychology Today, 1,* 48–51, 66–68.

deVilliers, J. G., & deVilliers, P. A. (1978). *Language acquisition.* Cambridge, MA: Harvard University Press.

Dublinske, S. (1981). Action: School services. *Language, Speech, and Hearing Services in Schools, 12,* 192–200.

Durkin, D. (1966). *Children who read early.* New York: Teachers College Press.

Ehri, L. C. (1996). Development of the ability to read words. In R. Barr, M. Kamil, P. Mosenthal, & P. D. Pearson (Eds.), *Handbook of reading research* (Vol. II, pp. 383–417). Mahwah, NJ: Lawrence Erlbaum Associates.

Gates, A. I., Bond, G. L., & Russell, D. H. (1939). *Methods of determining reading readiness.* New York: Bureau of Publications, Teachers College, Columbia University.

Gillet, J. W., & Temple, C. (2000). *Understanding reading problems: Assessment and instruction.* New York: Longman.

Goodman, K. S. (1967). Reading: A psycholinguistic guessing game. *Journal of the Reading Specialist, 6,* 126–135.

Halliday, M. A. K. (1969). Relevant models of language. *Educational Review, 22,* 26–37.

Heath, S. B. (1983). *Ways with words: Language, life, and work in communities and classrooms.* Cambridge, England: Cambridge University Press.

Henderson, E., & Templeton, S. (1986). A developmental perspective of formal spelling instruction through alphabet, pattern, and meaning. *Elementary School Journal, 86,* 305–316.

LaBerge, D., & Samuels, S. J. (1974). Toward a theory of automatic information processing in reading. *Cognitive Psychology, 6,* 293–323.

Leske, M. C. (1981). Speech prevalence estimates of communicative disorders in the U.S. *ASHA, 23,* 229–237.

Lyon, G. R. (1998). Why reading is not a natural process. *Educational Leadership, 55,* 14–18.

Mason, J. (1984). Early reading from a developmental perspective. In P. D. Pearson (Ed.), *Handbook of reading research* (pp. 505–543). New York: Longman.

Menyuk, P. (1991). Linguistics and teaching the language arts. In J. F. Flood, J. M. Jensen, D. Lapp, & J. R. Squire (Eds.), *Handbook of research on teaching the English language arts* (pp. 24–29). New York: Macmillan.

Moll, L. C. (1994). Literacy research in community and classrooms: A sociocultural approach. In R. B. Ruddell, M. R. Ruddell & H. Singer (Eds.), *Theoretical models and processes of reading* (pp. 179–207). Newark, DE: International Reading Association.

Piaget, J. (1996). The language and thought of the child. In B. M. Power & R. S. Hubbard (Eds.), *Language development: A reader for teachers* (pp. 18–21). Upper Saddle River, NJ: Prentice Hall.

Piper, T. (1998). *Language and learning: The home and school years.* Upper Saddle River, NJ: Prentice Hall.

Rice, M. L. (1996). Children's language acquisition. In B. M. Power & R. S. Hubbard (Eds.), *Language development: A reader for teachers* (pp. 3–12). Upper Saddle River, NJ: Prentice Hall.

Rosenblatt, L. (1969). Towards a transactional theory of reading. *Journal of Reading Behavior, 1*(1), 31–49.

Rosenblatt, L. (1978). *The reader, the text, the poem: The transactional theory of the literary work.* Carbondale, IL: Southern Illinois University Press.

Rozin, P., & Gleitman, L. (1977). The structure and acquisition of reading II. The reading process and the acquisition of the alphabetic principle. In A. Reber & D. Scarborough (Eds.), *Toward a psychology of reading* (pp. 55–141). Hillsdale, NJ: Lawrence Erlbaum Associates.

Ruddell, R. B., & Ruddell, M. R. (1994). Language acquisition and literacy processes. In R. B. Ruddell, M. R. Ruddell, & H. Singer (Eds.), *Theoretical models and processes of reading* (pp. 83–103). Newark, DE: International Reading Association.

Samuels, S. J. (1994). Toward a theory of automatic information processing in reading revisited. In R. B. Ruddell, M. R. Ruddell, & H. Singer (Eds.), *Theoretical models and processes of reading* (pp. 816–837). Newark, DE: International Reading Association.

Snow, C. E., Burns, S., & Griffin, P. (Eds.). (1998). *Preventing reading difficulties in young children.* Washington, DC: National Academy Press.

Stanovich, K. (1996). Word recognition: Changing perspectives. In R. Barr, M. Kamil, P. Mosenthal, & P. D. Pearson (Eds.), *Handbook of reading research* (Vol. II, pp. 418–452). Mahwah, NJ: Lawrence Erlbaum Associates.

Stanovich, K. E. (1980). Toward an interactive-compensatory model of individual differences in the development of reading fluency. *Reading Research Quarterly, 16,* 32–71.

Stanovich, K. E. (1993–1994). Romance and society. *The Reading Teacher, 47,* 280–291.

Stein, J. (Ed.). (1983). *The Random House dictionary of the English language.* New York: Random House, Inc.

Vygotsky, L. S. (1978). *Mind in society: The development of higher psychological processes.* Cambridge, MA: Harvard University Press.

Wells, G. (1986). *The meaning makers: Children learning language and using language to learn.* Portsmouth, NH: Heinemann.

Yopp, H. K. (1988). The validity and reliability of phonemic awareness tests. *Reading Research Quarterly, 23,* 159–177.

C H A P T E R

Literacy Difficulties

2

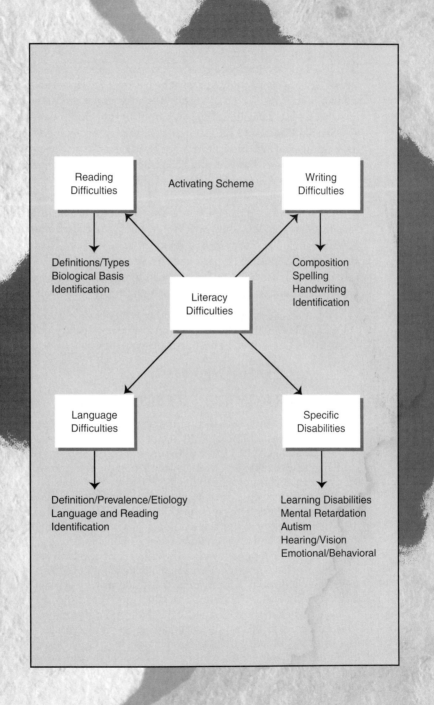

Reading
Difficulties

Activating Scheme

Writing
Difficulties

Definitions/Types
Biological Basis
Identification

Literacy
Difficulties

Composition
Spelling
Handwriting
Identification

Language
Difficulties

Specific
Disabilities

Definition/Prevalence/Etiology
Language and Reading
Identification

Learning Disabilities
Mental Retardation
Autism
Hearing/Vision
Emotional/Behavioral

The graphic representation indicates that the focus of this chapter is on literacy difficulties. There are four major subtopics: reading difficulties, writing difficulties, language difficulties, and literacy difficulties related to specific disabilities.

Steven is a 10-year-old boy in third grade. Steven struggles with reading. When asked to read material at his grade level, Steven reads slowly, with frequent stops and starts. It can take him several minutes to read one paragraph. Yet, after finishing the paragraph he can answer several questions about what he has read. Steven's teachers describe him as a good student who is motivated to read. He is achieving at grade level in math. Steven's father says that he had difficulty reading in school and still does not enjoy reading.

Sarah, a 12-year-old student in sixth grade, has significant difficulty writing. When asked to write an essay, her thoughts are not clearly expressed. There is a lack of connection between ideas. There is little or no elaboration of topics. Her spelling is poor, and words are frequently used incorrectly. Sarah does not like to write and has difficulty finding the errors in her writing.

Sarita is 8 years old and experiencing significant problems in school. Her teachers believe that Sarita understands what is going on in the classroom, but they just can't seem to get through to her. Sarita is very reluctant to talk in class. When she does talk she is so quiet that it is difficult to hear her. She also seems unable to follow directions in class. Sarita's hearing has been tested and is in the normal range. Her parents report that she talks a lot at home, although they notice that she is quiet around other people.

Why are these students having difficulty with reading, writing, and speaking? What, if anything, do they have in common? Most importantly, what can be done for students such as those described? These are questions that will be addressed in this chapter.

▪▪ WHAT ARE LITERACY DIFFICULTIES?

Each of the students described at the beginning of this chapter has some sort of difficulty with literacy. Literacy difficulties include problems with reading, writing, and spoken language. When these difficulties are so significant that they interfere with the student's ability to benefit from instruction in the classroom or affect social interaction, they may be considered disabilities.

Literacy difficulties are commonly thought of as including problems in reading and writing. We include language difficulties as well, because we believe that language ability is the foundation on which reading and writing skills are built. This broader view of literacy claims that there is an interactive relationship between language and literacy. Not only does spoken language influence written language, but the acquisition of written language skills affects the development of spoken language skills as well (Wallach & Butler, 1995). It should come as no surprise that students with spoken language difficulties have difficulty with written language acquisition and that difficulty with written language can have an impact on the continued acquisition and development of spoken language.

Difficulties in literacy—reading, writing, and language usage—occur at a surprisingly high frequency. Although it is not easy to assign an exact number to the frequency of literacy difficulties, the National Assessment of Education Progress (NAEP) has indicated that in 2000 37% of all fourth graders fell below the "basic" level of proficiency. Other estimates have put the prevalence of reading disabilities at between 5 to 20% of

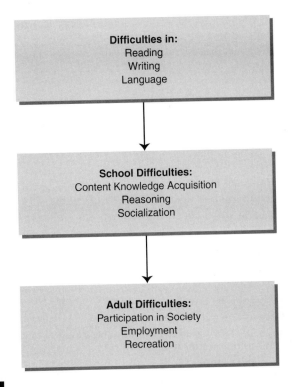

FIGURE 2.1

The impact of literacy difficulties

the school-age population (Shaywitz et al., 1992). Although the precise numbers are difficult to determine because of problems in definition and measurement, there can be little doubt that literacy difficulties are a significant problem.

Literacy disabilities may have profoundly negative effects on the success of children in school. For example, children with significant reading difficulties are at risk for failure in all of the school content areas that rely on textbooks (Blanton & Blanton, 1994). In addition, students with difficulties in reading may be unable to demonstrate higher-order thinking abilities because they lack the vocabulary and concept knowledge that accrue through reading (Snider & Tarver, 1987).

The impact of literacy difficulties is not limited to school or to children. Researchers who have followed children with reading difficulties have found that deficits in reading and spelling can persist into early adulthood (Korhonen, 1995). Similarly, studies of adults with learning disabilities have found that these difficulties do not disappear but, for many individuals, continue to cause problems in domains such as employment, leisure activities, and relationships (White, 1992; Cronin & Patton, 1993).

In summary, many children experience difficulty with early literacy development. These difficulties cause children to fail not only in reading and writing, but in all of the subject areas because of the effects on knowledge acquisition. Moreover, as illustrated in Figure 2.1, literacy difficulties may continue throughout life and limit one's knowledge of and participation in school, work, and the community.

Thus far, we have considered literacy difficulties as a whole to emphasize the interrelatedness among literacy skills. However, much of the research on literacy difficulties has been conducted within specific disciplines such as reading, writing, and language. Therefore, in the next section we will examine research on these specific skills.

READING DIFFICULTIES
Definition and Types

Think back to the case of "Steven" that is described at the beginning of this chapter. What might be causing Steven's difficulties with reading? His teacher reports that he seems to understand what is being said in class. He can answer questions when they are given to him orally. He has no apparent speech or language difficulties. He appears to be motivated to read. Yet, when given a grade-level passage to read, Steven struggles to identify the words. He reads painfully slowly, attempting to sound out each word as he goes. He substitutes sounds; for example, reading *monkey* as *donkey* and sometimes misreading entire words (e.g., *their* read as *through*). Despite these errors, when he finishes a paragraph, he can actually remember quite a bit of what he has read.

Cases such as Steven's have puzzled and challenged the medical and educational communities for more than a hundred years. Similar cases have been reported throughout history (Box 2.1). In all of these cases, the individuals involved appeared to have average to above-average intelligence, had no apparent disabilities, and appeared to have no surface impediments to successful reading. Yet, they struggled to read.

Box 2.1

A REPORT OF ALEXIA (READING DISABILITY)

In October 1887, Monsieur C., a French businessman in his late sixties who had amassed a fortune selling woven goods, experienced several attacks of numbness in his right leg, some feebleness in his arms, and a slight difficulty in speaking. These symptoms soon disappeared, and C. went back to work and thought little more about it, until he discovered that, while able to distinguish objects and persons without any difficulty, he could not read a single word. C. made an appointment with his ophthalmologist in order to be fitted with an adequate pair of glasses.

Much to C.'s surprise, the ophthalmologist, the world-renowned Edward Landolt, did not prescribe glasses. Instead, after a careful examination, he referred C. to an equally eminent colleague, Joseph Dejerine, neurologist at the Bicetre Hospital in Paris. . . . C's reading difficulty, the two men agreed, could not be rectified by glasses because it had nothing to do with visual acuity. C. had suffered a relatively rare yet fascinating type of stroke, which, while having little effect on his general perceptual capacity, had made it impossible for him to see objects in one-half of his visual field and had destroyed his capacity to read. . . .

Surprisingly, however, C. was able to express himself without difficulty, to recognize and name instantaneously obscure technical and scientific instruments, to understand everything said to him, and to recall the most minute details of past events. Even more astonishingly, he could still write without difficulty, both expressing his thoughts spontaneously and describing what was dictated to him; yet he was quite unable to decipher his own handwriting.

Source: Gardner, H. (1974). *The shattered mind.* New York: Vintage (pp. 114–115).

Numerous labels have been applied to the difficulty experienced by students like Steven and the individuals described in the case studies discussed previously. Children like Steven may be called "poor readers," "reading disabled," or even "dyslexic."

Dyslexia is a controversial term that has been defined in various ways. In her review of the history of dyslexia, Sylvia Richardson (1992) explains that the term *dyslexia* was coined to describe patients who had difficulty reading due to cerebral disease. Until recently, researchers have generally assumed that dyslexia is a particular kind of severe reading disorder, distinct from other reading difficulties, with an underlying neurological cause. However, some researchers have now claimed that dyslexia is not a distinct disorder, but is simply a more severe form of reading disability (Shaywitz et al., 1992). Later in this chapter we will examine the research on dyslexia in more detail.

The *Diagnostic and Statistical Manual of Mental Disorders* (DSM-IV), defines reading disorder as "Reading achievement . . . that falls substantially below that expected given the individual's chronological age, measured intelligence, and age-appropriate education" (p. 48). The definition describes the oral reading of individuals with reading difficulties as "characterized by distortions, substitutions, or omissions" and describes both oral and silent reading as "characterized by slowness and errors in comprehension" (p. 48) (Table 2.1).

Note that this definition lists three criteria that must be met before a reading difficulty can be considered a disorder. The individual must:

- Be reading below chronological age
- Be reading below the level that would be expected for their level of intelligence
- Have received an age-appropriate education

TABLE 2.1	DSM-IV Definition of Reading Disorder

Diagnostic Features	
Criterion A:	Reading achievement . . . that falls substantially below that expected given the individual's chronological age, measured intelligence, and age-appropriate education.
Criterion B:	There is significant interference with academic achievement or with activities of daily living that require reading skills.
Criterion C:	For individuals with sensory deficits, the reading disorder is greater than would be expected due to the sensory disorder.
Oral reading:	Characterized by distortions, substitutions, or omissions.
Oral and silent reading:	Characterized by slowness and errors in comprehension.

Source: American Psychiatric Association (1994). *Diagnostic and Statistical Manual of Mental Disorders,* (4th ed.). Washington, DC: American Psychiatric Association.

Within this seemingly simple and straightforward definition are the seeds of great controversy about the definition of reading difficulties. Some of the issues raised by this definition are:

- **Discrepancy between reading performance and intelligence:** Must there be a discrepancy between intelligence and reading performance in order for a reading disorder to exist? Are there real differences between children who demonstrate this discrepancy and those whose reading performance and measured intelligence are similar?
- **Cause of reading difficulties:** The definition takes no position regarding the probable cause of reading difficulties. Although this is certainly a safe position, it is not helpful to those looking for ways to identify and remediate serious reading problems.
- **Distinction between dyslexia and other reading difficulties:** Is dyslexia a separate and distinct type of reading disorder or is it just another name for severe reading difficulties?

Each of these points will be examined in more detail.

Discrepancy Between Reading Performance and Intelligence

Most definitions of reading difficulties claim that there must be a discrepancy between reading achievement levels and intelligence level in order for a child to be identified as reading disabled. In other words, a child with average intelligence who is reading significantly below grade level would be considered to have a reading disorder. However, another child with below-average intelligence who was reading at the same level would not be considered to have a reading disability. They might be called just "poor readers" or, as Gough and Tunmer (1986) called them, "garden-variety" poor readers.

However, there is increasing evidence that there are few, if any, differences between children whose reading performance differs significantly from their measured intelligence and children whose reading scores and intelligence scores are both lower than expected (Stanovich, 1991; Fletcher, 1992). Although a few studies have reported specific differences (e.g., Aaron, 1987) most researchers have found no difference between students who had a discrepancy between intelligence and reading performance and "garden-variety" poor readers on reading, spelling, language, and cognitive measures (for example, Fletcher, 1992; Siegel, 1992).

The research suggests that it may not make sense to use intelligence as a factor in the determination of reading difficulties in beginning readers. Rather, what is most important is that the child is having difficulty reading. In addition, the research results imply that reading instructional methods may be useful for all students with reading difficulty.

Causes and Correlates of Reading Difficulties

The question of what causes reading difficulties has occupied researchers for many years. Two types of factors have generally been identified as contributing to reading disorders—**intrinsic** factors (those that are within the child) and **extrinsic** factors (such as reading instruction and the home environment).

Intrinsic factors: Throughout most of the history of research on reading difficulties, the prevailing view was that reading difficulties were caused by underlying visual deficits. In some cases, vision exercises were prescribed as a way of alleviating reading difficulties. However, with a few exceptions, research has failed to find significant visual processing problems in children with reading difficulties (Vellutino, 1979).

Cognitive factors, such as memory and attention, and perceptual abilities, including visual and auditory perception, have also been suggested as possible causes of reading difficulties. However, these problems seem to be more the result of other factors (e.g., overall intelligence and language abilities) rather than a direct cause of reading problems. Although children with reading difficulties are often reported to have a higher incidence of attention problems than good readers (e.g., Silver, 1981), there is little evidence that attention problems cause reading difficulties (Shaywitz et al., 1995). Likewise, although children with reading difficulties may have some difficulty discriminating letters and identifying speech sounds, there is little evidence for a general perceptual processing problem in most children with reading difficulties (Mody, Studdert–Kennedy, & Brady, 1997).

If cognitive and perceptual factors are not the cause of reading difficulties, what does underlie reading difficulty? There is a growing consensus that reading difficulties are caused by underlying language difficulties. Delays and/or differences in a number of language skills have been associated with reading disabilities, but the one language skill most frequently associated with reading difficulties is phonological processing (Olson, 1994).

In the process of language acquisition, children learn to identify the sounds of their language. Exactly how they do this remains a mystery, but that they do it is shown by their sensitivity to sound changes (Eimas et al., 1971) and their ability to identify where one word stops and the next begins. They have an implicit knowledge of the sound system of their language, but would be hard pressed to identify the individual sounds if asked to do so. However, when children begin to learn to read they are asked to make this implicit knowledge explicit. They are asked to break words down into their individual sounds (phonology) and to associate sounds with letters (phonics). The process of making implicit knowledge about the sound system (phonology) of the language explicit is called phonological (or phonemic) awareness.

Most children have little difficulty developing phonological awareness, but a significant number do have difficulty (Lyon, 1995). There is evidence that phonological processing is related to successful word reading (Liberman, Shankweiler, & Liberman, 1989) and that beginning readers with good phonological skills are more successful than children with poor phonological awareness (Byrne, Freebody, & Gates, 1992). Similarly, there are now dozens of studies that have found that poor readers have poor phonological awareness (e.g., Bradley & Bryant, 1978; Gough & Tunmer, 1986; Stanovich, 1991). Children with poor phonological skills are likely to have difficulty identifying sounds within words, breaking words down into smaller units (syllables and phonemes—individual sounds), and with rhyming. Even more significantly, several research studies have demonstrated that teaching phonological skills can have a positive effect on reading performance (e.g., Ball & Blachman, 1991; Bradley & Bryant, 1985; Torgesen, Morgan, & Davis, 1992).

The large and ever-growing research base on phonological processing, reading, and reading difficulties has led experts such as Sally Shaywitz and Keith Stanovich to conclude that dyslexia is caused by a deficiency in phonological processing (Shaywitz, 1996; Stanovich, 1991). This is not to say that there may not be other factors that contribute to serious reading problems. For example, naming speed has been implicated as a possible cause of reading difficulties by several researchers (Tallal, Stark, & Mellits, 1985; Wolf, 1991). However, phonological processing deficits are clearly the most frequently reported cause of serious reading difficulties.

In addition to the evidence that language may be a basis for reading difficulties, there is also increasing evidence that there may be a biological basis for reading problems. There is evidence, for example, that dyslexia may be inherited (Pennington et al., 1991) and have a genetic basis, specifically related to chromosome 6 (Cardon et al., 1994) and, perhaps, to chromosome 15 (Grigorenko et al., 1997). In addition, a number of studies have focused on possible differences in the structure and functioning of the brain of persons with dyslexia (e.g., Galaburda et al., 1985; Hynd et al., 1987; Flowers, Wood, & Naylor, 1991).

Although research on the biological basis of reading difficulties is still in its infancy, even now there is growing evidence for differences in the structure and function of the brain of individuals with reading disabilities. In the future, this research may allow us to identify at an early age those children with a biologically based reading disorder. This may enable intervention to take place before they experience reading failure.

Extrinsic Factors

There is reason to believe that factors such as home environment and the quality of instruction may contribute to the reading difficulties of many children.

The emergent literacy model has helped us to understand that children develop literacy gradually during the first few years of life. Reading does not begin in kindergarten or first grade; it begins with the early experiences of listening to others read and with a gradually developing knowledge of books. Therefore, we might expect that children who have fewer literacy experiences become less-skilled readers.

In a major study of home background and literacy development (Teale, 1986) reported that, although there was a variety of literacy materials in the homes of children across socioeconomic levels, there was great variation in the amount of exposure that children had to literacy and literacy experiences. Interestingly, Teale did not find a close relationship between social class and amount of literacy experience. In contrast, Chaney (1994) found that children from lower socioeconomic groups did have less print awareness than children from middle-class families, but that social class was not the only factor that affected literacy. Although literacy experiences are no doubt important to the development of reading skills, so far research has been unable to establish a clear link.

Another extrinsic factor that may cause or contribute to reading difficulties is the type and quality of reading instruction that children receive. This factor, too, is hard to demonstrate through a research paradigm. Although some researchers (e.g., Carbo, 1997) have claimed that children learn best when their "learning styles" are matched with instruction, research results have been inconsistent. However, there is evidence that early intervention can prevent or significantly reduce reading difficulties. For example, the *Reading Recovery* program has been found to successfully prevent reading difficulties in many children (Pinnell, Fried, & Estice, 1990) and Vellutino and his colleagues (1996) showed that remedial instruction can enhance the reading of some (though not all) children with reading difficulties.

Children who come to school with limited literacy experiences and who do not receive early and intensive intervention are surely "at risk" for reading difficulties. Unfortunately, once these children experience reading difficulties, they often fall further and further behind their peers. Stanovich (1986) has called this phenomenon the "Matthew Effect"—a reference to the Book of Matthew in which "the rich get richer and the poor get poorer."

Distinction Between Dyslexia and Other Reading Difficulties

Another important question that has challenged those interested in understanding more about reading difficulties is whether dyslexia is a type of reading disorder that is significantly different from other reading disabilities or whether it simply describes those children at the lower end of a continuum of reading difficulties. If dyslexia is a separate and distinct disorder, one would expect individuals with dyslexia to have a unique pattern of abilities and difficulties. It is also possible that they might benefit from certain types of instruction that would be of little or no help to other children with reading problems.

Although some researchers have claimed that dyslexia is a separate and distinct disorder (e.g., Aaron, 1987) most of the research on children with reading difficulties has failed to find consistent differences among groups. For example, when Shaywitz and her colleagues at Yale University (Shaywitz et al., 1992) examined data from a longitudinal study of Connecticut schoolchildren they found no clear cutoff in scores between poor readers and good readers. This does not mean that dyslexia does not exist. It means, as Keith Stanovich (1988) has argued, that we should think of dyslexia as more like obesity than measles. In other words, we are not dealing with a distinct entity that has a specific cause and cure, but rather with a disorder that lies on a continuum. The definition of obesity, unlike that of measles, is arbitrary and can change from time to time. So, too, can the definition of dyslexia. We establish arbitrary criteria (such as the amount of discrepancy between achievement and potential) and say that this is dyslexia. Individuals with dyslexia have a problem, but their problem does not differ significantly from other persons with reading difficulties any more than an obese person differs from a person who is very overweight.

The implication of this contemporary view of reading disorders is that, rather than spending our time looking for unique interventions to help individuals with dyslexia, we should be searching for methods that will enhance the performance of all poor readers. It is possible that research into the genetic and neurobiological basis of reading difficulties may ultimately reveal the existence of a distinct disorder (such as measles) called "dyslexia." But, until that time, practitioners would do well to focus their energies on effective reading instruction practices.

Conclusion

The research on reading disorders suggests that there are more similarities between students with reading difficulties than there are differences. In other words, poor readers are poor readers. Gough and Tunmer (1986) suggest that reading instruction should focus on the specific problem exhibited by the student—decoding, comprehension, or both. Rather than spending a great deal of time trying to identify the cause and type of the reading disorder, it may be more valuable to focus on helping students improve their skills in the areas in which they are having difficulty.

Identification of Students with Reading Difficulties

In their recently released (1998) "action plan," entitled *Every Child Reading*, the Learning First Alliance (a group of major education organizations) identified the essential skills that children need for beginning reading. These include:

- Language skills: Including oral language, vocabulary, and language concepts.
- Background knowledge: Including knowledge and understanding of their world
- Appreciation of stories and books: The result of experience with literature
- Concepts of print: left-to-right, spacing, correspondence between written and spoken word
- Phonemic awareness: The ability to identify and manipulate sounds within words
- Alphabet and letter sounds: Familiarity with the alphabet.

Using this list as a guide, we suggest that teachers can identify children "at risk" for reading problems by looking for the following:

- Difficulty following simple directions
- Unfamiliarity with age-level vocabulary
- Limited knowledge of and experience with the world
- Limited experience with books (e.g., does not know how to hold a book)
- Does not know that print goes from left to right
- Difficulty identifying sounds and rhyming
- Limited (or no) alphabet knowledge

■■ LANGUAGE DIFFICULTIES

Language is a uniquely human characteristic that enables us to communicate efficiently and effectively with others. Language, either spoken or signed, is critical for success in school, in the community, and in life. Most children acquire their first language with apparent ease. Somewhere around two years of age they begin to use words that are recognized by their parents. Single words grow into two-word and then multiword phrases, vocabulary expands, and children pick up the subtleties of human communicative interaction. Yet, some children struggle with language acquisition. Their development may begin later than other children. Once they begin to acquire language, they may progress more slowly. Some even develop unusual language characteristics or fail to develop language skills that are normally acquired in the language acquisition process. Some of these language difficulties are secondary to other disabilities such as mental retardation or autism. Others appear to be restricted to language, with no obvious cause or cure.

Language is a critical component of literacy. At one time, it was thought that reading and writing skills were dependent on the development of language skills and emerged only after a first language was largely acquired. Today, the view is somewhat different. Most researchers recognize the interrelatedness of language, reading, and writing (Silliman & Wilkinson, 1994). Although it is certainly true that language emerges first in most children, recent research on the emergence of literacy in young children has discovered that children begin to read symbols (for example, the "McDonald's" sign) and write (scribbles) long before they enter school or complete the preschool stages of language acquisition (Sulzby, 1986). Rather than being dependent on language development, it may be more accurate to describe the relationship between reading, writing, and language as one in which, as Wallach and Butler (1995) put it, "Spoken language influences written language growth and development and written language influences spoken language and development" (p. 3).

Further evidence for the critical role of language in the development of literacy skills comes from a large body of research that has established that many preschoolers with early speech and language problems experience academic learning difficulties, especially reading and writing difficulties, later in school (Aram & Hall, 1989). Furthermore, students identified as learning disabled have a higher incidence of language problems than other children (Schoenbrodt, Kumin, & Sloan, 1997). Specifically, children with early syntax and phonological problems are likely to become poor readers later in school (Scarborough, 1990; Scarborough & Dobrich, 1990).

There are important implications for teachers and clinicians from this research on language and literacy. For teachers of young children, the research suggests that early intervention for speech and language problems, especially for difficulties with syntax and phonology, might be important. Although the child may have only a mild or even a nonexistent language disorder, it is possible that this child had a more severe language disorder at an earlier age that has affected the development of literacy skills.

Definition, Prevalence, and Cause of Language Difficulties

As is the case with learning disabilities and reading difficulties, language difficulties have been difficult to define. Still, the effort may be worthwhile in order to pinpoint the population of students with whom we should be most concerned.

The American Speech-Language-Hearing Association, the professional organization of speech-language specialists, has defined language disorder as follows:

> A language disorder is impaired comprehension and/or use of spoken, written, and/or other symbol systems. This disorder may involve (1) the form of language (phonology, morphology, syntax), (2) the content of language (semantics), and/or (3) the function of language in communication (pragmatics) in any combination. (Ad Hoc Committee on Service Delivery in the Schools, 1993, p. 40.)

The ASHA definition states that language disorder includes both *comprehension* of language as well as language *production*. It includes *either* spoken or written language, and it indicates that language difficulties can occur in one or more of the specific aspects of language (such as syntax, semantics, etc.). Lahey (1988) suggests that language difficulties exist when the child's language is different from that which would be expected at the child's chronological age. Most definitions of language difficulties exclude children whose language difficulty is the result of another condition (such as hearing loss or emotional disturbance), and some suggest that a discrepancy between language and intellectual development be used to determine language disorder (Aram, Morris, & Hall, 1992). In other words, children should only be considered language disordered if their language skills lag significantly behind their level of cognitive development.

A word of caution—language difficulties are not the same as language differences. Some children come to school speaking a language other than English as their first language or a "nonstandard" dialect of English (see Chapter 10). Although these children may talk differently from their teachers or peers, they are not language disordered. On the other hand, if a child has difficulty acquiring his or her native language or dialect, he or she may have a language disorder.

Because language is such a broad and complex phenomenon, researchers and clinicians have sought to identify subtypes of children with language difficulties. Frequently, children with language difficulties are described as having either a "receptive" or "expressive" disorder. But few children have a pure receptive or expressive problem and many have difficulty with both expressive and receptive language. Lahey (1988) suggests that language difficulties should be divided into difficulties with language content (semantics), form (syntax, phonology, and morphology), and use (pragmatics).

At this time, there is no general agreement about the best way to describe and categorize the various types of language difficulties. The best advice to clinicians and teachers is to be aware of the variety of ways in which language difficulties can be manifested and try to describe the particular problems experienced by any individual child.

Research on the prevalence of language difficulties has found that between 1 to 12% of children may have language difficulties (Lahey, 1988). Most authorities agree that about 5 to 10% of children experience language difficulties so severe that their parents seek attention for their problems (Aram & Hall, 1989; Riccio & Hynd, 1993).

In most cases, it is difficult, if not impossible, to identify the cause of a language disorder in a child with apparently intact physical and cognitive abilities. There is, however, substantial evidence of a familial basis for language difficulties. Children with language difficulties are more likely to come from families where one or more of the parents has a history of language disorder, and siblings are also more likely to share a language disorder (Riccio & Hynd, 1993). Language disorders can be due to a genetic factor, to the language environment in the home, or to some combination of the two. At this point, there is no definitive evidence for a genetic basis for language difficulties, but as research in this field expands, it is possible that such a genetic link will be discovered. Even if this happens, however, the role of the home environment will still be critical to the child's language development.

Language and Reading Disabilities

Earlier in this chapter we reviewed evidence that supported the finding that reading difficulties are, to a large extent, the result of language difficulties. This research has consistently shown that most children with severe reading difficulties have a language-based problem. As Catts (1989) put it, ". . . dyslexia is more than a reading disability. It is a language impairment that manifests itself in difficulties in both written and spoken language development" (p. 422).

Although there is a growing consensus among researchers that severe reading difficulties are caused by language deficiencies, the exact nature of the underlying deficit is not entirely clear. Phonological processing has received most of the attention and, as we have seen, there is a good deal of research evidence that difficulty with phonological processing is a critical component of reading difficulties (for example, see Bradley & Bryant, 1978; Gough & Tunmer, 1986; Shaywitz, 1996). But there is also evidence that at least some children with reading difficulties have difficulty with other elements of language, including syntax, semantics, and pragmatics (Riccio & Hynd, 1993).

For professionals who are interested in helping children improve their reading, the research on language and reading has several implications. First, intervention to enhance phonological processing is essential for young children and children at the beginning stage of reading. Second, for children beyond the earliest stages of reading, other language skills, such as syntax, semantics, and pragmatics, may take on added importance. Efforts to enhance these skills may lead to continued improvement in reading. Third, we must always keep in mind that each child is an individual and that, for any individual child, generalizations about language and reading (or other skills) may not be true. Finally, it is important to keep the reading task in mind. The skills needed for decoding single words are not the same as those needed to read and comprehend an entire story. Different reading tasks require that the reader bring different sets of skills to the task.

Identification of Children with Language Difficulties

Children with language difficulties can have a number of different characteristics. As a result, they can be difficult to identify. Some children with language difficulties have difficulty with peer relationships. They may be shy and reluctant to approach others. Some are less attentive in the classroom and slower to respond. Some even exhibit classroom behavior problems because of their difficulty understanding others or expressing themselves.

Candler and Hildreth (1990) suggested nine characteristics that they claim are frequently found in children with language learning disabilities. They are:

- Trouble with word meanings: Difficulty with multiple meaning words and words used in a nonliteral manner are examples.
- Off-target responding: Responding inappropriately to someone else.
- Inaccurate word selection: Failure to use words in a precise manner.
- Difficulty with word finding: Problems recalling known words.
- Use of neologisms: Using words with idiosyncratic meanings (e.g., "Higher the window")
- Referent errors: Incorrect use of pronouns or failure to give enough information.
- Topic closure: Not knowing when or how to stop.
- Immature grammatical structures: For example, incorrect subject–verb agreement or less-mature forms.
- Disorganization: Talking around topics and difficulty sequencing events are examples.

The key to determining the seriousness of a language difficulty is to consider the impact on the child and on others. If the language difficulty is interfering with the child's ability to learn and/or socialize, if other children tease or reject the child, if the child's parents or the children themselves are very concerned, then the child may have a language disorder that requires the attention of teachers and other professionals.

A checklist of characteristics of language difficulties that might be observed by teachers and clinicians in the classroom is presented in Table 2.2.

TABLE 2.2   Characteristics of Children with Language Difficulties

Academic Performance

Reluctance to contribute to discussions

Difficulty organizing ideas

Difficulty recognizing phonemes

Difficulty producing sounds

Failure to follow directions

Difficulty finding the right word for things

Social Interaction

Reluctance to interact with other children

Exclusion or rejection by other children

Difficulty carrying on a conversation

Problems negotiating rules for games

Cognitive Functioning

Difficulty organizing information for recall

Slow responding

Inattentive

Behavior

High level of frustration

Gets into frequent arguments

Fights with peers

Withdraws from interaction

Source: Kuder, S. J. (1997). *Teaching Students with Language and Communication Disabilities.* Boston, MA: Allyn & Bacon. Used with permission.

▪▪ WRITING DIFFICULTIES

The ability to write, to express one's thoughts on paper (or on a computer screen), is a critical skill for success both in school and in life. More than ever, writing is an important means of social interaction. Although many have bemoaned the decline of letter writing, in its place has arisen e-mail and chat rooms. Many people today prefer to communicate by these methods rather than by telephone. The quality of computer-based communication may not match the elegance of 19th-century letter writing, but the ability to communicate accurately and succinctly has never been more important. Writing is also critical for school success. Written assignments, tests, and statewide testing programs that include a writing test all require good writing skills.

Despite its importance, writing has not been researched as extensively as reading, and writing difficulties have not received nearly as much attention as have reading difficulties (Berninger, Mizokawa, & Bragg, 1991). Yet, we know a lot about children with writing difficulties. We know that they often have difficulty with the act of composition itself (Graham, Harris, MacArthur, & Schwartz, 1991). We know that they also have difficulty with many of the cognitive processes that underlie writing—such as generating ideas and organizing their thoughts (Englert & Raphael, 1988). They also have limited knowledge about writing and about writers (Wong, Wong, & Blenkinsop, 1989). We will explore each of these areas in greater detail. Because most of the research on writing difficulties has been conducted on children already identified as learning disabled or reading disabled, it is difficult to determine whether writing difficulties exist independently from reading difficulties or some other type of disability. It is quite possible that there are children with significant writing difficulties who do not have other literacy disabilities. But this question has not been adequately explored in the research literature.

Studies of Composition

Prior to the 1980s, most of the research on writing focused on the product of writing, that is, on the number of words produced, on the quality of handwriting, and on mechanical aspects of writing, such as grammar and spelling. In general, students with writing difficulties have been found to have significant problems with the mechanical aspects of writing. For example, students with reading difficulties and learning disabilities have been found to produce fewer and shorter compositions than good readers and typical students (Newcomer, Barenbaum, & Nodine, 1988; Nodine, Barenbaum, & Newcomer, 1985). In the latter study, typically developing students used more than twice the number of words in their compositions compared to reading-disabled and learning-disabled writers. In addition, students with learning disabilities have been found to produce fewer sentences and to use a more limited variety of words in their writing than nondisabled students (Houck & Billingsley, 1989). Students with disabilities have also been found to make significantly more mistakes in grammar and in the use of punctuation (Johnson & Grant, 1989).

An interesting area of research that could have significant implications for classroom instruction has examined the extent to which the physical act of writing interferes with the ability of students with disabilities to express themselves. In one study (MacArthur & Graham, 1987) children with writing difficulties were asked to write stories using three different formats: dictating their story to a teacher, writing their story by hand, and writing using a computer-based word-processing program. The researchers found that dictated stories were longer, contained fewer grammatical errors, and were of generally higher quality than either handwritten or word-processed stories. In fact, there were no differences between the latter two methods of composition. On the other hand, other researchers (e.g., Newcomer et al., 1988) failed to find that the dictated stories of students with disabilities were longer or better than their written compositions. Clearly, this is an area that requires more study.

It may be that, for some children, mode of composition does make a difference. For example, children with significant motor difficulties are likely to benefit from the opportunity to dictate their compositions. For other children it is likely that factors other than those involved with production may be more important to success in writing.

Cognitive Processes and Writing

Recently there has been a profound shift in the research on writing from a focus on the written product to a focus on the process of writing. Researchers such as Graves (1983) and Hayes and Flower (1980) have turned their attention to the cognitive processes that underlie writing. They have explored how writers organize and plan their work, how they revise, and how they adjust their presentation for different audiences.

Unfortunately, a number of studies have confirmed that students with reading and learning disabilities have significant problems with the cognitive skills that are essential for good writing. They lack effective strategies for writing. For example, rather than planning their writing, they tend to engage in what Englert and Raphael (1988) have called, "knowledge-telling." That is, they tell everything they know about a topic in whatever order the ideas come to mind. They also have less-effective strategies for accessing information from memory and organizing this information into a coherent whole (Graham & Harris, 1989) and for revising what they have written (Graham et al., 1991).

One reason why students with disabilities may use less-effective writing strategies is that they may lack sufficient knowledge about the writing process. For example, compared to normally achieving students, students with learning disabilities have been found to have much more difficulty articulating what writing involves (Wong et al., 1989). Their conception of writing was focused primarily on the mechanical aspects of writing rather than on writing as self-expression. Similarly, Englert and her colleagues (1988) found that students with learning disabilities had limited knowledge about steps in the writing process, strategies for presenting ideas, and procedures for selecting and integrating information. More importantly, Englert and associates found that knowledge about many of these writing strategies correlated with writing achievement. In other words, there is evidence that students who understand the purpose of writing and strategies for writing are more effective writers.

The research on writing difficulties reviewed in this section indicates that students with disabilities have difficulty with both the mechanical and cognitive processes that contribute to writing. In the past, writing instruction has focused largely on the mechanical components while largely ignoring cognitive factors. The results of this kind of teaching are apparent in students with disabilities who do not understand the point of writing, are not familiar with the process of writing, and have ineffective writing strategies. The implication is that classroom teachers need to pay more attention to these factors while continuing to provide feedback on the mechanical components of writing.

Spelling

Writing is a complex act. Therefore, it can be difficult to study, to understand, and to teach. Perhaps it is because of the complexity of the writing process that, for many years, writing skills such as spelling received so much attention. At first glance, spelling seems rather straightforward and easy to understand. You either spell correctly or you do not. But, in fact, spelling is more complex than it may first appear.

There is a rich history of research on the development of spelling skills in children as well as on spelling disabilities and instructional methods (see, for example, Beers & Henderson, 1977; Gentry, 1978; Zutell, 1980). In brief, this research has found that the spelling development of most children goes through predictable stages. Good spellers are able to apply their linguistic knowledge to spelling. They can recall and revisualize words with little difficulty. When faced with unfamiliar words, good spellers use a variety of strategies to arrive at the correct spelling (Wong, 1986).

What about poor spellers? Children with spelling difficulties have been reported to have a limited repertoire of known words. They are not sensitive to underlying spelling rules and are not good judges of the correctness of their spelling (Bailet, 1990; Graham & Miller, 1979). Spelling problems tend to be long lasting and difficult to remediate.

What might underlie the problems of poor spellers? A number of researchers have examined this question. Many possible causes of spelling problems have been suggested, including memory limitations (retention and recall), speed of processing, and deficiencies in phonological processing. Cornwall (1992) found that phonological awareness was significantly related to spelling performance for a sample of children suspected of having a reading disability. Although speed of processing was related to reading performance, it was not closely associated with spelling. Memory abilities were not highly related to either reading or spelling performance. Phonological processing appears to be an important factor in spelling performance at all ages, and phonological processing ability can be used to predict which students are likely to have spelling difficulties (MacDonald & Cornwall, 1995).

The research reviewed so far makes a strong case for the central role of phonological awareness in spelling and spelling difficulties. That is, it appears that children with poor phonological skills are poor spellers. But the truth is not that simple. In fact, researchers have identified two major processes to be important in spelling: phonological processing (in which the child learns the relationship between sounds and letters) and visual processing (where letters and words are stored as a whole in memory and retrieved when necessary). Students with reading difficulties have been found to make both types of errors in their spelling (Boder, 1973). Recently, researchers have suggested that there may be a difference in the spelling strategies of poor spellers with reading disabilities and those without reading difficulties. Reading-disabled poor spellers use neither a phonological nor a visual-based strategy for spelling. On the other hand, poor spellers who are good readers tend to use a visual, whole-word strategy for spelling.

Two important conclusions can be drawn from the research on spelling and spelling difficulties. First, students with reading and spelling disabilities need to have instruction that focuses both on improving their phonological skills as well as on using a visually based strategy for spelling. Second, poor spellers who are adequate readers can be successful with a sight-based approach to spelling, but might also benefit from instruction in the use of sound–letter relationships in spelling.

Handwriting

How important is handwriting? Just asking this question can create a lot of uneasiness in teachers. Of course it's important, they insist. But why? Today we are relying more and more on electronic means of communication that utilize typing (or, more recently, voice activation) to produce the written word. If we need to write, we can always print. Yet, for a variety of reasons not always connected to the development of literacy skills, handwriting continues to be taught in most schools. Teachers and others interested in education should examine the role of handwriting in modern society and the amount of time that should be devoted to its teaching in school. However, at this time most schools continue to require handwritten work from students, so it is important that children develop adequate handwriting skills. Unfortunately, some children have considerable difficulty mastering this skill.

Handwriting is a complex act that requires the integration of several underlying skills. For example, Lerner (1997) suggests that writing requires adequate perception; good visual and motor skills; the coordination of eye and hand movements; good visual and kinesthetic memory ability; and control of arm, hand, and finger muscles. Most children begin writing before they enter school. Their scribbles show an awareness of writing and a desire to express themselves through print (Sulzby, 1986). In school, these early writing attempts are shaped and guided to match the adult form of writing.

Although many children struggle to refine their handwriting to the point where it is legible and fluid, most are able to acquire handwriting skills. But some students have significant difficulty producing acceptable handwriting, even with appropriate instruction and practice. Children with significant writing difficulties are sometimes said to have "dysgraphia," a writing disability in children with intact intelligence where there is no distinct neurological cause (Hamstra–Bletz & Blote, 1993). Dysgraphia can co-occur with severe reading disability (dyslexia) or exist by itself. According to Lerner (1997), dysgraphia can be caused by poor motor skills, faulty visual perception, and difficulty with visual memory. There are probably subtle neurological differences that underlie the performance difficulties of children with severe handwriting difficulties, but there is, as yet, no research to support this speculation.

Technological innovations such as word processing have made handwriting less important for success after school. However, handwriting is still necessary for some tasks and is a required subject in most schools. Unfortunately, some children experience significant difficulty mastering the complex motor activities needed for excellent handwriting. Although instruction should focus on helping children improve their handwriting, children with handwriting difficulties should be encouraged to use technological aids to express their thoughts in writing.

Identification of Children with Writing Difficulties

School-age children may have difficulty with one or more of the components of writing: written composition, spelling, and handwriting. Signs of possible difficulty with written expression include difficulty telling or retelling a story, identifying a topic for writing, or inability to identify errors in writing. Children who have difficulty identifying sounds in words or who cannot identify the word with a different spelling from among three words may be at risk for spelling difficulties. Children who have difficulty holding a pencil, tracing shapes, and who frequently stop and start as they write may have handwriting difficulties (Table 2.3).

TABLE 2.3	A Checklist of Beginning Writing Skills

Difficulty with written expression
Difficulty telling or retelling a story
Difficulty identifying a topic for writing
Inability to identify errors in writing
Spelling difficulties
Difficulty identifying sounds in words
Inability to identify a word with a different spelling from among three words
Handwriting difficulties
Difficulty holding a pencil
Difficulty tracing shapes
Frequent stops and starts when writing

A more systematic way to identify children at risk for writing difficulties is to use a screening procedure. Such a screening would vary somewhat due to the ages of the students, but it should include the following elements:

- "Automatic" writing: such as writing one's name
- Copying: Of letters, words, and/or paragraphs
- Writing from memory: for example, writing about a recently read story or about a movie
- Writing from dictation

Not only can the written product of the screening be evaluated, but the child's performance during writing tasks can also be observed. For example, pencil grip, speed of writing, and fluidity of writing can all be observed.

▪▪LITERACY DIFFICULTIES AND SPECIFIC DISABILITIES

Up to this point in the chapter we have examined difficulties with literacy from the viewpoint of the specific domain of literacy—reading, writing, or spoken language. We think that this is a useful way for teachers to think about the challenges that face some of their students. However, we recognize that many children with significant literacy difficulties are or will be classified for special educational services. Therefore, we will briefly examine a few of the specific disabilities that are most often linked with literacy difficulties.

Individualized instruction for students with literacy difficulties should be focused on the student's needs and abilities.

Learning Disabilities

Learning disability has been an elusive, and often controversial, label for children with learning difficulties. In the 1977–78 school year approximately 800,000 (or 1.8% of the school population) received special educational services as learning disabled. By the 1998–99 school year that number had grown to 2.8 million (or 6% of the school-age population)(U.S. Dept. of Education, 2000). In most states, the number of children classified as learning disabled continues to increase.

Individuals with learning disabilities exhibit a broad range of learning problems. Reading and writing difficulties are the most frequent academic problem experienced by students with learning disabilities, but they may have difficulty in any academic area. One of the major dilemmas that has continued to plague those interested in learning disabilities is developing an adequate definition. Since the label "learning disabilities" was first proposed by Samuel Kirk in 1963, several definitions have been proposed. The current definition that is included in the Individuals with Disabilities Education Act (IDEA), states:

> The term "children with specific learning disabilities" means those children who have a disorder in one or more of the basic psychological processes involved in understanding or in using language, spoken or written, which disorder may manifest itself in imperfect ability to listen, think, speak, read, write, spell, or to do mathematical calculations. Such difficulties include such conditions as perceptual handicaps, brain injury, minimal brain dysfunction, dyslexia, and developmental aphasia. Such term does not include children who have learning problems which are primarily the result of visual, hearing, or motor

handicaps, of mental retardation, of emotional disturbance, or of environmental, cultural, or economic disadvantage.

Although this definition may appear to be adequate, it has been found to be difficult to apply in practice. There is, for example, disagreement about what is meant by "basic psychological processes" and disagreement about whether such processes are even relevant. Other definitions for learning disabilities have been developed, but significant problems with definition remain.

Despite the difficulties with definition, there is general consensus that language difficulties are a significant factor in learning disabilities. Most states have adopted some version of the federal definition that states that learning disabilities are a language-based disorder (Schoenbrodt et al., 1997). The precise nature of the language disorder is still being debated, but there is general agreement that phonological awareness problems underlie one type of learning disability—dyslexia (or specific reading disorder) (Padget, 1998).

Because language disabilities are thought to be central to the definition of learning disabilities, it should not be surprising to find that a significant number of students with learning disabilities have literacy difficulties. Estimates of speech, language, and communication problems among students with learning disabilities have ranged as high as 96% (Gibbs & Cooper, 1989). Reading disability is the most common type of learning disability (Lerner, 1997). Writing difficulties, including composition, spelling, and handwriting, are also frequently found among students with learning disabilities (Padget, 1998).

Mental Retardation

Definitions of literacy difficulties have often excluded persons with mental retardation because the definition required that the literacy difficulty be "unexpected." In other words, when an individual with normal intelligence experiences a significant difficulty in reading, writing, or spoken language, this is a literacy disorder. What about persons with mental retardation? Even though their difficulties with literacy might be expected given their measured intellectual level, are they not still problems?

We contend that the literacy difficulties experienced by individuals with mental retardation should be taken seriously and that students with mental retardation should receive intensive instruction designed to help them reach their potential. We will have more to say about approaches for teaching individuals with moderate to severe mental retardation in a later chapter. For now, we will briefly examine some of the research on the literacy difficulties experienced by students with mental retardation.

The Individuals with Disabilities Education Act (IDEA), defines mental retardation as, ". . . significant subaverage general intellectual functioning existing concurrently with deficits in adaptive behavior and manifested during the developmental period that adversely affects a child's educational performance." Generally, IQ scores must be 70 or below in order for the individual to be classified as mentally retarded.

Most of the research on the literacy difficulties of persons with mental retardation has focused on their language and reading. There is very little research on writing skills. Recent research has suggested that some of our long-standing assumptions about the literacy skills of persons with mental retardation may not be accurate.

For example, one assumption has been that poor readers with mental retardation differ in significant ways from poor readers with normal intelligence. This assumption was examined in a study by Cawley and Parmar (1995). They compared the reading performance of good and poor readers with mild mental retardation to that of good and poor readers with average intellectual ability. The "good" readers with mental retardation had reading scores that were consistent with their mental age. They found that, whereas the good and poor readers in both groups clearly differed on reading performance, there were few differences between the students with mental retardation and those with average intellectual ability within either reading group. Cawley and Parmar suggest that we should be cautious in making assumptions about the reading abilities of persons with mental retardation based on IQ score alone. Instead, the individual performance of each child should be considered.

Studies of the language abilities of persons with mental retardation have also found a good deal of variation within the population. Although, in general, expressive language delays have been found to be greater than would be expected on the basis of intellectual performance, especially in the Down syndrome population, results have varied depending on the age of the children studied as well as the area of language examined (Chapman et al., 1998). Still, numerous studies have reported specific difficulty in phonology (Shriberg & Widder, 1990), syntax (Kamhi & Johnston, 1982), semantics (Ezell & Goldstein, 1991), and pragmatics (Abbeduto, 1991).

Persons with mental retardation generally lag significantly behind their intellectually normal age-mates in all domains of literacy. In addition, many (but not all) children with mental retardation have specific deficits in reading and in spoken language. However, the research on literacy and mental retardation suggests that we carefully examine each individual to discover their unique pattern of strengths and weaknesses. Additionally, there is evidence that many children with mental retardation who were previously thought to be unable to benefit from instruction can, in fact, do so.

Autism (Pervasive Developmental Disorder)

Autism is a type of pervasive developmental disorder that is characterized by significant deficits in language and in social interaction. At one time autism was considered a type of behavior disorder. Today, however, it is recognized as a separate disorder that affects many areas of functioning. According to the *Diagnostic and Statistical Manual of Mental Disorders* (DSM-IV), published by the American Psychiatric Association (1994), a child must exhibit symptoms that are distributed among three general categories:

1. Qualitative impairment in social interaction
2. Qualitative impairment in communication
3. Restricted repetitive and stereotyped patterns of behavior, interests, and activities

Recently, the federal government recognized autism as a distinct disorder in the Individuals with Disabilities Education Act (IDEA). The federal definition states that:

> Autism means a developmental disability significantly affecting verbal and nonverbal communication and social interaction, generally evident before age three, that adversely affects educational performance. Characteristics of autism include—irregularities and impairments in communication, engagement in repetitive activities and stereotyped movements, resistance to environmental change or change in daily routines, and unusual responses to sensory experiences.

Children with autism often share characteristics with other children with disabilities. As a result, it is often difficult, even for highly skilled professionals, to diagnose autism.

One of the primary characteristics of autism is serious language and communication problems. Approximately half of the population have no functional spoken language (Rutter & Schopler, 1987). Like individuals with mental retardation, children with autism have been found to have deficits in many areas of language, including phonology (Bartolucci et al., 1976), syntax (Bartak, Rutter, & Cox, 1975), semantics (Volden & Lord, 1991), and pragmatics (Tiegerman, 1993). Unlike children with mental retardation, children with autism usually fail to compensate for their language difficulties through nonverbal communication. Also, children with autism have been reported to have specific language characteristics, such as the persistent use of echolalia (in which words are repeated back just as they are spoken) and pronoun reversal (for example, saying "you" when referring to themselves).

We have little information about the reading and writing skills of children with autism. Occasionally, children with autism are "hyperlexic"; that is, they have extraordinary word-reading skills (O'Connor & Hermelin, 1994). But this is rare. Most children with autism can be expected to have very limited reading and writing skills.

Hearing and Vision Impairments
Students with Hearing Impairments

Individuals with hearing disabilities have been reported to have delays and, in some cases, specific deficits in the acquisition of spoken language. Children with hearing disabilities have been found to make more phonological errors and substitutions than hearing children (Smith, 1975). They are delayed in their development of syntactic (grammatical) structures and fail to develop some advanced structures (Quigley, Power, & Steinkamp, 1977). Delays in semantic development have been reported as well (Davis et al., 1986).

It should not be surprising to find that deaf persons experience difficulty with the acquisition of spoken language. After all, they have limited opportunity to hear the models that young children use to build their language. What may be surprising is the finding that the underlying language ability of most persons with serious hearing impairments is intact. We know this from research that has examined the acquisition of a signing system in deaf children. This research has discovered that seriously hearing-impaired children can acquire a sign language system at about the same rate as hearing children acquire spoken language (Klima & Bellugi, 1979). This means that, although children with hearing disabilities have difficulty acquiring spoken language and may be significantly delayed and/or have specific deficits, they can acquire language.

There has been a significant amount of research on the reading and writing performance of persons with hearing impairments. In general, this research has found that reading and writing difficulties are much more common in hearing impaired persons than in hearing persons. For example, one study reported that more than half of a sample of 20-year-old persons with hearing loss had a median reading comprehension grade level of 4.5 (Trybus & Karchmer, 1977). Similarly, Quigley and Paul (1990) have reported that the writing of deaf persons is shorter, less complex, and includes more errors than the writing of hearing persons. These findings suggest that teachers of students with hearing disabilities should provide their students with lots of literacy opportunities that include feedback and direct instruction in literacy skills.

Students with Vision Impairments

The language development of children with visual impairments is quite similar to that of sighted children. The rate and sequence of their early language developments is much like that of sighted children. However, there are some subtle differences. For example, children with visual impairments seem to learn words largely through imitation rather than through a process of overgeneralization and narrowing used by sighted children (Andersen, Dunlea, & Kekelis, 1984). Also, they have difficulty acquiring some words that require sight to be fully understood. As they grow older, children with visual impairments continue to develop language at a normal rate, although they may have subtle differences in syntax, semantics (Erin, 1990), and the pragmatic aspects of language (Parke, Shallcross, & Anderson, 1980).

In order for students with visual impairments to be successful in reading and writing, it is usually necessary to make some modifications. These may be as simple as larger print or a seat closer to the board or as complex as braille or the use of a device that converts print to speech. If appropriate modifications are made, there is no reason to believe that visually impaired students who have no other disability cannot be successful in reading and writing.

Students with Emotional/Behavioral Difficulties

Although there is a limited research base on the literacy difficulties of students with emotional or behavioral difficulties, the research suggests that literacy difficulties may be more common than might be expected. Until recently, most of the research on children with emotional/behavioral difficulties has focused on ways to intervene after the student exhibits inappropriate behavior. However, there is growing interest in examining factors that may underlie problem behaviors.

Most of the research on the literacy abilities of students with emotional or behavioral difficulties has focused on spoken language. This research is of two types. One type has examined the incidence of behavior problems in children with language difficulties. Studies have generally found a much higher incidence of behavior problems in children with early speech and language difficulties than is found in the general population. For example, in one study of 600 children who attended a speech and language clinic, some 50% were found to have identifiable psychiatric problems (Baker & Cantwell, 1987). The other type of research has examined the language performance of individuals with emotional or behavioral difficulties. Studies using both clinical and school-based populations have found high rates of difficulty in receptive and expressive language (Donahue, Cole, & Hartas, 1994). In one study, 71% of children with mild to moderate behavior difficulties scored more than two standard deviations below the mean on a standardized test of language (Camarata, Hughes, & Ruhl, 1988). Studies of the reading and writing skills of students with emotional or behavioral difficulties have also found that these children have significant problems with reading and writing (Kauffman, Cullinan, & Epstein, 1987).

The research on the literacy abilities of students with emotional or behavioral difficulties, although limited, suggests that literacy instruction should receive more emphasis than it traditionally has for this population. Although improvements in language, reading, and writing may not prevent all of the problems experienced by children with emotional or behavioral difficulties, it may help these children become more successful students.

▮▮ SUMMARY

In this chapter, research on literacy difficulties, including difficulties with reading, writing, and language, has been described and discussed. Information on the characteristics, causes, and etiology of reading, writing, and language problems has been presented. In addition, the relationship between specific disabilities and literacy development has been discussed.

A significant number of children experience difficulties with literacy acquisition. Some of these children have problems that are so pervasive and persistent that they may be called "disabled." Other children come to school with a disability such as mental retardation or autism that generally has a significant impact on literacy development.

We still do not have all of the answers on the causes and identification of literacy difficulties, but it seems clear that many children need assistance with the acquisition of literacy skills. Later in this book we will examine a number of techniques that have been developed to modify or replace instruction for students with literacy difficulties.

Linkages

1. List and briefly explain the three criteria used by the *Diagnostic and Statistical Manual of Mental Disorders* (DSM-IV) to define reading disorders.
2. If there is no such thing as a "specific reading disability," what are the implications for instruction?
3. What is phonological processing? How is it related to reading?
4. How could "extrinsic factors" contribute to reading difficulties?
5. Why should we be concerned about identifying and helping children with language difficulties?
6. How are reading and language related?
7. What factors may affect children's ability to write?
8. To what extent should schools teach handwriting?
9. Choose one of the disability types described in this chapter (e.g., learning disabilities, mental retardation, etc.) and discuss the impact of this disability on literacy development.

On the Web

Interactive Guide to Learning Disabilities
www.ldonline.org

International Dyslexia Society
www.interdys.org

Council for Exceptional Children
wwsw.cec.sped.org

National Information Center for Children and Youth with Disabilities
www.nichy.org

Autism Society of America
www.autism-society.org

References

Aaron, P. G. (1987). Developmental dyslexia: Is it different from other forms of reading disability? *Annals of Dyslexia, 37,* 109–125.

Aaron, P. G. (1995). Differential diagnosis of reading disabilities. *School Psychology Review, 24,* 345–360.

Abbeduto, L. (1991). Development of verbal communication in persons with moderate to mild mental retardation. *International Review of Research in Mental Retardation, 17,* 91–115.

American Psychiatric Association. (1994). *Diagnostic and Statistical Manual of Mental Disorders* (4th ed.). Washington, DC: American Psychiatric Association.

American Speech-Language-Hearing Association (1993). Definitions of communication disorders and variations. *ASHA, 35* (Suppl. 10), 40–41.

Andersen, E., Dunlea, A., & Kekelis, L. (1984). Blind children's language: Resolving some differences. *Journal of Child Language, 11,* 645–664.

Aram, D. M., & Hall, N. E. (1989). Longitudinal follow-up of children with preschool communication difficulties: Treatment implications. *School Psychology Review, 18,* 487–501.

Aram, D. M., Morris, R., & Hall, N. E. (1992). The validity of discrepancy criteria for identifying children with developmental language difficulties. *Journal of Learning Disabilities, 25,* 549–554.

Bailet, L. L. (1990). Spelling rule usage among students with learning disabilities and normally achieving students. *Journal of Learning Disabilities, 23,* 121–128.

Baker, L., & Cantwell, D. P. (1987). Factors associated with the development of psychiatric illness in children with speech/language problems. *Journal of Autism and Developmental Disabilities, 17,* 499–510.

Ball, E. W., & Blachman, B. A. (1991). Does phoneme awareness training in kindergarten make a difference in early word recognition and developmental spelling? *Reading Research Quarterly, 26,* 49–66.

Bartak, L., Rutter, M., & Cox, A. (1975). A comparative study of infantile autism and specific developmental receptive language disorder. I. The children. *British Journal of Psychiatry, 126,* 127–145.

Bartolucci, G., Pierce, S., Streiner, D., & Eppel, P. (1976). Phonological investigation of verbal autistic and mentally retarded subjects. *Journal of Autism and Childhood Schizophrenia, 6,* 303–316.

Beers, J. W., & Henderson, E. (1977). A study of developing orthographic concepts among first graders. *Research in the Teaching of English, 11,* 133–148.

Berninger, V. W., Mizokawa, D. T., & Bragg, R. (1991). Theory-based diagnosis and remediation of writing disabilities. *Journal of School Psychology, 29,* 57–79.

Blanton, L. P., & Blanton, W. E. (1994). Providing reading instruction to mildly disabled readers: Research into practice. In K. D. Wood & B. Algozzine (Eds.), *Teaching reading to high-risk learners* (pp. 9–48). Boston: Allyn & Bacon.

Boder, E. (1973). Developmental dyslexia: A diagnostic approach based on three atypical reading-spelling patterns. *Developmental Medicine and Child Neurology, 15,* 66–687.

Bradley, L., & Bryant, P. (1978). Difficulties in auditory organization as possible cause of reading backwardness. *Nature, 271,* 746–747.

Bradley, L., & Bryant, P. E. (1985). *Rhyme and reason in reading and spelling.* Ann Arbor: University of Michigan Press.

Byrne, B., Freebody, P., & Gates, A. (1992). Longitudinal data on the relations of word-reading strategies to comprehension, reading time, and phonemic awareness. *Reading Research Quarterly, 27,* 141–151.

Camarata, S., Hughes, C., & Ruhl, K. (1988). Mild/moderate behaviorally disordered students: A population at risk for language difficulties. *Language, Speech, and Hearing Services in Schools, 20,* 22–30.

Candler, A. C., & Hildreth, B. L. (1990). Characteristics of language difficulties in learning disabled students. *Academic Therapy, 25,* 333–343.

Carbo, M. (1997). Reading with style. *Principal, 76*(5), 12–14.

Cardon, L. R., Smith, S. D., Fulker, D. W., Kimberling, W. J., Pennington, B. F., & DeFries, J. C. (1994). Quantitative trait locus for reading disability on chromosome 6. *Science, 266,* 276–279.

Catts, H. W. (1989). Speech production deficits in developmental dyslexia. *Journal of Speech and Hearing Difficulties, 54,* 422–428.

Cawley, J. F., & Parmar, R. S. (1995). Comparisons in reading and reading-related tasks among students with average intellectual ability and students with mild mental retardation. *Education and Training in Mental Retardation,* 118–129.

Chapman, R. S., Seung, H-K, Schwartz, S. E., & Kay-Raining Bird, E. (1998). Language skills of children and adolescents with Down syndrome: Production deficits. *Journal of Speech, Language, and Hearing Research, 41,* 861–873.

Coltheart, M., Masterson, J., Byng, S., Prior, M., & Riddoch, J. (1983). Surface dyslexia. *Quarterly Journal of Experimental Psychology, 35,* 469–495.

Chaney, C. (1994). Language development, metalinguistic awareness, and emergent literacy skills of 3-year-old children in relation to social class. *Applied Psycholinguistics, 15,* 371–394.

Cornwall, A. (1992). The relationship of phonological awareness, rapid naming, and verbal memory to severe reading and spelling disability. *Journal of Learning Disabilities, 25,* 532–538.

Cronin, M. E., & Patton, J. R. (1993). *Life skills for students with special needs: A practical guide for developing real-life programs.* Austin, TX: PRO-ED.

Davis, J., Elfenbein, J., Schum, R., & Bentler, R. (1986). Effects of mild and moderate hearing impairments on language, educational, and psychosocial behavior of children. *Journal of Speech and Hearing Disorders, 51,* 53–62.

Donahue, M., Cole, D., & Hartas, D. (1994). Links between language and emotional/behavioral difficulties. *Education and Treatment of Children, 17,* 244–254.

Eimas, P., Siqueland, E., Jusczyk, P., & Vigorito, J. (1971). Speech perception in infants. *Science, 171,* 303–306.

Englert, C. S., & Raphael, T. E. (1988). Constructing well-formed prose: Process, structure, and metacognitive knowledge. *Exceptional Children, 54,* 513–520.

Englert, C. S., Raphael, T. E., Fear, K. L., & Anderson, L. M. (1988). Students' metacognitive knowledge about how to write informational texts. *Learning Disability Quarterly, 11,* 18–46.

Erin, J. (1990). Language samples from visually impaired four- and five-year-olds. *Journal of Childhood Communication Difficulties, 13,* 181–191.

Ezell, H., & Goldstein, H. (1991). Comparison of idiom comprehension of normal children and children with mental retardation. *Journal of Speech and Hearing Research, 34,* 812–819.

Fletcher, J. M. (1992). The validity of distinguishing children with language and learning disabilities according to discrepancies with IQ: Introduction to the special series. *Journal of Learning Disabilities, 25,* 546–548.

Flowers, D. L., Wood, F. B., & Naylor, C. E. (1991). Regional cerebral blood flow correlates of language processes in reading disability. *Archives of Neurology, 48,* 637–643.

Galaburda, A. M., Sherman, G. F., Rosen, G. D., Aboitiz, F., & Geschwind, N. (1985). Developmental dyslexia: Four consecutive patients with cortical anomalies. *Annals of Neurology, 18,* 222–233.

Gentry, J. R. (1978). Early spelling strategies. *The Elementary School Journal, 79,* 88–92.

Gibbs, D. P., & Cooper, E. B. (1989). Prevalence of communication difficulties in students with learning disabilities. *Journal of Learning Disabilities, 29,* 60–63.

Gough, P. B., & Tunmer, W. E. (1986). Decoding, reading, and reading disability. *Remedial and Special Education, 7,* 6–10.

Graham, S., & Harris, K. R. (1989). A components analysis of cognitive strategy instruction: Effects on learning disabled students' compositions and self-efficacy. *Journal of Educational Psychology, 81,* 353–361.

Graham, S., Harris, K. R., MacArthur, C. A., & Schwartz, S. (1991). Writing and writing instruction for students with learning disabilities: Review of a research program. *Learning Disability Quarterly, 14,* 89–114.

Graham, S., & Miller, L. (1979). Spelling research and practice: A unified approach. *Focus on Exceptional Children, 12,* 1–16.

Graves, D. H. (1983). *Writing: Teachers and children at work.* Exeter, NH: Heinemann Educational Books.

Grigorenko, E. L., Wood, F. B., Meyer, M. S., Hart, L. A., Speed, W. C., Shuster, A., & Pauls, D. L. (1997). Susceptibility loci for distinct components of developmental dyslexia on chromosomes 6 and 15. *American Journal of Human Genetics, 60,* 27–39.

Hamstra-Bletz, L., & Blote, A. W. (1993). A longitudinal study on dysgraphic handwriting in primary school. *Journal of Learning Disabilities, 26,* 689–699.

Hayes, J. R., & Flower, L. S. (1980). Identifying the organization of writing processes. In L.W. Gregg & E. R. Sternberg (Eds.), *Cognitive processes in writing* (pp. 3–30). Hillsdale, NJ: Erlbaum.

Houck, C., & Billingsley, B. (1989). Written expression of students with and without learning disabilities: Differences across the grades. *Journal of Learning Disabilities, 22,* 561–572.

Hynd, G. W., Hynd, C. R., Sullivan, H. G., & Kingsbury, T. (1987). Regional cerebral blood flow (rCBF) in developmental dyslexia: Activation during reading in a surface and deep dyslexic. *Journal of Learning Disabilities, 20,* 294–300.

Johnson, D. J., & Grant, J. O. (1989). Written narratives of normal and learning disabled children. *Annals of Dyslexia, 39,* 140–158.

Kamhi, A., & Johnston, J. (1982). Towards an understanding of retarded children's linguistic deficiencies. *Journal of Speech and Hearing Research, 25,* 435–445.

Kauffman, J. M., Cullinan, D., & Epstein, M. H. (1987). Characteristics of students placed in special programs for the seriously emotionally disturbed. *Behavioral difficulties, 12,* 175–184.

Klima, E., & Bellugi, U. (1979). *The signs of language.* Cambridge, MA: Harvard University Press.

Korhonen, T. T. (1995). The persistence of rapid naming problems in children with reading disabilities: A nine-year follow-up. *Journal of Learning Disabilities, 28,* 232–239.

Lahey, M. (1988). *Language difficulties and language development.* New York: Macmillan.

Learning First Alliance (1998). *Every child reading.*

Lerner, J. (1997). *Learning disabilities: Theories, diagnosis, and teaching strategies.* Boston: Houghton Mifflin.

Liberman, I. Y., Shankweiler, D., & Liberman, A. M. (1989). The alphabetic principle and learning to read. In D. Shankweiler & I. Y. Liberman (Eds.), *Phonology and reading disability: Solving the reading puzzle* (pp. 1–33). Ann Arbor: University of Michigan Press.

Lovett, M. (1987). A developmental approach to reading disability: accuracy and speed criteria of normal and deficient reading skill. *Child Development, 58,* 234–260.

Lyon, G. R. (1995). Why reading is not a natural process. *Educational Leadership, 55,* 14–18.

MacDonald, G. W., & Cornwall, A. (1995). The relationship between phonological awareness and reading and spelling achievement eleven years later. *Journal of Learning Disabilities, 28,* 523–527.

Mody, M., Studdert-Kennedy, M., & Brady, S. (1997). Speech perception deficits in poor readers: Auditory processing or phonological coding. *Journal of Experimental Child Psychology, 64,* 199–231.

Newcomer, P. L., & Barenbaum, E. M., & Nodine, B. F. (1988). Comparison of the story production of LD, normal-achieving, and low-achieving children under two modes of production. *Learning Disability Quarterly, 11,* 82–96.

Nodine, B. F., Barenbaum, E. M., & Newcomer, P. L. (1985). Story composition by learning disabled, reading disabled, and normal children. *Learning Disability Quarterly, 8,* 167–179.

O'Connor, N., & Hermelin, B. (1994). Two autistic savant readers. *Journal of Autism and Developmental Disabilities, 24,* 501–515.

Olson, R. K. (1994). Language deficits in "specific" reading disability. In M. A. Gernsbacher (ed.), *Handbook of psycholinguistics* (pp. 895–916). New York: Academic Press.

Padget, S. Y. (1998). Lessons from research on dyslexia: Implications for a classification system for learning disabilities. *Learning Disability Quarterly, 21,* 167–178.

Parke, K., Shallcross, R., & Anderson, R. (1980). Differences in coverbal behavior between blind and sighted persons during dyadic communication. *Visual Impairment and Blindness, 74,* 142–146.

Pennington, B. F., Gilger, J. W., Pauls, D., Smith, S. A., Smith, S. D., & DeFries, J. C. (1991). Evidence for major gene transmission of developmental dyslexia. *Journal of the American Medical Association, 266,* 1527–1534.

Pinnell, G. S., Fried, M. D., & Estice, R. M. (1990). Reading recovery: Learning how to make a difference. *The Reading Teacher,* 282–295.

Polloway, E. A., & Smith, T. E. C. (1992). *Language instruction for students with disabilities.* Denver: Love Publishing.

Quigley, S., & Paul, P. (1990). *Language and deafness.* San Diego, CA: Singular Publishing Group.

Quigley, S., Power, D., & Steinkamp, M (1977). The language structure of deaf children. *Volta Review, 79,* 73–84.

Riccio, C. A., & Hynd, G. W. (1993). Developmental language difficulties in children: Relationship with learning disability and attention deficit hyperactivity disorder. *School Psychology Review, 22,* 696–709.

Richardson, S. O. (1992). Historical perspectives on dyslexia. *Journal of Learning Disabilities, 25,* 40–47.

Rutter, M., & Schopler, E. (1987). Autism and pervasive developmental difficulties: Concepts and diagnostic issues. *Journal of Autism and Developmental Disabilities, 17,* 159–186.

Scarborough, H. S. (1990). Very early language deficits in dyslexic children. *Child Development, 61,* 1728–1743.

Scarborough, H. S., & Dobrich, W. (1990). Development of children with early language delay. *Journal of Speech and Hearing Research, 33,* 70–83.

Schoenbrodt, L., Kumin, L., & Sloan, J. M. (1997). Learning disabilities existing concomitantly with communication difficulties. *Journal of Learning Disabilities, 30,* 264–281.

Shaywitz, S. E. (1996). Dyslexia. *Scientific American,* 98–104.

Shaywitz, S. E., Escobar, M. D., Shaywitz, B. A., Fletcher, J. M., & Makuch, R. (1992). Evidence that dyslexia may represent the lower tail of a normal distribution of reading ability. *New England Journal of Medicine, 326,* 145–150.

Shaywitz, S. E., Fletcher, J. M., Holahan, J. M., Shneider, A. E., Marchione, K. E., Stuebing, K. K., Francis, D. J., Shankweiler, D. P., Katz, L., Liberman, I. Y., & Shaywitz, S. E. (1995). Interrelationships between reading disability and attention-deficit/hyperactivity disorder. *Cognitive Neuropsychology, 1,* 170–186.

Shaywitz, B. A., Shaywitz, S. E., Fletcher, J. M., Pugh, K. R., Gore, J. C., Constable, R. C., Fulbright, R. K., Skudlarski, P., Liberman, A. M., Shankweiler, D. P., Katz, L., Bronen, R. A., Marchione, K. E., Holahan, J. M., Francis, D. J., Klorman, R., Aram, D. M., Blachman, B. A., Stuebing, K. K., Lacadie, C. (1997). The Yale Center for the Study of Learning and Attention: Longitudinal and Neurobiological Studies. *Learning Disabilities, 8,* 21–30.

Shriberg, L. & Widder, C. (1990). Speech and prosody characteristics of adults with mental retardation. *Journal of Speech and Hearing Research, 33,* 637–653.

Siegel, L. S. (1992). An evaluation of the discrepancy definition of dyslexia. *Journal of Learning Disabilities, 25,* 618–629.

Silliman, E. R., & Wilkinson, L. C. (1994). Discourse scaffolds for classroom intervention. In G. P. Wallach & K. G. Butler (Eds.), *Language learning disabilities in school-age children and adolescents* (pp. 27–52). New York: Merrill/Macmillan.

Silver, L. B. (1981). The relationship between learning disabilities, hyperactivity, distractibility, and behavioral problems. *Journal of the American Academy of Child Psychiatry, 20,* 385–397.

Smith, C. (1975). Residual hearing and speech production in deaf children. *Journal of Speech and Hearing Research, 18,* 795–811.

Snider, V. E., & Tarver, S. G. (1987). The effect of early reading failure on acquisition of knowledge among students with learning disabilities. *Journal of Learning Disabilities, 20,* 351–356.

Stanovich, K. E. (1986). Matthew effects in reading: Some consequences of individual differences in the acquisition of literacy. *Reading Research Quarterly, 21,* 360–406.

Stanovich, K. E. (1988). Explaining the differences between the dyslexic and the garden-variety poor reader: The phonological-core variable-difference model. *Journal of Learning Disabilities, 21,* 590–604.

Stanovich, K. E. (1991). Discrepancy definitions of reading disability: Has intelligence led us astray? *Reading Research Quarterly, 26,* 7–29.

Sulzby, E. (1986). Writing and reading: Signs of oral and written language organization in the young child. In W. H. Teale and E. Sulzby (Eds.), *Emergent literacy* (pp. 50–89). Norwood, NJ: Ablex Publishing.

Tallal, P., Stark, R. E., & Mellits, E. D. (1985). Identification of language-impaired children on the basis of rapid perception of production skills. *Brain and Language, 25,* 314–322.

Teale, W. H. (1986). Home background and young children's literacy development. In W. H. Teale & E. Sulzby (Eds.), *Emergent Literacy* (pp. 173–206). Norwood, NJ: Ablex Publishing.

Tiegerman, E. (1993). Autism: Learning to communicate. In D. Bernstein & E. Tiegerman (Eds.), *Language and communication difficulties in children* (Chapter 13). New York: Macmillan.

Torgesen, J. K., Morgan, S., & Davis, C. (1992). The effects of two types of phonological awareness training on word learning in kindergarten children. *Journal of Educational Psychology, 84,* 364–370.

Trybus, R., & Karchmer, M. (1977). School achievement scores of hearing impaired children: National data on achievement status and growth patterns. *American Annals of the Deaf, 122,* 62–69.

U.S. Dept. of Education (2000). Twenty-Second Annual Report to Congress on the Implementation of the Individuals with Disabilities Act. Washington, D.C.

Vellutino, F. R., Scanlon, D. M., & Sipay, E. R., Small, S. G., Chen, R., Pratt, A., & Denckla, M. B. (1996). Cognitive profiles of difficult-to-remediate and readily remediated poor readers: Early intervention as a vehicle for distinguishing between cognitive and experiential deficits as basic causes of specific reading disabilities. *Journal of Educational Psychology, 88,* 601–638.

Vellutino, F. R. (1979). *Dyslexia: Theory and practice.* Cambridge, MA: MIT Press.

Volden, J., & Lord, C. (1991). Neologisms and idiosyncratic language in autistic speakers. *Journal of Autism and Developmental Disabilities, 21,* 109–130.

Wallach, G. P., & Butler, K. G. (1995). Language learning disabilities: Moving in from the edge. *Topics in Language Disorders, 16,* 1–26.

White, W. J. (1992). The postschool adjustment of persons with learning disabilities: Current status and future projections. *Journal of Learning Disabilities, 25,* 448–456.

Wolf, M. (1991). Naming speed and reading: The contribution of the cognitive neurosciences. *Reading Research Quarterly, 26,* 123–141.

Wong, B. Y. L. (1986). A cognitive approach to teaching spelling. *Exceptional Children, 53,* 169–173.

Wong, B. Y. L., Wong, R., & Blenkinsop, J. (1989). Cognitive and metacognitive aspects of learning disabled adolescents' composing problems. *Learning Disability Quarterly, 12,* 300–322.

Zutell, J. (1980). Children's spelling strategies and their cognitive development. In E. Henderson & J. Beers (Eds.), *Developmental and cognitive aspects of learning to spell: A reflection of word knowledge* (pp. 52–73). Newark, DE: International Reading Association.

CHAPTER
Assessment 3

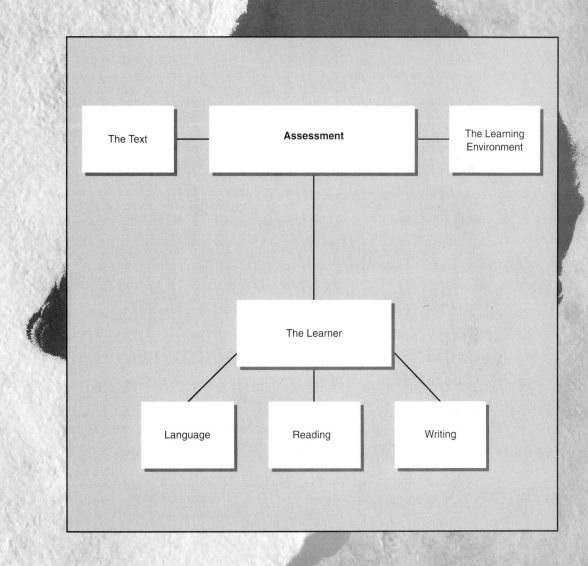

Before beginning this chapter, take a few minutes to jot down any words that you associate with the term *assessment.* What types of words did you write? Were they positive, neutral, negative? What feelings are associated with the word? Did you start to feel queasy? Did the word bring back memories of sleepless nights, of upset stomachs, of emotional upsets and worries? And as you thought back to specific tests, were these feelings reinforced by a sense of disappointment—that you were not able to demonstrate your true knowledge and hence your disappointment? If your associations were mainly negative, then you probably see assessment as detrimental to learning, as an instrument for separating and labeling learners. In this case, you are probably thinking of only one aspect of assessment; namely, evaluation. Evaluation entails making a judgment about another's abilities or mastery of a subject. This is one of the purposes of assessment. Although the evaluative aspects of assessment may have negative associations, evaluation *is* valuable in helping teachers gauge the effectiveness of their teaching. Assessment is also used for *placement,* to determine the appropriate educational context for the learner, and for *diagnosis,* to determine the learners' abilities, strengths, and weaknesses. This enables the teacher to provide appropriate instruction to support student learning.

Assessment may be conducted on a schoolwide basis by various educational specialists as well as by classroom teachers. Schoolwide testing and testing by specialists usually entails formal assessments, which are described in more detail later in this chapter. Classroom teachers generally engage in more informal assessments. Every time teachers look around the classroom to see if students appear to understand the lesson, they are engaging in a form of assessment. This type of observation is augmented by data gathering through paper and pencil tests, student work samples, and projects. Assessment, then, is the use of many tools and approaches to gather information about learners and the learning context in order to make instructional decisions that will ultimately maximize learning.

▌▌▌ A FRAMEWORK AND GENERAL PROCEDURE FOR ASSESSMENT

Assessment should not be viewed as separate from teaching and learning, but as a critical component. Decisions about *what* to assess and *how* to assess are based on one's conceptual framework about literacy and learning (Figure 3.1). Reviewing our assumptions about literacy practice, as discussed in Chapter 1, our conceptual framework for literacy is based on the following ideas:

- Reading, writing, and oral language are inextricably linked in literacy development.
- The reader's prior knowledge, expectations, and attitude toward reading affect literacy development.
- Literacy is a developmental process; students should have access to literacy at different stages, with appropriate instruction for their level of development.
- Reading/writing is a metacognitive act—mature readers are strategic, consciously using various types of knowledge, including decoding, vocabulary, and schema, to enable them to obtain meaning from print.

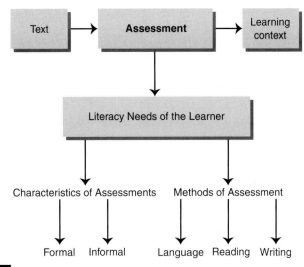

FIGURE 3.1

Assessment model based on conceptual framework.

- Reading/writing is a social act—the learning context and the participants (peers and teacher) all contribute to the development of literacy.

The statements preceding lead to four major concepts for assessment: (1) assessment must address oral language, reading, and writing, (2) assessment must include knowledge of students' developmental stages and knowledge of the different aspects of literacy, (3) assessment should incorporate information about the literacy development of the learner, the learning material, and the learning situation, and (4) assessment should be conducted by means of formal and informal measures. These measures include published assessments with standardized procedures and norms; various types of informal assessments, some of which are developed by the teacher and some that are published; observation of the learner's performance and behavior during instruction; and examination of instructional documents, such as writing samples.

Assessment should be a dynamic process whose purpose is to inform and improve instruction. It is an integral part of the learning situation, providing teachers with necessary information about the success of instruction for all children. By viewing assessment as a critical component of instruction and continually observing students and analyzing their performance, teachers make stronger instructional decisions. They learn to modify instruction, using their knowledge of the learners' abilities to remediate weaknesses. Appropriate assessment, conducted in the classroom, ensures that no learners are ignored or forgotten in the inclusive classroom.

Upon reading about the different types of assessment and areas that should be assessed, the reader may begin to develop the notion that good teachers spend most of their day assessing their students. You may begin to wonder how teachers ever find the time to teach. The following scenario should help you see how assessment is integrated with instruction.

In the classroom: Sharon G. is looking at the roster for her new second-grade class. Soon, she and twenty-five new individuals will be forming a classroom community. She starts to peruse the class list, making notes about the students, and thinking about the information she wants to gather as she begins the school year. She wants to know how the students feel about reading, what their oral reading is like—do they read fluently, how many words can they recognize on sight, what do they do when they don't know a word? She knows, though, that reading the words is not enough. So she wants to know how well they can understand a selection; specifically can they answer explicit and implicit questions about a selection, and can they retell a story they have either read or heard read to them? And, what about writing? Knowing their spelling level will help Sharon provide appropriate instruction. However, she also needs to know about their approach to writing and whether they view it as a communicative event. She puts her questions into categories and begins to look at the assessments that are already in each child's folder and decides how to gather information in the areas that are lacking.

Sharon's approach to her new class illustrates the principles of classroom assessment. To integrate assessment and instruction teachers should do the following:

- Gather background information about the students. This may include standardized test scores, previous report cards, and notes and assessments from prior-year teachers.
- Look at the curriculum to determine broad areas of emphasis and what children are expected to know and do. For example, teachers in a primary-level classroom will need to know more about children's phonemic awareness and decoding abilities. At the upper levels, the emphasis may be on students' comprehension of different types of texts.
- Analyze the means for gaining knowledge about the students through teaching. Decide whether to acquire the information from classroom assignments and work samples, from informal group and/or individual testing, or from observation of students as they work. Many forms of assessment can be obtained through the normal instructional sequence.
- Set up a time-frame for collecting information. Many teachers find that working with one child for fifteen minutes a day allows them to gather some initial information within a month. They then decide how often to update the information—quarterly, semi-annually, annually.
- Collaborate with other professionals, paraprofessionals, and volunteers when gathering the data.
- Create an organizational scheme for storing and retrieving data. They can use individual folders and class assessment forms to help them keep and use needed information.

▊▌ ASSESSMENT OF LEARNERS' LITERACY DEVELOPMENT

Definitions and Characteristics of the Different Types of Assessment

Formal Assessment

Formal (standardized) assessment can be defined as a published assessment developed by someone other than the practitioner. There are two types of formal, standardized tests: criterion-referenced tests, in which students' scores are based on mastery of a particular criteria; for example, knowledge of synonyms, and norm-referenced tests, in which students' scores reflect their performance comparative to a particular norming sample. Characteristics of formal assessments include standardized procedures for administration, norming samples, statistical information about reliability and validity, and standardized scoring.

In an attempt to prevent bias, formal assessments are generally field tested on a wide variety of students, with different demographic characteristics typical of the nation as a whole. Thus, one would see that the test has been given to children from different ethnic groups, socioeconomic levels, parental educational levels, types of community (urban, suburban, rural). Field testing also checks the *reliability* of the test, whether students' scores on the tests are relatively consistent, and the *validity* of the test, whether the test actually measures what it purports to. Any new items are generally field tested before they are added to a test. For example, many of you have taken the Scholastic Aptitude Tests (SATs). They always include a section which is not included in the score, although the test-taker is unaware of which one it is. That section consists of items that are being field tested before being included in new editions of the SATs.

Students' scores on formal assessments may be affected by factors that have little to do with students' abilities. Attitudes toward testing, willingness to take risks (guess at an answer), decoding ability, speed of work, physical and emotional state on the day of the test, and "testwiseness," are all factors external to the content being tested. You may recall being so fearful of standardized tests that your anxiety prevented you from demonstrating your true abilities. Have you ever seen the papers that are sent to parents to prepare children for tests? They include suggestions such as getting a good night's sleep, eating a good breakfast, in essence eliminating factors that have a deleterious effect on students' performance. One boy we know complained that he hated IOWA testing (a standardized achievement test) because his mother always gave him too much to eat for breakfast on the day of the tests!

With the widespread growth of standardized literacy tests today, particularly what is known as *high-stakes assessments,* there is much concern about their appropriate use and their impact on curriculum and student learning. High-stakes assessments are single test scores that are used to make important decisions about students. Many states use such scores to judge the effectiveness of teaching and the curriculum. Proponents maintain that these assessments monitor student learning and ensure that all students receive appropriate instruction to achieve a minimal level of basic competence. Critics claim that standardized tests are often biased, lead to low-level instruction, and are not true measures of students' learning, (Calkins, Montgomery, Santman, & Fulk, 1998).

There is particular concern about the influence on children with learning differences. A position paper on assessment for children in special education issued by the International Reading Association (IRA) states that children who experience learning difficulties should (1) have access to appropriate assessments for informing instruction, (2) be included in state and national assessments, and (3) receive accommodations and alternative assessment systems appropriate for their needs without distorting the skills, processes, and content being tested (International Reading Association, May, 2000). Accommodations include modification in time restrictions, having someone read the test to the learner, and out-of-level testing, in which learners are administered a test appropriate to their functioning level rather than their age level.

The IRA has also issued a position paper on high-stakes testing, expressing concern about the importance given to one measure of a student's achievement (Box 3.1) (International Reading Association, August 1999).

▮ Box 3.1

SUMMARY OF A POSITION STATEMENT OF THE INTERNATIONAL READING ASSOCIATION: HIGH-STAKES ASSESSMENTS IN READING (AUGUST 1999)

High-Stakes Testing

The International Reading Association strongly opposes high-stakes testing. Alarmingly, U.S. policy makers and educators are increasingly relying on single test scores to make important decisions about students. For example, if a student receives a high score on one high-stakes test, it could place him in a honors class or a gifted program. On the other hand, if a student receives a low score on one test, she could be rejected by a particular college. These tests can also be used to influence teachers' salaries, or rate a school district in comparison with others.

The Association believes that important conceptual, practical, and ethical issues must be considered by those who are responsibile for designing and implementing testing programs. Assessment should be used to improve instruction and benefit students rather than compare and pigeonhole them.

Among the Association's recommendations:

Teachers should:
> Construct rigorous classroom assessments to help outside observers gain confidence in teacher techniques.
> Educate parents, community members, and policy makers about classroom-based assessment.
> Teach students how tests are structured, but not teach to the test.

Parents and child-advocacy groups should:
> Ask questions about what tests are doing to their children and their schools.
> Lobby for the development of classroom-based forms of assessment that improve instruction and help children become better readers and learners.

Policy makers should:
> Design assessment plans that reflect the complexity of reading, learning to read, and teaching reading.
>
> Rely on multiple measures of assessment for decision making.
>
> Avoid using incentives, resources, money, or recognition of test scores to reward or punish schools or teachers.

Reprinted by permission of the International Reading Association, Newark: DE.

However, despite the many criticisms, standardized tests will not be eliminated any time soon. They are now a part of instruction and can be useful when used appropriately. When used in conjunction with other forms of assessment they provide additional information about the learner that the teacher could find helpful.

Informal Assessments

Informal assessments include teacher-made assessments such as worksheets, rubrics (which provide criteria for evaluating a task), and classroom tests as well as published assessments such as informal reading inventories, phonics inventories, interest inventories, and attitude surveys. Procedures for administering these assessments can be modified without affecting the validity of the results. They yield scores on certain criteria, not comparative scores, and can provide teachers with opportunities to observe student behavior in addition to obtaining a level. Informal assessments are generally more closely aligned with the curriculum. Because administration and scoring are not standardized, the skill of the examiner may affect the results of the assessment. Specific types of informal assessments will be discussed in greater depth later in this chapter.

Observations

Observations are another useful form of assessment. Teachers generally need some training in observational techniques in order to look closely at students' behavior and analyze their performance throughout the day. They need a systematic approach to gathering and recording data. This may include anecdotal records, checklists, and other organizational schemes. To increase the effectiveness of observation, teachers should have a system for collecting and storing observational data. Although some data collection will be spontaneous, it should be balanced with planned time to observe individual children as they engage in reading and writing. Teachers should constantly observe and analyze students' literacy behavior in order to plan more effective instruction.

Language Assessment

The assessment of language presents some difficult challenges for teachers and other education professionals. First, language is closely intertwined with the context in which language is used. Language in school may differ greatly from language used at home. Even different environments in the school (e.g., classroom, playground, lunchroom) may bring out different language usage. Second, language can vary in response to the listener. One may talk differently to a child than to an adult or to the school principal than to a classmate. Finally, language is closely related to other skills such as cognition, attention, and social skills, making it difficult to determine whether one is observing a language skill or another functional skill. Consider the following interaction that one of the authors witnessed in a kindergarten classroom:

Teacher (to a group of three students):   Can you get your books?
    (The students look at each other but make no response.)
Teacher (raising her voice):   Can you get your books!
    (Again, no response from the students.)
Teacher: Get your books and come here!
    (The students get their books and come forward.)

What happened? Were these students intentionally misbehaving (behavior problem)? Did they lack knowledge of what the teacher expected (cognition)? Or, did they fail to understand a complex linguistic structure (indirect request)? This example shows how difficult it can be to identify a language difficulty.

Despite the inherent difficulties in language assessment, it is essential that language be identified and described. Understanding a child's language skills and difficulties can provide insights into classroom behavior, socialization, and reading and writing difficulties as well as help identify the child's present language development. Like other skill areas, language can be assessed using both formal and informal techniques. Formal methods of assessment can be useful, especially for clinical diagnostic and prescriptive purposes. However, informal techniques, though difficult to use, may provide a richer picture of the child's language skills.

Formal Language Assessment Procedures

For assessing language we include standardized tests as well as structured observation systems in this category because both have a formal set of procedures and materials that must be used. Although formal language assessment procedures have the advantage of being relatively easy to use and interpret, some concerns about their use (and misuse) have been raised. Owens (1995) cited the following concerns:

- the validity of language assessment, that is, the effectiveness of the test in assessing the skill it purports to test.
- formal assessments test only a sample of a skill from which inferences are made about overall ability.
- many formal assessments do not reflect current definitions of the nature of language.
- formal assessments impose group criteria on individuals, thus obscuring the individual.

Despite the inherent limitations of standardized language assessment, it continues to be used widely. Therefore, it is important that education professionals have some knowledge of the range of formal assessment procedures that are available. Two types of formal assessment procedures are listed in Table 3.1. Tests of general-language functioning typically assess a wide range of language skills, often in both expressive (speaking) and receptive (listening) modes. They can be useful for giving an overall picture of the child's language development. Tests of specific language skills are often used to enhance the information provided by general tests. Because they have more test items that focus on the specific skill of interest, they can provide a more in-depth analysis of

TABLE 3.1   Formal Language Assessment Tests

Tests of General Language Skills

Name	Language Skill(s) Assessed	Age/Grade–Range
Bankson Language Test (2nd ed.)	Semantic knowledge morphological/syntactical rules pragmatics	3–0 to 6–11
Clinical Evaluation of Language Fundamentals (3rd ed.)	Receptive and expressive language content, form, and use	6–0 to 21
Clinical Evaluation of Language Fundamentals: Observational Rating Scale	Listening, speaking, reading, writing	6–0 to 21
Receptive-Expressive Emergent Language Test (2nd ed.)	Expressive and receptive language	Birth to 3–0
Test for Auditory Comprehension of Language—Revised	Word meanings, grammatical morphemes, complex sentences	3–0 to 9–11
Test of Adolescent and Adult Language (3rd ed.)	Listening, speaking, writing, vocabulary, grammar	12–0 to 24–11
Test of Early Language Development (3rd ed.)	Receptive and expressive language	2–0 to 7–11
Test of Language Development—Primary (3rd ed.)	Receptive and expressive: phonology, syntax, and semantics	4–0 to 8–11
Intermediate (3rd ed.)	Receptive and expressive: syntax and semantics	8–0 to 12–11

Tests of Specific Language Skills

Name	Language Skill(s) Assessed	Age/Grade–Range
Bankson-Bernthal Test of Phonology	Articulation and phonology	3–0 to 9–0
Boehm Test of Basic Concepts	Basic concepts	K to 2–0 (semantics)
Comprehensive Receptive and Expressive Vocabulary Test	Receptive and expressive oral vocabulary	4–0 to 17–11
Goldman–Fristoe Test of Articulation	Articulation	Above age 2
Peabody Picture Vocabulary Test	Receptive vocabulary	2–0 to adult
Test for Examining Expressive Morphology	Expressive morpheme development	3–0 to 7–0
Test of Phonological Awareness	Awareness of sounds in words	Grade K-2
Test of Pragmatic Language	Language in use	5–0 to 13–0
Wilson Syntax Screening Test	Grammatical morphemes	Pre-K to K

Teacher referral of children with possible language impairment

The following behaviors may indicate that a child in your classroom has a language impairment that is in need of clinical intervention. Please check the appropriate items.

_____ Child mispronounces sounds and words.

_____ Child omits word endings, such as plural -s and past tense -ed.

_____ Child omits small unemphasized words, such as auxiliary verbs or prepositions.

_____ Child uses an immature vocabulary, overuses empty words, such as *one* and *thing*, or seems to have difficulty recalling or finding the right word.

_____ Child has difficulty comprehending new words and concepts.

_____ Child's sentence structure seems immature or overreliant on forms, such as subject-verb-object. It's unoriginal, dull.

_____ Child's question and/or negative sentence style is immature.

_____ Child has difficulty with one of the following:

_____ Verb tensing	_____ Articles	_____ Auxiliary verbs
_____ Pronouns	_____ Irreg. verbs	_____ Prepositions
_____ Word order	_____ Irreg. plurals	_____ Conjunctions

_____ Child has difficulty relating sequential events.

_____ Child has difficulty following directions.

_____ Child's question often inaccurate or vague.

_____ Child's questions often poorly formed.

_____ Child has difficulty answering questions.

_____ Child's comments often off topic or inappropriate for the conversation.

_____ There are long pauses between a remark and the child's reply or between successive remarks by the child. It's as if the child is searching for a response or is confused.

_____ Child appears to be attending to communication but remembers little of what is said.

_____ Child has difficulty using language socially for the following purposes:

_____ Request needs	_____ Pretend/imagine	_____ Protest
_____ Greet	_____ Request information	_____ Gain attention
_____ Respond/reply	_____ Share ideas, feelings	_____ Clarify
_____ Relate events	_____ Entertain	_____ Reason

_____ Child has difficulty interpreting the following:

_____ Figurative language	_____ Humor	_____ Gestures
	_____ Emotions	_____ Body language

_____ Child does not alter production for different audiences and locations.

_____ Child does not seem to consider the effect of language on the listener.

_____ Child often has verbal misunderstandings with others.

_____ Child has difficulty with reading and writing.

_____ Child's language skills seem to be much lower than other areas, such as mechanical, artistic, or social skills.

FIGURE 3.2

Structured Observation Form

Source: Owens, R. E. (1995). *Language Disorders,* 2nd ed. Needham Heights, MA: Allyn & Bacon, p. 392.

that skill. Used carefully, formal assessments can help to build a profile of a child's language functioning. However, they should be combined with informal assessment to provide a more complete picture.

Informal Language Assessment Procedures

Considering the limitations of formal language assessments, it is essential that any assessment of language include informal assessment procedures. These allow the evaluator to go beyond the structured format and procedures of formal assessment and to observe the child in less structured, more naturalistic settings. Teachers and other education professionals can learn a great deal by observing children as they interact and by structuring classroom activities so that they elicit opportunities for language use.

Structured Observations

Whenever children are interacting with others there are opportunities for language assessment. The challenge is how to make these opportunities useful sources of assessment information. Figures 3.2 and 3.3 give two examples of structured observation forms that can be used in the classroom. The first asks the observer to give an overall judgment as to whether or not the child can perform a specific skill (Figure 3.2). The second example was developed by one of the authors and used in classrooms to observe interaction between students (Figure 3.3).

Structured Classroom Activities

Many classroom activities can be structured in such a way as to provide opportunities for language assessment. For example, following a lesson on the classification of plants, the teacher could place the children in small groups to prepare a chart that illustrates

	Obs 1	Obs 2	Obs 3	Obs 4	Obs 5	Obs 6	Obs 7	Obs 8
Initiation								
To Peer								
To Adult								
Response								
Positive								
Negative								
Ignored								

Note: Positive response = a response that is positive in tone and encourages additional interaction:
  e.g., "How are you today?" (initiation)
  "I'm fine. How are you?" (response)
 Negative response = a response that is negative in tone and discourages additional interaction:
  e.g., "How are you today?" (initiation)
  "Shut up!" (response)

FIGURE 3.3

Observation of Communicative Interaction in the Classroom

several of the plant groups. To enhance interaction, the teacher could provide groups of pictures from which the children need to choose one or two to illustrate each plant group. To further enhance interaction, the teacher could "sabotage" the activity by making sure that students did not have sufficient materials to complete the assignment. For example, there may be only one scissors, each child may have only one or two markers, and there may be no paste. To complete the assignment, students must share with each other and request missing materials from the teacher. During the activity, the teacher can observe language skills such as:

- initiating a language interaction
- making a request
- asking questions
- responding to a request or question
- turn-taking

Butler and Stevens (1997) give other examples of classroom-based activities that can be used to assess language, such as:

Book Talks: Students prepare an oral presentation about a book that they have read. Students are evaluated for both the content of their report and the delivery. Criteria for delivery can include:
- maintaining eye contact with audience
- demonstrating good posture
- using appropriate language for a formal presentation
- using appropriate voice level

Group Discussion Task: The authors suggest that a small group of students read a book or watch a video that leaves the ending unresolved. The students must participate in a group discussion to provide an ending. The teacher observes student interactions and rates them for:
- the quality and quantity of information contributed
- effectiveness in communicating information
- ease and flow of the student's speech

A rubric can be developed for each of these performance areas to guide the teacher's observations and feedback to the student. For example, for "quality and quantity of information contributed" Butler and Stevens suggest the following scale:

4 = *very elaborate* comments, opinions, solutions, or replies. Includes category #3 with greater elaboration.
3 = *elaborated* comments, opinions, solutions, or replies; e.g., opinions with reasons, solutions with explanations.
2 = *simple* comments, opinions, solutions, or replies. Complete sentences not necessarily used.
1 = *irrelevant* comments having little or nothing to do with the discussion.

Almost any classroom activity could be used as an opportunity for language assessment. All that is needed is the development of criteria for performance and careful observation and feedback.

Language Samples

Language samples are a potentially rich source of information about a child's language skills. Although a complete and detailed analysis of language samples requires

| **TABLE 3.2** | Calculation of Utterance Length |

Utterance length is usually found by using a measure called, "mean length of utterance" (MLU). MLU is calculated as follows:

1. Divide the language sample into utterances; i.e., spoken sentences.

2. Count the morphemes in each utterance (morphemes include words and word endings).

3. Add the total number of morphemes.

4. Divide by the number of utterances to derive the mean length of utterance.

Example　(Two boys playing with cars). Morphemes in parentheses.

Student 1:　Can it run on this place too? (7)

Student 2:　Yeah, go ahead. (3)

　　S 1:　Yeah, but I ... (3)

　　S 2:　This is your road. (4)
　　　　　This whole road is your road and this is my place, O.K.? (12)

　　S 1:　O.K. (1)

　　S 2:　All this road is yours. (5)
　　　　　This is where your cars drive. (7)

　　S 1:　Yeah. (1)

　　S 2:　You have a police station. (5)
　　　　　There's your, your fire station, your fire station. (5) (repeats not counted)
　　　　　I've got my police station and fire station. (9)

In this brief example, student 2 has an observed MLU of 6.25 (50 morphemes/8 utterances).

a significant amount of training, teachers can get useful information from a sample of language such as the following:

- number of times the child talks during an interaction
- average length of each utterance (see Table 3.2 for an example)
- type of sentences used (simple, compound, complex)
- variety and sophistication of vocabulary
- use of turn-taking

It is rarely possible to get a completely spontaneous language sample. Children just do not sit still long enough or talk at the time that the teacher is ready to observe. Therefore, it is usually necessary to structure the sample in some way. Owens (1995) suggests the use of activities that are meaningful to the child and contain numerous opportunities for interaction. For young children, this might include play with interesting toys. For older children this might include discussion of pictures or videos. In either case, there are some important factors to consider when choosing tasks for language sample elicitation, including:

- selecting toys with a variety of pieces that can be moved and interchanged
- using pictures that show several frames of continuing action rather than a static scene
- avoiding "story-telling" that might elicit a recitation of a writer's text rather than the child's language
- selection of conversational partners who will encourage interaction without talking for the child.

Assessment of language is important for establishing instructional goals for language instruction, identifying children in need of speech and language intervention, and understanding factors that may contribute to reading and writing difficulties. Although formal assessment can provide useful information, there are limitations that make informal assessment an important part of any language assessment. Routine classroom activities provide numerous opportunities for the observation of language when careful planning and setting of criteria are used to make the activity into an assessment procedure.

Reading Assessment

Emergent Level

At the emergent level of literacy development, children begin to acquire key concepts about language and print that create the foundation for literacy instruction. As noted earlier, children have to develop an understanding of the relationship between print and speech, understanding the concept of word, and word boundaries. They begin to recognize letters and the critical attributes of letters (that size, color, and thickness may not be important, but positioning and relationship of lines and curves are). Phonemic awareness should be evolving as well when children begin to understand that words are composed of sounds that can be manipulated to form new words. They should also become familiar with the format of books and print—position, directionality, page-turning etc.

One procedure for assessing word knowledge is the voice-pointing procedure (Gillett & Temple, 2000). In the voice-pointing procedure, children memorize a rhythmic poem or selection of text that they cannot yet read; for example, *Brown Bear* or *Twinkle, Twinkle Little Star*. The procedure consists of the following:

1. Pretest approximately eight words from the selection.
2. Recite text so that the child memorizes it without looking at it.
3. Read the lines aloud, pointing to each *line* as you read.
4. Have the child recite the lines, pointing to each *word* as he or she does so.
5. Read selected words aloud and ask the child to point them out.
6. Use word cards to post test word recognition.

This procedure assesses the child's concept of words, in addition to the child's ability to learn words from familiar context. Word concept can also be assessed during instruction by asking the student to point to each word as you read the selection together. Careful observation provides information of the student's strategies; that is, it will indicate if the student appears to be just telling a story or attempting to match his or her speech to the print in the text.

Knowledge of letters and phonemic awareness can be assessed through formal and informal measures, as well as embedded in instruction. Alphabet tasks can be as simple as asking students to identify upper- and lowercase letters and keeping a checklist of student responses. Phonemic awareness can be assessed through a number of formal assessments, such as *The Lindamood Auditory Conceptualization Test,* which is a criterion-referenced test that assesses an individual's abilities in auditory perception and phonemic awareness. These tests are generally individually administered and require from ten to thirty minutes to administer. Other less-formal assessments include the *Yopp–Singer Test of Phonemic Segmentation,* and the *Bruce Phonemic Deletion Test,* in which students are asked to manipulate phonemes to create new words (Yopp, 1988).

In the *Yopp–Singer Test of Phonemic Awareness,* students are presented with a word and are then asked to pronounce the component sounds of the word; e.g., *cat* is *c-a-t* (Box 3.2).

■ **Box 3.2**

WORDS USED IN YOPP–SINGER PHONEME-SEGMENTATION TEST

dog	zoo	wave
fine	job	that
she	ice	me
grew	top	race
red	do	three
sat	keep	in
lay	no	at
by		

Source: From "The Validity and Reliability of Phonemic Awareness Tests" by H. K. Yopp, 1988. *Reading Research Quarterly, 23*(2), p. 177. Copyright 1988 by the International Reading Association. Reprinted by permission of H. Yopp and the International Reading Association.

The *Bruce Phonemic Deletion Test* assesses a more complex ability in phonemic awareness. Children are presented with a word and are asked to delete a specific phoneme and indicate the word that remains. For example, when the *s* sound is removed from *stop,* the word *top* remains. To accomplish the task, children must segment the word into the component sounds, remove a sound, and then blend the remaining sounds to create a new word. Box 3.3 presents some tasks that have been used to test students' phonemic awareness.

▌Box 3.3

TECHNIQUES TO ASSESS PHONOLOGICAL AWARENESS

1. Division of bisyllabic words into CVC monosyllables.
   The children were given some examples of how to divide the words into parts using a puppet that modeled the correct response. Then the children were told to divide the following words into parts:

airplane	doctor
football	monkey
hotdog	pencil
pancake	window

2. Division of monosyllabic words into sounds (phonemes).
   The same preparation was used as that described previously. Then the children were told to divide the following words into their sounds:

plane	doc
foot	key
hot	pen
cake	dow

3. Elision task.
   The children were told, "I'm going to say a word to you. You say the word just like I do. Then I'm going to tell you a part to leave off, either at the beginning or the end of the word. You say the word, leaving off the part I tell you to." The children were given several examples, then were given the following words:

(t)old	(s)top	sun(k)	far(m)
(b)lend	(n)ear	bus(t)	car(d)
(t)all	(b)ring	pin(k)	for(k)
(n)ice	(s)pin	ten(t)	star(t)

4. Segmentation (tapping) task.
   The children were told, "Now we're going to play a tapping game. I'm going to say something to you—some play words—and then tap them after I say them. You need to listen carefully, so you can learn how to play the game."

   Example: The tester says, "oo" and taps one time.
            Then, the tester says, "boo" and taps two times.
            Then, "boot" and taps three times.

   The experimental items were:

ap	zan	leb	piv
em	ib	kest	kel
niz	polt	feh	kii
blim	wog	sput	mik

Source: Kamhi, A., & Catts, H. (1986). Toward an understanding of developmental language and reading disorders. *Journal of Speech and Hearing Disorders, 51*, 337–347.

Teachers can also assess phonemic awareness through classroom activities. The ability to rhyme is one of the most basic elements of phonemic awareness. Creating rhymes with children, asking them to supply the rhyming word in an unfamiliar nursery rhyme, and using songs can give important information to the observant teacher.

Another aspect of phonemic awareness is the manipulation of the initial consonant. Asking children to give examples of different words that begin with an initial consonant, using classifying activities such as providing some examples and then asking for another word that fits the category (boat, banana, ?), musical games such as the *Name Game* or *Willoby, Walloby, Woo,* in which children have to follow the pattern using their own name (*Lisa, Lisa, Bo Bisa, Banana Fanna, Fo Fisa, Lisa*) provide indications of children's abilities in this area.

A combination of writing and phonemic awareness assessment is the *Dictation Task* (Clay, 1993). In this task the examiner reads a sentence to the student and then dictates it slowly for the student to write. The test is scored by the number of phonemes represented in the child's writing. Norms are given for the test for 1st-grade students in New Zealand and the United States. An advantage of the *Dictation Task* is that although it may be preferable to use it individually, it can be used with the entire class to provide a quick indication for teachers of any children who may be having difficulty with this very important task.

Concepts about print or book knowledge can also be easily assessed by informal means. Some informal reading inventories, such as the *Bader Reading and Language Inventory,* have subsections for assessing book knowledge. The Concepts about print subtest in *An observation survey of early literacy achievement* (Clay, 1993) assesses students' awareness of print, directionality, concept of word, etc. There are special storybooks written for this test, which have interspersed upside-down words and letters, to determine if students notice the "odd" ones. Teachers can also assess students' knowledge through observation during instruction, or by informally asking students to point to the first or last word on a page, turn pages, or hold a book upside down.

Beyond the Emergent Stage

In Chapter 1, we postulated that literacy development is the strategic application of various types of knowledge and abilities. We have addressed language in an earlier section of this chapter. Now let's turn our attention to other components of literacy.

Assessment of Overall Reading Ability

Many schools use formal testing as a routine part of their assessment of children. Achievement tests, which include reading subtests, are often administered annually. If they are group norm-referenced tests, they may provide information on the different aspects of reading, but their main purpose is to determine an individual or a group's performance relative to a sample population. Thus, the scores that individuals receive are an indication of how they compared to others of the same age and grade. Take the case of Janna. Janna is a second-grade student who has taken a standardized achievement test. Her scores show that she has received a 3.0 grade equivalent in reading. Does this mean that she can read at the third-grade level? No, it indicates that she answered the same number of questions correctly as the median (50th percentile) child from the third grade. It does not, however, provide information on what she can read. Norm-referenced assessments, then, can provide an indication of a possible problem, or an indication that everyone is progressing similarly to the sample population, but they do not provide information for guiding instruction. The norm-referenced test may add additional information, but should never be used as the primary assessment tool for a student.

Some norm-referenced tests are administered individually. Their purpose is to generally provide a profile of strengths and weaknesses of a child, and may also be used as part of the procedure to determine if a learning disability exists. Tests such as the *Woodcock Reading Mastery Test* and the *Woodcock–Johnson Psychoeducational Battery (WJ-R)*, provide teachers with information on many of the areas of reading and skills that are related to reading. The Achievement Battery of the WJ-R, for example, includes subtests in the areas of *letter-word identification, passage comprehension, word attack,* and *reading vocabulary.* The value of these formal assessments, however, lies primarily in helping to identify a problem rather than informing instruction. Table 3.3. provides a partial listing of formal assessments in reading.

Teachers should supplement information from formal assessments of overall reading with a variety of informal measures. Informal measures encompass published assessments, teacher-made assessments, student work samples, and observational data. The *informal reading inventory* (IRI) is a published informal assessment. Although often commercially prepared and validated (they may however, be constructed by the teacher), informal reading inventories are informal in their administration (which can be modified as needed), their scoring, and their purpose (which is

TABLE 3.3   Some Commonly Used Formal Reading Tests

Name	Skills Assessed	Age/Grade–Range
Degree of Reading	Comprehension	Grades 1–12
Gates–MacGinitie Silent Reading Test	Vocabulary/comprehension	Grades k–12
Gilmore Oral Reading Test	Oral reading/comprehension	Grades 1–8
Iowa Tests of Educational Development	Comprehension decoding	Grades k–12
Nelson–Denny Reading Test	Vocabulary/comprehension	Grades 9–college
Slosson Oral Reading Test	Oral reading	Preschool–adult
Stanford Diagnostic Reading Test	Vocabulary/comprehension decoding/strategies	Grades 1–college
TerraNova	Comprehension	Grades k–12
Test of Reading Comprehension	Vocabulary/sequencing paraphrasing/comprehension	Ages 7–18
Woodcock Reading Mastery Test	Vocabulary/comprehension letter id/decoding	Grades k–12
Woodcock–Johnson Psychoeducational Battery	Letter id/decoding/ comprehension	Ages 3–80

mainly instructionally based). Based on the work of Emmett Betts and others (Manzo & Manzo, 1993) the purpose of the IRI is to:

- establish a student's independent, instructional, and frustration level for proper placement in reading material
- group students with similar abilities for instruction
- monitor students' progress in decoding and comprehension
- provide information to teachers about students' use of strategies while reading

IRIs consist of graded word lists and passages. They generally range from the preprimer to the junior high or high school levels, although at least one has been developed for secondary and college level. Word lists are used to determine automaticity and to provide information for beginning the paragraph reading. Although IRIs may differ, the paragraph assessment often has a background knowledge and prediction-making question, a passage, and comprehension questions. Some IRIs also ask for a retelling. When used qualitatively, IRIs can provide information about students' schema, their automatic sight vocabulary, their fluency and decoding ability, and strategies. Analysis of oral reading errors, sometimes called miscue analysis, gives the examiner insight into students' use of phonological, semantic, and syntactic cuing systems. IRIs also provide information about students' comprehension of explicit and implicit information, and their ability to retell a selection, selecting important information, and organizing it.

Many informal reading inventories have a number of forms, allowing the examiner to assess oral and silent reading comprehension. A number of them have narrative and expository text, providing information on students' abilities to comprehend different text structures. Administration of IRIs can be modified to meet students' needs. For example, the test can be segmented over various sessions, word lists may be retyped either in large print or on individual cards for students who become overwhelmed, questions can be reworded to help students more fully understand what is being asked, and students can use cards or placeholders for tracking as necessary.

Advantages of the IRI include the alignment of levels with graded instructional material, the closer resemblance to authentic text, and most critically, the opportunity to observe the reader to obtain a fuller picture of strengths, weaknesses, and the reader's strategies. Disadvantages include the uneven quality of passages and questions; the time it takes to administer the test (up to two hours for an individual student); the differences in assessment of miscues (e.g., some reading inventories count any deviation from text while others count only meaning-changing deviations); the dependence on the skill of the examiner for modifying administration, rewording questions, and analyzing responses; and the general disadvantages of one-time assessments. For the reasons above, IRIs are usually administered by reading specialists or learning consultants, not the classroom teacher. Used appropriately, however, the results can provide valuable information for the classroom teacher. Table 3.4 lists some common informal reading inventions currently in use.

An alternative to IRIs that can be administered by the classroom teacher is a running record. Any classroom text may be used for running records thus allowing a teacher to use it spontaneously as part of instruction. The teacher administers the running record individually, generally starting by having the student preview the text. The child reads orally as the teacher marks the miscues.

TABLE 3.4   Some common informal reading inventories

Name	Author	Levels/Grades	Publisher
Analytic Reading Inventory	Woods, M. L., Moe, A. J	Primer–grade 9	Merrill
Bader Reading and Language Inventory	Bader, L. A.	Preprimer–sr. high school	Prentice Hall
Basic Reading Inventory	Johns, J. L	Preprimer–grade 9	Kendall/Hunt
Qualitative Reading Inventory III	Leslie, L., Caldwell, J.	Preprimer–grade 9	HarperCollins
Secondary and College Inventory	Johns, J. L.	Grade 7–college	Kendall/Hunt

If the teacher has not made a copy of the text in advance, he or she uses check marks on a blank sheet of paper to record correct responses. A coding system similar to those used for informal reading inventories is used to record incorrect responses. Many teachers, however, have established benchmark books for running records that they have copied on paper to make recording easier. By keeping material for different leveled texts in folders, the teacher can quickly select an appropriate text for administration and scoring. Analysis of running records can provide an instructional level and information about the child's phonic knowledge and strategic knowledge during contextual reading. They are less cumbersome than IRIs and can provide relatively quick assessment for instructional purposes. Figure 3.4 is an illustration of a running record.

Miscue	Coding	Example
Omitted	——	~~slowly~~
Inserted	ʌ	ʌ small
Substitution	Miscue̲	slyly / ~~slowly~~
Self-correct	Miscue/sc̲	slyly sc / ~~slowly~~
Hesitate	H	
Appeal	A	
Repetition	⌐‾‾‾⌐	⌐He went⌐

H   so/sc   So   purple
They saw trees. Some were red. Some were green. They were pretty.

                                          the/sc   nest/sc
Pat and Sam saw birds too. Sam did not run after them. He was nice.

FIGURE 3.4

Running Record Example Coding System
Passage from: Johns, J. (1991). *Basic Reading Inventory.* Dubuque, IA: Kendall/Hunt, p. 130.

Assessment of Phonics   In an earlier section we examined whether students understood there was a sound system in spoken English. In this section we are looking at students' knowledge of sound-symbol relationships (phonological knowledge). There are a number of informal assessments for determining students' phonological knowledge. These tests are usually administered individually and provide information about students' strategies to decode unfamiliar words in isolation. Nonsense words are often used, which illustrate certain sound patterns, to eliminate the possibility of the child reading the word from memory. Tests using nonsense or pseudowords have been shown to help teachers identify students' strengths and weaknesses in phonics (Torgesen et. al., as cited in Gillet & Temple, 2000).

Because reading nonsense words is sometimes problematic for readers who understand that reading must make sense, an alternative test of phonic knowledge was developed by Cunningham (1990) called the *Names Test*. In this test, the examiner is directed to tell a student that he or she should pretend to be a teacher on the first day of school who needs to read the classlist. There are twenty-five first and last names on the test. Names were chosen to meet the following four criteria: (1) not some of the most common names, (2) fully decodable, (3) represent a sampling of phonics patterns, and (4) represent a balance of longer and shorter names (Duffelmeyer, Kruse, Merkley & Fyfe, 1994). Duffelmeyer et. al. (1994) enhanced it by adding ten additional first and last names, and providing a protocol sheet and scoring matrix for teachers.

TABLE 3.5   The *Names Test* (Cunningham, 1990 and as enhanced by Duffelmeyer et al., 1994)

Jay Conway	Cindy Sampson	Flo Thornton
Tim Cornell	Chester Wright	Dee Skidmore
Chuck Hoke	Ginger Yale	Grace Brewster
Yolanda Clark	Patrick Tweed	Ned Westmoreland
Kimberly Blake	Stanley Shaw	Ron Smitherman
Roberta Slade	Wendy Swain	Troy Whitlock
Homer Preston	Glen Spencer	Vance Middleton
Gus Quincy	Fred Sherwood	Zane Anderson
		Bernard Pendergraph

Additional Names:

Shane Fletcher	Bertha Dale	Joan Brooks
Floyd Sheldon	Neal Wade	Gene Loomis
Dean Bateman	Jake Murphy	Thelma Rinehart
Austin Shepherd		

Reprinted with permission: International Reading Association. Newark: DE

The test was validated for students with and without learning disabilities (Duffelmeyer & Black, 1996).

Assessment of Comprehension

Because comprehension is a complex task, teachers need to guard against overuse of simplistic comprehension measures. Many tools that encompass the various aspects of comprehension should be included in any system for assessing comprehension. Many formal assessments include comprehension testing as part of the reading battery. There are a number of difficulties associated with formal comprehension assessments, however. Because procedures are standardized, it is often difficult to determine the effect of decoding ability on comprehension results. Passages are generally short, having little relation to the type of reading in which learners usually engage. Literal-level questions may predominate for ease of scoring. Results are often reported in terms of percentiles, grade equivalents, standard scores and are not necessarily correlated with levels and types of texts used in school. Some of the state assessments and newer tests try to address these difficulties through longer passages, more open-ended questions, and assessment-through-criterion measures, rather than norm comparisons. They provide a better indication of a child's reading ability than previous tests.

As mentioned earlier, informal reading inventories can provide information on comprehension as well. Teachers can supplement information from these tests through classroom assessments, many of which often can be incorporated in instruction.

The cloze procedure may be used for instructional and assessment purposes. In the cloze procedure the reader is given a passage with deleted words and told to complete the passage. Students have to use their knowledge of grammar and the meaning of the passage to complete the task (Figure 3.5). When used to determine a student's reading level, it is called a cloze test. A cloze test may be group administered and may be easily developed by a teacher, using actual classroom material.

To create a cloze test, the teacher selects a passage of approximately 250 to 300 words. He or she types the first sentence intact, and beginning with a word in the second sentence, deletes every fifth word from the passage until there are fifty deletions. She then types one sentence intact after the sentence with the last deletion. Before

Because comprehension is a complex task, teachers need to guard against overuse of simplistic comprehension measures. Many tools that encompass the _____ aspects of comprehension should _____ included in any system _____ assessing comprehension. Many _____ assessments include comprehension testing _____ part of the reading _____. There are a number _____ difficulties associated with formal _____ assessments, however. Because _____ are standardized, it is _____ difficult to determine the _____ of decoding ability on _____ results. Passages are generally _____, having little relation to _____ type of reading learners _____ engage in. Literal-level questions may predominate for ease of scoring.

FIGURE 3.5

Example of cloze test

selecting the word for beginning deletions the teacher should peruse the selection to determine that proper nouns and numbers are not being consistently deleted. Scoring of the cloze test is more accurate when only exact word replacements are acceptable. Placement criteria are as follows (Bormouth, 1968):

independent level	57% or greater
instructional level	44 to 56%
frustration level	43 or less

Teachers may modify testing by constructing a maze test. In a maze test, there are twenty deletions from a passage of approximately 125 words. Children are provided with three choices for the deleted word: one word is the exact word, one word is syntactically acceptable, and one word is syntactically unacceptable. The placement criteria are as follows:

independent level	85% or greater
instructional level	50 to 84%
frustration level	49 or less

The maze procedure appears to be more effective for children below the third-grade level (McCormick, 1999).

Retellings may be used as a tool for comprehension assessment. To assess a student's retelling, the teacher should use a form to indicate the presence of the various elements of story grammar: setting, characters, theme, initiating event/problem, plot sequence, and resolution.

An important aspect of reading comprehension is metacognition. Metacognition includes the ability to be strategic in one's approach to reading, monitoring one's reading and knowing when comprehension has not occurred, and compensating for comprehension breakdown through the use of new strategies. In the *Metacomprehension Strategy Index* (Schmitt, 1990), students respond to a twenty-five item questionnaire, designed to assess the strategies they use before, during, and after reading. Four choices are provided for each question; one of them is an indication of awareness of metacognition strategies. Data analysis can be very useful for planning instruction (Harp, 2000).

Metacognitive awareness may also be assessed through teacher-constructed interviews (Paris, Wasik, & Turner, 1996). Interviews should assess students' understanding of the purposes of reading and their use of strategies for comprehension and for compensation. An advantage of the interviews is that the language of the interview can be tailored to the language of the child.

Assessment of Attitudes and Interests   Informal surveys and questionnaires may be used to assess children's attitudes toward reading. Some surveys for primary-level children use animal characters with different facial expressions or in different poses to indicate a feeling about reading in different contexts. Children work through the survey, circling the animal that most closely represents their feelings about different aspects of reading. For example, in response to the phrase "a rainy day is a good time to read a book" the children would choose either a very happy face, a happy face, a surprised face, a sad face, or an angry face.

Gambrell et al. (1996) have developed the *Motivation to Read Profile*, which can be used with older students. Through a questionnaire and conversational interview, the student's response provides an indication of the child's self-concept as a reader and his or her attitude toward reading. The interview is administered individually and usually takes about fifteen to twenty minutes. To save time, a classroom teacher might administer the survey to a group of students and conduct the interviews individually.

Attitudes may also be observed indirectly by keeping records of books read during a specified period of time and through observation of children during self-selected reading time.

Writing Assessment

A comprehensive assessment of writing should include assessment of the content of writing, mechanics (spelling, handwriting, grammar), and the learner's attitudes toward and knowledge of writing. However, in many cases, assessment focuses primarily on mechanics, sometimes to the exclusion of the other domains. The mechanical aspects of writing are easier to assess than content or factors intrinsic to the learner. Spelling and grammar errors are easily detected and many formal assessments of writing emphasize the detection of errors in spelling and grammar. However, assessment of content and of the learner, although more challenging, are equally important to the development of a complete picture of students' written expression skills.

Formal Assessment of Writing

As with language and reading assessment, there are both formal and informal techniques available for the assessment of written content. Many formal achievement tests include an assessment of writing. For example, the *Wechsler Individual Achievement Test*

A writing rubric provides a framework for assessment of a student's writing.

(WIAT) (Psychological Corporation, 1992) has a freewriting task that is assessed for the development of ideas and organization as well as capitalization and punctuation. The *Peabody Individual Achievement Test-Revised* (PIAT-R) (Markwardt, 1989) has both a copying and dictation task and a freewriting task.

More intensive assessment of writing skills is provided by tests such as the *Test of Written Language-3* (TOWL-3) (Hammill & Larsen, 1996). This test was designed to diagnose writing difficulties in students in grades 2 to 12. It is a standardized, norm-referenced test consisting of eight subtests:

- Vocabulary: students write sentences containing stimulus words.
- Spelling: students write sentences from dictation.
- Style: evaluation of punctuation in sentences written from dictation.
- Logical sentences: students rewrite illogical sentences so that they make sense.
- Sentence combining: students are asked to write one sentence based on several short sentences.
- Contextual conventions: evaluates students' use of spelling and punctuation in spontaneous writing.
- Contextual language: evaluates students' ability to construct grammatically correct sentences used in spontaneous writing.
- Story construction: evaluates student's spontaneous writing on the basis of plot, prose, development of characters, interest to the reader, and other compositional aspects.

Scores for each subtest, an overall writing score, and three composite scores (overall written language, contrived writing, and spontaneous writing) can be derived. A related test, the *Test of Early Written Language-2* (TEWL-2) is available to assess the writing skills of children from 3–7 years old.

In addition to formal assessments of general writing skills, there are tests of specific skills such as handwriting and spelling. For example, the *Zaner-Bloser Evaluation Scale* (1984) can be used with groups or individuals to assess handwriting skills. Students are asked to copy designated words or phrases from the board. Their handwriting is compared to a "standard" provided in the test manual.

The *Test of Written Spelling-3* (Larsen & Hammill, 1994) is a norm-referenced test of spelling skills designed for children from ages 6 to 18. The test utilizes both predictable words (those that conform to spelling rules) and unpredictable words. Some tests, such as the *Bader Reading and Language Inventory* contain spelling lists to assess students' ability to spell phonically regular words and common sight words. Bear et al. (2000) have developed elementary spelling inventories to assess students' developmental spelling levels. Through careful analysis of students' performance on these inventories and in their independent writing, teachers can design instruction appropriate to their stage of development.

Informal Assessment of Content

Assessment of content is complex and difficult but it is an essential part of a comprehensive assessment of writing. Fortunately, a number of techniques have been developed to assess writing content. We will examine a few of these methods in this section.

TABLE 3.6	Example of Holistic Scoring

3 = An introduction is apparent.
    At least three supporting ideas are expressed.
    Each idea is elaborated.
    A closing is evident.

2 = An introduction is apparent.
    There are 1–2 supporting ideas.
    Each idea is elaborated.
    A closing is evident.

1 = The main topic is addressed.
    No supporting ideas are expressed.
    No closing is evident.

0 = Off topic.

Holistic Scoring: In holistic scoring the evaluator considers the writing as a whole, rather than focusing on specific aspects of the written work. What is the overall impact of the writing? Is it clear, well-organized, and persuasive? Often, the writing is scored on the basis of broad categories (e.g., 1 = excellent; 2 = fair; 3 = poor). The criteria for scoring may be based on broad guidelines (see Table 3.6) or may be established using *benchmarks* (comparative papers that are chosen to represent each of the scoring levels).

Analytic Scoring: Although holistic scoring is useful for obtaining an overall impression of a students' writing, analytic scoring enables the evaluator to obtain information about specific writing skills. To use analytic scoring, writing must be analyzed into specific components and the criteria for each of these components specified. Examples of analytic approaches to writing assessment include *checklists* and *rubrics*. With a checklist, each desired element in the writing activity is identified and point values are assigned:

Introduction = 10 points
Ideas = 10 points
Elaboration = 20 points
Closing = 10 points

A more elaborate variation of the checklist approach is the rubric. As with checklists, one begins by identifying the target writing elements. Then, criteria for each element are established. For example, for the introduction section, an "excellent" level might be defined as consisting of an easily identified introduction that includes a main idea. A "satisfactory" level might have an implied introduction that states a main idea. A "poor" introduction would have no introduction or main idea stated. Although rubrics can be difficult to develop at first, they can be a very useful method both for assessing writing and for teaching students how to improve their writing. Table 3.7 gives an example of a rubric that is used in a statewide assessment of writing.

Self-Assessment   An important goal for any writer is to develop the ability to self-evaluate. Good writers are able to be critical about their writing and are able to edit their writing to improve the final product. These skills are not easily learned. Students can be helped to improve their writing by engaging in self-evaluation of their written work. Each of the preceding techniques described (holistic scoring, checklists, and rubrics) can be adapted for self-evaluation. In addition, teachers can ask students to reflect on their writing in a journal or as part of a periodic evaluation. Students might be asked to respond to questions such as:

- Which is your best piece of writing? Tell why.
- How can you make your writing better?

Portfolios   Portfolios have become a widely used method in literacy instruction. Portfolios include a collection of the students' work that shows change over time. Farnan, Flood, and Lapp (1994) suggest that writing portfolios should include the following elements:

- Writing samples: including both early and final drafts
- Writings completed and in progress: including a list of works completed and the type of work (essay, story, poem, etc.)
- Learning in progress: checklists of "what I do well" and "what I need to work on"
- Writing topics: lists of possible topics for future writing

If portfolios are to be used as an assessment tool, the writing must be evaluated in some way. Any or all of the procedures described previously could be used. In addition, both the teacher and the student could keep a reflective journal that comments on the student's work over time.

Informal Assessment of Mechanics

Informal assessment of writing skills such as handwriting, spelling, vocabulary, and grammar is used frequently in most classrooms. Any written product can be assessed for these elements. However, in many cases, teachers may want to focus their feedback on one or just a few of these elements and may want to provide more in-depth analysis of this skill.

When assessing handwriting, it is a good idea to use a variety of tasks. For example, students might be asked to:

- Write their name
- Copy a word from the board
- Copy a sentence from the board
- Write a word/sentence from dictation
- Write a paragraph in response to a picture

Each of these tasks taps a somewhat different set of skills. For example, when copying from the board, students have the model in front of them but writing from dictation requires that an image of the letters be generated internally. Teachers can examine students' handwriting to see if it differs when they have the model available to them or must recall it from memory.

TABLE 3.7 New Jersey Registered Holistic Scoring Rubric

In scoring, consider the grid of written language	Inadequate Command	Limited Command	Partial Command	Adequate Command	Strong Command	Superior Command
Score	1	2	3	4	5	6
Content and Organization	• May lack opening and/or closing • Minimal response to topic; uncertain focus • No planning evident; disorganized	• May lack opening and/or closing • Attempts to focus • May drift or shift focus • Attempts organization • Few, if any, transitions between ideas	• May lack opening and/or closing • Usually has single focus • Some lapses or flaws in organization • May lack some transitions between ideas	• May lack opening and/or closing • Single focus • Ideas loosely connected • Transitions evident	• Generally has opening and closing • Single focus • Sense of unity and coherence • Key ideas developed • Logical progression of ideas	• Has opening and closing • Single, distinct focus • Unified and coherent • Well-developed • Logical progression of ideas
	• Details random, inappropriate, or barely apparent	• Details lack elaboration, i.e., highlight paper	• Repetitious details • Several unelaborated details	• Uneven development of details	• Details appropriate and varied	• Details effective, vivid, explicit, and/or pertinent
Usage	• No apparent control • Severe/numerous errors	• Numerous errors	• Errors/patterns of errors may be evident	• Some errors that do not interfere with meaning	• Few errors	• Very few, if any, errors
Sentence Construction	• Assortment of incomplete and/or incorrect sentences	• Excessive monotony/same structure • Numerous errors	• Little variety in syntax • Some errors	• Some errors that do not interfere with meaning	• Few errors	• Very few, if any, errors

In scoring, consider the grid of written language	Inadequate Command	Limited Command	Partial Command	Adequate Command	Strong Command	Superior Command
Score	1	2	3	4	5	6
Mechanics	• Errors so severe they detract from meaning	• Numerous serious errors	• Patterns of errors evident	• No consistent pattern of errors • Some errors that do not interfere with meaning	• Few errors	• Very few, if any, errors

NON-SCORABLE RESPONSES*

(FR) Fragment — Student wrote too little to allow a reliable judgment of his/her writing

(OT) Off Topic/Off Task — Student did not write on the assigned topic/task, or the student attempted to copy the prompt.

(NE) Not English — Students wrote in a language other than English.

(NR) No Response — Student refused to write on the topic, or the writing task folder was blank.

Content/Organization
- Communicates intended message to intended audience
- Relates to topic
- Opening and closing
- Focused
- Logical progression of ideas
- Transitions
- Appropriate details and information

Usage
- Tense formation
- Subject-verb agreement
- Pronouns usage/agreement
- Word choice/meaning
- Proper Modifiers

Sentence Construction
- Variety of formations
- Correct construction

Mechanics
- *Skills intact in:*
- Spelling
- Capitalization
- Punctuation

Source: NJ State Department of Education.

Similarly, an informal spelling assessment should include both analysis of spelling from dictation as well as choosing the correctly spelled word from a set of options and detection of spelling errors. Some students may have a great deal of difficulty recalling words from memory but may do better when the correct answer is available to them.

Methods for the informal assessment of vocabulary and grammar may be less familiar but can also be valuable. For example, a *type–token ratio* can be calculated to give a measure of vocabulary. In order to calculate a type–token ratio, the number of different words (the first appearance of each word) in a written sample is divided by the total number of words in that sample (see Table 3.8). *T-unit length* is calculated by dividing the total number of words in a sample by the number of thought (T) units. A thought unit is an idea. A sentence such as, "My friend came over to my house and we played baseball" consists of 11 words, one sentence, and two thought (T) units.

In addition to assessment of content and mechanics, it may be useful to gather information about the learners themselves. This could include evaluating their attitudes toward writing, their knowledge of the writing process, and their cognitive and motor skills. Students might be asked questions such as:

- How do you feel about writing?
- Why do people write?
- What do you like best about writing?
- What do you find difficult about writing?
- How should you begin to write?
- Where can you find ideas for writing?

Although there are numerous formal tests of cognitive and motor skills available, the most valuable information for understanding these factors in students' writing may

---

TABLE 3.8   Examples of Type–Token Ratio and T-Unit Calculation

Story by 3rd-grade male:

The Story is about a girl named Megan and her father Mike. Megan's father works at a leather shop wher then make belts, shoes, and bags out of leather. Megan would work with he dad she would make lunch and clean up the leather that would fall on the floor after work they would go to the beach and make a trail in the wet sand.

Type–Token Ratio Calculation:

    type = 45 (different words)

    token = 66 (total words)

    ratio = 45/66 = .68

T-Unit Calculation:

    Thought units = 8

    Average length of T-unit = 66 words/8 = 8.25

    Number of sentences = 5

come from observation. Teachers might look at how the student holds the pencil, whether written output improves when the student uses a computer for word processing, whether handwriting and spelling differ in relation to the type of task (copying or dictation). Each of these can give some insight into understanding what might be limiting a student's written expression. In addition, students can be asked to self-report about what they find challenging in writing.

▋▋ASSESSMENT OF THE TEXT

One of the purposes for assessing the reader is to ensure proper placement in a reading text. To accomplish this, however, one must understand the characteristics of easy and difficult texts for evaluating reading material. Before you continue, think about your own texts. Do you find they are all at the same difficulty level, or are some easier for you to read than others? What makes a textbook easy or difficult for you to read? Jot down your ideas, and after reading this section, see if your thoughts match the authors'.

Readability

One of the ways that texts are evaluated is through a process that determines their readability. Readability is generally calculated through a formula that assesses word difficulty and sentence complexity. Two major assumptions inherent in common readability formulas used today are (1) that longer words and multisyllabic words are more difficult, and (2) longer sentences are more complex and thus, more difficult. A readability formula that is easy to use is the Fry Readability Graph (Fry, 1968, 1977).

▌ Box 3.4

FRY READABILITY GRAPH

Directions for Use

Randomly select three 100-word passages from a book or an article.

Plot the average number of syllables and the average number of sentences per 100 words on the graph to determine the grade level of the material.

Choose more passages per book if great variability is observed and conclude that the book has uneven readability.

Few books will fall into the solid black area, but when they do, grade level scores are invalid.

Additional Directions for Working Readability Graph

Randomly select three sample passages and count exactly 100 words beginning with the beginning of a sentence. Don't count numbers. Do count proper nouns.

Count the number of sentences in the hundred words, estimating length of the fraction of the last sentence to the nearest 1/10th.

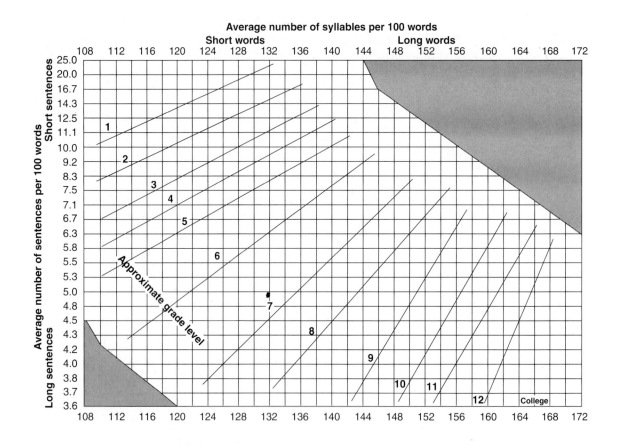

Count the total number of syllables in the 100-word passage. If you do not have a hand counter available, an easy way is to simply put a mark above every syllable over one in each word, then, when you get to the end of the passage, count the number of marks and add 100.

Enter graph with average sentence length and number of syllables; plot dot where the two lines intersect. Area where dot is plotted will give you the approximate grade level.

If a great deal of variability is found, putting more sample counts into the average is desirable.

Source: Fry, E. B. (1968). A readability formula that saves time. *Journal of Reading, 11,* 513–516, 575–578.

Certain word processing programs, such as *Microsoft Word* also provide information about readability. Type in three 100-word passages from the text and then select spelling and grammar from the tools bar. In addition to checking for grammar mistakes, the program will also provide readability information, based on the *Flesch–Kincaid* readability formula.

Readability formulas cannot be used with texts at the emergent levels. At the emergent levels one looks for lines of print, repetitiveness of words and patterns, and strong graphics support. Fountas and Pinnell (1996) provide descriptions of readers and text at various emergent literacy levels. Guided by their work, the authors have simplified and condensed categories for use with children at this stage (Table 3-9).

A cautionary note: Readability formulas only assess one small part of the factors that affect comprehension. Thus, they should at best be viewed as estimates of reading difficulty. They provide a guide for teachers in text selection and making instructional decisions, but should never be considered the final word on the difficulty level of a text.

Text considerateness encompasses many factors that affect the difficulty of a text. When assessing texts for classroom use, teachers should consider the following:

- Is the vocabulary appropriate for specific learners?
- Are appropriate assumptions made about students' background knowledge?
- Are there sufficient concrete examples to help make concepts more meaningful?
- Is the organizational structure of the book apparent and useful for the students?
- Does the text contain elements such as graphic organizers, summaries, and subheadings to enhance the reader's comprehension?
- Is the book interesting?
- Is the book physically attractive, with an easily readable typeface and an appropriate thickness of paper?

The factors above are only a sample of areas to look at. Review your list. Is it similar? If not, what elements do you have on your list that should be included here?

▪▪ASSESSMENT OF THE LEARNING ENVIRONMENT

So far we have examined students' literacy abilities and the characteristics of the text that affect learning. Sociolinguistic theory tells us that the context of instruction also affects learning. Thus, we need to look at the classroom, the participants in the learning situation, and the use of instructional methods that support children in their literacy development.

Physical aspects of the class should be assessed in terms of a literate environment. Are books displayed invitingly, are students' works displayed, and if so, which students? Do bulletin boards show that all members of the class are a part of the literacy community? Grouping procedures should also be assessed to ensure that students are not segregated by reading and writing ability; instead, all students should have opportunities at different times to interact with one another as equals. Teachers should observe interactions throughout instruction. Teachers may want to create rubrics for assessing the learning and communication in cooperative learning groups, which are discussed in later chapters. In addition, teachers should assess their own interactions with students. At times, the teacher's purpose for an interaction may vary significantly from the students' perception (Good & Brophy, 1997). For example, a teacher may feel that he or she is protecting a low-achieving child from embarrassment by not asking the child to perform publicly, but the child may interpret that to mean that the teacher does not believe the child is capable. Examining activities to determine if they provide support for students is an important aspect of assessment as well. Gathering data on students and texts should lead to instructional decisions for furthering all students' literacy development. Evaluating our role in the classroom is integral to the assessment process.

TABLE 3.9   Literacy Levels for Beginning Readers

Characteristic of Reader	Characteristic of Text
Beginning Emergent	
Can locate print	One line of print
Can match voice to print with help	Picture and text match
Can identify front of book	Repetitive, one word change
Knows left-to-right orientation	
Knows some letters	
Knows where to start reading	
Emergent	
Identifies title/cover	One line of print
Aware of word/syllable segments in oral language	Picture and text match
Identifies word, letter, space	Repetitive, one word change; one or two deviations
Identifies oral rhyming of words	
Early	
Identifies word and letter, and begins to understand sentence	One–two lines of print
	Picture and text match
Uses picture cues and attempts to use consonants	Repetitive, one to two word changes; few, if any, deviations
Becomes aware of sight vocabulary	
Understands concepts of sentence, word, letter	Two lines of print
Uses picture cues and consonants	Picture and text match
Is developing sight vocabulary	Repetitive, two word changes, some deviations
Uses language structure	Two–four lines of print
Has a beginning awareness of sound segments or phonemes	Less picture and text match
	Repetitive word or phrase changes
Begins to apply initial and final sounds	
Uses self-correction	
Begins to apply learned, high frequency words	
Beginning Fluent	
Uses more text to get meaning	Four–six lines of print
Uses various cuing systems (pictures, semantic, syntactic, grapho-phonemic)	Some picture and text support
Self-corrects while reading	Text may repeat stanzas but mostly only high frequency words are repeated
Understands inflectional endings	
Uses short, long, r-controlled vowels	
Is developing vocabulary	

A Final Note

As you read through this chapter, you may have noticed that there was little direct attention paid to children with special needs. Aside from modification for testing procedures, the assessment of all children is more alike than different. Assessment should be integrated with instruction and teachers should be encouraged to develop assessment systems for the students in their classes to enhance learning for all students.

▮▮ SUMMARY

Assessment should be placed within a conceptual framework for teaching/learning. Based on the conceptual framework posited in Chapter 1, assessment should include examination of the learner, the text, and the learning environment in relation to language, reading, and writing development. Assessment includes formal assessment, informal published assessments, and classroom assessments. Through observation and analysis of student work, teachers gather the information needed to improve literacy for all the students in the classroom.

▬▬▮▮ Linkages

In the text
1. List the different types of assessments and discuss the advantages and disadvantages of each.
2. A child in your first-grade classroom is having difficulty with reading. What areas should be assessed and what are some of the instruments you would use?
3. What is the purpose of assessing both the text and the learning environment?

Outside the text
1. Observe an at-risk reader in the classroom. How is the classroom environment supporting or hindering the child's literacy development?
2. Interview a classroom teacher about the assessment techniques he or she uses. Classify the procedures as formal, informally published, or classroom assessments.
3. Select some content-area textbooks. Use the Fry readability chart to determine reading level.

▬▬▮▮ On the Web

A university website presents rubrics
edweb.sdsu.edu/triton/july/rubrics/Rubrics_for_Web_Lessons.html

Prentice Hall website for evaluating cooperative learning
www.phschool.com/professional_development/assessment/rub_coop_process.html

Classroom assessments
www.rmcdenver.com/useguide/assessme/online.html

Sample rubrics for different subjects
bard.huensd.k12.ca.us/html/writingrubrics.html

Educator's site with the Fry chart
school.discovery.com/schrockguide/fry/fry.html

University website; by searching portfolio assessment will link to various articles on the use of portfolios
www.uncg.edu/home.html

References

Bear, D. R., Invernizzi, M., Templeton, S., and Johnston, F. (2000). *Words their way: Word study for phonics, vocabulary, and spelling instruction.* Upper Saddle River, NJ: Merrill/Prentice Hall.

Bormouth, J. R. (1968). The cloze readability procedure. In J. R. Bormouth (Ed.), *Readability in 1968.* Champaign, IL: National Council of Teachers of English.

Butler, F. A., & Stevens, R. (1997). Oral language assessment in the classroom. *Theory into Practice, 36,* 214–219.

Calkins, L. M., Montgomery, K., Santman, D., & Falk, B. *A teacher's guide to standardized reading tests: Knowledge is power.* Portsmouth, NH: Heinemann.

Clay, M. M. (1993). *An observation survey of early literacy achievement.* Portsmouth, NH: Heinemann.

Cunningham, P. (1990). The names test: A quick assessment of decoding ability. *The Reading Teacher, 44,* 124–129.

Duffelmeyer, F. A., & Black, J. L. (1996). The names test: A domain-specific validation study. *The Reading Teacher, 50,* 148–150.

Duffelmeyer, F. A., Kruse, A. E., Merkley, D. J., & Fyfe, S. A. (1994). Further validation and enhancement of the names test. *Reading Teacher, 48,* 118–128.

Farnan, N., Flood, J., & Lapp, D. (1994). Motivating high-risk learners to think and act as writers. In, K. Wood and B. Algozzine (Eds.), *Teaching reading to high-risk learners* (pp. 291–314). Boston: Allyn & Bacon.

Fountas, I. C., & Pinnell, G. S. (1996). *Guided reading: Good first teaching for all children.* Portsmouth, NH: Heinemann.

Fry, E. B. (1968). A readability formula that saves time. *Journal of Reading, 11,* 513–516, 575–578.

Fry, E. B. (1977). Fry's readability graph: Clarifications, validity, and extension to level 17. *Journal of Reading, 21,* 242–252.

Gambrell, L. B., Palmer, B. M., Codling, R. M., & Mazzoni, S. A. (1996). Assessing motivation to read. *The Reading Teacher, 49,* 518–533.

Gillet, J. W. & Temple, C. (2000). *Understanding reading problems: Assessment and instruction.* NY: Addison Wesley Longman.

Good, T. L. & Brophy, J. E. (1997). *Looking in classrooms.* NY: Addison-Wesley.

Hammill, D. & Larsen, S. (1996). *Test of written language* (3rd ed.). Austin, TX: Pro-Ed.

Harp, B. (2000). *The handbook of literacy assessment and evaluation.* Norwood, MA: Christopher-Gordon.

International Reading Association (Aug. 1999). Position paper on high-stakes testing [http://www.ira.org/positions/high_stakes.html].

International Reading Association (May 2000). Assessment in the U.S. for children in special education experiencing reading difficulties. [http://www.ira.org/positions/spec_assess.html].

Johns, J. (1991). *Basic reading inventory.* Dubuque, IA: Kendall/Hunt.

Larsen, S., & Hammill, D. (1994). *Test of written spelling* (3rd ed.). Austin, TX: Pro-Ed.

Manzo, A. V. & Manzo, U. C. (1993). *Literacy disorders: Holistic diagnosis and remediation.* NY: Harcourt Brace Jovanovich.

Markwardt, F. (1989). *Peabody individual achievement test—revised.* Circle Pines, MN: American Guidance Service.

McCormick, S. (1999). *Instructing students who have literacy problems.* Upper Saddle River, NJ: Merrill/Prentice Hall.

Owens, R. E. (1995). *Language disorders* (2nd ed.). Needham Heights, MA: Allyn & Bacon.

Paris, S. G., Wasik, B. A., & Turner, J. (1996). The development of strategic readers. In R. Barr, M. L. Kamil, P. Mosenthal, & P. D. Pearson (Eds.), *Handbook of reading research* (Vol. II, pp. 609–640). Mahwah, NJ: Lawrence Erlbaum Associates.

Psychological Corporation (1992). *Weshsler individual achievement test.*

Schmitt, M. C. (1990). A questionnaire to measure children's awareness of strategic reading processes. *The Reading Teacher, 43,* 454–461.

Yopp, H. K. (1988). The validity and reliability of phonemic awareness tests. *Reading Research Quarterly, 23,* 177.

Enhancing Emergent Literacy

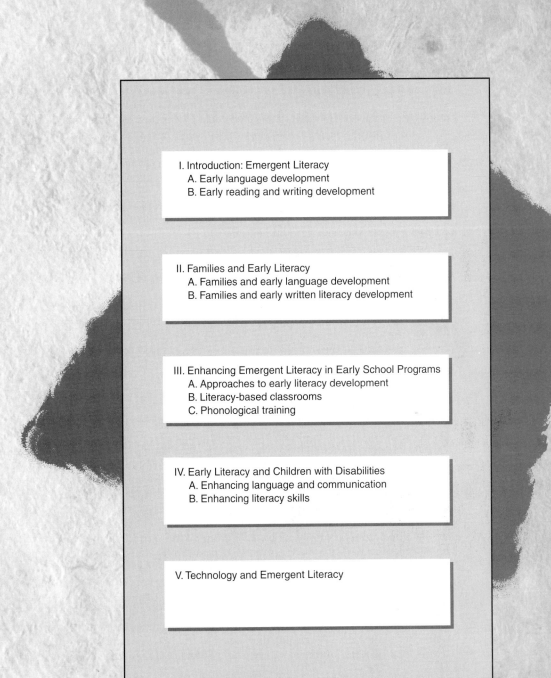

I. Introduction: Emergent Literacy
   A. Early language development
   B. Early reading and writing development

II. Families and Early Literacy
   A. Families and early language development
   B. Families and early written literacy development

III. Enhancing Emergent Literacy in Early School Programs
   A. Approaches to early literacy development
   B. Literacy-based classrooms
   C. Phonological training

IV. Early Literacy and Children with Disabilities
   A. Enhancing language and communication
   B. Enhancing literacy skills

V. Technology and Emergent Literacy

▪▪ INTRODUCTION: EMERGENT LITERACY

Throughout most of the 20th century, the prevailing model of early literacy develop-ment was that of "reading readiness." According to this model, the primary purpose of the preschool years in regard to literacy development was to prepare mentally for the introduction of reading that came with formal schooling. Preschoolers were expected to develop the cognitive, perceptual, and motor skills that were presumed to be pre-requisites for successful reading. Because most of this development was thought to be the result of physiological maturation of the brain, there was little that parents or pre-school teachers could do other than provide a healthy environment and numerous ex-periences that would provide stimulation for the developing brain (Teale & Sulzby, 1986). Teale (1995) has summarized the main principles of the reading readiness model of early literacy as follows:

- Learning to read begins only after a set of prerequisite reading readiness skills have been mastered.
- Children become proficient in oral language first and then learn to read (and then learn to write).
- Reading and writing are learned by young children as a series of abstract, separate skills in a decontextualized fashion.
- During the prereading period, skill in visual and auditory discrimination and knowledge of letters and sounds are the essential building blocks of eventual reading ability.
- Children follow the same skills path into reading, and their progress through this hierarchy should be carefully monitored with periodic testing.

By the 1970s, it was apparent to many that there were significant limitations to the reading readiness model of early literacy development. Many parents noticed that their preschool children could name common symbols (for example, McDonald's "Golden Arches") and even read some words prior to formal schooling. Parents and preschool teachers alike reported that many children seemed to understand the concept of letters and tried to write, even though they had received no formal writing instruction. More-over, researchers in the new field of psycholinguistics were describing children who seemed to develop abstract grammatical rules and test hypotheses about language at an age when the cognitive theorists said that such thinking skills were not possible.

These and other observations led to the development of an alternative model of literacy development known today as "emergent literacy." This model views literacy development as part of a developmental continuum that begins with the earliest par-ent–child interactions and continues through the school years. There is no clear dis-tinction made between reading and prereading. Instead, both are seen as part of the same sequence of literacy development. Another important distinction between the readiness model and the emergent literacy model is the notion that reading, writing, and spoken language are viewed as developing concurrently and in relationship to each other, rather than separately and independently (Whitehurst & Lonigan, 1998).

Teale (1995) has summarized the main tenets of the emergent literacy model as follows:

- Learning to read and write begins very early in life for almost all children in a literate society. Children use legitimate reading and writing behaviors in the informal settings of home and community, as well as in preschool or school settings.

- Literacy development is the more appropriate way to describe what was previously called reading readiness: The child develops as a reader/writer. The notion of reading preceding writing, or vice versa, is a misconception. Reading, writing, and oral language develop concurrently and interrelatedly from the beginning rather than sequentially.
- Literacy develops in real-life settings for real-life activities in order to "get things done." Therefore, the meaningful/functional/purposeful bases of early literacy are a critically important part of learning to read and write and must be emphasized so that children learn strategies within such contexts, not in isolation.
- Children learn written language through active engagement with their world. They interact socially with adults in writing and reading situations; they explore print on their own, and they profit from modeling of literacy by significant adults, particularly their parents.
- A much broader range of knowledge, dispositions, and strategies is involved in young children's becoming literate, including, among other things, the functions of language and literacy, knowledge of stories and how they work, understanding the nature of written language, and developing concepts about print, as well as phonemic awareness and knowledge of letters and sound-symbol relationships.
- Although children's learning about literacy can be described in terms of generalized stages, children become literate at different rates and take a variety of different paths to conventional reading and writing. Any attempts to "scope and sequence" instruction should take this developmental variation into account.

The emergent literacy model has significant implications for parents seeking to help their children develop early literacy skills, for preschool teachers and curriculum, and for parents and teachers of children with developmental delays and differences. According to the emergent literacy model, parents play a crucial role in the early literacy development of their children. Parents serve as the primary language partners for children in the very earliest stages of language development. They also provide their children with their first exposure to printed materials. Research has found significant relationships between the literacy environment in the home and preschool children's language and literacy development (Whitehurst & Lonigan, 1998). Preschool learning environments have also been found to significantly influence emergent literacy skills. Preschool programs that include a significant amount of exposure to print, including listening to and discussing stories, phonological training activities, and writing opportunities, can lead to enhanced literacy skills (Dickinson & Tabors, 1991).

The emergent literacy model also has important implications for understanding and teaching children with literacy difficulties. The model suggests that deficiencies in the child's literacy environments, at home and in school, can contribute to the child's literacy difficulties. Moreover, the model implies that children with delays in their development of literacy skills can benefit from enhanced literacy environments. However, these implications, although logical, remain largely untested.

Early Language Development

The emergent literacy model emphasizes the interrelationships between language, reading, and writing, but it seems clear that language provides the early framework on which developing literacy skills are built. In most children, language, in its spoken form, emerges first (usually before age 2) and the major elements of language are mastered long before the beginning of formal schooling. It is estimated that by 18 months the typical child has a receptive vocabulary (comprehension) of about 100 words and a spoken vocabulary of about 50 words. By first grade this vocabulary has expanded to between 7,800 and 13,000 words (Anglin, 1993). But children are not only acquiring vocabulary during the first 5 years of life. They are simultaneously learning about the sound system of their language (phonology), about word formation rules (morphology), about sentence structures (syntax), and about meaning (semantics). In addition, preschool children are learning the very complex rules of human language usage known as *pragmatics.*

What is even more amazing is that children are acquiring all of this knowledge about language at an age that some cognitive psychologists have described as prelogical. That is, in domains other than language, children of 2 or 3 years of age rarely exhibit the ability to develop and use rules for problem solving. Yet, in the domain of language learning they appear to act as if they know the rules. Look at the following example that might be used by a typical 3-year-old: "I see deerses." This child has learned that if you add an "s" to the end of the word it means "more than one." The child appears to have learned a rule for pluralization, but has not yet learned that there are exceptions to the rule.

During the preschool years, children progress through stages of language development that begin with the earliest cries and vocalizations of the newborn and continue through the sophisticated language usage of school-age children. One of the most fundamental, yet still largely unanswered, questions about early development is, How do children learn language? What enables children to develop the many complex rules of language at an age when they are not supposed to be thinking in logical, rule-governed ways? How do they aquire language so quickly and without formal instruction?

There have been many theories proprosed to answer these questions, but none has yet been able to fully account for the wonder of language development. The *behavioral* model of language development (Skinner, 1957) contends that children learn language primarily by imitating what they hear and receiving some sort of response that either encourages further language use (reinforcement) or discourages it (punishment or being ignored). Although this model seems to make sense, as parents often report that their young children seem to imitate what they hear, the model fails to explain certain curious developments in early language. For example, why is it that children often make "mistakes" that they have never heard before (recall the "deerses" example)? Because children should say those words that they hear the most, why is it that 2- and 3-year-olds rarely use words such as "the" and "A"—the most frequently heard words in English?

The *psycholinguistic* (or "innatist") model of language acquisition was developed in an attempt to address these and other shortcomings of the behavioral model (Chomsky, 1968). This theory of language acquisition has at its core the belief that language is an innate human characteristic. Moreover, there is a specific neural mechanism that Chomsky called the "language acquisition device," which contains the basic rules common to all languages and enables the infant to begin processing language right from birth. Although this model does a good job of explaining the speed of language acquisition and the ability of very young children to develop language rules, it gives little attention to the role of parents and others in the child's environment.

The more recent *interactionist* model of language acquisition holds that communication with parents and others is the motivating factor for early language development. Children talk, it is claimed, because they want to be involved in communicative interaction. According to this model, parents and others persons in the child's environment play a crucial role by simplifying their language to match the child's ability to understand and by responding to children as if they were competent language users.

Each of these models describes a portion of the language acquisition process, yet none can fully describe all of the elements and complexity of early language development. On the other hand, each of the theories contributes something to our understanding of how children learn language. Undoubtedly, children imitate many of the things they hear. At the same time, neurological development enables them to become more sophisticated in their language usage. Interaction with parents and others may provide the motivation to engage in language interaction. All of these elements are necessary in order for the child to develop early language skills.

At the beginning of this section, it was claimed that language development provides the framework for early literacy development. It is hard to imagine how a child could develop significant literacy skills without considerable knowledge of language, as reading and writing are language-based skills. However, language development does not take place in a vacuum. At the same time that children are developing significant spoken language skills, they are having experiences with written language. For example, children listen to and participate in story reading. They are bombarded by text, from *Sesame Street* to the mall. Although it remains difficult to demonstrate the precise connection between early language development and early literacy skills, many researchers believe that not only does reading facilitate literacy acquisition, but that reading and writing also influence spoken language development (e.g., Teale & Sulzby, 1986).

Early Reading and Writing Development

The emergent literacy model claims that reading and writing skills emerge during the preschool years as a natural consequence of early learning experiences. What does this early literacy development look like?

Think for a moment about all of the early encounters that young children have with print. They are constantly exposed to the printed word: They see words (and other symbols) on signs; they encounter letters and words on television and among their toys. The written word is all around them. Until recently, it was thought that children paid no attention to the signs and symbols in their environment. However, many parents and researchers recognize that children often attend and respond to the symbols around them. What parent has not heard their child cry out with anticipation as they passed the sign for a favorite fast-food establishment? How does the child know what lies beyond the sign? Clearly they have learned to associate the sign with a meaning (food). Goodman (1986) reported that some 60% of 3-year-olds in her studies could recognize environmental print in context and that by age 5 80% of her subjects could read

A. Writing sample of a 3-year-old child.

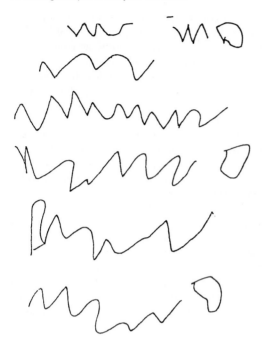

B. Writing sample of a 3-and-a-half-year-old child.

C. Writing sample of a 4-year-old child.

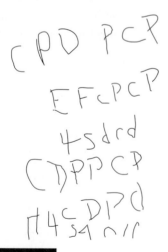

D. Writing sample of a 4-year-old child.

FIGURE 4.1

Examples of Early Writing

Source: Examples A, B, & C from: Morrow, L. M. (1989). *Literacy Development in the Early Years.* Upper Saddle River, NJ: Prentice Hall, p. 150. Example D from: Neuman, S. B., & Roskos, K. A. (1993). *Language and Literacy Learning in the Early Years.* Ft. Worth, TX: Harcourt Brace Jovanovich, p. 45. Used with permission.

environmental print. In addition to print recognition, Goodman also reported that young children were learning important literacy skills such as how to handle books and the meaning of words such as *read, book,* and *story.*

Similarly, children demonstrate some writing skills prior to formal instruction in writing. Just as the earliest sounds of spoken language gradually take on the sound characteristics of adult words, the early scribbles of young children gradually take the shape of recognizable words. Look at the examples of early writing in Figure 4.1. Example A shows an early attempt at writing by a 3-year-old child. She certainly appears to have the idea that writing moves along lines and has begun to alternate some circles with curved lines. Example B shows that this child has begun to form one of two recognizable letters. Example C, taken from a 4-year-old child, shows the use of more letters in configurations that begin to look like words, although they are only random combinations of letters. Finally, example D shows a transition from random letters to recognizable words.

Although not all children progress through such clear stages of writing, it seems apparent that many children acquire basic ideas about writing long before they receive formal instruction in it. Children move from the random creation of scribbles to forming letterlike shapes, to drawing actual letters, to stringing letters together in a stage sometimes called "phonetic"(or "invented") spelling. Just as with language acquisition, we might ask, How do children acquire early literacy skills? In the next section, we will examine the role of parents and the home environment in early literacy development.

▪▪ FAMILIES AND EARLY LITERACY

Families and Early Language Development

There is an old folktale (some say it is true) that long ago, in a faraway country, a king decided to determine once and for all what was the true language of God. So he ordered that a pregnant woman be locked up in a tower until she gave birth to her child. As soon as the child was born, he was spirited away by the king's guards, who were under strict orders not to speak in the child's presence. From that day on, the child was fed and cared for, but never spoken to. Much to the King's surprise, not only did the child not reveal the true language of God, the child did not speak at all.

Sadly, from time to time there have been real-life cases that come close to repeating the tragedy of the king's folly. One of the best-known cases is that of "Genie," a child who was discovered by authorities at 12 years of age locked in her room, where she had apparently been kept from a very early age (Curtiss, 1977). Lacking almost all opportunities for human contact, "Genie" had developed almost no language skills beyond a few grunts, as well as significant social and emotional difficulties.

These stories are presented to illustrate in the most extreme form the crucial role that parents play in their child's language acquisition and development. A less-dramatic, though no less important example, has been provided by a monumental research study undertaken by Betty Hart and Todd Risley (1995). The researchers and their colleagues intensively studied language interaction in 42 families during a 2 1/2-year period. These families were carefully chosen to represent levels of socioeconomic status ranging from upper class to families on welfare. Additionally, the researchers made sure that there were both white and African-American families represented within each socioeconomic level. During their monthly 1-hour observations, the researchers attempted to record everything that was said between the children and their parents.

The findings of this study are both dramatic and disturbing. Children from the higher socioeconomic groups, regardless of race, developed a far larger vocabulary than did children in families that received welfare. Children from middle-class families were right in the middle of the spectrum of vocabulary development. Similarly, parents from higher socioeconomic families engaged in more language interaction with their children than did parents of children from welfare or from middle-class families. There were also a number of qualitative differences in the way that parents from upper socioeconomic families interacted with their children. For example, these parents talked to their children at all times, not just when they were trying to manage their children.

There are many ways to look at the results of this study. Most importantly, it demonstrates very clearly that early experiences are important in shaping language development. In addition, it indicates that socioeconomic status, not race, is the most influential factor in shaping interaction differences. It is important to understand, however, that Hart and Risley are not saying that it is one's socioeconomic status itself that determines how quickly a child will develop language competence. Rather, it is the amount and quality of interaction that shapes language development. It just happens that parents from higher socioeconomic groups have a different interaction style than do parents from lower socioeconomic groups. These differences may be the result of factors such as the amount of leisure time available, the number of children in the family, health status, and a variety of other variables.

Hart and Risley are not the first or the only researchers to find a link between parent–child interaction and language development. There has long been a recognition that parents talk to their children in special ways—ways that encourage and enhance language interaction. Parents of young children slow down their speech and use a greater range of intonation, more restricted vocabulary, and simpler grammatical structures (Newport, Gleitman, & Gleitman, 1977). This phenomenon has come to be called "motherese" (or, more accurately, "parentese"). Look at the parent–child interaction presented in Box 4.1. Note how the mother guides the interaction through the use of questioning. She also uses short utterances, most of which refer to items in the child's immediate environment.

▌Box 4.1

PARENT–CHILD CONVERSATION

This exchange took place between a mother and her 21-month-old child during lunch.

Mother (M):	Hi baby. Want some lunch? (Taking child from crib.)
Child (C):	Yunch! (Arms outstretched to mother.)
M:	Would you like some turkey and cheese?
C:	Chee! Mmm! Cuppy? Cuppy? (Pointing to cup.)
M:	Yes honey, you can have your cuppy. Do you want juice or milk?
C:	Mook? Mook! (Clapping and smiling.)
M:	Mommy loves you. You're such a happy baby!

> C: Happy! Monkey? Monkey? (Looking around.) Monkey?
> M: Where's monkey? Did you leave him upstairs?
> C: Up? Monkey? (Hands out as if saying, "I don't know.")
> M: OK honey, mommy will look upstairs. Want to come with mommy?
> C: Uppy, come? Come? (Arms outstretched to mother.)
> M: Let's go find monkey so we can have a happy baby.

The evidence from tragic cases of neglect as well as from careful observations within typical families show that parents play a crucial role in their child's language acquisition and development. The amount and quality of their interactions strongly influence their child's language growth. Although there appear to be differences in language interaction that are the result of socioeconomic conditions, it may be possible to help parents develop interaction styles that will lead to greater growth in their child's language skills.

The best advice for parents who are interested in helping their children to develop language skills may be by providing their children with numerous opportunities for language interaction and being responsive to their child. Parents who truly engage their children in communicative interaction, who initiate interactions that are related to their child's interests, and respond when their child attempts to communicate are being most helpful to their children.

Families and Early Written Literacy Development

In addition to influencing the language development of their children, parents also play a very important role in shaping emerging written literacy skills. Research has found that children who enter kindergarten with a solid knowledge of print and its uses are generally more successful than other children in acquiring formal literacy skills and on standardized tests of achievement (Purcell–Gates & Dahl, 1991). Parents help their children develop knowledge about print in many ways, including through their language interaction, through exposure to print materials, and through shared book reading.

Language and Early Reading

There is evidence that the child's early language environment can influence written literacy development. Much of the evidence for this claim comes from studies of children who begin to read at an early age. For example, when Davidson and Snow (1995) studied children who were early readers, they found that there were small but consistent differences in the language environments of early readers as compared to typically developing readers. Parents of early readers tended to engage their children in more prolonged and more complex interactions. Look at the following interaction described by Davidson and Snow:

> **Child (C):** Do you know what sharks' chunks weigh?
> **Mother (M):** Shark's what?
> C: When they eat it.

M:	Shark's what?
C:	Chunks when they eat it.
M:	When they eat what?
C:	You know how much their chunks weigh?
M:	No, how much does a chunk weigh?
C:	Fifteen pounds.
M:	A chunk of...
Father: (F)	. . . a shark can take a fifteen-pound bite out of another fish?
M:	Really?
C:	Uh huh.

This is an example of a rich and extended language interaction. The parents appear to be really trying to understand what their child is saying. They respond to and comment on attempts at interaction. This is the sort of communicative interaction that Davidson and Snow found in the families of children who were early readers.

Children who are included as conversational partners, whose contributions to the conversation are encouraged and acknowledged, have greater opportunities to be exposed to the richness and complexity of language. As they begin to read and write, they are able to apply their sophisticated language skills to print.

The Print Environment

Researchers have consistently found that children who come from home environments in which there is a variety of print materials tend to have better-developed reading and writing skills (Durkin, 1966, Morrow, 1983; Purcell–Gates, 1996). Print materials include not only books but also newspapers, magazines, television guides, religious materials, and all of the other objects that contain print. These types of materials are present in every home. It is often assumed that families in lower socioeconomic communities have fewer print materials in their home. Although it is true that families with limited means generally have fewer books (and fewer children's books) than more well-to-do families, they often have a variety of print materials in the home (Teale, 1986). In his study, Teale reported that, although the amount of print materials varied considerably from home to home, there were many homes that contained a wealth of written materials.

Unfortunately, the presence of print materials in the home is not sufficient to ensure the development of literacy skills. What is even more important is the extent to which the materials are available to and used with the child. Purcell–Gates (1996) reported that children from lower socioeconomic families who had more opportunity to interact with print had a better understanding of the purpose of printed materials. Therefore, it appears to be important to remind parents to use the print materials in their home with their children. Parents can use the many natural opportunities that occur throughout the day to model reading for the child and to engage their child in early print activities. For example, parents could point to the name of their child's favorite show in the television guide or ask their child to name a food pictured on a label. Unfortunately, many families provide their children with limited opportunities to experience printed materials.

Book Reading

Reading books to children provides parents and their children with an important opportunity to share a few moments of time together in a very busy day. But more than that, book reading plays an important role in building literacy skills. Referring to the skills of reading and writing, the International Reading Association (IRA) and the National Association for the Education of Young Children (NAEYC) (1998) stated that, "The single most important activity for building these understandings and skills essential for reading success appears to be reading aloud to children" (p. 33). Children who are read to frequently during their preschool years have been found to have better language skills and reading comprehension when they enter school (Wells, 1985). Moreover, these advantages appear to persist into the later school years (Stevenson & Newman, 1986).

Why is storybook reading so important to early literacy development? What do children learn from this activity? One of the primary effects of shared reading is on language growth. Reading time provides an ideal time for parents to interact with their children. Observations of parents and their 2-year-old children have found that language interaction during book reading can account for as much as 5% of the daily speech between parents and their children (Wells, 1985). Storybook reading also exposes the child to more-complex language and new vocabulary. Researchers have found that shared reading fosters vocabulary development (Senechal & Cornell, 1993) as well as overall language development (Bus, van Ijzendoorn, & Pellegrini, 1995).

The second major benefit of shared reading is enhanced knowledge about books and about print. By engaging in shared reading, children learn about books—what they are, how to hold them, how to turn the pages. In addition, children learn the important principle that print is the written form of language and that it can be read and said.

It is interesting to note that studies of storybook reading between parents and their preschool children have found that not all shared reading interactions are equally constructive. Parents who engage their children in interaction during storybook reading appear to be more effective in helping their children develop language and literacy skills than parents who simply read the book to their (mostly passive) child (Whitehurst et al., 1988). Parents engage their children in interaction by doing some of the following during reading:

- Asking them "what" questions ("What's happening now?") rather than "yes–no" questions ("Do you like this story?").
- Giving them "informative" feedback (for example, expanding on what the child says or providing corrective modeling).
- Asking the child to *predict* what will happen next in the story and *discuss* what actually did happen.

Social Class and Emergent Literacy

According to some reports, as many as one-third of children enter school each year with such low levels of skill and motivation in literacy that they are at risk for significant academic difficulties (Carnegie Foundation, 1991). Many of these children come from lower-socioeconomic-status families. Children from such families tend to lag behind in their development of both language and written literacy skills. This is the bad news;

TABLE 4.1	Dialogic Reading Procedures

Ask who, what, and when questions, not yes–no or where questions.

Follow the child's answers with more questions.

Repeat what the child says.

Help the child with answers as needed.

Praise and encourage.

Follow the child's interests.

Have fun.

Source: Whitehurst, G. J., Epstein, J. N., Angell, A. L., Payne, A. C., Crone, D. A., & Fischel, J. E. (1994). Outcomes of an emergent literary intervention in Head Start. *Journal of Educational Psychology, 86,* 542–555.

however, the good news is that these deficiencies appear to be caused primarily by the early language and literacy experiences that children receive rather than directly by socioeconomic status. We have already reviewed research on differences in language interaction. There are similar findings for reading as well. That is, parents of children from lower socioeconomic groups tend to engage their children less frequently in shared reading experiences (Whitehurst & Lonigan, 1998).

This is more good news for teachers and other education professionals because it suggests that intervention could make a difference. For example, Whitehurst and associates (1994) trained both parents and preschool teachers in a reading method they called "dialogic reading" (Table 4.1). Using this technique, adults were taught to engage children in interaction during reading. The results showed that children who were read to by trained adults both at home and in school performed better on a vocabulary test than did children who were read to only at school or those whose teacher and parent received no training. This is just one example of the kind of training that might help parents from lower socioeconomic communities become more effective transmitters of literacy skills to their children.

Conclusion   Parents play a very important role in stimulating and supporting the early literacy development of their children. The amount and quality of communicative interaction with their child influences the child's language growth and development. Children benefit from a home environment that is rich in print materials but, even more importantly, they need parents or others who read with them and engage them in the reading process as they read.

The International Reading Association (IRA, 1986) has suggested that positive home environments that support emergent literacy:

- Provide a wide variety of reading and writing materials that are readily available to the child.
- Have parents (and other family members such as siblings and grandparents) who themselves engage in a variety of reading and writing activities.

- Have parents who read to the child on a regular basis.
- Encourage the child's reading and writing activities.
- Have responsive parents who answer the child's questions about language, books, reading, and writing.

In Chapter 11 we will discuss in greater detail the role of parents in enhancing literacy during the preschool and school years.

ENHANCING EMERGENT LITERACY IN EARLY SCHOOL PROGRAMS

Unfortunately, not every home provides the ideal environment for emergent literacy growth. Fortunately, most children attend preschool and/or kindergarten programs that can supplement the literacy experiences of early childhood. The importance of early literacy experiences cannot be overemphasized. Numerous studies have found that children with superior early literacy skills are more likely to become proficient readers and writers. Similarly, children who lack essential literacy skills are at serious risk for reading and writing difficulties (Butler et al., 1985).

Children have opportunities to work with letters and words in literacy-based early childhood programs.

Approaches to Early Literacy Development

In the beginning of this chapter we discussed the major competing theories of early literacy. The "reading readiness" or maturationist model claims that, as children mature, they gradually acquire the prerequisite skills that enable them to read and write. Implicit in this theory is the belief that children cannot read and write until they have acquired these prerequisite skills. In contrast, the "emergent literacy" model emphasizes the importance of early literacy experiences and their evolution toward more adult forms of literacy.

These competing theories of early reading are reflected in early childhood educational programs (Table 4.2). "Skills-based" programs emphasize the acquisition of specific (prerequisite) skills that are thought to underlie reading. These programs often begin with instruction on skills that are thought to be prerequisites to reading. Instructional activities might include cutting and coloring geometric forms and developing auditory discrimination skills by learning to identify sounds in the environment. Later, children are taught specific skills such as letter recognition, letter-sound correspondence, and conventional spelling and punctuation. These programs often use basal readers as the primary reading material in the classroom.

In contrast, early childhood programs that are based on emergent literacy principles generally use a "whole-language" approach to instruction. That is, teachers emphasize the importance of gaining meaning from text rather than focusing on individual letters and words. Typically, children learn through experiences that expose them to print. Classrooms based on this model often have a variety of learning centers at which children can explore and experiment. These centers may include print and writing materials that the children are encouraged to explore and use. Teachers read frequently to the children and engage them in discussions of the text.

Thomas and Barksdale–Ladd (1997) described two actual kindergarten classrooms that demonstrate the contrast in approaches. In the skills-based classroom each child

TABLE 4.2   Early Childhood Literacy Approaches

Skills-Based	Emergent Literacy
Teach prerequisite skills:	Learning centers:
• Identification of geometric forms	• Exploration
• Developing auditory discrimination skills	• Print materials
	• Writing materials
Teach specific skills:	Frequent reading and discussion of text
• Letter recognition	
• Letter-sound correspondence	
• Conventional spelling and punctuation	
Use basal readers	Use a "whole-language" approach

Descriptions adapted from Willis, 1994 and Haggerty, 1995

had an assigned seat with his or her name carefully printed on a name tag. In addition, each child had a model alphabet taped to his or her desk. The room was decorated primarily with commercially produced materials, including phonics guides. There was a small classroom library that contained some big books and trade books. The whole-language classroom had no desks. Instead, the room contained movable chairs and four round tables that served as activity centers. A set of risers that served as audience seating for plays stood against one wall. There was a play corner that contained old clothing that the children could use for playacting and a corner that contained puppets and props for plays. The walls were covered with children's drawings and stories.

These classrooms differed not only in physical appearance but also in what went on during the day. In the skills-based classroom, each week begins with the introduction of a new letter. On Monday the children work on visual discrimination activities (coloring in workbooks) related to the letter. On Tuesday the sounds associated with the letter are introduced. Wednesday brings review on the visual discrimination activities and letter formation. On Thursday the children continue to practice letter formation. Review and games related to the letter take place on Friday. In contrast, on Monday in the whole-language classroom children talk about what they did over the weekend, giving one sentence that is copied for them and hung on the wall. On Tuesday the class reads news stories and on Wednesday they copy the stories. The teacher uses opportunities provided by the stories to illustrate specific items (such as the spelling of a word). Each day children listen to a story read by the teacher, then go to listening stations where they have a chance to hear the book once again. Each day also brings a writing opportunity that is followed by the children acting out their story.

In addition to describing the classrooms, Thomas and Barksdale–Ladd (1997) were interested in looking at the effect of these approaches on students' literacy skills. Not surprisingly, the children in the skills-based classroom were far ahead of the children from the whole-language classroom on a phonemic segmentation task (dividing a word into its constituent sounds). In addition, children in the skills-based class also outperformed the other children on a word recognition task. On the other hand, when asked to write a story, almost one-quarter of the children from the skills-based classroom refused to do so. They said that they did not know how to write or could not spell. None of the children from the whole-language class refused the opportunity to write. In addition, many of the children from this class produced a recognizable story line whereas most of the children from the skills-based class who attempted to write simply labeled their pictures.

These results suggest that both the skills-based and the whole-language approach have something to contribute to the development of literacy in children. The skills-based approach may be best for teaching specific phonics and vocabulary skills whereas the whole-language method may enhance students' ability to derive meaning from print and to produce written work. In the sections that follow we will examine additional specific techniques that have been used to enhance literacy and the outcomes of these instructional methods.

Literacy-Based Classrooms

Preschool and kindergarten classrooms that are based on an emergent literacy model have as their primary goal the development and enhancement of literacy in young children. Teale and Sulzby (1986) suggest five principles that should underlie the development of literacy-based classrooms. These are:

- An understanding of young children as literacy learners—recognizing that literacy learning can take place in many environments and activities throughout the day.
- Reading and writing programs must be developmentally appropriate—they should use methods and materials appropriate for the preschool and kindergarten child, not traditional, formal reading instruction.
- Programs must use functional, meaningful activities that involve reading and writing in a variety of ways—programs should reemphasize skills such as letter discrimination and letter names.
- The curriculum must set a high priority on getting children actively involved in literacy—children need opportunities to experiment with reading and writing.
- Learning should not be confused with teaching—that is, the child's activities (rather than the teacher's strategies) should be the focus.

Most literacy-based, early childhood classrooms adhere to these or similar principles in developing their curriculum and learning activities. Teachers in these classrooms use numerous techniques and a variety of materials to engage children in reading and writing. For example, they use multiple and varied stimuli for reading. They use a variety of books, including predictable books, touch-and-smell books, "big" books, point-and-say books, picture storybooks, and rhythmical language books (see Table 4.3). Reading is generally a one-on-one or small-group activity. Reading may occur at any time during the day, not just during a designated period. Of course, teachers and other staff do more than just read to the children. Teale and Sulzby (1986) suggest that adults who read to children should preview the book with the child, briefly introduce the book, read with expression, and engage the child in discussion of the story and pictures. In addition to books, literacy-based classrooms typically contain a variety of print materials. These might include child or adult-authored stories, notes, or messages; lists; classroom rules; recipes; schedules; and labels.

Literacy-based classrooms also provide children with many opportunities to write. Many classrooms provide writing centers that contain a variety of writing materials (lined and unlined paper, a chalkboard, a computer) and instruments (pencils, markers, crayons) that the young child can use. The writing center may provide suggestions for writing activities (e.g., write a grocery list, copy a recipe, write your name). Many teachers also ask their children to keep writing journals. Bouas, Thompson, and Farlow (1997) describe journal writing in a typical kindergarten classroom. Children may include drawings, scribbles, and conventional forms of writing in their journal. The teacher provides a time each day for children to write in their journals. A key principle of writing in early childhood, literacy-based classrooms is to accept any form of writing, from scribbles to conventional letters, while encouraging the children to progress to the more adult form of writing. At first, children might be encouraged to "Do it your way." As they become more comfortable with writing, they might be encouraged to "Write it so I can read it too."

In addition to providing opportunities for exposure to and practice with written language, literacy-rich early childhood classrooms also help children continue their development of spoken language skills. Teachers actively engage children in conversation and encourage children to talk both to adults and with other children. They also

TABLE 4.3　Examples of Early Childhood Reading Books

Type of Book	Description	Examples
Predictable	Use repetitive language to model language and give child opportunity to repeat a phrase	*Brown Bear, Brown Bear, What Do You See?* (Martin, 1967) *The Gingerbread Boy* (Galdone, 1975)
Touch-and-smell	Provide opportunities for children to use their senses in reading	*Pat the Bunny* (Kundhardt, 1962) *Where's My Fuzzy Blanket?* (Carter, 1991)
"Big" books	Large-size books with large pictures that can be displayed by the teacher	Publishers include: SRA; Houghton-Mifflin; DLM, Scholastic; Curriculum Assoc.
Point-and-say	Use simple illustrations that ask child to "point to the . . ."	*What Is It?* (Hoban, 1985) *Family* (Oxenbury, 1981)
Picture storybooks	Use few words per page with simple illustrations	*The Runaway Bunny* (Brown, 1972) *The Snowy Day* (Keats, 1962)
Rhythmical language	Books that use rhyme	*The Three Little Kittens* (Cauley, 1982)

Source: Kupetz, B. N., & Green, E. J. (1997). Sharing books with infants and toddlers: Facing the challenges. *Young Children, 52,* 22–27.

provide an environment in which conversation is encouraged and expected. The environment can be arranged into center or group activities that encourage communicative interaction. Teachers can prompt interaction through active questioning and by responding to requests from the children. Some preschool and kindergarten classrooms ask that children give a brief verbal report about their play experiences in which they describe what they did.

The classroom environment, including room arrangement and materials, can be a powerful influence on literacy activity in the early childhood classroom. Neuman and Roskos (1992) have suggested the following guidelines for designing literacy-based classrooms:

- The play space should be arranged so as to encourage sustained play interactions, yet allow for adequate adult presence and supervision: Small, intimate play areas encourage more sustained play.
- Literacy enrichment should include play settings that reflect authentic literacy contexts: Real-life literacy situations, such as libraries or offices, provide good play opportunities.
- The literacy environment should include a network of common literacy objects in appropriate contexts that are safe for children to use: Items should be familiar to the child and commonly found at home.

Neuman and Roskos found the classrooms that used these principles enhanced young children's literacy activity during play.

Phonological Training

In addition to providing a supportive environment in which literacy can develop, preschool programs can help young children develop the phonological (phonemic) skills that are essential for beginning reading. As we discussed earlier, phonological skills include the ability to recognize sounds within words, to divide words into their sound units, and to blend sounds together to make words. By the time children enter preschool or kindergarten programs, most have an extensive spoken language vocabulary. However, that does not necessarily mean that they can analyze the sound structure of words. In fact, researchers have found that only 17% of typical kindergarten students can segment words into their sound components (e.g., "cat" is made up of the sounds k/a/t) (Liberman, Shankweiler, Fischer, & Carter, 1974). Phonological awareness requires that the children go beyond their implicit knowledge of language to the point where they can explicitly divide words into sounds and blend those sounds together to make words.

In Chapter 2 we discussed the importance of phonological awareness for beginning reading. Several studies have found that children with poor phonological skills are more likely to have reading difficulties (for example, Fox & Routh, 1980; Kamhi & Catts, 1986). All of this research evidence points out the important role that phonological skills play in beginning reading.

At the same time, several studies have found that children with poor phonological skills are more likely to have reading difficulties (for example, Fox & Routh, 1980; Kamhi & Catts, 1986). All of this research evidence points out the important role that phonological skills play in beginning reading.

Fortunately, phonological skills can be taught. A number of research studies have shown that systematic training in phonological skills can enhance the ability of preschool (Byrne and Fielding–Barnsley, 1993) and kindergarten (Torgesen, Morgan, & Davis, 1992; O'Connor, Notari–Syverson, & Vadasy, 1996) children to recognize and blend sounds. Moreover, researchers have found that children who receive early training in phonological skills are more likely to become better readers (Byrne & Fielding–Barnsley, 1995; Lundberg, Frost, & Petersen, 1988; Lyon & Moats, 1997).

Let's look at one of these phonological training studies in more detail to see how they try to help children develop phonological skills. In the study by Torgesen and associates (1992) cited earlier, kindergarten children who were identified as having poor phonological skills were divided into three groups. One group received instruction only in blending. Children in this group identified words pronounced in a segmented form by their teacher by choosing the correct picture from sets of two or three pictures. A second group of children received this instruction in combination with word analysis training. These children were taught to identify and pronounce the beginning, ending, or middle sounds in words of two or three phonemes. A third group of children engaged in a variety of language-experience activities that focused on getting meaning from stories. At the end of the training period, the researchers found that the children who received both the word analysis and blending activities were better than either of the other two groups in segmenting words into their parts and in learning new words.

Drawing on research such as that just described, Busink (1997) has suggested several activities to build phonological awareness that can be included in early childhood programs, including:

- Learning about words as "sound objects": Activities include using nursery rhymes to learn about rhythm and rhyme in language. Busink suggests that children can clap the rhymes or march to the words as ways of identifying rhythm. Children can be asked to fill in the blanks in a well-known rhyme such as "Jack and Jill went up the _____." or make up silly rhymes that go with their name.
- Segmenting activities: Children can clap the names of their fellow class members, later learning to count the claps as they recognize the syllables. They might experiment with changing the first or last sounds of familiar words to see what happens (e.g., substitute the /m/ sound for the /k/ sound in the word *cat*.
- Phoneme identification activities: Children can be taught to identify individual sounds by labeling the sounds. This is the approach used in a phonological training program called the *Lindamood Phoneme Sequencing Program for Reading, Spelling, and Speech* (LiPS) (Lindamood & Lindamood, 1998). For example, children are taught that the /t/ and /d/ sounds are "tongue tappers."
- Phoneme manipulation activities: As children say the sounds within words they can be taught to move colored blocks that represent the sounds. As they become more proficient at this skill, they can move the blocks around, saying the sounds that result.

There is no reason that training in phonological skills has to be done in isolation from other literacy activities. In fact, phonological training is likely to be more successful when it is combined with meaningful literacy experiences. It is important that children are helped to understand that the segmentation and blending skills they are learning are related to the reading and writing activities in which they are engaged. In order to do this, teachers can use the opportunities that are naturally presented during reading and writing activities. For example, while listening to a story, children can be encouraged to listen for a target sound.

▌▐ EARLY LITERACY AND CHILDREN WITH DISABILITIES
Enhancing Language and Communication

Many children with disabilities enter their first school experience with limited language skills. As a result, many early childhood programs for children with disabilities place a heavy emphasis on the development of language and communication skills. Teachers can support the development of these skills by structuring the classroom environment to promote communication and by interacting with children in ways that enhance communication.

Ostrosky and Kaiser (1991) suggest seven strategies that preschool teachers can use to enhance the communicative environment for young children with disabilities:

1. **Use interesting materials:** Because young children are most likely to talk about things that interest them, toys and materials that children prefer should be

readily available. Some children with disabilities may be unable to express their preferences verbally, so careful observation will be needed to identify their preferred objects and activities.

2. **Put some items out of reach:** Placing some items in view but out of reach will prompt children to make requests. Children with very limited language skills can point, whereas those with more advanced language skills can be encouraged to make a verbal request.

3. **Provide inadequate portions:** Give small but inadequate portions of blocks, crayons, snack items, or preferred activities (e.g., playing a song) as another way to encourage the child to communicate.

4. **Provide opportunities for choice making:** Present the child with two choices and wait for (or ask the child to) make a choice. For example, during snack time in a classroom with preschool children with severe disabilities, the teacher asked each child to choose either crackers or cookies. Children with very limited language could point. Other children were required to make a verbal response.

5. **Create situations in which children need assistance:** A windup toy, a tape-recorded song, or a new game provide opportunities for children to request the teacher's assistance.

6. **"Sabotage" situations:** Do not provide all the materials that are needed for an activity, making it necessary for the children to request them. If the children do not recognize that they need something or fail to make a request, they can be prompted to do so.

7. **Create "silly" situations:** For example, the adult can wear a silly hat or crawl on the floor as a way of encouraging the child to make a comment.

Environmental arrangements can be a useful way to prompt interaction, but will only be useful if adults respond to children in ways that encourage continued interaction. In general, adults can enhance interaction by making frequent attempts to initiate interaction, by responding to children when they make attempts to communicate, and by talking about things in which the child is interested. Unfortunately, in some classrooms children's attempts at communication are frequently ignored or even actively discouraged. At other times, most of the talk is directed at the child for management purposes (e.g., "sit down, "be quiet") rather than in a way that enhances interaction (e.g., "Tell me what you did at the dress-up corner"). Some specific strategies for enhancing expressive and receptive language are presented in Table 4.4.

Enhancing Literacy Skills

Children with disabilities are likely to come to the preschool and kindergarten classroom with a range of literacy skills. Some may have acquired little, if any, knowledge and skill in reading and writing. Others will have acquired a number of emergent literacy skills. Therefore, it is always important to be aware of each individual's knowledge and skills rather than making generalizations based on disability levels.

There is a growing consensus among researchers that children with disabilities develop emergent literacy skills in much the same way as typically developing children (Katims, 1994). That is, they go through the same steps of early reading and writing skill, although at a slower pace in some cases. This belief has led to significant changes

TABLE 4.4   Strategies to Enhance Language

Expressive Language Strategies

Child's Desired Behaviors	Teachers' Verbal Prompts	Classroom Activities
Speaks in complex sentences	"I'm not sure what you mean. Tell me more." "Start with _____ and tell me again." (Give child appropriate word or phrase with which to start a complex sentence.) "Do you mean _____? . . . Can you tell me _____?" (Give child appropriate sentence for repetition.)	• Read aloud literature that contains descriptive language and complex sentence forms. • Perform choral reading/speaking activities so children can hear and use expressive language. Young children can use poems with repetitive phrases. Older children enjoy Paul Fleischman's *Joyful Noise: Poems for Two Voices*. • Memorize chants and rhymes. Tap out rhythms to improve fluency.
Uses specific vocabulary such as names, pronouns, possessive markers	"I asked _____ [where/when/who/how many/etc]. Tell me a _____ [place/time/name/number/etc.]." "You said he/she. What person do you mean? Tell me his/her name." Who does that belong to? Is it Susan's or Tom's?"	• Role-play situations in which children ask questions of others. • Have children generate questions and then interview peers or adults. Tape interviews for later review. • Use cooperative groups to solve mysteries by connecting clues to answers: who, what, when, where, and so on. Children can create questions for other groups. • Encourage dialogue through class meetings, cooperative group work, and literature discussion. • Use a Who-What-When-Where analysis chart for literature. Young children can chart these with the teacher. • Play 20 Questions: Teacher or child thinks of a secret topic. Children can ask up to 20 yes/no questions to solve the mystery topic.
Joins in conversations with peers and adults	"Please tell _____ to _____." (Give the child practice approaching and speaking to others.) "You're going to be a team leader. Who would you like in your group?" (Choose an activity in which the child succeeds easily; ask the child privately to name classmates with whom she/he feels comfortable.) "Ms. _____ wants someone to teach her children to _____. I know you are good at that. Let's pretend you are teaching this puppet to _____. How would you teach the puppet to _____?"	• Teach bridging phrases such as "I agree with Julie because . . ." or "In addition to what you said, I . . ." to facilitate discussion. • Have the children respond to each other's stories during Author's Chair time. • Teach cooperative group skills. Assign each group member a role and task (e.g., leader, recorder, encourager, presenter) and have children complete a group project. • Use math manipulatives to develop strategies for problem solving. Have children share their reasoning with each other.

TABLE 4.4   Continued

Expressive Language Strategies

Child's Desired Behaviors	Teachers' Verbal Prompts	Classroom Activities
Provides more information when asked	"I don't understand. Can you tell me with different words?" "Do you mean ____?" (Requires only yes/no response.) "Do you mean ____ or ____?" (Requires child to rephrase original statement.)	• Have children ask and answer questions during Author's Chair time, sharing time, or book discussions. • Have children respond to questions from teacher/peers in dialogue journals (written or audiotaped) or during editing activities. • Have children explain their strategies and/or reasoning when giving an answer or comment. • Encourage questions and answers after oral presentations or during sharing time.
Participates appropriately in conversations (takes turns, stays on topic, does not interrupt others)	"It's ____'s turn now. You can have your turn after ____." "We are talking about ____ [e.g., going to the grocery store]. What can you tell us about that?" "It's your turn now. Can you tell us ____?" (Gain child's attention and repeat question to prompt memory.)	• Class meetings: Use a "turn stick" that children pass to the person whose turn it is to talk. • At the beginning of a discussion, give each child three tokens. A child spends one token per turn. Turns are over when all of the tokens have been spent. • Cooperative group work: Assign rules of leader, recorder, questioner, etc., to ensure that each child has a participatory role. • Use round-robin techniques for brainstorming. Drawing names from a holder ensures each child an opportunity to speak.

Receptive Language Strategies

Child's Desired Behaviors	Teachers' Verbal Prompts	Classroom Activities
Signals when information is not understood	"Show me with your hands: Do you want a lot of help, a little help, or no help?" "Show me with your hands: Did you understand all of that, a little of that, or none of that?" "Tell me as much as you can. I'll help if it gets confusing."	• Seat a child in front row or close to teacher; establish a signal for the child to indicate a need for help (e.g., tap on teacher's shoe, tug on right ear). • Have children paraphrase and repeat directions. • Give incomplete directions: "What else do you need to know?" Children ask for information. • Give incomplete information for an activity: Children work in cooperative groups to determine what additional information is needed.

Receptive Language Strategies		
Child's Desired Behaviors	*Teachers' Verbal Prompts*	*Classroom Activities*
Gives appropriate responses when asked questions	"That tells me ____. Right now I want to know ____. Can you tell me ____?" (Credit child with answering a question but clarify desired information; then repeat/reword original questions.) "I can tell you're trying, but I want to know ____. Can you tell me ____?" (Credit child's effort, clarify, and repeat/reword original question.) "That's interesting. Sounds like you were reminded of ____. But right now, we're discussing ____. Tell me ____." (Credit effort and association with general topic but clarify specific topic and repeat/rephrase question.)	• Create a concentration game: Match questions and answers to form pairs. With nonreaders this can be done on a pocket chart. • Practice peer interviews for a Meet Your Classmate book. • Have children keep dialogue journals in which the teacher responds to children's reflections. In addition, have both teachers and children write at least one question per entry for the reader to answer. • Read and discuss *Martha Speaks* by Susan Meddaugh, in which Martha the dog gains the ability to speak by eating alphabet soup.
Follows multistep instructions without visual cues or repetition of directions	"Tell me what you have to do." "Tell me what you will do first." Have child signal teacher as soon as step is completed. Gradually expand the number of steps child completes before signaling teacher. "Great!" You have already followed the first direction. Now you have to ____. Tell me what you must do now." (Credit partial success, repeat next step[s]. Immediately check for understanding.)	• Have children retell stories in proper sequence. Have children give explanatory "how-to" speeches for completing tasks like tying shoes, folding origami cranes. • Tell/write naratives of the steps followed to get ready for school, make Jell-o, etc. • Play Simon Says using more than one command (e.g., "Simon says to touch your toes and wave your hand").
Recognizes and adapts to subtle changes in classroom activities	"What did I do differently today? What do you think that means?" "I changed something this morning. Point to what I changed." "We have a visitor coming today. How should we change our schedule?"	• Use nonverbal cues such as a bell, music, or clapping to signal transition times in the classroom. • Develop a signal that children can use to help manage the classroom (e.g., voice-level chart, traffic signal, or bell to signal when classroom is too noisy.) • Use signs or other visual cues.

Source: Howard, S., Shaughnessy, A., Sanger., D., & Hux, K. (1998). Let's talk: Facilitating language in early elementary classrooms. *Young Children, 53,* 34–39. Used with permission.

in instructional approaches to literacy development for children with disabilities. As Katims (1994) explains, there has been a shift from breaking literacy down into isolated, often abstract, skills (such as letter-sound identification, word analyses, and structural analysis) to supporting and encouraging the development of emergent literacy skills through literacy experiences. At the same time, it is clear that many children with disabilities will need more structure and support in order to acquire emergent literacy skills. The challenge for teachers is in how to provide a supportive environment for emergent literacy while also incorporating the more-structured guidance that many children with disabilities require.

It is often possible to use the routine activities within the preschool and kindergarten classroom as the basis for more-structured instruction. For example, in one preschool program for children with significant disabilities, the traditional "circle time" is used as an opportunity to teach word recognition. When a bell sounds, the children have to find their place in the circle by identifying their name written on a card. Later, when the "job chart" is discussed, the label for each job is placed next to a picture of the job and the name of the child to whom the job has been assigned. In this same preschool classroom, three literacy/communication centers have been developed: an art and writing center, a role-playing center, and a book and library center. At the art and writing center children are encouraged to label their pictures. Teachers help to translate the marks into words that become stories that can be used during reading time (Watson, Layton, Pierce, & Abraham, 1994).

Like all children, those with disabilities should have many opportunities to interact with books. They can be read to, listen to books on tape and on the computer, or watch video adaptations of stories (such as those from the PBS program, *Reading Rainbow*). But exposure to reading is not enough. Children need to be involved in reading. Teachers can enhance involvement by asking children to predict what may happen in the story from looking at pictures from the book, by asking questions as they go along, and by prompting the child to recall the story through writing or role-playing activities.

Katims (1994) demonstrated the efficacy of engaging children with disabilities in structured reading activities in a study of 14 children with a variety of significant disabilities. The children were exposed to a literacy-rich preschool environment that included daily usage of a classroom library and frequent group storybook readings that featured interactive dialogs to engage the children in discussion of the story and "imitative" readings in which children were directed to repeat words, phrases, or sentences immediately after hearing an adult read them. Katims found that there were significant improvements in the children's knowledge of books and print as the result of their experiences in the preschool classroom. This study confirms what many parents and teachers have claimed—that children with disabilities can acquire emergent literacy skills when given frequent and structured opportunities to participate in literacy activities.

■■ TECHNOLOGY AND EMERGENT LITERACY

A number of new and emerging technologies are now available to support and enhance emergent literacy in young children. Although these resources and activities may not replace traditional books and writing, they can supplement the traditional materials and make literacy more accessible for all children, including those with disabilities.

CD-ROMs

One example of these new technologies is CD-ROM storybooks and skill-building programs on CD. CD-ROM storybooks typically present pictures, words, and an audio soundtrack, which can be used or turned off depending on the child's reading abilities. Often there are "help" buttons that assist the reader with the pronunciation or meaning of a word. Some of the programs include activities in which the child can participate before and after the story. For example, the Discis Books series includes classic stories (e.g., Poe's, "The Tell-Tale Heart"), poetry, and contemporary stories in an interactive format. Teachers or parents can customize the story presentation by changing the font, size, and/or line spacing of the print. When a child clicks on a word, the word is pronounced for this child. This feature can be customized to present the word by syllables or provide an explanation of the word. For many stories, music and sound effects are available, or these can be turned off if the teacher/parent believes that they may be distracting. Other CD-ROM products provide similar options (Table 4.5).

A number of programs are now available that provide activities for emergent literacy skill development. For example, the *Reader Rabbit* (The Learning Company) and *Arthur* series (Broderbund) provide CD-ROM programs for the very young child through second grade. *Reader Rabbit Playtime for Baby & Toddler* provides activities in 20 skill areas, ranging from colors and shapes to language development and early vocabulary. The program is designed to be simple enough that young children can play on their own. At higher levels, early reading and writing skills are presented in an interactive game format. "Simon Sounds It Out" (Don Johnston) uses a friendly on-screen tutor who teaches the student to recognize and use beginning sounds and word families. The program uses pictures to support the spoken sounds and offers positive feedback and motivational activities to keep the student interested. The program automatically adjusts the difficulty level of the words based on the student's responses and keeps track

TABLE 4.5 Examples of Early Literacy Computer Programs

Program	Publisher	Age–Range
Arthur's:	Broderbund	
Preschool		3–5
Reading Games		3–7
Discis Books	Discis	6–12
Rainbow	Curriculum Associates	5–9
Reader Rabbit:	The Learning Company	
Playtime		9 mo. to 2 yr.
Kindergarten		5–7
First Grade		5–8
Phonics		4–6
Reading Blaster	Davidson	4–7
Wiggleworks	Scholastic	5–8

of their progress. The *Wiggleworks* program (Scholastic) combines CD-ROM storybooks, literacy activities, and word processing to provide a comprehensive literacy development system. The publishers present research that suggests that the program can be very effective in enhancing the reading and writing of children in first grade.

In addition to using commercially prepared materials, teachers can develop their own computer-based literacy materials. Eisenwine and Hunt (2000) describe how they developed interactive books for their first-grade students using Hyperstudio (Roger Wagner). They used the program to illustrate and animate their stories as well as to provide sound. They found that their students really enjoyed stories presented in this format.

CD-ROM storybooks and skill-development programs have features that can make them very attractive to teachers and parents. The ability to customize print, sound, and graphics and to retrieve information on a student's progress can be very valuable. In the future, DVD and other emerging technologies are likely to expand the options for computer-based literacy instruction.

Internet

The Internet can be an excellent source of information about educational approaches, activities, and materials. However, it is often difficult to search, and caution must be used in evaluating the source of information. Because the Internet is so large and unregulated, information can be posted with no screening. Therefore, it is important to try to determine the source of information that appears on a Web page.

With these limitations in mind, the Web can still be an excellent tool. Information on preschool instructional activities can be found on sites such as perpetual-preschool.com and creativeprek.com. Information on publishers and materials can also be found on the Internet. Increasingly, publishers are developing early literacy programs that utilize computer-based software and Internet resources. For example, The *Wiggleworks* early literacy program from Scholastic, www.scholastic.com, allows the text in stories to be enlarged, changed in color or highlighted, or read aloud by the computer. The *Invitations to Literacy* program from Houghton Mifflin, www.eduplace.com, includes Web links to supplementary activities, research on the program, and discussion sites. These and many other programs are enabling teachers to provide children with a broader range of literacy experiences with modifications that enable all children to participate.

Word Processing

Many companies have developed word-processing programs that are specifically designed for young children. For example, *Storybook Weaver* (Broderbund) provides thousands of images that can be used as the stimulus for writing activities. A text-to-speech feature lets the students hear the story they have written. The *Write:OutLoud* (Don Johnston) uses a spell checker, dictionary, and homonym checker to support students' writing. Specifically designed for students who are experiencing difficulty with writing, the program reads text out loud to students as they write.

Most word-processing programs for young children have simple directions or symbols on the screen that allow children to easily cut and paste and perform other editing tasks that facilitate composition and revision. Spellcheckers and grammar checkers provide support that can also be valuable for young writers.

▌▌SUMMARY

The emergent literacy model views the acquisition and development of reading and writing skills as a gradually emerging process that is closely linked to the development of language skills. Rather than viewing reading and writing as the outcome of the accumulation of specific "readiness" skills, the emergent literacy model views the early identification of symbols and early attempts at writing as significant steps in the emergence of adult forms of literacy.

From the emergent literacy perspective, the role of parents and early childhood teachers is to provide numerous opportunities for literacy experiences. Children develop literacy skills, it is claimed, through exposure to print and to writing. Opportunities for learning increase when parents and teachers engage their children and students in discussions during reading and provide feedback for writing. Children with disabilities also can develop literacy skills through experiences with print but may, in some cases, need more structured activities and environments. In addition to engaging in literacy experiences, research has demonstrated that many children can benefit from instruction that focuses on the development of phonological skills. This instruction can be integrated with other literacy activities.

In this chapter we have described a number of methods that teachers and parents can use to enhance literacy. Our hope is that all children will have an optimal environment in which to develop those literacy skills, which are essential both for success in school and for enrichment throughout their lives.

▌▌ Linkages

1. How does this emergent literacy model differ from the reading readiness model of child literacy development?
2. According to the emergent literacy model, what role do parents play in the emergence of their child's literacy skills?
3. Contrast the behavioral, psycholinguistic, and interactionist models of child language acquisition.
4. What evidence supports the notion that reading and writing skills begin to develop before formal schooling begins?
5. What are the implications of Hart and Risley's research for teachers of young children?
6. Earlier in this chapter, the following statement was made: "The presence of print materials in the home is not sufficient to ensure the development of literacy skills." What does this statement mean? What does it indicate about the role parents should play in enhancing literacy?
7. Contrast a "skills-based" approach to a "whole-language" approach to initial instruction in reading.
8. What does research suggest about the relationship between phonological skills and beginning reading?

On the Web

Broderbund, a publisher
www.broderbund.com

Don Johnston Incorporated, a publisher
www.donjohnston.com

The Learning Company, a publisher
www.thelearningcompany.com

Preschool Education lists activities for teachers
www.preschooleducation.com

The Perpetual Preschool lists activities for teachers
www.perpetualpreschool.com

National Association for the Education of Young Children
www.naeyc.org

National Institute on Early Childhood Development and Education
www.ed.gov/offices/OERI/ECI/

Head Start website
www.acf.dhhs.gov/programs/hsb

References

Anglin, J. (1993). Vocabulary development: A morphological analysis. *Monographs of the Society for Research in Child Development, 58* (10), Serial No. 238.

Bouas, M. J., Thompson, P., & Farlow, N. (1997). Self-selected journal writing in the kindergarten classroom: Five conditions that foster literacy development. *Reading Horizons, 38,* 3–12.

Bus, A. G., van Ijzendoorn, M. H., & Pellegrini, A. D. (1995). Joint book reading makes for success in learning to read: A meta-analysis on intergenerational transmission of literacy. *Review of Educational Research, 65,* 1–21.

Busink, R. (1997). Reading and phonological awareness: What we have learned and how we can use it. *Reading Research and Instruction, 36,* 199–215.

Butler , S. R., Marsh, H. W., Sheppard, M. J., & Sheppard, J. L. (1985). Seven-year longitudinal study of the early prediction of reading achievement. *Journal of Educational Psychology, 77,* 349–361.

Byrne, B., & Fielding-Barnsley, R. (1993). Evaluation of a program to teach phonemic awareness to young children: A 1-year follow-up. *Journal of Educational Psychology, 85,* 104–111.

Byrne, B., & Fielding-Barnsley, R. (1995). Evaluation of a program to teach phonemic awareness to young children: A 2- and 3-year follow-up and a new preschool trial. *Journal of Educational Psychology, 87,* 488–503.

Carnegie Foundation for the Advancement of Teaching. (1991). *Ready to learn: A mandate for the nation.* New York: Author.

Chomsky, N. (1968). *Language and mind.* New York: Harcourt, Brace, & World.

Curtiss, S. R. (1977). *Genie: A linguistic study of a modern-day "wild child."* San Diego: Academic Press.

Davidson, R. G. & Snow, C. E. (1995). The linguistic environment of early readers. *Journal of Research in Childhood Education, 10,* 5–21.

Dickinson, D. K., & Tabors, P. O. (1991). Early literacy: Linkages between home, school, and literacy achievement at age five. *Journal of Research in Childhood Education, 6,* 30–45.

Durkin, D. (1966). *Children who read early.* New York: Teachers College Press.

Eisenwine, M. J., & Hunt, D. A. (2000). Using a computer in literacy groups with emergent readers. *The Reading Teacher, 53,* 456–458.

Fox, B., & Routh, D. (1980). Phonemic analysis and severe reading disability. *Journal of Psycholinguistic Research, 9,* 115–119.

Goodman, Y. M. (1986). Children coming to know literacy. In W. Teale & E. Sulzby (Eds.), *Emergent literacy: Writing and reading* (pp. 1–14). Norwood, NJ: Ablex.

Hart, B., & Risley, T. R. (1995). *Meaningful differences in the everyday experience of young American children.* Baltimore: Paul H. Brookes.

Howard, S., Shaughnessy, A., Sanger, D., & Hux, K. (1998). Let's Talk: Facilitating language in early elementary classrooms. *Young Children, 53,* 34–39.

International Reading Association (1986). IRA position statement on reading and writing in early childhood. *The Reading Teacher, 39,* 822–824.

International Reading Association & National Association for the Education of Young Children. (1998). Learning to read and write: Developmentally appropriate practices for young children. *Young Children, 53,* 40–46.

Kamhi, A., & Catts, H. (1986). Phonological deficiencies in children with reading disability: Evidence from an object-naming task. *Journal of Speech and Hearing Disorders, 51,* 337–347.

Katims, D. S. (1994). Emergence of literacy in preschool children with disabilities. *Learning Disability Quarterly, 17,* 58–69.

Kupetz, B. N., & Green, E. J. (1997). Sharing books with infants and toddlers: Facing the challenges. *Young Children, 52,* 22–27.

Liberman, I., Shankweiler, D., Fischer, F., & Carter, B. (1974). Reading and the awareness of linguistic segments. *Journal of Experimental Child Psychology, 18,* 201–212.

Lindamood, P., & Lindamood, P. (1998). *The Lindamood Phoneme Sequencing Program for Reading, Spelling, and Speech.* Austin, TX: Pro-Ed.

Lundberg, I., Frost, J., & Petersen, O. (1988). Effects of an extensive program for stimulating phonological awareness in preschool children. *Reading Research Quarterly, 23,* 263–284.

Lyon, G. R., & Moats, L. C. (1997). Critical conceptual and methodological considerations in reading intervention research. *Journal of Learning Disabilities, 30,* 578–588.

Morrow, L. M. (1983). Home and school correlates of early interest in literature. *Journal of Educational Research, 76,* 221–230.

Morrow, L. M. (1989). *Literacy development in the early years.* Upper Saddle River, NJ: Prentice Hall.

Neuman, S. B., & Roskos, K. (1992). Literacy objects as cultural tools: Effects on children's literacy behaviors in play. *Reading Research Quarterly, 27,* 202–225.

Neuman, S. B., & Roskos, K. A. (1993). *Language and literacy learning in the early years.* Ft. Worth, TX: Harcourt Brace Jovanovich.

Newport, E., Gleitman, A., & Gleitman, L. (1977). Mother I'd rather do it myself: Some effects and non-effects of maternal speech style. In C. Snow & C. Ferguson (Eds.), *Talking to children: Language, input, and acquisition* (pp. 109–149). New York: Cambridge University Press.

O'Connor, R., Notari-Syverson, A., & Vadasy, P. (1996). Ladders to literacy: The effects of teacher-led phonological activities for kindergarten children with and without disabilities. *Exceptional Children, 63,* 117–130.

Ostrosky, M. M., & Kaiser, A. P. (1991). Preschool classroom environments that promote communication. *Teaching Exceptional Children, 24,* 6–11.

Purcell-Gates, V. (1996). Stories, coupons, and the *TV Guide*: Relationships between home literacy experiences and emergent literacy knowledge. *Reading Research Quarterly, 31,* 406–428.

Purcell-Gates, V., & Dahl, K. (1991). Low-SES children's success and failure at early literacy learning in skills-based classrooms. *Journal of Reading Behavior, 23,* 1–34.

Senechal, M., & Cornell, E. H. (1993). Vocabulary acquisition through shared reading experiences. *Reading Research Quarterly, 28,* 360–375.

Skinner, B. F. (1957). *Verbal behavior.* New York: Apple-Century-Crofts.

Stevenson, H. W., & Newman, R. S. (1986). Long-term prediction of achievement and attitudes in mathematics and reading. *Child Development, 57,* 646–659.

Teale, W. H. (1986). Home background and young children's literacy development. In W. Teale & E. Sulzby (Eds.), *Emergent literacy* (pp. 173–206). Norwood, NJ: Ablex Publishing.

Teale, W. H. (1995). Young children and reading: Trends across the twentieth century. *Journal of Education, 177,* 95–127.

Teale, W. H., & Sulzby, E. (1986). *Emergent literacy.* Norwood, NJ: Ablex Publishing.

Thomas, K. F., & Barksdale-Ladd, M. A. (1997). Plant a radish, get a radish: Case study of kindergarten teachers' differing literacy belief systems. *Reading Research and Instruction, 37,* 39–60.

Torgesen, J. K., Morgan, S. T., & Davis, C. (1992). Effects of two types of phonological awareness training on word learning in kindergarten children. *Journal of Educational Psychology, 84,* 364–370.

Watson, L. R., Layton, T. L., Pierce, P. L., & Abraham, L. M. (1994). Enhancing emerging literacy in a language preschool. *Language, Speech, and Hearing Services in Schools, 25,* 136–145.

Wells, G. (1985). *Language development in the preschool years.* New York: Cambridge University Press.

Whitehurst, G. J., Epstein, J. N., Angell, A. L., Payne, A. C., Crone, D. A., & Fischel, J. E. (1994). Outcomes of an emergent literacy intervention in Head Start. *Journal of Educational Psychology, 86,* 542–555.

Whitehurst, G. J., Falco, F. L., Lonigan, C., Fischel, J. E., DeBaryshe, B. D., Valdez-Menchaca, M. C., & Caulfield, M. (1988). *Developmental Psychology, 24,* 552–559.

Whitehurst, G. J., & Lonigan, C. J. (1998). Child development and emergent literacy. *Child Development, 69,* 848–872.

CHAPTER 5
Developing Literacy

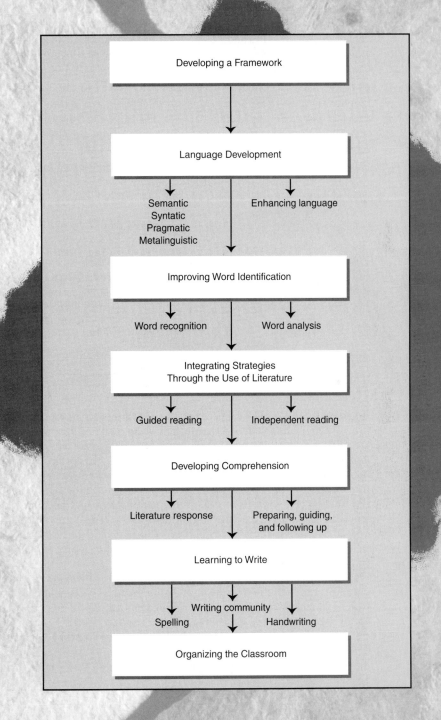

Developing a Framework

Language Development

Semantic
Syntatic
Pragmatic
Metalinguistic

Enhancing language

Improving Word Identification

Word recognition

Word analysis

Integrating Strategies
Through the Use of Literature

Guided reading

Independent reading

Developing Comprehension

Literature response

Preparing, guiding,
and following up

Learning to Write

Writing community

Spelling

Handwriting

Organizing the Classroom

It's the beginning of August, and for Sharon G., a second-grade teacher, as for many other teachers, August 1 brings thoughts of the new school year. As in past summers, Sharon had attended a workshop this summer and is excited to try out some of the new ideas and techniques she had learned. As she peruses her class list, she notices that she has a wide range of reading abilities again this year. Six of her 25 students receive special education services. There will be a special education teacher, Barbara, there for part of the day to support the instruction. Sharon makes a note to herself to call Barbara for the two of them to plan together. There are another three children in the class who had received supplementary instruction in reading last year. She knew they still needed further assistance to maintain their progress. And, finally, there was one new student this year. Sharon needed to find out more about him. As Sharon begins her preliminary planning, she thinks about ways to incorporate the various strategies she has learned into her own philosophy of teaching. She reviews her "standards" guide to help her set appropriate goals for the children for the year.

Let's leave Sharon now, but before you continue, look back at Chapter 1. How does an understanding of literacy and literacy development influence the decisions that Sharon will have to make about structuring her class? List three concepts that you believe will have instructional impact.

▌▌▌DEVELOPING A FRAMEWORK FOR BEGINNING TO READ

Before planning instruction for students, you should always consider your conceptual framework. Think of your ideas about literacy, literacy development, and your broad, general ideas about learning and the learning environment. Review Chapter 1, looking carefully at the top-down, bottom-up, and interactive models of reading and the linguistic, cognitive, and sociocultural factors impacting literacy development. Use this information, along with your own experiences, to help you begin to think about a conceptual framework. The formulation of a conceptual framework (Figure 5.1) enables one to make informed, logical, instructional decisions. It enables teachers to evaluate teaching methods and materials, preventing the use of random activities because they "sound cute." This is particularly critical in the Internet age when teachers have access to so many new ideas, many of which have never been critically evaluated.

Conceptual frameworks do not remain static, however. As people have wider experiences and acquire greater knowledge, some aspects of the conceptual framework should change. However, even an initial framework will help you think more critically about the instructional decisions that you need to make.

As you read this chapter think about the nine assumptions that were posited in Chapter 1. Throughout this chapter, those assumptions will be referred to and woven into the principles and techniques for learning to read that will be presented here. These assumptions are significant factors in developing a conceptual framework.

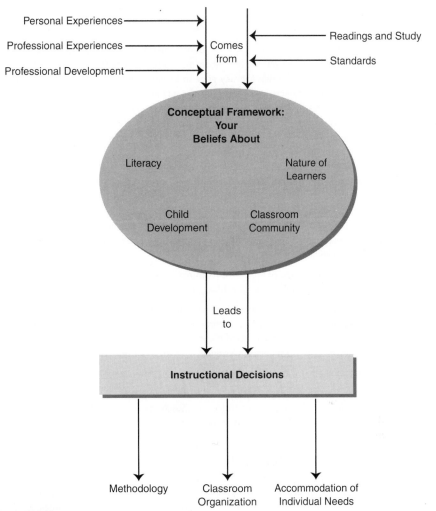

FIGURE 5.1

Conceptual Framework

The Standards Movement

The standards movement has affected education throughout the United States in the various content areas. The standards movement is a national and state effort to define the knowledge and abilities that students should possess at different levels within the various content areas. It has affected many academic areas. Table 5.1 shows the national standards for literacy/language arts that have been developed jointly by the National Council of Teachers of English and the International Reading Association (International Reading Association and National Council of Teachers, 1996).

TABLE 5.1 IRA/NCTE Standards for the English Language Arts

The vision guiding these standards is that all students must have the opportunities and resources to develop the language skills they need to pursue life's goals and to participate fully as informed, productive members of society. These standards assume that literacy growth begins before children enter school as they experience and experiment with literacy activities—reading and writing, and associating spoken words with their graphic representations. Recognizing this fact, these standards encourage the development of curriculum and instruction that make productive use of the emerging literacy abilities that children bring to school. Furthermore, the standards provide ample room for the innovation and creativity essential to teaching and learning. They are not prescriptions for particular curriculum or instruction.

Although we present these standards as a list, we want to emphasize that they are not distinct and separable; they are, in fact, interrelated and should be considered as a whole.

1. Students read a wide range of print and nonprint texts to build an understanding of texts, of themselves, and of the cultures of the United States and the world; to acquire new information; to respond to the needs and demands of society and the workplace; and for personal fulfillment. Among these texts are fiction and nonfiction, classic and contemporary works.

2. Students read a wide range of literature from many periods in many genres to build an understanding of the many dimensions (e.g., philosophical, ethical, aesthetic) of human experience.

3. Students apply a wide range of strategies to comprehend, interpret, evaluate, and appreciate texts. They draw on their prior experience, their interactions with other readers and writers, their knowledge of word meaning and of other texts, their word identification strategies, and their understanding of textual features (e.g., sound-letter correspondence, sentence structure, context, graphics).

4. Students adjust their use of spoken, written, and visual language (e.g., conventions, style, vocabulary) to communicate effectively with a variety of audiences and for different purposes.

5. Students employ a wide range of strategies as they write and use different writing process elements appropriately to communicate with different audiences for a variety of purposes.

6. Students apply knowledge of language structure, language conventions (e.g., spelling and punctuation), media techniques, figurative language, and genre to create, critique, and discuss print and nonprint texts.

7. Students conduct research on issues and interests by generating ideas and questions, and by posing problems. They gather, evaluate, and synthesize data from a variety of sources (e.g., print and nonprint texts, artifacts, people) to communicate their discoveries in ways that suit their purpose and audience.

8. Students use a variety of technological and informational resources (e.g., libraries, databases, computer networks, video) to gather and synthesize information and to create and communicate knowledge.

9. Students develop an understanding of and respect for diversity in language use, patterns, and dialects across cultures, ethnic groups, geographic regions, and social roles.

10. Students whose first language is not English make use of their first language to develop competency in the English language arts and to develop understanding of content across the curriculum.

11. Students participate as knowledgeable, reflective, creative, and critical members of a variety of literacy communities.

12. Students use spoken, written, and visual language to accomplish their own purposes (e.g., for learning, enjoyment, persuasion, and the exchange of information).

By examining these standards, one sees that the goal of literacy instruction and the generic types of experiences that students must engage in are clear, but the standards are general enough to allow for many types of instructional procedures.

In addition, various states have developed their own standards and many have developed assessments throughout students' schooling to determine whether they have met the standards. Most of the state standards also allow for different instructional applications. Many schools are requiring teachers to align their instruction with the state standards, explicitly indicating the correlation on their lesson plans.

The standards movement has impacted the education of children with learning differences in two major ways. First, it has provided broad goals for literacy development for all children. When children have difficulty learning to read, there is a tendency to focus on the child's area of weakness and segment the task into small attainable units. Although segmenting is not necessarily harmful, it sometimes results in children losing the purpose of reading. The expression "they can't see the forest for the trees" aptly describes the instruction for many children (Figure 5.2). As a result, the children have a skewed view of the reading process (Palincsar, 1993).

Second, many states have severely limited the exemptions granted for state assessments, thereby informing school systems that all students, except for the very severely disabled, are required to meet the standards. Teachers must then consider the needs of all their students and develop instructional strategies to enable all of them to meet the literacy standards. This is no small feat, but it is extremely powerful in determining that all children must be taught to allow them to reach their potential.

Knowledge of Special Needs

Barbara, the special education teacher who will be working with Sharon, is also beginning to plan for September. She and Sharon have a true collaborative relationship. Both of them take responsibility for the class and respect each other's knowledge. They spend a great deal of time planning together. As Barbara looks over the class roster she focuses her attention on the children who receive special services. She studies their Individual Educational Plans (IEPs) and begins to make some tentative decisions about modifications for them in the classroom. Barbara uses her conceptual framework about special education to guide these decisions.

In inclusive classrooms, teachers may see students with various disabilities. In Chapter 2 you read about many disabilities and their impact on reading. The most common ones, called higher-incidence disabilities, are: communication disorders, learning disabilities, mental retardation (for the most part mild or moderate), and serious emotional disturbance. These disabilities comprise about 90% of students with disabilities under IDEA (Mastropieri & Scruggs, 2000). Of these, teachers mainly encounter children with communications disorders and learning disabilities in inclusive classrooms. The following paragraphs provide a brief review of the characteristics described in Chapter 2.

Students with *communications disorders* have difficulty with speech or language. Speech disorders affect articulation; that is, pronunciation of words, fluency (for example, stuttering), and voice-pitch, volume, and quality. Language difficulties may

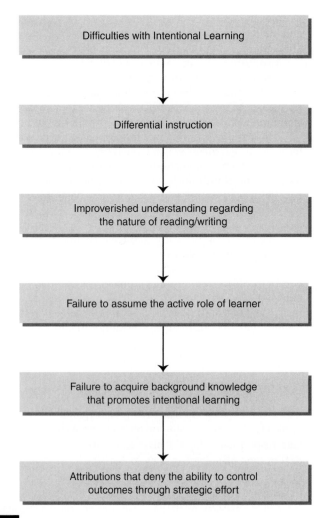

FIGURE 5.2

Learning Profiles of Children with Disabilities
Source: Palincsar, A. S. (1993). Friendship and literacy through literature: Responses of special education students. Paper presented at the annual convention of the International Reading Association, San Antonio, TX. Used with permission.

affect different components of language such as phonology, syntax, semantics, and pragmatics. A number of these problems impact on the social area.

Learning disabilities refers to a wide range of difficulties in which students have academic and cognitive difficulties despite average or above average intelligence, no serious emotional problems, and adequate environmental, cultural, and economic conditions (Federal Register, 1977). They may manifest themselves in the areas of academics, cognition, and the social-emotional realm. Children with learning disabilities may also exhibit language difficulties. Their language may develop more slowly than their peers, they may have difficulty with word retrieval, and they may have difficulty with pragmatics or the use of language in social situations.

▌▌LANGUAGE DEVELOPMENT IN THE EARLY SCHOOL YEARS

By the time they enter formal schooling, most children have acquired a sophisticated spoken language system. They can understand and use thousands of words, pronounce most of them accurately, use them in a variety of sentence types, and communicate appropriately in a variety of settings with many different types of people. Yet, language learning is not complete. During the school years children continue to acquire a significant number of language skills.

Semantic Development

One of the best-documented areas of language development in the school years is vocabulary growth. Research has determined that children in first grade have an average spoken language vocabulary of approximately 10,000 words. By the end of grade 5, their vocabulary has expanded to almost 40,000 words (Anglin, 1993). Much of this growth comes from learning to make new words by combining a known root word (e.g., *bake*) with a word ending (e.g., *er*) to create a new word (*baker*). Additionally, word growth comes from exposure to new experiences and new concepts in domains such as social studies and science.

Although growth in vocabulary during the school years is dramatic, it is not the only semantic language development taking place. During the school years most children demonstrate a shift in the way they understand words. When they are beginning to acquire words, young children tend to focus on the visual and perceptual features of the item. Thus, when asked to group things that go together, young children might place all of the red objects in one group and all of the blue in another group. Later (usually around age 6) they begin to put more emphasis on the function of the object. For example, they might group all of the items that are used in school and all of the items that are used to cook. The final stage of semantic-cognitive development (usually beginning around age 10) is reached when children begin to use language labels to categorize words. Now they may say, "these are all utensils" (Owens, 1992). This development marks a significant change in the way children understand the world around them.

Another significant semantic language achievement during the school years is the understanding and use of figurative language and humor. Both figurative language and humor require the child to move from a rigid to a more flexible understanding of words. Figurative language includes linguistic devices such as simile and metaphor—items that break the standard rules and cannot be interpreted literally. As children progress through school, they may encounter these linguistic devices in their reading and may be called on to use them in their own writing. The accuracy with which they understand and use figurative language indicates increasing sophistication of language usage.

Humor, too, is a sign of semantic growth. Humor often requires understanding double meanings [e.g., "What's black and white and read (red) all over?"] and semantic-pragmatic structures (e.g., "Knock-knock." "Who's there?" "Boo." "Boo who?"). Young children sometimes figure out the form of the joke before they understand the meaning (e.g., "Knock-knock." "Who's there?" "Me.") or fail to "get it" because they lack knowledge of the possible dual meaning of a word. Researchers have documented the growth of the understanding and use of humor during the school years (e.g., Fowles & Glanz, 1977).

Syntactic Development

Most children come to school having acquired the major syntactic structures of their first language. They can accurately form a variety of sentences including questions and complex sentences. For the most part, growth during the school years consists of a refinement of these basic structures. Some of the specific developments in the school years include:

- *Gerunds:* Gerunds are verbs to which "-ing" is added to produce a noun. For example, "Fish*ing* is fun."
- *Passive voice:* In a passive sentence the direct object and indirect object switch positions. Thus, the object of the action appears before the performer of the action (e.g., "The ball was hit by the girl").
- *Embedded sentences:* Although the rudiments of sentence embedding are acquired prior to the school years, some forms, such as center embedding ("The book that Joe read was interesting") are acquired during the school years.

Pragmatic Development

Perhaps the greatest language growth during the school years comes in the area of pragmatic language. As both their language skills and their opportunities to use language in increasingly varied ways increase, pragmatic language skills develop rapidly during the school years. Children learn the rules for telling and retelling stories, for recognizing the structure within texts (story grammar), for talking to people of different ages and levels of authority, and for entering, exiting, and repairing conversations. Often, these pragmatic rules are taught explicitly (as when parents and teachers teach the "politeness" rules of saying "thank you"). At other times, the rules are acquired through interaction (e.g., indirect requests such as, "Can you sit down!").

The school environment is an important venue for the acquisition of pragmatic language skills. In school, children learn such essential skills as how to wait your turn, how to respond when addressed by the teacher, and how to stay on the topic. When children experience difficulty with the acquisition of pragmatic language skills, they run the risk of failure in school and estrangement from their peers.

Metalinguistic Awareness

Another important language development during the school years is that of metalinguistic awareness—the ability to reflect on language itself. As we noted earlier, most children enter school with a large spoken language vocabulary that they can pronounce reasonably well. However, in school we ask that children do something they have never done before—recognize the individual sounds that make up these words. We then ask that they use this new skill to "sound out" the written word. This is one type of metalinguistic (metaphonetic or "phonological") skill. Other metalinguistic skills that develop during the school years include semantic and syntactic awareness. Menyuk (1995) illustrates the growth in these skills in children at ages 3, 5, and 7. In her study, children were asked to repeat sentences and then asked to say whether the sentence was right or wrong. Here are some of the responses she received to the sentence, "I see two cat":

At age 3: "It's wrong because you can't say that."
At age 5: "It's wrong because you say two cats. You can say one dog but you've got to say two cats."
At age 7: "It's wrong because there's more than one. You can say one cat but two cats, one dog but two dogs, two shoes."

These examples show the growing ability of children to reflect on language—metalinguistic ability.

Enhancing Language Skills

The school environment provides many opportunities for children to learn and practice their language skills. Circle times, group projects, interactive learning centers, and field visits all provide rich opportunities for language growth and development.

However, the school environment also presents challenges for many children. In some classrooms, teachers use a highly structured style of interaction in which the teacher dominates the conversation and students' responses are limited to one or a few words. Some children may come from cultural or language backgrounds that differ from those of the teacher and other students. These children may bring different experiences and a different style of interaction to the classroom. What can teachers do to enhance children's opportunities for continued language growth and development in school?

Dudley–Marling and Searle (1988) have provided four suggestions that teachers can use to enhance the language-learning environment in the classroom. They suggest that:

1. *The physical setting must promote talking:* Classroom organization can enhance interaction by providing activity areas such as learning centers or grouped seating arrangements where children can interact.
2. *The teacher must provide opportunities for children to interact and use language as they learn:* Teachers can use strategies such as "think alouds," brainstorming, and cooperative learning to provide opportunities to use language in the classroom.
3. *The teacher needs to provide opportunities for children to use language for a variety of purposes, and for a variety of audiences:* Activities such as authors' "teas," where parents are invited to hear their children read what they have written, and cross-age tutoring, where children work with younger or older students, provide opportunities for children to expand their language skills.
4. *The teacher needs to respond to a student's talk in ways that encourage continued talking:* When teachers acknowledge the child's contribution, extend the

conversation by asking a follow-up question, or ask the child to elaborate on a response, they are providing opportunities for enhanced language interaction.

▌▌ IMPROVING WORD IDENTIFICATION

Word identification is an essential skill for early literacy development. But how do children learn to identify words? Experts in reading have identified two types of word identification strategies—*immediate* and *mediated.* Immediate word identification (sometimes called "automatic" or "sight word" recognition) is used for those words that you know on sight, that is, words that can be identified with little or no hesitation. Mediated word identification (also called "word analysis," "decoding," or "phonetic analysis") is used for unfamiliar words. For the mature reader, that would include specialized vocabulary or words that are encountered rarely in print. For a long time there was a dispute between the better method for teaching children to read, by sight or through decoding (Chall, 1967). It is clear now, however, that proficient readers use both approaches as they read. As young readers develop, they need to be helped to use both immediate and mediated word recognition strategies.

Rationale for Teaching Word Recognition

Teaching word recognition is also called teaching sight vocabulary. There are a number of reasons for teaching sight vocabulary or teaching some words as wholes:

1. It is developmentally easier to conceptualize words as wholes than to examine word parts. Research supports phases of word learning, with the earliest stage being the logographic—selective cue stage. Children at this stage and at the rudimentary—alphabetic stage rely heavily on learning words as wholes as they engage in literacy acts. Thus, teaching sight word recognition is developmentally appropriate for many children (Ehri, 1991).
2. Learning sight words can provide the foundation for later developing word analysis strategies. Studies have shown that students who have acquired some sight vocabulary use this knowledge to develop word attack strategies more quickly (Ehri & Wilce, 1985).
3. There are a number of high-frequency words that are not phonetically regular, such as *of, what,* and *the.* These words are encountered often in reading and are most efficiently learned by sight.

Principles and Techniques for Teaching Word Recognition

Students need many opportunities to interact with whole text as their sight vocabulary broadens. Students learn about words by seeing and hearing them in meaningful contexts. Exposure to literature is particularly important to children with reading difficulties by providing them with the necessary experiences on which reading builds.

Read-Alouds

Reading to children provides them with many opportunities to hear language and to recognize words within context. The use of *big books* gives children a chance to see the print as the teacher reads. When reading aloud, teachers should be careful to engage children in the reading by activating their prior knowledge (schema) of the subject and asking for predictions. All children should be able to see the print as teachers slide their hands under the words while reading. This will increase the children's understanding of word concept and left-to-right directionality. At first, teachers may read the entire book to the class, but as children become more familiar with the text, there should be opportunities for them to participate in the reading in various ways, as discussed next.

Choral Reading

After reading a book several times, the teacher can involve students by having them read along with the teacher. In choral reading the teacher and the students read in unison. In order to scaffold the experience for students, the teacher may begin the reading alone and have students choral read for certain parts. With each successive reading the students will read more parts of the text with the teacher.

Echo Reading

In echo reading the teacher reads a part of the book and then the students echo the teacher's part. The entire book is read in this manner: a sentence or two is read by the teacher, then echoed by the students. This allows for more independence because the students do not have the teacher's simultaneous support.

Reading Familiar Words or Refrains

In this rereading of the book, the teacher reads but then waits for students to read a familiar refrain, rhyming word, or other predictable word. Students can read them in unison, in small groups, or individually. By carefully selecting the parts for the children to read, the teacher can ensure that all children are successful with this activity (Box 5.1).

Smaller copies of the big book should be in the classroom library to enable children to practice reading. The books can be used for shared reading or for individual reading time. Having heard the story read a number of times by the teacher and participating in the reading in various ways provides children with needed support before practicing to read the book without the teacher.

❚ Box 5.1

CHICKEN SOUP WITH RICE

Mrs. R. takes out the big book, *Chicken Soup with Rice* (Sendak, 1962). She asks the children what kind of soup they like. She may jot a few ideas down on the board, but that is not the focus of the lesson. She reads the story through to the end, turning each page carefully and allowing the children to see the pictures as she does so. As she reads each line, she moves her hands under the print to raise children's awareness of word boundaries. After the first reading, she asks the children what is the little boy's favorite soup. There is a very brief discussion of the boy's favorite soup and when he likes to eat it. She asks the children if they notice any other pattern with the book, notably the organization around the months of the year.

For the second reading the children read in unison with the teacher. Because Mrs. R. has assigned the students' places she has put "good" readers in close proximity to children having more difficulty. Mrs. R. listens carefully during this reading to make sure all students are participating. For the third reading, Mrs. R. reads a phrase, "In January it's so nice." The children repeat the phrase, then Mrs. R. continues "while slipping on the sliding ice."

She then tells them to pay very close attention because they are going to help her read the book. As she reads the fourth time, she pauses before the refrain, "chicken soup with rice" to allow the children to say it in unison. For the fifth reading individual children are given a chance to be readers. Thus, when the lesson is concluded all children have been exposed to the book five times.

There are many small copies of *Chicken Soup with Rice* in the classroom library. Mrs. R. notices with satisfaction that when she reads the big book, the children are then eager to practice the small book either in dyads or individually.

Words should be taught in both isolation and context and reinforced often. There is disagreement about the most effective way to teach sight words, either in isolation or in context. The research is conflicting, with some research studies indicating that sight words are learned more quickly in isolation. Other research indicates that there is either no difference or that sight words are learned more quickly in context (McCormick, 1999). Hence, it appears that students should be exposed to words under both conditions, isolation and context. Research has also shown that instruction alone may not be sufficient for many students to retain a sight vocabulary, but that the students need many opportunities to practice their acquired words (Lemoine & Hutchinson, 1993; Cunningham & Stanovich, 1990).

General Procedure

When teaching sight words the following steps can be useful:

a. Select the words to be presented from high-frequency word lists or common words in the literature being read by the children.
b. First present the word in oral context. Use a sentence from familiar literature.
c. Present the word in written context. Have children practice reading the sentence with the target word.
d. Focus children's attention on the target word. Discuss the meaning of the word and visual and phonetic features.
e. Put the word on a word wall to which the children can refer for various classroom reinforcement activities.
f. Have children write the word for their word box for group and individual reinforcement activities. (If students are paired, one student can be the scribe.)
g. Have children read the word in a new written context.

Use of Word Walls

A word wall is a systematically organized collection of words that is displayed in large letters either on a wall or other large display area in the classroom (Cunningham, 1995). It may be organized alphabetically or around other phonic elements, by themes, or in any other appropriate way to support the reading and writing of children. Fountas and Pinnell (1998) refer to an "interactive word wall" that supports children's increasing knowledge of words by providing a visual map to help them remember the characteristics of words that will help them form categories. If you refer back to the information gained from Piaget, you can see the critical importance of aiding in the formation of categories. Daily activities based on word walls make them most effective (Wagstaff, 1997).

Multisensory Techniques

Some children will have difficulty learning words with common methods. They sometimes benefit from multisensory techniques, particularly those that add the kinesthetic sense. Although the research is inconclusive, many teachers have found them effective. Students can look at, say, and trace words. The kinesthetic sense can be enhanced by using textured materials such as salt, sand, and glitter pens. Shaving cream can also be used effectively for tracing words. In addition, some children have acquired difficult sight words by learning sign language. They look at the word, make the sign for the word, and say the word. A clinical multisensory technique that has been effective for severely disabled readers is the Fernald method. This technique was established at the UCLA reading clinic in the 1940s. It is a four-stage method that requires one-on-one instruction.

> Stage 1—The child learns individual words, then when ready dictates his or her own story. Words that the child cannot read are placed on 8 × 2-inch strips of paper. The child is directed to look at the word and trace it while saying each word segment. Decoding individual letter sounds is discouraged. The child traces the word as often as needed until the child can write the word twice from memory. This stage continues as long as the child needs to trace words to learn them. As the tracing begins to decrease, the teacher should look to move to the next stage.
>
> Stage 2—Language experience is continued, but words are now placed on index cards and learned through looking and saying the word without tracing. The child continues to write the words twice.
>
> Stage 3—Books are used, rather than the child's own story, but words are still taught by placing them on index cards.
>
> Stage 4—The emphasis is on generalizing from the known to the unknown. The children are required to do their own reading. Teachers supply words if a child is having difficulty, but phonic analysis is forbidden. The emphasis is on the use of context. Children study "words" if they are common enough to be important.

Language experience stories, stories that students generate from their own experiences, can provide a foundation for developing sight vocabulary. Teachers need to be careful to construct activities that require the students to attend to individual words as well as the entire message. In beginning a language experience story, teachers often first provide the experience, such as an excursion outside on school grounds to notice the trees, playground, and parking lot. By providing a planned experience, the teacher is ensuring that all children have access to the same experience. After the children return to the classroom, the teacher asks the students to talk about the experience and from this generates a three- or four-sentence story. Because the story uses the students' own language, the words are easier to learn (Allen, 1976). The students read through the story a number of times.

The next day the teacher may put up the story again, but this time certain words are masked. Individual children are given the words on word cards and are asked to put them in the correct place in the story. The children need to work together to do so. The entire class then reads the story aloud to determine if it makes sense. The students are then given sentence strips with the individual sentences of the story. In groups, they work with the sentence strips to reconstruct the story. All groups share their work with the class.

On the third day, students are divided into dyads. Each dyad is given an envelope with the individual words of the story. They are to put the words together to reconstruct the story. The envelopes may have subdivisions so that the words are organized according to sentence. This allows the children to work with smaller numbers of words at one time.

Reinforcement Activities for Sight Vocabulary Development

Words should be reinforced frequently through various activities and through the children's reading and writing for students to retain them. Many of the following activities can be conducted through cooperative learning groups and pairs. Because they have various purposes, they engage students who may need less practice with the words themselves. The activities generally require students to have word cards with their sight words. These can be kept in a file box or on a binder ring.

Adaptation of Games

Many common card games can be adapted for sight words. Two of the most common ones are *Go Fish* and *Memory*. Children play the games the same as usual, but instead of using playing cards or pictures, sight words are used. The games can be modified to include using the word in a sentence before the pair is kept. Board games such as *Candyland* can also be modified for word reinforcement.

Word Sorts

Word sorting is an activity that can be adapted for a number of purposes, some of which will be addressed later in this chapter and in later chapters. In a word sort the children must separate their cards into various categories. There are two types of word sorts—closed and open. In the closed word sort, the teacher provides the categories, such as all the color words, all the sensory words, or function words. In the open word sort the children devise their own categories for separating their words. They need to justify their categories and the placement of the words when finished.

Word Hunts

Children look through a familiar children's book to find target words. As a variation, certain words can be chosen for the week, and children should note every time the word is seen in print. This will also help them focus their attention on the words.

Sentence Creation

Children can use their word cards to create numerous sentences. Students can work with their words individually, in pairs, or in an activity called *living sentences*. In this activity each child is given a large word card and the children need to arrange themselves to create a sentence.

There are many imaginative ways that teachers can find for reinforcing sight vocabulary. They should be careful, however, to vary the activities to require children to use the words both in isolation and in context.

Teachers should adapt the quantity of words taught at any one time to the needs of the students. In observing classrooms, one sometimes sees teachers "overwhelming" students with 10 to 15 or more sight words presented at one time. The number of words taught should be limited to ensure success. By teaching only five sight words a week, within half a year a teacher can establish the basic sight vocabulary needed for half the words children usually see in print. Children who have difficulty acquiring a sight vocabulary could be presented with one to three words per week with many opportunities for reinforcement. Students with learning difficulties often need more repetitions to learn a sight word. Hargis (1982) found that the number of repetitions correlated with IQ levels, ranging from 20 for students with IQs over 120 to 55 for students in the 60–69 IQ range.

High-frequency words are often characteristic of the most difficult words to learn. Words that are concrete, can be visualized, are spelled regularly, and have high emotionality (evoke a feeling in the reader) are the easiest to learn. Having these characteristics, long words are sometimes easier to attain than shorter ones. If you are not sure about this, watch 4- and 5-year-olds who can easily read the names of the dinosaurs, finding *tyrannosaurus* more easily recognizable than the common word *the*. The high-frequency words generally lack these characteristics. Fortunately, only 10 words—*a, and, in, is, it, of, that, the, to,* and *you*—are used in about 25% of all the words in children's reading and writing (Cunningham, Moore, Cunningham, & Moore, 1995). One hundred words (Table 5.2) account for 50% of them (Fry, Kress, & Foukouditis, 1993).

There are a number of specialized techniques that can be used when children have difficulty learning high-frequency words. The techniques are often very time consuming and should only be used for useful words that are particularly problematic or for children who have extreme difficulty retaining words. The specialized techniques generally have the following characteristics in common:

a. They are multisensory in that they involve looking at words, saying and often writing words, or engaging in a physical activity with the words.
b. Words are addressed in a variety of ways. Students are asked to perform multiple activities that focus their attention on the word to be learned.
c. Attention is generally focused on the words as a whole as well as parts of the words (letters and/or sounds).

TABLE 5.2   100 Most Common Words

The first 25 words make up about one-third of all printed material. The entire list makes up about half.

1–25	26–50	51–75	76–100
the	or	will	number
of	one	up	no
and	had	other	way
a	by	about	could
to	word	out	people
in	but	many	my
is	not	then	than
you	what	them	first
that	all	these	water
it	were	so	been
he	we	some	call
was	when	her	who
for	your	would	oil
on	can	make	its
are	said	like	now
as	there	him	find
with	use	into	long
his	am	time	down
they	each	has	day
I	which	look	did
at	she	two	get
be	do	more	come
this	how	write	made
have	their	go	may
from	if	see	part

common suffixes: s, ing, ed, er, ly, est

Source: Fry, E. B., Kress, J. E., Fountoukidis, D. L., (1993). *The reading teacher's book of lists.* Upper Saddle River, NJ: Prentice Hall. Reprinted with permission.

Special Procedures

Cloze Procedure   The cloze procedure, in which one omits parts of a word or sentence, has many functions. It may be used for facilitating word retention in the following way: First the student is presented with the word as a whole. Looking at a model of the word, the child recreates the word using letter tiles, plastic letters, or other manipulatives. Next the child is presented with the word with the vowels missing, and the child must add the appropriate vowels. Third, the child is presented with the word with the consonants deleted and must add the consonants. Finally, the child must create the word without a model. When the child accomplishes that, he or she writes the word.

McNinch Procedure (McNinch, 1981)
1. The teacher presents the word in oral context, then written context.
2. The word is written in isolation, then questions are asked to focus attention; for example, What is the first letter? The last letter? How many letters? Can you spell the word? Trace the word?
3. Students practice reading the word in sentences and phrases.
4. Students practice reading the words in actual text with the teacher directing students to the words through questioning.
5. Students do independent practice.

Word Analysis

Although mature readers can recognize many words instantly, there are times when they must analyze the word to decode. An example is reading a textbook on reading disabilities and encountering the word *strephosymbolia*. You were probably able to decode the word, but were not able to do so instantly. You, however, developed a strategy for decoding, most probably segmenting the word into syllabic units and then using your knowledge of letter-sound relationships to read each syllable. The decoding may have been so rapid that you were hardly aware of doing so. But, in order to be successful, you needed to know common sound-letter relationships. You used your knowledge of the graphophonemic system.

Instruction in Word Analysis—Yes or No?

The explicit teaching of word analysis has had a very controversial history in our educational system. Within the last 50 years there have been a number of paradigm shifts in terms of word analysis (phonics). At times, experts have emphasized the teaching of phonics (e.g., 1960s to mid-1970s, mid-1990s to present). At other times, phonics instruction was deemphasized in favor of whole word and "whole language" approaches (e.g., 1950s, mid-1970s to mid-1990s). Particularly in the last few years the media has fueled this controversy with strident attacks on the supposed lack of phonics instruction in our schools. As you might assume, however, actual research and instruction in literacy development is much less polarized. Studies of teacher practices show that effective teachers generally use a variety and balance of methods in their classrooms (Pressley, Rankin, & Yokoi, 1996).

There is considerable research that supports the effectiveness of explicit instruction in word analysis *as part of a total reading program* for developing children's reading ability (Chall, 1967; Adams, 1990). This may be particularly true for children who are at risk for later reading failure (Foorman, Francis, Fletcher, Schatschneider, & Mehta, 1998, Sacks & Mergendoller, 1997). Effective programs provide consistent, systematic instruction in word analysis and the application to real text.

Phonic Elements

The English language system can be analyzed into several components. These components can, in turn, be used as the basis for teaching phonics. The major elements are:

> Consonants—there are 21 consonants in the English langauge, with two of the consonants, *y* and *w,* sometimes functioning as vowels. Consonants are generally consistent in their sounds and appear to be easier for children to acquire. They cannot be pronounced in isolation, however, and must be attached to a vowel sound.
> Vowels—the letters *a, e, i, o, u,* sometimes *y* (e.g., *fly, baby),* and sometimes *w* (e.g., *cow).* Vowels may have a number of sounds, depending on their placement within the word or the etymology of the word. Vowels may be particularly difficult for some children to access within the word and learn.
> Consonant blends—two or three consonants adjacent to one another in which the sound of both letters is heard (e.g., *st, sk, sm, bl, cl, fl, tr,* and *str,*). Blends usually include the letters s, l, n, or r.
> Consonant digraphs—two consonants adjacent to one another that create one third sound (e.g., *th, ch,* and *sh).*
> Vowel digraphs—two vowels that are adjacent to one another in which *usually* the sound of one of the vowels is heard (e.g.. *oa, ee, ai,* and *ea).*
> Vowel diphthongs—two adjacent vowels that create a third sound, which is a combination of the two (e.g., *oy* and *oi).*
> Syllable—a combination of letters containing a vowel sound and pronounced as a unit. Syllables may have different patterns, such as CVC (consonant-vowel-consonant; e.g., bat) CVCe (consonant-vowel-consonant-silent e; e.g., bake); CCVC (consonant blend or digraph-vowel-consonant; e.g., that or stop); CVVC (consonant-vowel digraph or diphthong-consonant; e.g., keep or boil).
> Onset—an initial consonant, consonant blend, or digraph (e.g., the *h* in the word *hat,* and *sh* in *shop).*
> Rime, phonogram, syllable pattern—a group of letters that have the same vowel and ending pattern as, for example, *at, in, ake.* Generally, phonograms or rimes are commonly added to onsets to create word families.

Analytic and Synthetic Approaches to Phonics Instruction

There are two main approaches to teaching phonics: analytic (implicit) phonics instruction and synthetic (explicit) phonics instruction (Box 5.2).

In analytic phonics, the sounds of the words are taught in the context of words. Students are presented with words that illustrate a certain sound such as *book, baby,* and *boy* for the sound *b.* Through these examples and direct teacher questioning, students are expected to ascertain the sounds within the words. As they learn the different sounds, students use their knowledge to substitute the sounds to read new words. For example, if students can read *baby* and *look,* they should then be able to decode the word *book.* This had been the preferred method for teaching phonics in the basal reading series in the 1970s and 1980s (Vacca, Vacca, & Gove, 2000).

In synthetic phonics, sounds are taught in isolation. Students receive practice in the sounds of the letters and provide examples of words that contain the sounds. When letter sounds are firm, they are then combined to create words. Students engage in blending the sounds to read the word. Synthetic phonics has been found to be more effective than analytic phonics (Chall, 1967; Adams, 1990). Two major concerns with the synthetic phonics approach have been that isolating consonant sounds distorts the language, and that instruction has sometimes centered on phonics rules so that learning phonics has been seen as the goal rather than a strategy for reading. In effective synthetic phonics instruction, students are given many opportunities to practice blending the sounds to create words. In the aggregate, synthetic phonics may be preferable, but for children having difficulty, other approaches may be helpful.

▌Box 5.2

EXAMPLE OF AN ANALYTIC PHONICS LESSON

Mrs. K. put the following words on the board: *book, bat, baby.* She pronounced each word and asked the students if they could hear the similarity among them. She then asked the students if they could give her other words that had the same similarity. She then wrote the following sentences for the students to practice reading:

> He had a book in his hand.
> The big boy played ball.

The students provided more sentences with words beginning with b. The class read all the sentences together.

Example of a Synthetic Phonics Lesson

Mrs. K. put the word *bat* on the board. She asked the students to listen carefully as she read the word *bat.* As she read she stretched the word so that the three sounds were audible. She asked the students what sound they heard at the beginning of *bat.* Students responded. She then asked them for the middle sound of *bat,* and then the ending sound. The students read *bat* by stretching the word. Then they blended the sounds to read the word *bat.* They then read a little story with many *b* words in it.

Principles and Techniques for Teaching Word Analysis

Principle I Phonics instruction should be appropriate for the students' developmental levels. Chapter 1 identified five levels of word learning: logographic/selective cue, rudimentary alphabetic, alphabetic, orthographic, and automatic (McCormick, 1999; Ehri, 1994). In first- and second-grade classrooms, most students are at the rudimentary alphabetic stage. Children are becoming aware that words consist of letters and sounds. They begin to include letter cues in their attempts to recognize words. They are not consistent in their ability to do so, however, only partially using letter cues present within the word. Many are also at the alphabetic stage (children have developed greater proficiency with letter-sound correspondences and apply them consistently and in an orderly sequence when attempting to read unfamiliar words) with many students progressing to the orthographic and automatic stages. There may be students at each of the different levels, however, and the phonics instruction should be adapted as necessary. As you look at the activities presented in the remainder of this section, consider the suitability for the different levels and the appropriate modifications that you can make to accommodate students at different levels.

Principle II   Sufficient grounding in the internal structure of words—both letters and sounds should be systematically taught and practiced (Osborn, Stahl, & Stein, 1977; Adams, 1990; Gibson & Levin, 1975). Using plastic letters and other manipulatives (Clay, 1985), forming letters through different art media, associating letters with key pictures and key words, and creating personal dictionaries in which children paste pictures of appropriate objects for letters learned, all provide students with experiences with letters and sounds. Students who have difficulty acquiring letter and sound knowledge should receive reinforcement and if necessary, use multisensory activities such as skywriting or tracing letters.

Parents and teachers are often concerned when young readers confuse letters such as *b, d; p, q;* and *n, u.* They are fearful that this may be a symptom of a severe reading disability. However, recent research indicates that these fears are unfounded (McCormick, 1999). Letter reversals are characteristic of young readers and reflect a level of development, rather than a disability. When helping children discriminate between confusing letters, it is often best to firmly establish one letter before attempting to teach the other. After each letter has been learned, the child then should engage in discrimination activities such as letter sorts. Mnemonic devices may also be helpful for particularly troublesome pairs.

Principle III   Programs should provide students with instruction in segmenting and blending. Students should be able to segment words into their component sounds and blend the sounds to create a meaningful word. The phonemic awareness activities mentioned in Chapter 4 provide the basis for acquiring these skills.

Instruction in blending should include explicit instruction in onsets and rimes (syllable patterns). In her oft-quoted work, *Beginning to Read: Thinking and Learning about Print,* Adams (1990) looked at the consistency of letter sounds in the English language. She concluded that there were many irregularities at the letter level in English, but when one looked at letter combinations in rimes, there was far greater consistency. Gibson & Levin (1975) found that maturing readers analyzed words in increasingly larger orthographic units. Working with onsets and rimes provides children with experiences to allow them to view words beyond letter by letter. Approximately 500 primary words can be derived from 37 rimes (Wylie & Durrell, 1970), as shown in Box 5.3.

Rimes are easier to recognize than individual phonemes (Barr & Johnson; 1991, Rozin & Gleitman, 1977) and appear to be used successfully by young children with some decoding skill and sight vocabulary (Ehri & Robbins, 1992; Goswami, 1986; Goswami & Mead, 1992; McClure, Ferreira, & Bisanz, 1996; Moustafa, 1995; Treiman, 1985). Although some students appear to use the onset and rime strategy spontaneously (Bruck & Treiman, 1992), instruction is necessary and effective for children with reading and learning difficulties including Down syndrome (Barr &

Johnson, 1991; Greany, Tunmer, & Chapman, 1997; Oelwein, 1995; Peterson & Haines, 1992). A sample lesson is shown in Box 5.4.

▌Box 5.3

BASIC RIMES

Nearly 500 primary-grade words can be derived from this set of only 37 rimes:

-ack	-all	-ain	-ake	-ale	-ame
-an	-ank	-ap	-ash	-at	-ate
-aw	-ay	-eat	-ell	-est	-ice
-ick	-ide	-ight	-ill	-in	-ine
-ing	-ink	-ip	-ir	-ock	-oke
-op	-ore	-or	-uck	-ug	-ump
-unk					

▌Box 5.4

ZEHAVA'S WEEKLY LESSON ON WORD FAMILIES FOR STUDENTS WITH DOWN SYNDROME

After observing her students in a previous lesson, Zehava decided that the students needed to be trained step-by-step with a focus on one word family at a time. She first consulted with the speech therapist to create an appropriate sentence for introducing the "an" family.

She began her lesson with the sentence, *Fran wanted to cook for her man.* Then the words *Fran, man, pan, can,* and *ran* were introduced. Each rhyming word had an accompanying picture. Students then had to identify one picture from a group of four that had an "odd" sound. Rhyming words were reviewed.

At the next session the students had an activity sheet with pictures that did and did not illustrate the *an* sound. Zehava held up a picture of a fan, asked the students to listen carefully to the sounds and then circle the pictures of words that contained those sounds, and cross out the pictures that did not contain the *an* sound. Words were reviewed and written on the board with *an* written in a different color.

Zehava reflected on the previous lessons. She realized the lessons needed to be very explicit with only a small number of words targeted. Enlarged pictures should accompany the targeted words. The students needed a great deal of reinforcement with different activities.

The original story was reviewed. The students helped by providing the rhyming word in each sentence. The teacher then showed the students objects and pictures. The students matched the flash cards to them. Then the students created a silly story by finishing a sentence starter with a rhyming word. At the next session the students made a flip book with the rhyming words. In session six the students blended and segmented the *an* family words. The lesson was presented visually and auditorily. The students practiced with the big posters. There was further practice and then the students were asked to spell the words.

In session seven, the teacher reviewed segmenting and blending by covering parts of the words and asking students to pronounce only the visible part. Students worked with this until they were able to do it correctly. At the next session the *op* family was introduced. Students made words for the *op* words by following the principles introduced for *an*. They spelled the words and wrote them in sentences. Additional activities included word sorts, word hunts, picture sorts, and writing rhyming poems. In the assessment of the lesson the students read the targeted words and, in addition, were able to read some words that were not taught explicitly.

Activities for Developing Word Analysis Abilities

Word Making   In the word-making activity, students are provided with a limited set of letters on cards from which to create their own words. For example, Terri takes a blank sheet of paper and divides it into eight sections. On each section she writes either an onset or a rime, using *p, t, m, s, at, ake, it, ad*. She cuts up the paper and distributes them to pairs of students. Their task is to manipulate the cards to create as many words as they can, writing the meaningful words. At the end of the activity she discusses the students' results by asking for the number of words that they found and the strategy they used to create the words (Botel & Seaver, 1977). A variation of this activity is provided by Cunningham and Cunningham (1992) who have students write individual letters on each card for word making. Other variations on the word-making activity include the use of phonic wheels, slotters, and common card and board games such as Tic Tac Toe and Candyland (Figure 5.3).

Word Sorts   Word sorting can be adapted for word analysis by supplying students with the categories for the sort (Bear, Invernizzi, Templeton, & Johnston, 2000; Santa, 1998). Teachers can use sorts to reinforce various syllable patterns. Students should sort the words and then read down each list to ensure that they are reading the words, not merely sorting words by their visual cues. The difficulty level can be adapted, beginning with picture sorts to increasingly more complex word patterns. Teachers should maintain a balance of two known to one unknown pattern in creating the sorts.

Word Play   Engaging children in word play activities heightens their awareness of the internal structure of words and provides enjoyable and meaningful practice in word analysis. One example is *Hink Pinks*, in which students are given clues that are solved by a rhyming pair (e.g., an unhappy father, *sad dad,* an overweight kitten, *fat cat*) (Pearson & Johnson, 1978; von Hoff Johnson, 1999).

Principle IV   Attention should be paid to writing words, sentences, and longer discourse. Writing, and particularly invented or temporary spelling, provides children with opportunities to apply their phonic knowledge and to focus their attention on let-

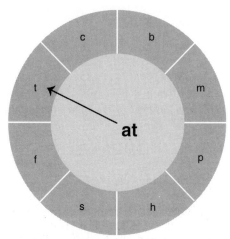

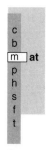

Students spin the spinner and read the word that is formed. If it is a real word they write it down. Two players can see how many words they make.

Students move the strip through the slotters and read the words. If the words are real, they write them down.

FIGURE 5.3

Example of Phonics Wheels and Slotters

ters and sounds. Students may write their own books similar to pattern books they have read, applying various phonic generalizations they have learned. Poetry writing also allows them to use their developing knowledge of phonics.

Principle V   Another approach to the development of work analysis skills is the use of a cognitive strategy. With this technique students learn how and when to use their knowledge of the internal structure of language. When teaching word analysis one should teach the following:

What is being taught: for example, the rime *ad*.
Why it is being taught: so that students can use their knowledge of *ad* to read unfamiliar words with *ad* in them.
How to use their knowledge: Teachers should model the thinking processes they engage in when encountering unfamiliar words.
When to use the strategy: when they see words such as *mad, lad, had*.

Principle VI   Students should have opportunities to practice and expand their knowledge through word play and application to extended text. Students should have opportunities to read books that illustrate the phonic elements that they have learned. This can be accomplished through decodable text (Box 5.5), text that is written to provide practice with particular phonic elements, or poetry, and appropriately selected children's literature.

▌Box 5.5

EXAMPLE OF DECODABLE TEXT

Jim's Bank Job

Jim was in bed. The bell rang at six A.M. He sank in his bed. Jim had a job at the bank but he did not think much of his job. He did not wish to go. Then the bell rang again, and he had to get up in a rush.

Source: Wilson, B. A., Student Reader Two, *Wilson Reading System.* Millbury, MA: Wilson Language Training. Reprinted with permission.

Principle VII   Teachers need to adjust the amount of time spent on teaching word analysis to the needs of the student. The essential principle for appropriate phonics instruction is "just enough." However, that may vary considerably for different students. Some students who have come from rich literacy environments appear to need very little phonics instruction before they generalize the various sounds and apply them appropriately to their reading. Other students from similar environments may need a great deal of instruction. Many students who are learning disabled require more intensive instruction in word analysis to become proficient readers.

Using Technology to Increase Word Proficiency

Using computer programs can give students the extra practice they may need to improve their word recognition and word analysis skills. Drill and practice programs use graphics and games to motivate children to continue with a task that they find difficult. Tutorial programs such as *Supersonic Phonics* (Curriculum Associates) can provide additional instruction. Criteria for selection should include:

- Easy-to-read screens
- Consistency
- Logical labels
- Instructional choices
- Auditory cues
- Alternatives to the mouse
- Visual cues
- Options to make the cursor more visible or easier to manipulate
- Ability to create custom programs (Alliance for Technology Access, as cited in Male, 1997)

It is also important to evaluate the nature of the graphics and sound effects to determine if they enhance learning, not detract from it. In addition to the general guidelines for evaluating computer programs, teachers should consider the following before selecting programs for literacy development:

- Sequencing of skills
- Different levels of difficulty within skills
- Easily identifiable pictures

- Opportunity to apply skills in reading and writing
- A management system for teachers
- Access to a dictionary
- Use of words in students' speaking vocabulary (Fox & Mitchell, 2000)

USING LITERATURE AS THE BASIS FOR WORD IDENTIFICATION INSTRUCTION

In Chapter 1 we noted that reading is much more than applying the rules of phonics. Although word recognition and word analysis instruction are critical elements in a reading program, they are not sufficient for the development of readers. Phonemic awareness development, word recognition and word analysis instruction, and reading literature complement one another. Phonemic awareness and word recognition and analysis improve reading abilities, whereas reading familiar text aids in the development of these skills (Weaver, 1998).

Phonemic awareness abilities should not be a prerequisite for opportunities to read.

> To put it even more bluntly, the ability to do phonics and identify words easily was used as a gatekeeper, on the assumption that "of course" children couldn't read whole books until they had developed better word-reading skills. This, in turn, served to perpetuate their status as poorer readers (Weaver, 1998, p. 365).

All children should have many opportunities for wide reading within their classroom appropriate to their development. In addition to the whole-class reading activities mentioned earlier, children should have access to books to read either with teacher guidance or independently.

Leveling of Books for Guided Reading

As children are learning to read, one component of the reading program should be leveled, focused instruction. Basal readers or leveled books similar to those used in *Reading Recovery* (Clay, 1993) or *Guided Reading* (Fountas & Pinnell, 1998) may be used for this facet of the program. Books should be at a comfortable level for the students, which is defined as the level at which students can read with 90% accuracy in word recognition. Reading books at an appropriate level allows children to consolidate and extend their strategies. When students are continuously exposed to books that are too difficult, they actually begin to lose the skills they have attained (Clay, 1979). Think of yourself learning a new skill, such as tennis. You worked with your instructor on your forehand and backhand and played some matches where the instructor hit the ball slowly so that you were able to return it. As you played, you became more proficient at focusing on the ball, moving into position, adjusting your form, and placing the ball. Now, suppose, you played an expert tennis player who hit the ball with all her power and speed. You barely had time to move out of the way to avoid being hit by the ball. Were you able to use the skills you learned? Not at all. If you continued to play only with this person, you would have no opportunity to practice; thus, the skills you have learned would fall into disuse. After several weeks you would probably be worse at tennis than before. That is what happens to students who are always given books that are too difficult. They may learn new skills, but because their attempts to practice them lead to failure, they tend to lose them.

Within these lessons, instruction should focus on strategy development. Readers should learn to integrate picture cues, visual cues, syntactic cues, and semantic cues with increasing efficiency. They use their background knowledge and make predictions about the reading. They monitor their reading by engaging in cross-checking behaviors by using more than one cuing system to confirm their responses. Marie Clay (1985) lists seven strategies that developing readers use: monitoring reading, searching for cues, discovering new things for themselves, cross checking, repeating, self-correcting, and solving. Teachers *guide* children through the use of these strategies to help them to develop independence.

In conducting guided reading lessons the teachers should allocate most of the time to reading (Box 5.6). Although prereading and follow-up activities are important, care must be taken so that these activities do not overwhelm the lesson. These activities should provide support for the lesson, but should not be the main focus of it.

▌ Box 5.6

GUIDED READING LESSSON

Mrs. M. calls a small group of first-grade students to the carpet to work with her. It is February so the students are very comfortable with the routine. They are reading *The Seven Sillies*. The students had looked over the story the day before. She begins the lesson by discussing the strategies the students can use to help them figure out words: (1) Find little words inside big words—the students practice using *inside* as an example. (2) Skip the word and return to it—one student pretends she did not know the word *dog* in the sentence, *the dog barked*. Mrs. M. tracks the sentence as she rereads to help her read it. (3) Stretch it—the students draw out the word, saying it very slowly while stretching rubber bands to accentuate the sounds. (4) Look at the pictures. (5) Use phonics cards with long or short vowel sounds. (6) If all else fails, ask a friend.

The students engage in partner reading today. They choose partners and may read anywhere on the floor. Each partner reads the whole story at least once. Mrs. M. circulates and listens to them read. When they have finished reading, they return to the carpet. Mrs. M. asks if anyone feels comfortable doing a retelling of the story. One student volunteers.

The students now begin a response to *The Seven Sillies*. They begin with characters, listing them on one page and drawing them on the facing page. On the next page she asks for the setting, first reviewing what the setting is. They are told to write a sentence telling where the story takes place. Mrs. M. asks the students what she will be looking for. They respond with period at the end, capital in the beginning, not all capitals in a word, spaces, capitals for names. Finally the students are asked to write their favorite part.

Wait Time

All too often when children miscue or hesitate in their oral reading, well-meaning instructors immediately correct or provide the word to prevent disruption in the reading. An unfortunate result of the immediate help is learned helplessness. Learned helplessness is the reaction of people to situations in which they feel unable to affect the results (Seligman, 1975). It has been applied to children who are learning disabled who, when help is provided too soon, begin to believe that they cannot learn (Thomas, 1979). When children have difficulty with oral reading, teachers should wait before providing any help. (Five seconds has been used as a guideline.) This enables the children to begin to use the strategies that they have been taught.

Independent Reading

The primary classroom library should have books at different levels for independent reading. Teachers may wish to color code books by level and then organize the books in the library by themes and/or genres. All students should have time for independent reading of material of their choice every day. Independent reading should be an integral part of the day and should not be used as a reward for finishing one's work. Teachers should observe children during independent reading, asking questions such as: Is the child reading during this time or is the child leafing through books with little attention to the text? Does the child tend to choose books at an appropriate level? Is the child reading a variety of books? Can the child share during book-sharing time? Does the child engage in many off-task behaviors during this time? Based on the response to these questions, the teacher may need to modify the time frame or actively guide children in selecting more appropriate books.

Buddy Reading

A variation of independent reading is buddy reading where two or more children read a book together. Fountas and Pinnell (1998) present four options for buddy reading:

1. Partners with the same book can read it to one another, one at a time.
2. Partners with different books can take turns reading the whole book while the partner looks at the pictures.
3. Partners with the same book can alternate pages.
4. Partners may read the book in unison.

Less-abled readers may be paired with more-abled readers (Topping, 1989) or students of similar abilities may be paired (Winter, 1988). Teachers should teach students about pacing, error correction, and the use of praise before beginning this procedure.

▌▐ DEVELOPING COMPREHENSION

The main purpose of reading is to obtain meaning from print. At the developing literacy stage children exhibit their understanding of their reading by associating the reading with their own experiences, predicting what will happen next, monitoring their reading and correcting errors as necessary, and retelling the story in their own words. It is difficult at this stage to determine if children have difficulty with comprehension because of language or learning problems, with general comprehension processes or if it is a result of their laboring word recognition abilities (Snow, Burns, & Griffin, 1998). To improve both comprehension and word recognition, classrooms should provide many opportunities for meaningful reading.

Preparing Students for Reading

When developing and activating schema, teachers should identify the key elements and themes of the story and determine that students are familiar with them. Students sometimes have difficulty in three areas relative to schema: the development of schema, the activation of schema, and the maintenance of the appropriate schema. Some students in the class may not have had the background experience for the story, as one of our preservice teachers learned when tutoring a child who had never been to the zoo or seen pictures of one. The student had no schema for the concept of zoo, rendering the story meaningless. When this occurs, the teacher can provide the background through the use of pictures, objects, or discussion. Students may engage in picture walks in which they peruse the book before reading and make predictions about the reading from the pictures. Prereading activities activate schema for readers by providing clues to the main themes of the story and set a purpose for the reading.

Guiding Students Through the Reading

Depending on its length and complexity, the teacher may need to segment the story and guide students as they read or listen. Stories may be segmented by teacher- or student-generated questions, predictions, or written activities. It is important, however, that the teacher's guidance aid students' understanding of the story, not interfere with it by fragmenting it.

Extending the Reading

Response to literature may take many forms. It should capitalize on students' strengths and provide opportunities for the students to bring personal response to the text.

- *Cooperative learning:* Students in the primary grades may work in cooperative groups to relate the story to their own lives. Take, for example, the story *Wilfrid Gordon McDonald Partridge* (Fox, 1984), in which the little boy, Wilfred, helps an elderly friend remember her past by bringing her some simple objects that are precious to him. The woman associates the objects with events that have happened in her life. To utilize concept learning with this book, the teacher would first read the story to the class. The class would then be divided into heterogenous groups, with the teacher paying careful attention to the social makeup of these groups. In their groups the children would be asked what they would put in a basket of gifts. They would discuss what objects they would bring as a gift to someone special and why these objects are important to them. One person in the group could be the scribe who records the others' responses. By first reading the story to the children and appointing one child as the scribe, the teacher is allowing all children to participate in the activity independent of their reading ability. All children could be contributing members of the group. Students may work in cooperative learning groups to solve problems about the reading or extend the reading through writing, discussion, and different media. The considerable research on cooperative learning finds that opportunities to work together to achieve a common goal benefits both higher- and lower-achieving students. (Pearson & Fielding, 1994).

To maximize the benefits of cooperative learning the teacher should consider:

The composition of the group:
- Size—how many students are needed to complete the assignment? What is the optimal size for ensuring that the group remain on task?
- Criteria for grouping—is there a mix of "leaders" and "followers"? Are some students' personalities inhibiting for others? Are there any specific conflicts between group members that would affect members' performance? Are the groups balanced by ability? Does the task require special responsibilities (such as artwork), and do all groups have members who can fulfill them?

Preparation for cooperative learning:
- Behaviors for group work
- Individual and group responsibilities
- Appropriate interactions
- Problem solving

Assignment:
- Goals—are they clear to the students? Do the students understand the steps needed to achieve the goals?
- Task analysis—are students given individual tasks to complete that contribute to the group achieving its goal? Do all students have a task at which they may be successful?

The teacher should carefully monitor group interactions and progress toward completion of the assignment, intervene as necessary, evaluate, and guide individual and group evaluations of their performance.

- *Retelling stories:* Story maps can be an effective tool for guiding students' story retellings. They provide a pictorial representation of the essential elements of any story—the setting, the characters, the goal or problem, the plot sequence, and the resolution. When teachers introduce the story map before the story is read, they can guide children's thinking to attend to these critical elements. After the story is read, the story map helps organize the students' thoughts before retelling a story. Giving students incomplete story maps or sentence strips for adding, deleting, and organizing story events can further scaffold the task for students.

A variation on story retelling that is particularly appealing to young children is the use of drama to respond to the literature. Stories become more concrete for students, and by rereading stories in preparation for acting them out, students become more aware of story elements (McMaster, 1998).

■■ LEARNING TO WRITE

Reading and writing are reciprocal processes. When students have opportunities to write, their knowledge of language increases, thereby improving their reading abilities. Students may begin writing before they have become proficient readers. In fact, writing will aid in the development of reading proficiency. Many children who are learning disabled, however, have great difficulty with writing. They have difficulty with syntax, vocabulary, cohesion, revision, and mechanics (Singer, 1995). Their stories are often shorter than those of their peers (Barenbaum, 1987). Through the use of various interventions, teachers will enable these students to view themselves as writers.

Establishing a Writing Community

In a writing community, students engage in various types of writing. There may be class writing in which the whole class composes a piece together, there may be short, individual pieces such as message writing, there may be time for process writing, and there may be time for writing instruction. With appropriate modifications and support, all members of the class can be part of the writing community.

Class Writing

Language experience stories are a type of class writing. Individual members contribute to one class composition. They may compose ideas orally or may write individual words or sentences. Class writing gives all children an opportunity to participate at a level in which they are comfortable. It also gives them a chance to learn about language in different ways. As the students compose, teachers can teach students about language features by, for example, pointing out how *book* has the same syllable pattern as a word with which they're familiar, *look*.

Short, Individual Writing

In short, individual writing or message writing, children write one sentence, often from a story they have read. Through message writing, children become more aware of the

Children should have many opportunities to write throughout the day.

letters and sounds within words. In *Reading Recovery* (Clay, 1993) students hold a notebook vertically to write their message. The bottom page is used for the message. The top page is used to help students problem solve to spell the word. Thus, if a child wants to write "The dog ran after the bus" and has difficulty with the word *dog*, the teacher would draw three boxes for the word. The child would write the letter(s) for any recognized sound(s), and the teacher would complete the word for the child (Figure 5.4).

The teacher provides support for the child, helping the child to attend to the letters and extend language knowledge. Variations on message writing could include having secret pen pals or having a suggestion box in the classroom.

Process Writing

Children need time for longer, sustained writing: time to select a topic, plan their writing, draft, revise, and edit. They need time to move back and forth among stages as necessary. Take a minute and think about some of the research papers you have written. Have you ever completed the research (the planning stage), begun to write the paper, and then realized that you need to complete more research in a different area? This happens to many writers and is a normal part of the writing process. By focusing on writing as a process, teachers can segment and provide support for children as necessary. The process writing approach can be effective for diverse learners (Zaragoza & Vaughn, 1992).

Selecting a Topic   Students' writing improves when they have ownership of it. By allowing children to select their own topics they write about subjects that are personally meaningful for them. Because not all children can automatically think of topics to write about, teachers can provide support by brainstorming with the class, keeping a topic notebook for children to browse, conferencing with children, or allowing them to partner to discuss possible topics. Teachers need to believe that children have the ability to choose their own topic, with support if necessary, and convey that belief to their students.

Prewriting   In the prewriting stage children *collect* the information that they want to convey and then *connect* it. Students activate schema and increase their involvement with a story through prewriting (Noyce & Christie, 1989).

Children may collect information through many means such as reading, brainstorming, talking, and drawing. It is common in primary classrooms to hear teachers tell students to draw a picture before writing. This helps many students gather their

Child fills in w, t, r, sounds that he or she hears. Teacher fills in a, e.

He had ~~wt~~.

FIGURE 5.4

Sound Boxes

thoughts through a concrete medium. Students should be allowed to use diverse means for collecting the information. Using a tape recorder or an adult as a scribe will facilitate this stage for children with writing difficulties and who have trouble remembering their thoughts before actually writing them.

Connecting refers to the organization of one's thoughts. Too often, children attempt to move directly from the collecting phase to the drafting stage. Their writing then tends to look like a listing of their thoughts, not a coherent piece. In a study conducted in the reading clinic of one of the authors, tutors were taught to use semantic webbing to help their students write (Figure 5.5). First, the tutors discussed the piece with their students. Then they selected an appropriate web design. The students completed the web, and then began writing. Using the web increased the length, organization, and quality of language of the students' writing (Hasit, 1994).

Drafting   Children should be encouraged to "just" write their thoughts. Showing them how to skip lines and write on only one side of a page, use a word processor, or dictate to another person as they draft simplifies the next stage of revision and editing.

Revision and Editing   After the students have recorded their thoughts they then can revise their writing. Revision refers to the content of the message: Did the student sequence the writing correctly? Is it clear to the reader? Only after the student revises the writing should the student begin to edit the paper, or look at the form of the message. Teachers should limit revision and editing to a few key points for children who have difficulty with writing to avoid overwhelming them at this stage.

Spelling Development

Spelling appears to play a major role in many students' concepts of themselves as writers. Spelling is an important skill for effective writing. Writing that contains many spelling errors is more difficult to understand and may create a negative impression that interferes with the intended message being conveyed by the writer. It also affects some students' self-concept as a writer. Unfortunately, many students, including some identified as learning disabled, experience significant difficulties with spelling, especially when they have to use spelling in their own writing (Ehri & McCormick, 1998). Spelling requires memory, phonological awareness, graphemic capability, and metacognition, all of which may be areas of weakness for children with learning disabilities (Mastroprieri & Scruggs, 2000). Students do not become proficient spellers through attention to isolated drills and practice and memorization of spelling lists (Graves, 1983). They need opportunities to apply spelling strategies in meaningful tasks.

Invented spelling reflects the natural spelling development of the child. As children's literacy develops they begin to attend to the letters and sounds within words and their spelling more closely approximates correct spelling. At the same time, the use of invented spelling encourages them to attend to the letters and sounds. Encouraging the use of invented spelling along with classroom resources, such as word walls, allows children with spelling difficulties to view themselves as writers.

Word study incorporates the integration of spelling, phonics, and vocabulary instruction (Bear et al., 2000). Students are actively involved in categorizing words and examining sounds, structure, and meaning. Students who were involved in word study

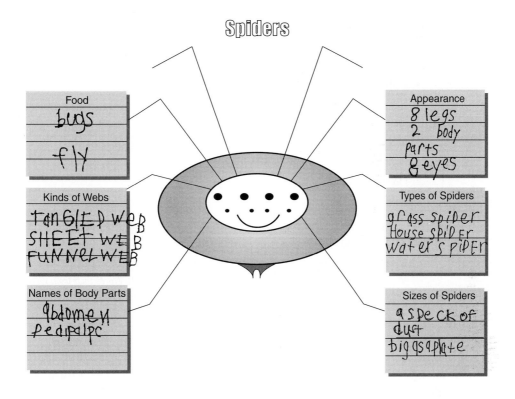

Spiders

Food	Appearance
bugs	8 legs
fly	2 body parts 8 eyes

Kinds of Webs	Types of Spiders
TanGlED weB SHEET WEB FuNNeL WEB	grass spiper House spiper water spiper

Names of Body Parts	Sizes of Spiders
qbdomey pedipalpc	a speck of dust big qsaplate

Spiders have 8 legs, two body parts and 8 eyes.

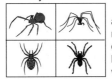

Spiders eat bugs and flies. There are many types of spiders, grass spiders, house spiders, and water spiders. Some kinds of webs are the funnel web, the sheet web, and the tangle web. A spider can be as small as a speck of dust.

FIGURE 5.5

Semantic Webbing

instruction were found to pay more attention to sounds when attempting new words (Fresch & Wheaton, 1992). Word study instruction proceeds from knowledge of the child's developmental spelling level (Table 5.3). Instruction is tailored to use what the child knows about words in order to extend the child's knowledge of words' internal structure. Most children in the primary classroom are in the early phonemic to the within-word stages of spelling development.

TABLE 5.3 Word Study

1. Look for what students use but confuse.

2. A step backward is a step forward.

3. Use words students can read.

4. Compare words "that do" with words "that don't."

5. Sort by sight and sound.

6. Begin with obvious contrasts first.

7. Don't hide exceptions.

8. Avoid rules.

9. Work for automaticity.

10. Return to meaningful texts.

Source: Bear, D. R., Invernizzi, M., Templeton, S., & Johnston, F. (2000). *Words their way: Word study for phonics, vocabulary, and spelling instruction.* Upper Saddle River, NJ: Merrill/Prentice Hall. Reprinted with permission.

Activities for the early phonemic (letter-name alphabetic) speller: Instruction should center on initial consonant sounds, then blends and digraphs, short vowels in word families, then out of word families and integration of the preceding (Bear et al., 2000). Picture and word sorts, developing word banks, and personal readers enable children to concentrate on appropriate sound patterns while also building students' sight vocabulary.

Activities for the within-word phase of the transitional speller: Instruction should center on long vowels, *r*-controlled vowels, diphthongs and other vowel digraphs, homophones, and homographs. Word sorts, word-study notebooks in which students reflect on their sorts, word hunts, and various games that are adapted to provide practice with learned patterns (e.g., *Jeopardy, Uno*) are examples of the types of activities appropriate for learners at this stage.

Adapting Spelling Instruction for Students with Special Needs

Bos and Vaughn (1998) suggest several principles for adapting spelling instruction for students with spelling difficulties:

- Teach in small units—three words a day, rather than four or five
- Provide sufficient practice with feedback
- Select appropriate words—they should be words within students' reading and oral vocabulary
- Teach spelling through explicit instruction
- Maintain previously learned words
- Teach for transfer of learning
- Motivate students to spell correctly
- Teach students how to use the dictionary

Specialized Techniques for Spelling

As you read in the section on word recognition, there are a few key words that account for most of the vocabulary in our reading and writing. Learning how to spell these words facilitates the writing process for students who have writing disabilities. Cunningham and associates (1995) suggest doing daily activities with high-frequency words on word walls to support the spelling of these words. Students should then be held accountable for the correct spelling of these words in their writing.

There are a number of other specialized techniques for learning to spell key words. They are multisensory and focus children's attention on the letters within the word and on the word as a whole (see Table 5.4).

Handwriting

Handwriting may be very laborious and difficult for some children with disabilities. Difficulties arise in copying from the board, near point copying, and forming letters from memory (Hallahan, Kauffman, & Lloyd, 1996). When providing instruction in handwriting, the teacher should focus on the importance of fluent, legible handwriting to facilitate communication of the writer's message. Handwriting instruction should thus be embedded in general writing instruction. In order to acquire legible handwriting, students should understand its characteristics. Citing Barbe, Wasylyk, Hackney, and Braun's work, Tompkins (2000) describes the six characteristics of legible handwriting: letter formation, size and proportion, spacing, slant (differing for right- and left-handed students), alignment, and line quality. A two-step process of having students (1) examine a model of a letter with numbered arrows to indicate the form, order, and direction of the strokes and (2) reproduce the letter from memory with increasingly longer intervals between seeing the model and writing the letter, has been successful with developing writers who are at the at-risk level (Berninger, 1999; Graham, 1999). The characteristics can be taught through minilessons and then practiced and self-monitored by children through the use of handwriting checklists. In summarizing Graham and Weintraub's research on handwriting, Mastropieri and Scruggs (2000) suggested the following techniques for students who continue to have difficulties:

- Use paper with more space between the lines.
- Provide models for the order, number, and direction of strokes.
- Provide sufficient practice tracing, copying, and writing from memory.
- Use behavioral techniques such as cueing, shaping, and positive practice.
- Teach self-regulation behaviors such as self-verbalizations.
- Use self-assessment, self-instruction, and self-correction as part of the instruction.

▓▌ ORGANIZING THE CLASSROOM

Many procedures have been presented here for meeting the needs of the diverse learners in the classroom. There is no time in the day to use all of the strategies. Teachers need to select appropriate strategies, and organize the classroom and instruction for successful implementation. A model, developed by Friend and Bursuck (1996), for systematically adapting instruction for students with special needs is helpful for guiding

TABLE 5.4

Fitzgerald Method (Fitzgerald, 1951a)

1. Look at the word carefully.
2. Say the word.
3. With eyes closed, visualize the word.
4. Cover the word and then write it.
5. Check the spelling.
6. If the word is misspelled, repeat steps 1–5.

Horn Method 1 (E. Horn, 1919)

1. Look at the word and say it to yourself.
2. Close your eyes and visualize the word.
3. Check to see if you were right. (If not, begin at step 1.)
4. Cover the word and write it.
5. Check to see if you were right. (If not, begin at step 1.)
6. Repeat steps 4 and 5 two more times.

Horn Method 2 (E. Horn, 1954c)

1. Pronounce each word carefully.
2. Look carefully at each part of the word as you pronounce it.
3. Say the letters in sequence.
4. Attempt to recall how the word looks, then spell the word.
5. Check this attempt to recall.
6. Write the word.
7. Check this spelling attempt.
8. Repeat the above steps if necessary.

Visual-Vocal Method (Westerman, 1971)

1. Say word.
2. Spell word orally.
3. Say word again.
4. Spell word from memory four times correctly.

Gilstrap Method (Gilstrap, 1962)

1. Look at the word and say it softly. If it has more than one part, say it again, part by part, looking at each part as you say it.
2. Look at the letters and say each one. If the word has more than one part, say the letters part by part.
3. Write the word without looking at the book.

Fernald Method Modified

1. Make a model of the word with a crayon, grease pencil, or magic marker, saying the word as you write it.
2. Check the accuracy of the model.
3. Trace over the model with your index finger, saying the word at the same time.
4. Repeat step 3 five times.
5. Copy the word three times correctly.
6. Copy the word three times from memory correctly.

Cover-and-Write Method

1. Look at word. Say it.
2. Write word two times.
3. Cover and write one time.
4. Check work.
5. Write word two times.
6. Cover and write one time.
7. Check work.
8. Write word three times.
9. Cover and write one time.
10. Check work.

Source: S. Graham and L. Miller, "Spelling Research and Practice: A Unified Approach," *Focus on Exceptional Children,* 13(2), (1980): 11. Reprinted with permission.

decisions for instruction. Called **INCLUDE**, the model is comprised of seven steps that can be applied to various disabilities and in varied classroom environments:

1. **I**dentify classroom environmental, curricular, and instructional demands. Look at classroom organization such as physical organization, routines, nonacademic activities, classroom climate toward differences, and classroom rules. Examine classroom grouping. Review instructional strategies, materials, and student evaluation.
2. **N**ote student learning strengths and needs. One looks at academic areas such as acquisition of basic skills, cognitive and learning strategies, knowing the "unwritten curriculum" (e.g., regular attendance, completing assignments). A second area to look at is socioemotional development, which includes classroom behavior and interpersonal skills. Students' physical development should also be assessed.
3. **C**heck potential areas for student success. In this step the teacher analyzes student strengths relative to the classroom demands. The teacher finds areas in which the student can perform successfully and ascertains that students will have opportunities to do so.
4. **L**ook for potential problem areas. The teacher analyzes student problem areas relative to the classroom demands. The teacher checks for mismatches and identifies areas to modify curriculum or provide additional support.
5. **U**se information to brainstorm adaptations. If necessary, develop bypass strategies that allow students to compensate for areas of disability (e.g., a tape-recorder for writing). Adapt classroom organization and instruction. Select critical adaptations to increase the likelihood of success.
6. **D**ecide which accommodations to implement. Use these guidelines to help you select appropriate adaptations: select the easiest accommodations first, select age-apprpropriate adaptations, and select adaptations within your conceptual framework.
7. **E**valuate student progress. Use various measures for evaluating student progress. Use tests, a variety of written classroom assignments, observations, and student self-assessments. Develop a plan for systematic evaluation.

A look at Sharon and Barbara's collaboration shows how the INCLUDE model provides a framework for their instruction.

Sharon and Barbara now meet to plan for the year. They know that they will be meeting weekly and conferencing on the phone whenever they cannot meet in school. Ongoing collaboration between the two professionals in the classroom is critical for maximizing the instruction for all students. They both realize that there are some essential decisions that must be made now to get the class off to the right start.

First, Barbara and Sharon examine the roster together. They review the records from the previous teachers and the assessment results in order to obtain a general picture of literacy levels, strengths, and weaknesses. They make some tentative decisions about initial grouping for cooperative learning and for homogeneous instruction. Next, they carefully read the IEPs for the students who receive special education services. They discuss goals, general adaptations within the classroom, and referral for specialized programs and services. They determine that Barbara will be the liaison between the classroom and the special services, communicating and planning to enable the professionals to provide integrated instruction for the students.

Using the INCLUDE framework from the beginning of the chapter, Barbara and Sharon examine the demands of the literacy program relative to the strengths and weaknesses of the students. Specifically, they look at:

- Appropriateness of materials—they confirm that there are sufficient materials at various levels of difficulty that are organized to make it easier for the students to select appropriate ones.
- Grouping of students—they balance whole-class, homogeneous, and heterogeneous groups for different literacy activities. They establish different collaborative groups to meet the social and academic needs of the students. They set up buddies to help the students participate in activities. They determine which teacher will be initially responsible for each group.
- Modification of assignments and activities for students as necessary. Using the IEPs as the guide, they determine which assignments should be modified and how to provide extra support as necessary. Barbara and Sharon share in the teaching of all the students. And when students receive extra instruction to acquire certain skills, they use classroom materials and lessons for application.
- Finding time to provide extra help for all children who need it. They use the services of the reading specialist or basic skills teacher and coordinate lessons to avoid fragmented instruction.
- Evaluation of student progress—they develop plans for systematically gathering data about student performance through observation, collection of work samples, and the use of various assessments.

▌▌SUMMARY

In selecting instructional techniques and materials to help all children develop literacy, the teacher must first develop a conceptual framework. This framework should include knowledge of literacy, of learning, of special needs, and of general guidelines for providing education for all children in the classroom.

Literacy development includes language development. Language growth and development does not stop when children enter formal schooling. On the contrary, language continues to develop in sophistication and use during the school years. There is much that teachers can do to provide a supportive environment for continued language development. By doing so they enhance not only language skills but all areas of literacy development.

Using the framework first developed in Chapter 1, the teacher needs to plan a balanced program for literacy development. This includes instruction in improving children's word identification abilities, in integrating strategies through the use of literature, in developing comprehension, and in increasing writing ability.

As literacy develops, students increase their word recognition and word analysis abilities. Word recognition is the instant recognition of words; analysis is looking at the parts of words to determine the word. Word analysis is also referred to as decoding. Instruction in both of these areas should include explicit, systematic instruction along with many opportunities to apply learned skills and strategies in connected text.

Literature is the foundation of the reading program. Teachers should select appropriate material for students in which they may feel successful. In addition, students should have opportunities in the classroom for reading self-selected texts. Comprehension activities should help students retell texts, connect their own experiences with the text, and extend the text.

Writing is a major component of literacy development. Teachers should create a writing community in the classroom that provides students with opportunities to engage in various writing activities. Spelling and handwriting instruction should be incorporated in writing and should be developmentally appropriate.

As teachers plan instruction for literacy development, they should organize their classrooms to allow for flexible grouping, cooperative learning, individual instruction where needed, and whole-class instruction in order to provide the varying amounts of support that different students will need to succeed.

Linkages

In the text
1. Research a literature-based series in terms of word identification instruction. Using the guidelines for word recognition and word analysis in this chapter, examine the scope and sequence of skills instruction and the activities for developing the skills. Does the series meet the guidelines that are set forth here? If not, how would you supplement instruction for students who needed it?
2. Choose a piece of literature that is appropriate for a group of students who are developing literacy. Plan a lesson that engages students in word identification and comprehension strategies for the literature.
3. Plan a spelling lesson for beginning spellers. Develop different types of activities to meet students' different needs.

Outside the text
1. Observe a classroom for children who are developing literacy. Create a chart of literacy activities for a day. Include in the chart the different grouping arrangements that are being used.
2. Interview a teacher who is working in an inclusive classroom. Determine the procedure for pairing teachers, the preparation and training that was provided for inclusive education, and the planning that the two teachers engage in.

On the Web

National Center to Improve Practice
    www2.edc.org/NCIP/tour/Susan.html
In conjunction with Duke University, provides a tour of a primary teacher's classroom.

The Children's Literature Web Guide
    www.acs.ucalgary.ca/~dkbrown/index.html
Provides information on children's literature, includes award winners, databases, and teaching ideas.

Mrs. McGowan's First Grade
    myschoolonline.com/folder/0,1872,34898-119831-38-35031,00.html
A glimpse into a poetry lesson in a first-grade classroom; winner of the "miss rumphius award."

Teachers.Net
    teachers.net

A commercial website that provides chatrooms, lesson plans and articles on teaching literacy.

LD Resources
>   www.ldresources.com/readwrite/index.html
A commercial website with many ideas for teaching reading and writing to children with disabilities in the classroom.

Ask Eric
>   ericir.syr.edu/cgi-bin/lessons.cgi/Language_Arts/
Website from the ERIC clearinghouse providing lesson plans in the areas of reading/ writing—teachers may submit their own plans.

References

AAMR Ad Hoc Committee on Terminology and Classification. (1992). *Mental retardation: Definition, classification, and systems of support.* Washington, DC: American Association on Mental Retardation.

Adams, M. J. (1990). *Beginning to read. Thinking and learning about print.* Cambridge, MA: MIT Press.

Allen, R. V. (1976). *Language experiences in communication.* Boston: Houghton Mifflin.

Anglin, J. (1993). Vocabulary development: A morphological analysis. *Monographs of the Society for Research in Child Development, 58,* Serial No. 238.

Barenbaum, E. (1987). Children's ability to write stories as a function of variation in task, age, and developmental level. *Learning Disability Quarterly, 10,* 175–188.

Barr, R., & Johnson, B. (1991). *Teaching reading and writing in elementary classroom.* New York: Longman.

Bear, D. R., Invernizzi, M., Templeton, S., & Johnston, F. (2000). *Words their way: Word study for phonics, vocabulary, and spelling instruction.* Upper Saddle River, NJ: Merrill/Prentice Hall.

Berninger, V. W. (1999). Coordinating transcription and text generation in working memory during composing: Automatic and constructive processes. *Learning Disability Quarterly, 22,* 99–122.

Bos, C. S., & Vaughn, S. (1998). *Teaching students with learning and behavior problems.* Needham Heights, MA: Allyn & Bacon.

Botel, M., & Seaver, J. T. (1977). *Literacy plus.* Washington, DC: Curriculum Development Associates.

Bruck, M. & Treiman, R. (1992). Learning to pronounce words: The limitations of analogies. *Reading Research Quarterly, 27,* 374–388.

Chall, J. S. (1967). *Learning to read: The great debate.* New York: McGraw-Hill.

Clay, M. M. (1979). *Reading: The patterning of complex behavior.* Auckland: Heinemann.

Clay, M. M. (1985). *The early detection of reading difficulties: A diagnostic survey with recovery procedures.* Portsmouth, NH: Heinemann.

Clay, M. M. (1993). *Reading recovery: A guidebook for teachers in training.* Portsmouth, NH: Heinemann.

Cunningham, A., & Stanovich, K. E. (1990). Assessing print exposure and orthographic processing skill in children: A quick measure of reading experience. *Journal of Educational Psychology, 82,* 733–740.

Cunningham, P. M. (1995). *Phonics they use: Words for reading and writing.* New York: Harper Collins.

Cunningham, P. M., & Cunningham, J. W. (1992). Making words: Enhancing the invented spelling-decoding connection. *Reading Teacher, 46,* 106–115.

Cunningham, P. M., Moore, S. A., Cunningham, J. W., & Moore, D. W. (1995). *Reading and writing in elementary classroom: Strategies and observation.* White Plains, NY: Longman.

Dudley-Marling, C., & Searle, D. (1988). Enriching language learning environments for students with learning disabilities. *Journal of Learning Disabilities, 21,* 140–143.

Ehri, L. C. (1991). Development of the ability to read words. In R. Barr, M. L. Kamil, P. Mosenthal, & P. D. Pearson (Eds.), *Handbook of reading research* (Vol. II, pp. 383–417). Mahwah, NJ: Lawrence Erlbaum Associates.

Ehri, L. C. (1994). Development of the ability to read words: Update. In R. B. Ruddell, M. R. Ruddell, & H. Singer (Eds.), *Theoretical models and processes of reading* (4th ed., pp. 323–358). Newark, DE: International Reading Association.

Ehri, L. C., & McCormick, S. (1998). Phases of word learning: Implications for instruction with delayed and disabled readers. *Reading and Writing Quarterly, 14,* 135–163.

Ehri, L. C., & Robbins, C. (1992). Beginners need some decoding skill to read words by analogy. *Reading Research Quarterly, 27,* 13–27.

Ehri, L. C., & Wilce, L. S. (1985). Movement into reading: Is the first stage of printed word learning visual or phonetic? *Reading Research Quarterly, 20,* 163–179.

Federal Register. (1977, December 29). *Procedures for evaluating specific learning disabilities.* Washington, DC: Department of Health, Education, and Welfare.

Fielding, L. G., & Pearson, P. D. (1994). Reading comprehension: What works. *Educational Leadership, 51,* 62–68.

Foorman, B. R., Francis, D. J., Fletcher, J. M, Schatschneider, C., & Mehta, P. (1998). The role of instruction in learning to read: Preventing reading failure in at-risk children. *Journal of Educational Psychology, 90,* 37–55.

Fountas, I. C., & Pinnell, G. S. (1998). *Guided reading.* Portsmouth, NH: Heinemann.

Fowles, L., & Glanz, M. (1977). Competence and talent in verbal riddle comprehension. *Journal of Child Language, 4,* 433–452.

Fox B. J., & Mitchell, M. J. (2000). Using technology to support word recognition, spelling, and vocabulary acquisition. In S. B. Wepner, W. J. Valmont, & R. Thurlow (Eds.), *Linking literacy and technology* (pp. 42–75). Newark, DE: International Reading Association.

Fox, M. (1984). *Wilfrid Gordon McDonald Partridge.* Australia: Omnibus Books.

Fresch, M. J., & Wheaton, A. (1992). Open word sorts: Helping third-grade students become strategic spellers. ERIC Document Reproduction Service No. ED353554.

Friend, M., & Bursuck, W. (1996). *Including students with special needs: A practical guide for classroom teachers.* Needham Heights, MA: Allyn & Bacon.

Fry, E. B., Kress, J. E., & Fountoukidis, D. L. (1993). *The reading teacher's book of lists.* Upper Saddle River, NJ: Prentice Hall.

Gibson, E. J. & Levin, H. (1975). *The psychology of reading.* Cambridge, MA: MIT Press.

Goswami, U. (1986). Children's use of analogy in learning to read: A developmental study. *Journal of Experimental Child Psychology, 42,* 73–83.

Goswami, U., & Mead, F. (1992). Onset and rime awareness and analogies in reading. *Reading Research Quarterly, 27,* 153–162.

Graham, S. (1999). Handwriting and spelling instruction for students with learning disabilities: A review. *Learning Disability Quarterly, 22,* 78–98.

Graves, D. (1983). *Writing: Teachers and children at work.* Portsmouth, NH: Heinemann.

Greaney, K. T., Tunmer, W. E., & Chapman, J. (1997). Effects of rime-based orthographic analogy training on the word recognition skills of children with reading disability. *Journal of Educational Psychology, 89,* 645–651.

Hallahan, D. P., Kauffman, J. M., & Lloyd J. W. (1996). *Introduction to learning disabilities.* Needham Heights, MA: Allyn & Bacon.

Hargis, C. H. (1982). Word recognition development. *Focus on Exceptional Children 14*(9), 1–8.

Hasit, C. (1994). *Graphic organizers: Supporting process writing for at-risk readers and writers.* Paper presented at the annual meeting of the College Reading Association, New Orleans, LA.

International Reading Association and National Council of Teachers of English. (1996). *Standards for the English Language Arts.*

Lemoine, B. L., & Hutchinson, A. (1993). Increasing the naming speed of poor readers: Representations formed across repetitions. *Journal of Experimental Child Psychology, 55,* 297–328.

Male, M. (1997). *Technology for inclusion: Meeting the special needs of all students.* Needham Heights, MA: Allyn & Bacon.

Mastropieri, M. A., & Scruggs, T. E. (2000). *The inclusive classroom: Strategies for effective instruction.* Upper Saddle River, NJ: Merrill/Prentice Hall.

McClure, K. K., Ferreira, F., & Bisanz, G. L. (1996). Effects of grade, syllable segmentation, and speed of presentation on children's word-blending ability. *Journal of Educational Psychology, 88,* 670–681.

McCormick, S. (1999). *Instructing students who have literacy problems.* Upper Saddle River, NJ: Merrill/Prentice Hall.

McMaster, J. C. (1998). "Doing" literature: Using drama to build literacy. *The Reading Teacher, 51,* 574–584.

McNinch, G. H. (1981). A method for teaching sight words to disabled readers. *Reading Teacher, 35,* 269–272.

Menyuk, P. (1995). Language development and education. *Journal of Education, 177,* 39–62.

Moustafa, M. (1995). Children's productive phonological recoding. *Reading Research Quarterly, 30,* 464–476.

Noyce, R. M., & Christie, J. F. (1989). *Integrating reading and writing instruction in grades k–8.* Needham Heights, MA: Allyn & Bacon.

Oelwein, P. (1995). *Teaching reading to children with down syndrome: A guide for parents and teachers.* ERIC Document Reproduction Service No. ED379902.

Osborn, J., Stahl, S., & Stein, M. (1977). *Teachers' guidelines for evaluating commercial phonics packages.* Newark, DE: International Reading Association.

Owens, R. E. (1992). *Language development: An introduction* (3rd ed.). New York: Merrill/Macmillan.

Palincsar, A. S. (1993). *Friendship and literacy through literature: Responses of special education students.* Paper presented at the annual convention of the International Reading Association, San Antonio, TX.

Pearson, P. D., & Johnson, D. D. (1978). *Teaching reading comprehension.* New York: Holt, Rinehart & Winston.

Peterson, M. E., & Haines, L. P. (1992). Orthographic analogy training with kindergarten children: Effects on analogy use, phonemic segmentation, and letter sound knowledge. *Journal of Reading Behavior, 25,* 109–127.

Pressley, M., Rankin, J., & Yokoi, L. (1996). A survey of instructional practices of outstanding primary-level literacy teachers. *Elementary School Journal, 96,* 363–384.

Rozin, P., & Gleitman, L. (1977). The structure and acquisition of reading: II. The reading process and the acquisition of the alphabetic principle. In A. Reber & D. Scarborough (Eds.), *Toward a psychology of reading* (pp. 55–141). Hillsdale, NJ: Erlbaum.

Sacks, C. H., & Mergendoller, J. R. (1997). The relationship between teachers' theoretical orientation toward reading and student outcomes in kindergarten children with different initial reading abilities. *American Educational Research Journal, 34,* 721–739.

Santa, C. (1998). *Early steps: Learning from a reader.* Kalispell, Montana: Scott Publishing Co.

Seligman, M. E. P. (1975). *Helplessness: On depression, development, and death.* San Francisco: W. H. Freeman.

Singer, B. D. (1995). Written language development and disorders: Selected principles, patterns, and intervention possibilities. *Topics in Language Disorders, 16,* 83–98.

Smith, T. E. C., Polloway, E. A., Patton, J. R., & Dowdy, C. A. (1995). *Teaching students with special needs in inclusive settings.* Needham Heights, MA: Allyn & Bacon.

Snow, C. E., Burns, M. S., & Griffin, P. (1998). *Preventing reading difficulties in young children.* Washington, DC: National Academy Press.

Thomas, A. (1979). Learned helplessness and expectancy factors: Implications for research in learning disabilities. *Review of Education Research, 49,* 208–221.

Tompkins, G. E. (2000). *Teaching writing: Balancing process and product.* Upper Saddle River, NJ: Merrill/Prentice Hall.

Topping, K. (1989). Peer tutoring and paired reading: Combining two powerful techniques. *Reading Teacher, 42,* 488–494.

Treiman, R. (1985). Onset and rimes as units of spoken syllable: Evidence from children. *Journal of Exceptional Child Psychology, 39,* 161–181.

U.S. Department of Education. (1996). *Eighteenth annual report to Congress on the Implementation of the Individuals with Disabilities Act.* Washington, DC: U.S. Department of Education.

Vacca, J. L., Vacca, R. T., & Gove, M. K. (2000). *Reading and learning to read.* New York: Addison-Wesley-Longman.

von Hoff Johnson, B. (1999). *Wordworks: Exploring language play.* Golden, CO: Fulcrum Resources.

Wagstaff, J. M. (1997). Building practical knowledge of letter-sound correspondences: A beginner's word wall and beyond. *Reading Teacher, 51,* 298–304.

Weaver. C. (1998). Experimental research: On phonemic awareness and on whole language. In C. Weaver (Ed.), *Reconsidering a balanced approach to reading* (pp. 321–371). Urbana, IL: National Council of Teachers of English.

Winter, S. (1988). Paired reading: A study of process and outcome. *Educational Psychology: An International Journal of Experimental Educational Psychology, 8,* 135–151.

Wylie, R. E., & Durrell, D. D. (1970). Teaching vowels through phonograms. *Elementary English, 47,* 787–791.

Zaragoza, N., & Vaughn, S. (1992). The effects of process writing instruction on three 2nd-grade students with different achievement profiles. *Learning Disabilities Research and Practice, 7,* 184–193.

Transitional Literacy

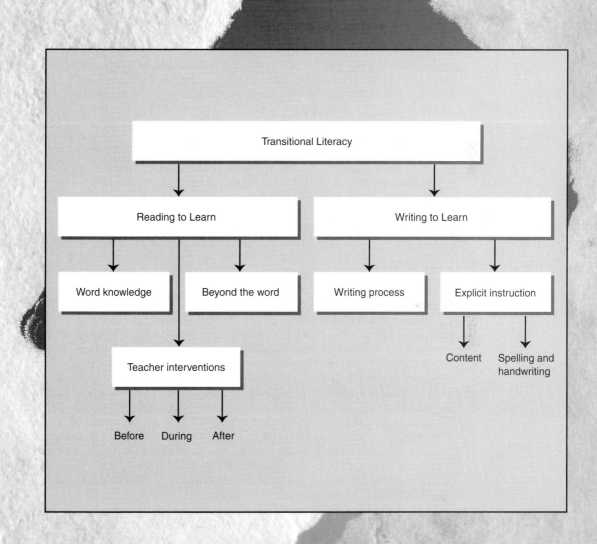

Initial reflection: Before you begin, think about the title of this chapter. What does the word *transitional* mean? How do you think the focus of this chapter will be different from the one before it? Make a prediction about some of the major concepts that you would expect to see in this chapter.

The dictionary definition for *transition* is "movement from one position, state, stage, subject, concept, etc. to another; change" (Random House Dictionary, 1983, p. 1505). In literacy, transition implies the movement from emphasizing basic literacy development, or learning to read and write, to using literacy to enhance learning, or reading and writing to learn. The teaching focus changes to higher-order thinking for reading and writing. The transitional literacy stage is characteristic of many learners from the end of second through fifth grade (Cooper & Kiger, 2001). But, because we know that literacy does not develop in lockstep fashion, we should not be surprised if some students have characteristics of different stages. Further, as the grades increase, the range of reading competencies within the same class tends to broaden. Thus, within classrooms in which the majority of children are in the transitional stage, teachers should expect to see some children at the developing literacy stage and others at the advanced stage. As you read through this chapter, consider the ways for providing additional support for students who need it and enrichment for students at the higher end of the range.

■ ■ COMPREHENSION

Comprehension is the main purpose of reading. Comprehension development should thus comprise a major portion of the instructional day. But consider the following scenario:

Students are directed to take out their social studies texts and read Chapter 3 silently. When finished reading, they are told to answer the questions at the end of the chapter. The teacher allows a sufficient amount of time for most students to complete the assignment. She then reviews the answers with the students, calling on different students to share their responses. If a student gives an incorrect response, the teacher calls on someone else who provides the correct answer for everyone. At the end of the session, all of the students should have written the correct answers to all the questions.

Does this scenario seem familiar to you? Does it remind you of lessons you have observed or perhaps remember from your school days? It might. Delores Durkin (1978) studied comprehension instruction in many schools. The lesson just described was typical of the lessons that she saw. Unfortunately, if you examine the lesson, you see that the teacher did not help students develop their comprehension. She assigned a reading and then assessed their understanding of the reading through questioning. If a student answered incorrectly, another student provided the correct answer. But there was no explanation of how the answer was derived. Durkin concluded that most of the lessons that she observed consisted of comprehension *assessment*, not comprehension *instruction*. Comprehension instruction consists of teaching students basic comprehension processes and supporting students in their attempts to compensate for difficulties that may affect comprehension.

In the Classroom

Kelley and Debbie meet to discuss the students in their fourth-grade class. They are particularly concerned about five students who are having difficulty understanding their literature books, and social studies and math texts. They begin their planning by discussing observations and analyzing work samples for these particular students.

Gina: Gina seems to have a lot of trouble with her texts. She rarely answers questions or contributes to the classroom discussions. She does, however, appear to be more involved when she reads with Tameka, who often reads parts to Gina. Debbie had conducted a running record for Gina and found that Gina miscued over 20% of the words in the text. In addition, her reading was very slow and labored.

Bryan: Bryan also has difficulty. He has a lot of trouble understanding who the characters are in a story. He can answer literal questions in which the answer is found in one sentence, but cannot answer questions when he has to look at two sentences. He often has difficulty following narratives and directions. In looking at his responses Kelley and Debbie also saw that he has a lot of trouble with vocabulary questions.

Shana: Shana is a very fluent reader. She reads accurately and with expression. She can answer many of the comprehension questions at the end of each chapter. Her retellings of stories are very full, in fact perhaps too full. She appears to have memorized the stories and relates every event that has taken place. Her retellings are so long, that the reader finds it difficult to understand the main points from them.

Jason: Jason also appears to be a fluent reader. His oral reading is accurate, but at times it lacks expression. Lacking expression appears to characterize Jason's whole approach to reading. He approaches all reading tasks without enthusiasm. He reads to answer the questions in the book and is generally accurate. On further examination of his responses, however, Kelley noted that his answers were very short and never went beyond the literal level. This was confirmed by observations that he very seldom contributes any of his own thoughts or experiences to discussions.

Leslie: Leslie is very eager to read and approaches all tasks with enthusiasm. She can often answer questions immediately after she has read something, but cannot remember very much about her reading from one day to the next. At other times if you ask her if she has understood what she has read she says yes, but then cannot tell you anything about the selection.

As you can see from the preceding scenarios, comprehension is quite complex. Instruction must be multifaceted. Gina has difficulty with the words in the selection. She cannot decode important words, struggles with others, and devotes so much attention to decoding that she does not understand what she reads. Bryan has difficulty making connections from one part of a text to another. His limited vocabulary also tends to disrupt the meaning for him. Shana's problems are more subtle. On the surface she appears to comprehend well. However, one sees that she cannot distinguish important from unimportant information and seems unable to determine the main points of a selection. Jason is also a good "surface" comprehender. He can answer literal-level questions, but has a poor attitude toward reading and does not make connections between the text and his background knowledge. His purpose for reading appears to be limited to looking only for explicit information in the text. Leslie's memory appears to interfere with her reading. She can remember details if asked immediately after reading, but seems to have difficulty storing information in her long-term memory to retrieve at a later time. Further, Leslie does not know whether she has understood something and often proceeds without any true understanding of her reading. Comprehension instruction needs to address all of these difficulties.

Looking at Words
Developing Fluency to Aid in Comprehension

In Chapter 1 the theory of automaticity and phases of word learning were introduced. Students in the transitional literacy stage are generally at the alphabetic, orthographic, and automatic phases of word learning. According to LaBerge and Samuels (1974) students must develop automaticity in their word recognition to facilitate comprehension. When word recognition is not automatic, students attend to decoding and, thus, have less attention to give to comprehending the material. Unfortunately, instruction in word recognition strategies often ends before many students have acquired automaticity. As the vocabulary load greatly increases at this stage, reading becomes extremely burdensome for these students. Compensatory strategies that helped students through lower-level material often fail to help them meet the challenges of the higher-level texts. Fortunately, providing systematic, explicit instruction at appropriate developmental levels for students has been found to improve overall reading ability for struggling readers (Curtis & Longo, 1999). Thus, even at the transitional literacy stage teachers should continue word recognition instruction to help children acquire automaticity.

Readers at the alphabetic phase of word learning use letter-sound correspondences to read new words. Their phonetic knowledge enables them to acquire sight words more rapidly than at previous stages. Their decoding may still be relatively inefficient, however, as they tend to decode letter by letter, rather than in larger units. Instruction at this phase should center on helping students recognize known letter patterns and segmenting words into parts. Working with onsets and rimes and using analogies of words and word parts to determine unknown words is effective for helping students progress through this stage (Ehri & McCormick, 1998). Programs such as the Benchmark Word Identification program, which is more fully described in Chapter 8, teach students how to use analogy for more effective decoding. Because students at this phase have difficulty with decoding relative to their classmates, instruction often centers on decoding skills in isolation. It is critical to provide decoding instruction, but not exclusively. Students must practice their developing skills in connected text. The reading program for students at this stage should consist of explicit instruction in language structure applied to meaningful text. Instruction should provide sufficient time for students to practice reading easier texts fluently as well as engaging in comprehension of age-appropriate works. Emphasis should be placed both on structure and meaning (Moats, 2001). Reading text should provide opportunities for students to use their sight word knowledge, their developing phonetic abilities, and then context to confirm their choices. Because readers at this phase still tend to overrely on context, with limited attention to graphophonic analysis, teachers should monitor instruction to strengthen students' phonic knowledge and encourage its use during contextual reading (Ehri & McCormick, 1998; Stahl, 1998).

Readers at the orthographic phase focus on spelling patterns as they read, chunking words into larger units rather than letter by letter. There is greater understanding of the structure of English, such as the influence of final *e*. Teaching rules may help students acquire greater facility with multisyllabic words, but the most important instructional strategy is to provide practice with larger unknown words. Students' facility with the use of analogies should be refined at this stage as they advance from making analogies from prompts, to consciously making them independently, to unconsciously using them (Ehri & McCormick, 1998). Students at this stage should also receive instruction in, and practice, segmenting multisyllabic words including recognition and application of prefixes and suffixes.

Developing Fluency   Readers who are at the automatic phase of word learning are generally fluent readers. Fluency has been described as the ability to identify words quickly, with good pacing and appropriate phrasing and expression (Zutell & Rasinski, 1991). Table 6.1 represents a rating scale for fluency based on Zutell and Rasinski's work.

In contrast, dysfluent reading is often characterized by inappropriate pauses, conscious decoding of words, multiple attempts at a word, and inappropriate patterns of stress or intonation (Aulls, 1978). As you have read in previous chapters, developing fluency (automaticity) aids in comprehension by freeing the reader to attend to comprehension, rather than word identification. Although fluency has been recognized as a necessary aspect of proficient reading, fluency development is often neglected in the classroom (Allington, 1983).

TABLE 6.1   Multidimensional Fluency Rating Scale

Phrasing

1. Monotonic; generally word-by-word reading
2. Choppy—improper stress and intonation, inattention to punctuation at the end of sentences
3. Well-phrased; good expression

Smoothness

1. Hesitations; repetitions
2. Difficulties with certain words
3. Generally smooth, quick self-corrections

Pace

1. Slow and laborious
2. Combination of slow and fast reading
3. Consistently conversational

Source: Zutell, J. & Rasinski, T. (1991). Training teachers to attend to their students' oral fluency. *Theory Into Practice, 30,* 211–217.

Repeated readings are an effective way to develop fluency (Chomsky 1976; Dowhower, 1987; Samuels, 1979, 1997), particularly for struggling readers and those with learning disabilities (Herman, 1985; Rashotte & Torgesen, 1985). Samuels' model begins by listening to children read a story on their instructional level and recording the miscues. The child practices rereading the selection, either orally or silently. The child rereads the selection orally while the listener records the miscues and the rate. Miscues and rate are plotted on a chart. The student is given feedback on the miscues and reading rate. Students repeat the procedure until reaching the goal of 85 words per minute (wpm) and decreased miscues. Students then move to another instructional level passage. Samuels found that the number of repetitions needed to achieve automaticity decreased with successive repeated readings and transference improved between stories.

There have been a number of variations of repeated readings used with similar success. Chomsky used recorded books with students who were accurate, but not automatic, decoders. Students simultaneously listened to a tape-recorded reading and read aloud. They practiced this procedure until they felt competent with the passage at which time rate and miscues were recorded (Chomsky, 1976).

In paired repeated reading, the repeated reading technique is combined with peer tutoring. Children of different levels engage in repeated reading. Research on peer tutoring indicates that it is beneficial for both tutor and tutee (Ezell, Kohler, & Strain, 1994; Sheehan, Feldman & Allen, 1976; Simmons, Fuch, Fuch, Mathes, & Hodge 1995; Topping, 1989). Taking the role of tutor may increase poorer readers' motivation as their self-images as readers improve. Paired repeated reading consists of the following steps:

- Each reader chooses a passage on his or her instructional level to read. The partners then decide who will be first reader.
- Both readers read their passages silently.
- Reader one begins by orally reading the passage and then evaluating the reading on a scale of one to five. This is repeated two more times.
- At the conclusion of the third reading, the reader marks the scale, and the listener completes an evaluation checklist.
- The listener then verbally expresses comments to the reader.
- The second reader begins and the process continues (Figure 6.1).

One difficulty with repeated readings is that students often tire of the procedure. For some students repeated readings are similar to practicing the same piece of music many times, a tedious procedure unless one has a purpose such as an audition or performance. The use of drama may provide the purpose for repeated reading as students reread to reach an attainable goal (Bidwell, 1990). Readers' theatre is a classroom adaptation of drama that is uniquely suited to encouraging repeated readings. In readers' theatre the goal is to bring characters to life through expressive reading of the text. Without the requirements of memorization of parts, search for costumes, or the design of sets, the main focus of readers' theatre is on the students' *reading* of their roles. In selecting materials for readers' theatre, the teacher should allow students to choose material that excites them. It should be on the students' instructional level and should have sufficient characters to ensure that all students have parts. Students should have sufficient opportunity to practice their parts with feedback and support from the teacher and the group to allow all students to be comfortable with their reading. In some cases, teachers may want to provide students with tape recordings of their parts

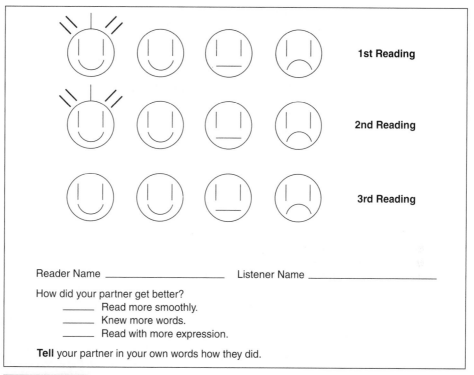

1st Reading

2nd Reading

3rd Reading

Reader Name _____   Listener Name _____

How did your partner get better?
_____ Read more smoothly.
_____ Knew more words.
_____ Read with more expression.

Tell your partner in your own words how they did.

FIGURE 6.1

Fluency Rating Sheet

to allow students to practice at home. Readers' theatre culminates with a performance within the classroom or to an external audience. See Box 6.1 for an example of a Reader's theatre presentation.

❙ Box 6.1

READERS' THEATRE IN THE CLASSROOM

Cheryl introduced Readers' theatre by administering a questionnaire to determine personal interest and prior knowledge related to putting on a play. Students were enthusiastic about the idea and made suggestions from the literature-based series, novels, and read-alouds. They ultimately chose a selection related to Black History Month. To prepare students for the play, Cheryl first discussed Frederick Douglas, slavery, and the play's content. She then modeled play parts and discussed characterization. The class created a word web for characterization by brainstorming ways in which an author provides information about characters. An exploratory phase followed with children trying out different parts, switching among themselves. Along with providing time to practice the play, Cheryl taught minilessons on punctuation cues and phrasing. Modeling was done with examples from the play. She used overheads to illustrate pauses, inflection, and intonation. Students were given a marking system to highlight different cues. The students practiced until they were satisfied with their reading while Cheryl provided feedback and coaching. The activity culminated with a performance for a fourth-grade class. They received rave reviews from peers and teachers.

Developing Knowledge of Word Meanings to Aid in Comprehension

Lack of word knowledge is another area that may interfere with comprehension. As you read in the section of Chapter 5 on language development, most children know the meanings of about 40,000 words at this stage. Many of these words are learned incidentally; that is, through conversation and through reading. Unfortunately, many students with reading difficulties tend to read less than their peers, thus learning fewer words. In addition to knowing fewer words, their knowledge of words is often superficial. Dale (1965) described four stages of knowledge of word meanings: (1) never having seen it; (2) having heard the word, but not knowing its meaning; (3) having a vague knowledge of the word in context; and (4) knowing it well. Knowing a word well encompasses knowing the definition and related aspects of the word, the appropriate definition for the context, and the strategies to use, such as contextual analysis, structural analysis, or a reference to access the meaning if needed (Ruddell, 1994).

Many poorer readers have stage 2 understanding for many vocabulary words (Beck & McKeown, 1991). Furthermore, many students with difficulty in reading cannot derive word meanings naturally and are unaware of the processes needed to determine meaning (Carnine, Kameenui, & Coyle, 1984; Stahl & Fairbanks, 1986). There has been substantial research to support a connection between vocabulary knowledge and reading comprehension (Freebody & Anderson, 1983; Davis, 1968; Sternberg & Powell, 1983). Students who have insufficient knowledge of words and strategies for determining meaning when unknown words are encountered in text find reading more difficult and less enjoyable. They then read less. One can see how this cycle can lead to the widening gap between good readers and poorer readers at the transitional stage.

Vocabulary Instruction   Although substantial evidence exists that there is a connection between reading comprehension and vocabulary development (Beck & McKeown, 1991; Laflamme, 1997), vocabulary instruction does not always lead to gains in reading comprehension (Beck, Perfetti, & McKeown, 1982; Jenkins, Pany & Schreck, 1978). Readers must learn words well to apply their knowledge appropriately and strategically. Studies have shown that explicit instruction in using context can improve vocabulary development for readers in the transitional stage of literacy (Carnine, Kameemui, & Coyle, 1984). However, characteristics of the text and of the context clue affect students' ability to effectively use context. Studying natural text with various types of context clues, Beck and associates (1983) found that the type of context clue affected students' ability to infer the meaning. Factors such as proximity of the context clue, connectivity, explicitness, and completeness increase the effectiveness of the clue (Konopak, 1988).

Instructional strategies should engage students in relating words to their prior knowledge. Linking words with their own experiences, linking words to one another or classifying them, and becoming actively involved in manipulating words appear to be particularly important for students with reading difficulties (Eeds & Cockrum, 1985; McKeown, Beck, Omanson, & Perfetti, 1983).

Guidelines for Explicitly Teaching Vocabulary To teach vocabulary sufficiently well to aid in reading comprehension teachers should:

- Teach words in depth. Definitions are often only the first step in learning about a word. Knowing words well involves knowing related terms and various meanings and connotations for the words.
- Help students link words to their schema to aid in long-term memory.
- Provide explicit instruction in the strategies needed for word learning such as contextual and structural analysis and the use of references (Baumann & Kameenui, 1991). Explicitly teaching strategies will enhance students' abilities to acquire vocabulary through their readings.
- Provide students with many opportunities to use the words in diverse ways through writing and oral language. Students should be encouraged to experiment with words and use them in different contexts. Vocabulary-building activities should create interest in words, raising students' awareness of the etymology and structure of words.
- Be selective. Teachers should consider the importance and frequency of the words for understanding text. Time should be allocated to teaching select words in depth, rather than many words superficially.

Brainstorming Before having the students read the selection, the teacher should select five or six key terms that are critical for understanding the selection. Students should write each term and then write down any term that they can associate with it. In some cases it may be a definition, in others a word that sounds like the key term. After a few minutes, students should share their associations. Through teacher-guided discussion of students' responses, brainstorming provides opportunities for students to learn from one another and build shared knowledge. In addition, teachers become aware of misconceptions that may interfere with comprehension and can address them prior to the reading. For example, when asked to write associations for the word *sarphcophagus*, many students wrote a body part, linking it to esophagus.

Semantic Maps and Concept Maps By creating semantic maps, students organize their knowledge about words through a visual representation. A number of studies cited the benefits of this technique for developing both vocabulary and comprehension (Ruddell, 1994). Pearson and Johnson (1978) postulate that our knowledge of words can be categorized by the larger class that the word belongs to, characteristics or attributes of the word, and examples of the word. This can be translated into words such as *is a part of, looks like, sounds like,* and *consists of* when used with students at the transitional stage of literacy. When students are actively engaged in constructing concept maps, the maps are used in integrating their knowledge leading to greater understanding of the concept (Figure 6.2).

Semantic feature analysis focuses students' attention on the critical attributes of a concept and links new words with students' prior knowledge (Johnson & Pearson, 1984). Its effectiveness has been shown with elementary-aged students (Johnson, Toms–Bronowki, & Pittelman, 1982 as cited in Ruddell, 1994) and students with

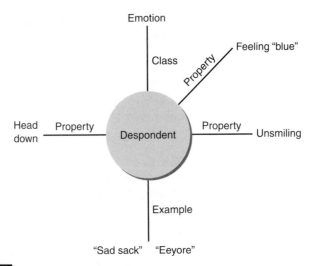

FIGURE 6.2

Concept Map

learning disabilities (Anders, Bos, & Filip, 1984 as cited in Ruddell, 1994). In a semantic feature analysis chart (Figure 6.3), the students look at groups of words in relation to the absence or presence of various attributes (e.g., a group of animals in terms of size, egg-laying, presence of hair, etc.). As students work through the chart, teachers and students become aware of incomplete knowledge and can integrate knowledge of the word into a larger group.

Word sorting was introduced in Chapter 5 as a method to help children with sight word and phonic development. It can also be adapted to increase knowledge of word meanings. The technique is the same as that used for increasing decoding ability, but words are now sorted according to their semantic similarities. Similar to sight word and phonics sorts, teachers may provide categories (closed sort) or may provide structure for the sorts (e.g., at least two words per category, words may be used more than

	large	alive today	eats meat	has fur	lays eggs
dog	maybe	yes	yes	yes	no
elephant	yes	yes	no	yes	no
frog	no	yes	yes	no	yes
dinosaur	maybe	no	maybe	no	yes
platypus	no	yes	yes	yes	yes

FIGURE 6.3

Semantic Features Analysis

once, all words must be used), while permitting students to develop their own categories (open sort). When allowed to work in cooperative groups to complete the sort, students deepen their understanding through creativity, conversation, and justification of their choices.

In the *key-word strategy* (Pressley, Levin, & Delaney, 1982) students are taught ways for remembering vocabulary words through mnemonic devices. They are taught to develop visual images to link a word with its definition. The visual image, which may be related to the sound of the word, creates the link between the word and definition. For example, to remember the word *car*nivore, a child may visualize a *car*rot biting into a large piece of steak.

Teaching Morphemic Analysis of Words to Develop Vocabulary

Through morphemic or structural analysis of words, students are taught to divide words into their morphemic parts—prefix, suffix and base (a part of a word that may stand alone; e.g., *play* in *playing*), or root (a part of a word that comes from another language and is not a word by itself; e.g., *path* in *sympathy*). In providing rationale for instruction in morphemic analysis Cunningham (1998) cites Nagy and Anderson's 1984 study analyzing words found in texts used by students in grades three to nine. Although they estimated that students encountered approximately 400,000 distinct words, many of the words were semantically related. By understanding semantic relationships, learners could reduce the number of distinct words to 54,000. Further, Nagy and Anderson (1984) found that the meanings of approximately 60% of the words encountered by students in the transitional literacy stage could be determined by knowledge of the word parts. In reviewing this research Cunningham (1998) concludes that readers' ability to gain meaning through morphemic analysis increases their effectiveness in working with new, multisyllabic words.

Many of you might remember being taught structural analysis in school. Unfortunately in many classrooms instruction consisted of having students memorize lists of Latin or Greek prefixes, suffixes, and bases or roots. It was pretty tedious and often not very helpful, as certain morphemes were very seldom enountered in reading. Fortunately, by applying our knowledge of schema theory to morphemic analysis, we can create more interesting and effective strategies to help students analyze words.

In planning instruction for children one should consider the utility of the prefixes and suffixes (Table 6.2). Four prefixes, *un, re, in,* and *dis,* account for 58% of prefixed words, 16 other prefixes account for 39% of prefixed words. Three suffixes, *s(es), ed,* and *ing,* account for 65% of suffixed words (White, Sowell, & Yanagihara, 1989).

Rather than teaching students to memorize affixes that may have little utility, instruction should focus on the most useful affixes and then teaching children to use their knowledge of affixes within common words to create analogies for understanding new ones. For example, look at the word *gynecocracy.* You may never have seen it before, but you can probably determine its meaning by relating it to parts of words that you do know. Perhaps you've seen the words *gynecologist* or *misogynist*; a gynecologist is a doctor for women and a misogynist is someone who hates women, so "gyne" probably relates to women. Look at the word *democracy*—that is government by the people—autocracy, a dictatorship, or government by one person. "Ocracy" probably relates to government, thus gynecocracy is a government by women. Years ago many students tried to spell *antidisestablishmentarianism,* which had the distinction of being the longest

TABLE 6.2   Most Common Prefixes and Suffixes

Prefixes		Suffixes	
un	pre	s (es)	ible (able)
re	inter	ed	al
in (im, ir, il)	fore	ing	y
dis	de	ly	ness
en (em)	trans	er (or)	ity
non	super	ion (tion)	ment
in (im)	semi		
over	anti		
mis	mid		
sub	under		

Source: Cunningham, P. (1998). The Multisyllabic Word Dilemma: Helping Students Build Meaning, Spell, and Read "Big" Words. *Reading and Writing Quarterly: Overcoming Learning Difficulties, 14,* 189–218.

word in the dictionary. Very few, however, tried to determine its meaning. But if you know that "arianism" is a particular church doctrine then you should have no trouble with the word. *Anti*socialism is against socialism, to *dis*inherit is to remove someone's right to inherit. Therefore, antidisestablishmentarianism is against removing the establishment of a particular church doctrine—in simpler terms, against the separation of

Working in pairs, students help one another become familiar with the most common morphemes.

church and state. By teaching children to chunk words and then using their knowledge of more common words, you are providing them with a strategy for independently determining the meaning of "long" words.

Instructional Procedures for Morphemic Analysis

Incidental Morpheme Analysis was developed by Manzo and Manzo (1990) to help students learn new words while reading. It consists of four steps.

- Write the word on the blackboard underlining meaningful word parts. Example: bi <u>cent</u> <u>ennial</u>
- Ask students if the underlined parts will help them determine the meaning. Even if predicted correctly, continue with steps three and four.
- Give students additional clues for figuring out the meaning. These are level one clues that are words that may be in their vocabulary and contain these word parts. Example: <u>bicycle</u>, <u>century</u>, <u>perennial</u>
- Write level two clues below the level one clues. These clues are the meanings of the word parts. Continue to encourage predictions until the correct meaning is ascertained. Write the meaning beneath the clues.

Word Trees. In constructing a word tree (Figure 6.4), students collect as many words as they can with a common base or root to complete the branches of a tree (Bear, Invernizzi, Templeton, & Johnston, 2000).

Procedure for constructing a word tree

1. Construct a tree, either laminating it or adding velcro to the branches and root to target different bases/roots.
2. Determine the base or root to highlight, beginning with more common ones.

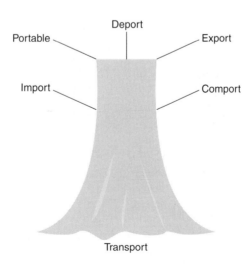

Portable   Deport   Export

Import   Comport

Transport

FIGURE 6.4

Word Tree

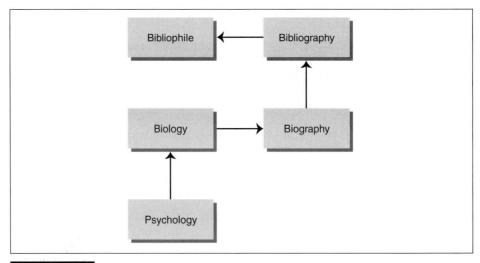

FIGURE 6.5

Word Web

3. Write the base/root at the bottom of the tree, thinking of as many forms as possible.
4. Write each form on a different branch.
5. Display the word tree for a few days, then create another one.

A *word web* is a visual representation of the relationship between words (Figure 6.5). Through construction of the web, students can begin to see words in families. For example, if you know the word *carnivore* means a meat or flesh eater, then you can relate it to *omnivore*, something that eats everything, and *reincarnation*, or becoming flesh again. *Omnivore* relates to *omniscient*, or all-knowing, *reincarnation* relates to *reform*, etc. Word webs should first be conducted through the whole class, but can then be applied to individual work or cooperative teams. Box 6.2 is an example of a fifth-grade lesson in morphemic analysis.

▌ Box 6.2

MORPHEMIC ANALYSIS LESSON—GRADE 5

Several dictionaries were at the tables that the children shared. Then their teacher, Jon, distributed a copy of the following poem to the class while he read from the poem on the overhead:

Misunderstood History?

Some say Columbus was the man who **discovered,**
But we say he was the man who simply **uncovered.**
The civilization was **preexisting.**
He was annoyed at their resisting.
Ever since then, the natives have never **recovered.**

Jon and the other fifth grade teachers had written the poem because it illustrated prefixes and tied in with their social studies unit.

Students were then asked to jot down anything they noticed. They shared with their small group, and then the large group discussed what they recognized. Student responses were written on chart paper. In their groups the students developed a definition of prefix. After a class discussion, Jon clarified the definition and listed it on the chart. Students drew a line after each prefix in the poem. Selected students modeled this for the class. Jon then had each group select a prefix from a hat (*mis, un, re, dis*). Each group collaborated to list as many words as possible. Words were charted, and Jon encouraged the students to orally use the words in a sentence. Students then played "prefix mix and match" in which they selected prefixes and matched them to base words to create a new valid word. Dictionaries were used to confirm their responses. The class then added new words to the chart. The lesson concluded with a review of the term *prefix*, and the specific prefixes used.

Use of Reference Materials

At times, readers will not be able to determine the meaning of a word from contextual or morphemic analysis. They will need to know how to use the dictionary to learn or confirm word meaning. Many learners at the transitional stage know how to use the dictionary and understand how it is organized. Teachers should check, however, to see if that is true for all students in the class. Instruction should focus on (a) knowing when to use the dictionary and (b) knowing how to select the appropriate meaning of a word for the context of the reading selection. Many teachers at this stage remark that when asked to write a definition for a word from their readings, students often write either the first definition or the shortest! One technique to use is to have students replace their word with the definition and then reread the sentence to see if it makes sense.

Before reading the next section, determine the key vocabulary terms used in this chapter thus far. Which of the preceding techniques do you think would be most useful for you to remember the words? Try the technique with your key words.

▒▉DEVELOPING UNDERSTANDING BEYOND THE WORDS

Although accessing word meaning is a critical factor in general comprehension, it is not the only factor. It is quite possible to read and understand all the words in a selection, but still not understand the meaning. An example familiar to many of us is the beginning of Hamlet's soliloquy, "To be or not to be, that is the question." Each individual word is understandable, but unless you are familiar with the play and know the context, you may not be exactly sure of the message. Many students who seemed able to comprehend material at the lower levels begin to have difficulty at this stage as the texts they read become increasingly complex. At this stage children encounter more expository text, which tends to be more challenging because of its concept density and less-familiar organizational structure.

Yuill (1991) described three main areas of weakness that children with reading problems often have:

1. Difficulty integrating information from different parts of the text. When good readers read they create mental models of their reading, which is putting the reading into their own words. They use these mental models to remember what they have read and connect new text to the old. Students with reading difficulties do not build mental models as they read.
2. Poor working memory efficiency. The students do not have or use strategies for moving information from short-term to long-term memory (Swanson & Berninger, 1995).
3. Poor metacognitive skills. The successful reader is actively involved in the reading, setting purposes for the reading, constructing meaning, monitoring one's own comprehension, and using remediation strategies when reading breaks down. Metacognition may also relate to motivation as students' understanding of the usefulness of the learning and their means of attaining it leads to feelings of empowerment and increased motivation (Roehler & Duffy, 1996). Students with poor metacognitive skills generally do not understand that the purpose of reading is to attain meaning, or cannot access appropriate strategies for doing so.

In addition to the above-mentioned difficulties, students may have inadequate schema for their reading or difficulty activating and using appropriate schema. Difficulties with identifying themes (Williams, 1998) and distinguishing between important and unimportant information are also exhibited.

Fortunately, there is a great deal of evidence that teachers can intervene to enhance the comprehension of difficult text for students with or without learning disabilities for difficult text. Instruction should center on procedures for guiding children through text and explicitly teaching students the comprehension strategies that mature readers use to construct meaning. Explicit instruction in strategies (explaining *what, why, how* through modeling, guided practice and independent practice, and *when* through application in authentic texts) improves students' reading comprehension (Swanson, 1999; Pearson & Camperell, 1994). Teachers can affect children's comprehension and provide children with access to more difficult material by the instructional decisions that they make to:

- Introduce the reading (prereading procedures and strategies)
- Guide the reading (during reading procedures and strategies)
- Provide for student response (postreading procedures and strategies)

Using Procedures to Introduce the Reading

Instructional strategies to introduce the reading should:

- Help students develop and activate appropriate schema
- Provide information about key concepts and vocabulary
- Provide necessary information about the text structure to help students organize information as they read
- Help students set a purpose for the reading
- Enhance motivation by relating the reading to prior knowledge and future needs

When used as a prereading activity, *semantic maps and webs* aid in comprehension by directing readers to the key concepts of the text and enabling students to predict the types of information that will be found. Teachers should construct incomplete maps with the students. The key concept should be the central focus of the map with lines indicating the types of information that might be found in the text. Through brainstorming, the teacher would elicit the students' prior knowledge of the topic, placing the information in the appropriate part of the map. The students would then read the selection to complete the sections of the map. The graphic organizer on page 173 at the beginning of this chapter is an example of a semantic map.

In *previewing and predicting*, students peruse the selection before reading, attending to pictures, graphs, subheadings, and words in bold print. Based on the information from these sources students would make predictions about the reading. Predictions should then be organized by categories.

Anticipation guides activate schema for a reading selection and provide motivation for students to read the selection. In an anticipation guide the teacher selects a few important concepts for engaging the students prior to reading (Box 6.3). These concepts are transformed into a series of short sentences to which the students then react. They may write their reactions individually and then discuss them as a group prior to reading. The students then read the selection to confirm or modify their responses.

▌ Box 6.3

An Example of an Anticipation Guide

Anticipation Guide

Directions: Read each statement carefully and decide whether you agree or disagree with it, placing a check mark in the appropriate *Before Reading* column. When finished reading and studying the chapter, return to the guide and decide whether your anticipations need to be changed by placing a check mark in the appropriate *After Reading* column.

	BEFORE READING		AFTER READING	
	Agree	Disagree	Agree	Disagree
1. Students are better able to read at higher levels than in the past.	_____	_____	_____	_____
2. Literacy means being able to read words correctly.	_____	_____	_____	_____
3. All teachers should reinforce literacy skills for students.	_____	_____	_____	_____
4. *Aliteracy* means being unable to read.	_____	_____	_____	_____
5. Literacy can be used to achieve social and economic improvement.	_____	_____	_____	_____
6. Learning is most effective when students learn on their own.	_____	_____	_____	_____

Source: Brozo, W. G., & Simpson, M. (1999). *Readers, teachers, learners: Expanding literacy across the content areas.* Upper Saddle River, NJ: Merrill/Prentice Hall, p. 3.

An often neglected technique for preparing students at the transitional level for content-area reading is the use of picture books—informational storybooks (Leal, 1996). Informational storybooks can provide necessary background information for the more complex content text in a manner that is more easily comprehended and can lead to a deeper level of involvement (Leal, 1992). Reading aloud picture books on a similar topic to the content text engages even older students in the topic, providing access to the concepts needed for comprehension.

Enhancing Comprehension Through Guidance of the Reading

As students read a selection, the teacher can guide them to use the strategies that mature readers use. These include predicting, self-questioning, using mental models to connect and remember text, and monitoring one's comprehension.

Question–Answer Relationships (Raphael, 1982, 1984, 1986; Raphael & Pearson, 1982) help students create better questions and understand the source for the responses. Many students can answer questions when the answer is directly stated in the selection, but have difficulty with higher-order questions that require integration of textual information with prior knowledge. In the Question–Answer Relationships (QAR) procedure, students are taught four types of questions:

- *Right there*—the answer can be found in one sentence (literal and explicit).
- *Think and search*—the answer can be found in the text, but requires searching in different places (literal and implicit).
- *Author and you*—the answer requires integration of information from the text and from the reader's prior knowledge (inferential).
- *On your own*—the answer is derived from the reader's prior knowledge.

The four question types are categorized into two major divisions, "In the Book" and "In My Head." Begin by introducing these two major categories, and then demonstrate the relationship to the students. Raphael suggests the following instructional sequence for teaching QARs and providing practice through scaffolded instruction:

- Model the procedure by providing the text, questions, answers, label, and reason for the label.
- Provide the text, questions, answers, and label. Students provide the reason for the label.
- Provide the text, questions, and answers. Students supply the labels and the reasons.
- Provide the text and questions. Students provide the answers, labels, and reasons.

The activity can be further extended by asking students to work in pairs to create and share questions and responses. By raising children's metacognitive awareness of the range of thinking required to question appropriately and providing a common language for questions, teachers enhance students' questioning abilities for the techniques that follow (Figure 6.6).

	Right There Was Jamie taller than Jeb? (Answer is found in one sentence.)	**Author and You** Was Jamie a good friend? (Need to use the information in the book and your prior experiences.)
	Think and Search Describe Jamie. (Need to look in different sentences.)	**On Your Own** Does Jamie remind you of anyone you know? (Answer comes from your schema.)

(Left margin, vertical: In the Book) (Right margin, vertical: In My Head)

FIGURE 6.6

Question–Answer Relationships

The ReQuest procedure, Reciprical Questioning (Manzo, 1969; Manzo & Manzo, 1993) helps students to develop their own purposes for reading through self-questioning. Its base can be found in psychoeducational and sociocultural theories (Manzo & Manzo, 1993). Through teacher-led and then gradual release of the questioning to the students, ReQuest encompasses comprehension intervention, self-monitoring, and collaborative learning strategies for facilitating comprehension (Gersten & Baker, 1999). The instructional sequence of ReQuest consists of:

- Teacher and students preview the selection by reading title, first sentence, and examining graphics.
- Students are directed to ask as many "teacher-type" questions that they wish. Students have their copy of the selection in front of them.
- The teacher answers the students' questions fully without referring back to the selection.
- The teacher then asks additional questions to focus students and set a purpose for reading.
- Teachers and students continue the same procedure throughout the selection.

The value in ReQuest lies in guiding students to the most important concepts of the selection and in scaffolding effective self-questioning techniques. Teachers should be cognizant of the types of questions that they ask about the selection ensuring that the questions require literal, inferential, and evaluative responses.

In the *reciprocal teaching* procedure teachers model and guide students in the comprehension processes used by mature readers through collaborative groups. The use of collaborative groups allows for instructional conversation about content and strategic reading. Palinscar and Brown (1984) identified six characteristics of comprehension: understanding the goal of reading is *constructing meaning, activating* appropriate schema, *focusing* on *major ideas, integrating and evaluating* ideas with prior knowledge, *inferencing*, and *monitoring* ones' meaning. The six characteristics of the mature reader were then combined into teaching four strategies for students to use while reading from their texts: *summarizing* the information in one sentence, *questioning*—developing one or two good questions about the selection, *clarifying* any unclear information, and *predicting* what the next selection will be about. The following sequence is used to implement reciprocal teaching:

- The teacher meets with a small group of students, all of whom are reading the same selection. After they read a section of the text, the teacher models the four strategies for the students.
- A member of the group becomes the new "teacher." At the conclusion of the reading the student summarizes, questions, clarifies, and predicts. The other students encourage the leader to clarify the text and provide feedback. If necessary, fix-up strategies are used.
- Each member of the group takes a turn as teacher, following the same procedure.

The effectiveness of reciprocal teaching has been shown with remedial and nonremedial students at the transitional stage of literacy development (Bruce & Chan, 1991; Palincsar & Brown, 1984; Speece, MacDonald, Kilsheimer, & Krist, 1997).

Students' reading can also be guided by teaching them to summarize and paraphrase while they read and create mental images of the reading selection. Many students with learning disabilities do not develop these skills naturally, however. In reviewing the research on summary instruction Pearson and Fielding (1996) conclude that explicit instruction rather than mere practice is needed to improve students' performance. Mastropieri & Scruggs (2000) cite studies where summarization and paraphrasing have been successfully taught to students with learning disabilities at the latter part of the transitional literacy stage. Summarizing strategies generally include the following steps:

- Deleting unimportant and redundant information
- Creating a category for classifying the information
- Finding or creating a topic sentence

Constructing mental images also appears to help students with disabilities to integrate material (Pressley, 1977; Yuill, 1991). Manzo and Manzo (1993) provide a model for guided imagery instruction:

- Have students relax and concentrate.
- Use a brief example, to model the concept of imaging.
- Read a second selection and have students construct images of selected concrete objects.
- Have students broaden their images.
- Have students describe additions to their images in sensory terms (see, hear, feel, smell).
- Have students represent images in stick-figure drawings before class-sharing.

Activities for Responding to the Reading

Literature circles can be a very effective means for stimulating student response to readings. Literature circles are "small, temporary discussion groups who have chosen to read the same story, poem, article, or book" (Daniels, 1994, p. 13). They can engage students in meaningful talk, provide student responsibility for decisions affecting learning, and allow students to hear different interpretations of text (O'Flahavan,

1994). Students' comprehension increases through opportunities to collaborate among peers, take ownership to construct meaning, and have their voices heard (Englert & Tarrant, 1994; Evans, 1996; Lewis, 1997; Miller & Meece, 1997). In addition to improvement in comprehension, students' motivation and enthusiasm for books also increase through sharing their feelings and experiences, making personal connections with text, and discussing topics that were relevant to them (Roller & Beed, 1994; Scharer & Peters, 1996).

At the transitional stage of literacy, groups generally consist of four to five participants. Each participant has a distinct role to play. Daniels (1994) provides eight basic roles for fiction and five for nonfiction (Box 6.4). Various combinations may be used for different pieces of literature. By carefully selecting and assigning roles, teachers ensure that there is a comprehensive discussion of the selection and that every member has a unique contribution to make to the group.

▌Box 6.4

SAMPLE LITERATURE CIRCLE ROLES

Artful Artist—draws a picture related to the reading; the artist presents the picture without comment, inviting the others to connect it with their understanding; the artist then tells what it means.

Discussion Director—develops questions for the group to discuss; is encouraged to ask questions linking schema and feelings to text and focusing on major ideas.

Passage Master—selects passages of the text for oral reading; decides whether to read alone, ask someone else to read, or engage in shared or choral reading.

Creative Connector—makes connections between the book and the reader's own life; specific suggestions can be made.

Word Wizard—looks for special words in the story, which could be unfamiliar vocabulary, unusual words, or words that are particularly descriptive.

Source: Daniels, H. (1994). *Literature circles: Voice and choice in the student-centered classroom.* York, ME: Stenhouse Publishers.

The effectiveness of literature circles increases through teacher-led discussion before, during, and after the activity. Discussions should focus on the content and process of interactions. Teachers should carefully monitor the social interactions within the circle to ensure that all voices are heard.

Retellings facilitate students' understanding and memory for the selection through building mental models of the reading, using elements of the organizational format, and distinguishing important from unimportant elements. Retellings can be improved through explicit instruction and group collaboration. An instructional sequence based on *Read and Retell* (Brown & Cambourne, 1987) can consist of introducing the parts of a retelling (events, details, characters, and descriptions) and modeling and practicing with the class by:

- Showing students the title of the short story or fable and having them individually write a prediction.
- Allowing students in small groups to "share and compare" their predictions.

- Orally reading the selection to the students while they read along silently.
- Telling students to compose a retelling for a reader with no background knowledge or experience with the text. The teacher should also stress the importance of using their own words, rather than trying to memorize the selection.
- Encouraging students to create "mental maps" and then writing the retelling.
- Pairing students to read and compare their partner's retelling. Pairs complete a "share and compare" sheet for each retelling.

This procedure can be modified by originally providing more time for students to complete the task and then gradually shortening the time to focus their retellings on the most important information.

Procedures That Extend Through All Phases of the Reading

Directed-reading-thinking activity (DRTA) is a group activity that prepares, guides, and helps students assimilate the reading through the use of predictions (Stauffer, 1975). By reading to confirm or reject their predictions, students are actively engaged in setting the purpose and monitoring their reading. Teachers prepare for the DRTA by determining appropriate points in the story for segmenting the reading based on the plot.

In the DRTA students begin by previewing title, illustrations, and possibly the first sentence or paragraph of the selection. Based on their preview, they are asked to form a prediction about the selection. Students then read to the preselected part of the story and confirm or reject their prediction. They are asked to provide the reasons for their choice, giving specific evidence from the selection. They are then asked to form a new prediction. This begins the cycle for the DRTA of *predicting, reading, confirming or rejecting, proving,* and *predicting.* The procedure concludes by reviewing predictions or follow-up discussion.

Know, Want to Know, and Learn (K-W-L) (Carr & Ogle, 1987; Ogle, 1986) is a procedure developed to prepare students for reading, guide their reading, and record and remember the information gleaned from the reading. The later version of the K-W-L consists of the three categories in K-W-L as well as summarizing and/or mapping the information to aid students' long-term memory. The K-W-L chart is a simple chart with three columns, *K* (what I know), *W* (what I want to know) and *L* (what I have learned). Prior to reading, the teacher introduces the topic for the text. Through teacher-guided discussion, students share their prior knowledge of the subject. The teacher should probe students about how they have acquired that knowledge. As the students share, the information should be listed in the *K* column. At the conclusion of the brainstorming stage, students discuss the categories of information they expect to obtain. Students then discuss what more they wish to learn about the subject. For very reluctant readers, it is sometimes beneficial to reword this section to *what I think I will learn.* The information is listed in the *W* column before students begin to read. As they read the information they note the information they have learned in the *L* column. This should be followed by class discussion of the information in relation to the questions listed in the *W* column. At the conclusion, students should construct a summary or map of the selection. This activity may be implemented as a whole class, in cooperative learning groups, or individually as needed.

Look back at the students described at the beginning of this chapter. Has our instruction focused on remediating all their areas of difficulty? We have described procedures for improving word identification and enhancing fluency. We have suggested ways to help students link the reading with their schema, develop purposes for reading, and respond beyond the literal level. There have been suggestions for improving students' recall of their reading, and monitoring their reading. But what about Jason? Have we addressed all his needs? What about his attitude toward reading? What can be done for the Jasons in our classrooms who are apathetic toward reading, seeing very little value in it?

Increasing Motivation to Read

Motivation for a task increases when there is an authentic purpose, when the task captivates one's interest, and when one feels successful with the task. The purpose can vary from learning more about a particular subject and using knowledge to accomplish something, to being part of a social or learning group. When teachers provide students with time and opportunities for choice, when they consider ways to "hook" students on a particular topic or reading selection, when they help students set their own purposes, and value the students' decisions, students begin to develop a sense of themselves as readers.

In a *readers' workshop* teachers provide large blocks of time for students to read and respond to selections of their choice. Responses are often shared with peers through conversation or writing. Readers' workshop encourages students to take ownership of their reading and make connections between the reading material and their own lives (Atwell, 1987; Taylor & Nesheim, 2000–2001). Taylor & Nesheim (2000–2001) posit five key elements for initiating a readers' workshop: time, choice, response, community, and structure. Careful attention to classroom climate, organization, and structure maximizes the benefits of the readers' workshop. The classroom library should be plentiful and arranged to allow children to select appropriate material. Student folders should be readily accessible, and the structure of the workshop time should be developed. Expectations for performance and collaboration should be shared by all participants. Often, readers' workshop consists of three parts, a minilesson, reading time, and sharing or response time.

Read-alouds are usually an integral part of the developing literacy stage, but often begin to disappear at the transitional literacy stage either from perceived lack of time or concern that it is no longer appropriate. How many of us, however, have fond memories of a book that a special teacher had read to us, carefully changing voices, adding inflection, and creating a special atmosphere? And how many of us then went on to read other books by the same author? As in the earlier stages of literacy, read-alouds can provide children with access to materials that may be difficult for them to read, but which appeal to their interests. They may also initiate a desire to work through difficult material (Renninger, as cited in Wigfield & Guthrie, 1997). As mentioned earlier with informational storybooks, reading aloud fictional material on a related content-area topic increases schema and may raise students' desire to learn about a topic. For example, *The Slave Dancer*, by Paula Fox, provides a chilling picture of life in the slave ships by describing how slaves were forced to dance at night to prevent their otherwise shackled muscles from atrophying, which would render them useless as slaves.

Attention to motivation is critical at the transitional stage of literacy. Although skill and strategy instruction may be necessary to help some of our students become literate, it is seldom sufficient. Numerous studies have indicated that interest is often the key to unlocking literacy for struggling readers (Fink, 1995–1996). Activities that increase motivation should be an integral part of the reading program at this stage.

USING WRITING TO LEARN

As we have stressed in this and previous chapters, reading and writing are reciprocal processes. Reading helps students to write, writing helps students to read. Writing should, thus, have a central place in literacy instruction. In the transitional literacy stage writing tasks become increasingly complex. Students are asked to write for different purposes, for different audiences, and in different genres. State and national standards at this level often indicate that students should be able to communicate effectively, using different organizational structures as necessary. The increased complexity of the assignments may make writing appear to be a very burdensome task for some students.

There are many elements to good writing. The writer must focus on the content of the message, determining the salient points and deciding how to organize and sequence it coherently for the audience. At the same time the writer must consider the form of the message: grammar, usage, spelling, and handwriting.

To review Chapter 2, we find that students with learning disabilities often have difficulties with all of the aspects of writing. They do not view themselves as writers, thus having low motivation to write (Zhang, 2000). They have difficulty with the content of writing. Their essays are often short, contain little elaboration, and are poorly organized (Barenbaum, Newcomer, & Nodine, 1987). They seem to lack knowledge of the structure and framework of text (De La Paz, 1999) and do not have a clear focus or sequence. They have difficulty with planning, typically approaching writing by retrieving from memory whatever seems appropriate and writing it down. Each idea then generates the next with little attention to the purpose or goal of the writing (De La Paz & Graham, 1997). Revising is often limited to changes in spelling and other mechanical items (Wong, 1997). The mechanics of writing, particularly spelling, are other troublesome aspects for children with writing difficulties. These children may have difficulty representing phonemes, accessing visual memory, and knowing the "rules" of the language. Handwriting may also continue to present a problem.

Writing Instruction

The first axiom for writing instruction in the transitional stage of literacy is that in order for children to improve, they must write. Comparable to reading instruction, explicit writing strategy instruction has been beneficial to students with difficulties. And, comparable to reading, the instruction should be incorporated into a total writing program. As we examine writing, let us first look at general writing activities and procedures and then proceed to specific interventions for students with writing disabilities.

Journal writing at this stage of literacy development may take different forms: personal journals, learning logs, dialogue journals, or literature response. Although often used for personal reflection, they should also be seen as a tool for increasing comprehension through personal construction of meaning (Hancock, 1993; Wells, 1993). In personal journals, the student's audience is the self. The writing may be informal; form may not be important. The purpose of the journal is to express oneself. In dialogue journals the audience is another. Form takes on greater importance in dialogue journals as the writer considers the needs of the audience. Learning logs serve still another purpose. They help the learner reflect on learning and verbalize the concepts learned. Literature response is often used as part of readers'/writers' workshop. The literature response journal should help the reader extend his or her understanding of the text by making personal connections with the text. When the teacher is the audience for these journals, the response should focus on the content of the message. Responses should be supportive, validating the writer's thoughts and feelings. Strategy instruction through minilessons, which include modeling of types of responses and opportunities for student practice, develop students' abilities to think more deeply about text and take risks with their writing.

Process writing was introduced in Chapter 5. If necessary, review the descriptions of the different steps in process writing: preparing, organizing, drafting, revising, and editing. There should be much opportunity at this stage for students to work through a piece of writing, culminating with publication or another form of public sharing.

The writing workshop is an effective format for implementing process writing by providing opportunities for explicit instruction in writing strategies and sufficient time to develop a student's own piece of writing. Components of the writing workshop include writing, sharing, minilessons, and read-alouds (Tompkins, 2000). Read-alouds expose children to different types of writing and techniques. Encouraging students to read like a writer focuses their attention on the craft of writing (Nia, 1999).

Effective writing workshops are generally characterized by providing students with time to engage in extended writing, choice of topic and genre, and opportunities to confer with the teacher and peers. Teachers in writing workshops are lifetime readers and writers who encourage children to develop their own authentic writing, rather than teaching "writing formulas" (Atwell, 1991). They share the diverse writing tasks that writers engage in, encouraging students to extend their writing into different genres and for different purposes and audiences.

The teacher's role is critical during minilessons and sharing/conferencing. Providing explicit instruction in how to plan, draft, and edit, through modeling and think-alouds and collaboratively written and edited pieces, facilitates students' acquisition of the underlying processes for process writing (Singer, 1995). It allows students with writing difficulties to be full members of the writing community. To avoid writing prescriptions, teachers must be cognizant of asking the right types of questions during conferencing (Box 6.5). Questions about topic sentences, number of paragraphs, and other formulaic responses should be bypassed in order to help the writers focus on recognizing their success in achieving their own purpose. Suggestions for writing conferences include the following:

- Have the child read the piece aloud—listen carefully.
- Ask questions about the child's feelings about the piece and process; then follow up if necessary with clarifying questions.
- Help the child discover changes needed to improve the writing.
- End the conference by asking for the child's plan for improving the writing (Tully, 1996).

■ Box 6.5

CONFERENCE QUESTIONS TO EXTEND STUDENTS' WRITING

Questions are designed to help students tell their story better.

- How's it coming?
- What's the most important thing you're trying to say?
- What is this piece of writing really about?
- Do you have more than one point or story here?
- What's your favorite part?
- How can you cut to the chase?
- I don't understand X. Put your draft aside and tell me about it.
- What else do you know about this topic? How could you find out more?
- Why is X significant to you or others? Why does it matter?
- How did you feel when X happened?
- I'm confused at the end; I'm left wondering about X. How can you clear this up?
- Why are you writing about this? What makes this a subject you want to write about?
- What will you do next?

Source: Atwell, N. (1988). *In the middle: Writing, reading, and learning with adolescents.* Portsmouth, NH: Heinemann.

Procedures for Helping Children with Writing Difficulties

Self-regulated strategy development (SRSD) is an instructional model that has been validated for transitional readers/writers with learning disabilities (Graham & Harris, 1999; Troia, Graham, & Harris, 1999). SRSD consists of explicit instruction in writing strategies in conjunction with regulating the use of these strategies. The model includes schema activation, metacognitive development, and collaborative learning. Planning strategies are taught by teaching students goal-setting, brainstorming, and sequencing techniques while writing. They may be assigned a writing task in which they would have to complete three steps for planning and writing: consider audience and purpose (why am I writing this and for whom?), plan, and write and extend writing. The explicit instruction model is used to present strategies such as mnemonics, self-statements, visualization, and note taking for completing these steps. Self regulation of the planning phase may be taught by having students:

- Compare the model strategy to their strategy
- Identify the reason for using the strategy
- Determine their own ways to enhance strategy learning
- Monitor their use of the strategy
- Consider application and modification of the strategy
- Think about other methods for improving performance (Troia, Graham, & Harris, 1999)

Students are taught specific revision strategies by focusing on the meaning of the selection, which are then implemented through peer revision.

The *sharing chair* is an opportunity for children to share their writing with their peers and receive feedback from the teacher and peers. Based on sociocultural theories of zone of proximal development and socially constructed meaning, it has been found to be successful with students with learning disabilities at the transitional stage of literacy (Mariage, 2000). After engaging in free-writes children read their journals to their peers, inviting questions and comments. Journals are then reviewed by the teacher who provides written comments. The sharing chair promotes academic discourse and the building of a writing community for all levels of writers within a classroom.

Spelling and Handwriting

The relationship between spelling and handwriting to writing is similar to that of decoding and fluency to reading. Correct spelling and legible handwriting are essential to the communicative act of writing. They enable the reader to obtain meaning from the writer's message. In addition, similar to the theory of automaticity for reading, automatic spelling and handwriting enable the writer to focus on the content of the writing. Comparable to decoding and fluency, writers who are burdened with spelling and writing difficulties tend to attend to the mechanics, leaving less attention for the substance of their writing. Berninger (1999) provides three criteria for predicting handwriting proficiency at the transitional stage: (1) matching strings of alphanumeric symbols, (2) writing briefly displayed words or letters from memory, and (3) retrieving and producing letters from memory. Fine motor skills are much less influential at this stage than previous ones.

Spelling Development

The spelling program at this level should have many facets. Students need to develop their automatic spelling vocabulary, should continue applying phonological knowledge, and should learn the different strategies that good spellers use to determine spellings of words. Although spelling continues to develop through wide reading and writing, natural, incidental learning is not sufficient for all students. As with many of the strategies discussed previously, explicit instruction may be necessary to enable students to progress in their spelling abilities.

As a basis for spelling at this stage, students should be able to spell the most commonly used words in writing (Horn, 1926). These words (Table 6.3) can be learned through multisensory techniques, or if they continue to present difficulties, should be readily accessible to students. They should be visible on wall charts, on reference cards for students, or in personal dictionaries.

Explicitly teaching strategies for learning spelling words can be effective for a wide range of writers (Graham & Harris, 1999). In Chapter 5, a number of specialized approaches to spelling were presented. Allowing children to select the most effective approach and then using the explicit instruction model to develop independence in using the approach gives children control over their learning.

Phonological knowledge should continue to evolve at the students' developmental spelling level. As noted earlier, Bear and associates have described the various stages of spelling development. Many children at the transitional stage of literacy are at the transitional and derivational stages. These may be further segmented to within words, syllables, and affixes, and derivational relations stages of spelling development

TABLE 6.3   Most Frequent Words for Writing

a	for	man	them
about	from	me	then
after		mother	there
all	get	my	they
am	got		things
an		no	think
and	had	not	this
are	have	now	time
around	he		to
as	her	of	too
at	here	on	two
	him	one	
back	his	or	up
be	home	our	us
because	house	out	
but	how	over	very
by			
	I	people	was
came	if	put	we
can	in		well
come	into	said	were
could	is	saw	what
	it	school	when
did		see	who
didn't	just	she	will
do		so	with
don't	know	some	would
down			
	like	that	you
eat	little	the	your

(Bear, Invernizzi, Templeton, & Johnston, 2000). The teacher should assess students' spelling to provide developmentally appropriate instruction.

Children at the within-word stage are generally competent with short vowels, consonants and consonant clusters, and frequently used long vowels. As they progress through this stage their mastery of long vowel patterns increases. At the syllable and affixes stage most of the patterns within single syllables have been mastered. The focus of instruction should be on multisyllabic words, although students may still have difficulty with consonant doubling, schwas, and some prefixes and suffixes. At the derivational relations stage most words are spelled correctly, except for occasional schwas, suffixes and prefixes, and silent letters. Instruction centers on the derivation of words and lexical relationships. Word sorts, syllable sorts, and semantic sorts are among the types of activities that help students become more cognizant of spelling patterns and automatic with their spelling.

Because some children with learning disabilities may not always represent all the sounds within the word, strategies such as the use of sound boxes as used in reading recovery may be helpful. They enable the writer to focus on the number of phonemes in the word and then represent each phoneme graphemically.

There are a number of strategies used by good spellers when they encounter a word they are unsure of. They may use their phonological knowledge; they may use visual memory by either picturing the word in their minds, or writing the word. Have you ever had the experience of sudden hesitancy with a word such as accommodate? Sometimes you need to write it out—is it *accomodate* or *accommodate*? When examining the choices in isolation, the correct choice (*accommodate*) becomes more obvious. Spelling by analogy is another useful strategy. Teaching children to think of other words with similar sound patterns may help children spell unfamiliar words or sylla-bles. Certain spelling rules and mnemonic devices may also help us spell. How many of us spell *deceive* without thinking of *i before e except after c*? Mnemonic devices can help spellers with words that often present difficulty. For example, *their* is easier to re-member if you know that the three homonyms (*their, there, they're*) all have the word *the* in them. Consideration of lexical relationships and affixes creates a logic in English spellings that seems to be lacking when considering sounds alone. Knowing that *sign* and *signal* have similar meaning or that *condemn* and *condemnation* are related helps one include the silent letters. When students are uncertain of the spelling of a word, rather than directing them to "sound it out," teachers should direct them to "think it through" to consider what strategies to use.

When used purposefully, technology has had some beneficial effect on spelling within context. Spelling programs such as *Spell-it Deluxe* (produced by Davidson), which allows teachers to customize instruction, provides motivation for students to practice as needed. Spellcheckers eliminate many of the difficulties of using dictionar-ies and may be programmed to verbalize the possible choices for students who cannot recognize them in writing. Students, however, may need instruction in using spellchecks and in procedures to use when the spellcheck does not appear to produce the correct spelling. One such approach is teaching students to use the mnemonic CHECK:

- **C**heck beginning sounds.
- **H**unt for correct consonants.
- **E**xamine vowels.
- **C**hanges in word list should be used to get hints.
- **K**eep repeating steps 1–4 (Ashton, 1999).

Word-processing programs effectively improve children's writing when used in conjunction with a process approach and strategy instruction (MacArthur, Graham, Schwartz, & Schafer, 1995; Zhang, 2000). They increase motivation to write and sim-plify the revision and editing stages, leading to a greater willingness for students to sus-tain the writing process. Multimedia programs such as *Hyperstudio* and *PowerPoint* can be easily taught to students at this age and will increase motivation by incorporating pictures, sound effects, movies, and other visual items to create a product for the stu-dent that "looks professional" and can be shared with others. In one of the author's ex-periences with both programs in our reading clinic, both programs are grasped quite easily by many students: They create an authentic purpose for the writing as well as a desire to share the writing and they increase students' willingness to attend to form and content in their writing. Programs such as *Storybook Weaver Deluxe* (produced by MECC), in which students create a storybook, and *Hollywood* (produced by Theatrix), in which they write a play, choosing characters and character moods, settings, and writing dialogue that will then be acted out on screen, have heightened enthusiasm for writing among reluctant writers. The programs provide the "bells and whistles" that increase students' interest, leading to increased receptivity to instruction and practice.

ORGANIZING THE CLASSROOM

Kelly and Debbie are grateful for their common planning time, which affords them the opportunity to collaborate and modify instruction to help all the students become more successful. As they look at their students' literacy needs they realize that many of the students are having difficulty truly comprehending their texts. They examine the different comprehension procedures and select appropriate ones for each unit. They decide to share the presentation of the techniques and both monitor the collaborative groups, flexibly moving from group to group in order to watch all the interactions. They also determine the students who would benefit from additional prereading and organizational support. They develop strategy guides to help these students read the difficult material. Finally, they decide which activities can be accomplished within the classroom by giving students options, and what instruction should occur separately. They decide that Gina still needs additional instruction in word analysis and set aside time each day for individual instruction. During writing time, Debbie gives particular attention to the reluctant writers and the two teachers tailor minilessons to small-group and individual needs. Finally, they agree to return the following week to discuss their assessment of students' performance and continue to modify instruction as needed.

SUMMARY

The literacy focus in the transitional stage moves from learning to read and write to reading and writing to learn. There are a number of factors that affect comprehension. At the word level these include decoding abilities, degree of fluency, and word knowledge. Students also need to know how to comprehend and integrate longer pieces of discourse and how to be strategic readers. Teachers can increase students' comprehension through activities conducted before reading, during the reading, and after the reading. As reading and writing are reciprocal processes, writing should be an integral part of the classroom instruction. The most effective techniques combine a process writing approach with explicit instruction in ways to improve content and mechanics, particularly spelling. Finally, technology can be used to enhance students' motivation to write and help them overcome some of their difficulties.

Linkages

In the text
1. Review all the procedures in this chapter for developing comprehension. Which procedures do you feel would have been most useful for you to understand the key facets of

this chapter? Working with a small group of other students teach this chapter to your peers.
2. How would you organize your classroom for writing instruction? What are the key components you would emphasize to help all students be full members of the writing community?

Outside the text
1. Delores Durkin's research was conducted in the 1970s. Visit a classroom today. Describe the comprehension instruction that you observe. Is there comprehension instruction or is it still merely assessment?
2. Interview an intermediate-level teacher about her class. What reading problems does she see? What is she doing to help students who have difficulty with reading?
3. Observe writing instruction in a classroom. What model is being followed? Are you seeing process writing coupled with explicit instruction? If not, what is the teacher doing to improve children's writing?
4. Take a writing lesson from the teacher and enhance it to make writing easier for students with difficulties.

On the Web

Teaching Reading in every classroom
www.sdcoe.k12.ca.us/trec/
An educational website from the California Department of Education geared to literacy for grades 4–6.

Apple Learning Interchange
ali.apple.com/ali/
A commercial website with many resources for teachers.

Iditarod.com
www.iditarod.com/index.shtml
A commercial website, giving information about the Iditarod. Can be used to supplement novels with that subject.

Discovery School.com
school.discovery.com/lessonplans/k-5.html
A commercial website with literacy lesson plans that can be adapted for diverse learners.

References

Allington, R. L. (1983). Fluency: The neglected goal. *Reading Teacher, 36,* 555–561.

Ashton, T. M. (1999). Spell CHECKing: Making writing meaningful in the inclusive classroom, *Teaching Exceptional Children, 32,* 24–27.

Atwell, N. (1987). *In the middle: Writing, reading, and learning with adolescents.* Portsmouth, NH: Heinemann.

Atwell, N. (1991). *Side by side: Essays on teaching to learn.* Portsmouth, NH: Heinemann.

Aulls, M. W. (1978). *Developmental and remedial reading.* Needham Heights, MA: Allyn & Bacon.

Barenbaum, E., Newcomer, P., & Nodine, B. (1987). Children's ability to write stories as a function of variation in task, age, and developmental level. *Learning Disability Quarterly, 10,* 175–188.

Baumann, J. F., & Kameenui, E. J. (1991). Research on vocabulary instruction: Ode to Voltaire. In J. Flood, J. M. Jensen, D. Lapp, & J. R. Squire (Eds.), *Handbook of research on teaching the English language arts* (pp. 604–632). New York: Macmillan.

Bear, D. R., Invernizzi, M., Templeton, S., & Johnston, F. (2000). *Words their way:Word study for phonics, vocabulary, and spelling instruction.* Upper Saddle River, NJ: Merrill/Prentice Hall.

Beck, I. L., & McKeown, M. G. (1991). Conditions of vocabulary acquisition. In R. Barr, M. Kamil, P. Mosenthal, & P. D. Pearson (Eds.) *Handbook of reading research,* Vol. II (pp. 789–814). Mahwah, NJ: Lawrence Erlbaum Associates.

Beck, I. L., McKeown, M. G., & McCaslin, E. S. (1983). Vocabulary development: All contexts are not created equal. *Elementary School Journal, 83,* 177–181.

Beck, I. L, Perfetti, A. A., & McKeown, M. G. (1982). Effects of long-term vocabulary instruction on lexical access and reading comprehension. *Journal of Educational Psychology, 74,* 506–521.

Berninger, V. W. (1999). Coordinating transcription and text generation in working memory during composing: automatic and constructive processes. *Learning Disability Quarterly, 22,* 99–122.

Bidwell, S. (1990). Using drama to increase motivation, comprehension, and fluency. *Journal of Reading, 34,* 38–41.

Brown, H., & Cambourne, B. (1987). *Read and Retell.* Portsmouth, NH: Heinemann.

Brozo, W. G., & Simpson, M. (1999). Readers, teachers, learners: Expanding literacy across the content areas. Upper Saddle River, NJ: Merrill/Prentice Hall, p. 3.

Bruce, M. E., & Chan, L. K. S. (1991). Reciprocal teaching and transenvironmental programming: A program to facilitate the reading comprehension of students with reading difficulties. *Remedial and Special Education, 12,* 44–54.

Carnine, D., Kameenui, E. J., & Coyle, G. (1983). Utilization of contextual information in determining the meaning of unfamiliar words. *Reading Research Quarterly 19,* 188–203.

Carnine, D., Kameenui, E. J., & Coyle, G. (1984). Utilization of contextual information in determining the meaning of unfamiliar words. *Reading Research Quarterly, 19,* 188–203.

Carr, E., & Ogle, D. M. (1987). K-W-L Plus: A strategy for comprehension and summarization. *Journal of Reading, 30,* 626–631.

Chomsky, C. (1976). After decoding: What? *Language Arts, 53,* 288–296, 314.

Cooper, J. D., & Kiger, N. D. (2001). *Literacy assessment: Helping teachers plan instruction.* Boston, MA: Houghton Mifflin Co.

Cunningham, P. M. (1998). The multisyllabic word dilemma: Helping students build meaning, spell, and read, "big" words. *Reading and Writing Quarterly, 14,* 189–218.

Curtis, M. E., & Longo, A. M. (1999). *When adolescents can't read: Methods and materials that work.* Cambridge, MA: Brookline Books.

Dale, E. (1965). Vocabulary measurement: Techniques and major findings. *Elementary English, 42,* 895–901, 948.

Daniels, H. (1994). *Literature circles: Voice and choice in the student-centered classroom.* York, ME: Stenhouse Publishers.

Davis, F. (1968). Research in comprehension in reading. *Reading Research Quarterly, 3,* 499–545.

De La Paz, S. (1999). Teaching writing strategies and self-regulation procedures to middle school students with learning disabilities. *Focus on Exceptional Children, 31,* 1–16.

De La Paz, S., & Graham, S. (1997). Strategy instruction in planning: Effects on the writing performance and behavior of students with learning difficulties. *Exceptional Children, 63,* 167–181.

Dowhower, S. L. (1987). Effects of repeated reading on second-grade transitional readers' fluency and comprehension. *Reading Research Quarterly, 22,* 389–403.

Durkin, D. (1978). What classroom observations reveal about reading compehension instruction. *Reading Research Quarterly, 14,* 481–533.

Eeds, M., & Cockrum, W. A. (1985). Teaching word meanings by expanding schemata vs. dictionary work vs. reading in context. *Journal of Reading, 28,* 492–497.

Ehri, L. C., & McCormick, S. (1998). Phases of word learning: Implications for instruction with delayed and disabled readers. *Reading and Writing Quarterly: Overcoming Learning Difficulties 14,* 135–164.

Englert, C. S., & Tarrant, K. L. (1994). Lesson talk as the work of reading groups: The effectiveness of two interventions. *Journal of Learning Disabilities, 27,* 165–194.

Evans, K. S. (1996). Creating spaces for equity? The role of positioning in peer-led literature discussions. *Language Arts, 73,* 194–203.

Ezell, H., Kohler, F., & Strain, P. (1994). A program description and evaluation of academic peer tutoring for reading skills of children with special needs. *Education and Treatment of Children,* 52–67.

Fink, R. P. (1995–1996). Successful dyslexics: A constructivist study of passionate interest reading. *Journal of Adolescent & Adult Literacy, 39,* 268–280.

Freebody, P., & Anderson, R. C. (1983). Effects of vocabulary difficulty, text cohesion and schema availability on reading comprehension. *Reading Research Quarterly, 24,* 277–294.

Gillet, J. W., & Temple, C. (2000). *Understanding reading problems: Assessment and Instruction* (5th ed.). New York: Addison-Wesley-Longman.

Gersten, R. & Baker, S. (1999). Reading comprehension instruction for students with learning disabilities. In *Two decades of research in learning disabilities: Reading comprehension, expressive writing, problem solving, self-concept. Keys to successful learning. A national summit on research in learning disabilities.* New York, NY: National Center for Learning Disabilities, Inc. (ERIC Document Reproduction Service No. ED 430 365).

Graham, S., & Harris, K. R. (1999). Assessment and intervention in overcoming writing difficulties: An illustration from the self-regulated strategy development model. *Language, Speech, and Hearing Services in Schools, 30,* 255–264.

Hancock, M. R. (1993). Exploring the meaning-making process through the content of literature response journals: A case study investigation. *Research in the Teaching of English, 27,* 335–367.

Herman, P. A. (1985). The effect of repeated reading on reading rate, speech pauses, and word recognition accuracy. *Reading Research Quarterly, 20,* 553–565.

Horn, E. (1926). *A basic writing vocabulary.* Iowa City: University of Iowa Press.

Jenkins, J. R., Pany, D., & Schreck, J. (1978, August). Vocabulary and reading comprehension; instructional effects (Tech Rep. No. 100). Urbana: University of Illinois, Center for the Study of Reading.

Johnson, D. D., & Pearson, P. D. (1984). *Teaching reading vocabulary* (2nd ed.). New York: Holt, Rinehart & Winston.

Konopak, B. C. (1988). Effects of inconsiderate vs. considerate text on secondary students' vocabulary learning. *Journal of Reading Behavior, 20,* 25–41.

Laflamme, J. G. (1997). The effects of the multiple exposure vocabulary method and the target reading/writing strategy on test scores. *Journal of Adolescent & Adult Literacy, 40,* 372–381.

LaBerge, D.& Samuels, S. J. (1974). Toward a theory of automating information processing in reading. *Cognitive Psychology, 6,* 293–323.

Leal, D. J. (1992). The nature of talk about three types of text during peer group discussions. *Journal of Reading Behavior, 24,* 313–338.

Leal, D. J. (1996). Transforming grand conversations into grand creations: Using different types of text to influence student discussion. In L. B. Gambrell & J. F. Amasi (Eds.), *Lively conversations! Fostering engaged reading,* (pp. 149–168). Newark, DE: International Reading Association.

Lewis, C. (1997). The social drama of literature discussions in a fifth/sixth grade classroom. *Research in the Teaching of English, 31,* 163–203.

MacArthur, C. A., Graham, S., Schwartz, S. S., & Schafer, W. D. (1995). Evaluation of a writing instruction model that integrated a process approach, strategy instruction, and word processing. *Learning Disability Quarterly, 18,* 278–291.

Manzo, A. V. (1969). The ReQuest procedure. *Journal of Reading, 13,* 367–369.

Manzo, A. V., & Manzo, U. C. (1990). *Content area reading: A heuristic approach.* Columbus, OH: Merrill.

Manzo, A. V., & Manzo, U. C. (1993). *Literacy disorders: Holistic diagnosis and remediation.* Fort Worth, TX: Harcourt Brace Jovanovich.

Mariage, T. V. (2000). Constructing educational possibilities: A sociolinguistic examination of meaning-making in "sharing chair." *Learning Disability Quarterly, 23,* 79–103.

Mastropieri, M. A., & Scruggs, T. E. (2000). *The inclusive classroom: Strategies for effective instruction.* Upper Saddle River, NJ: Merrill/Prentice Hall.

McKeown, M. G., Beck, I. L., Omanson, R. C., & Perfetti, C. A. (1983). The effects of long-term vocabulary instruction on reading comprehension: A replication. *Journal of Reading Behavior, 15,* 3–17.

Miller, S. D., & Meece, J. L. (1997). Enhancing elementary students' motivation to read and write: A classroom intervention study. *Journal of Educational Research, 90,* 286–315.

Moats, L. C. (2001). When older students can't read. *Educational Leadership, 58,* 36–39.

Nagy, W., & Anderson, R. C. (1984). How many words are there in printed school English? *Reading Research Quarterly, 19,* 304–330.

Nia, I. T. (1999). Units of study in the writing workshop. *Primary Voices K–6, 8,* 3–10.

O'Flahavan, J. F. (1994). Teacher role options in peer discussions about literature. *The Reading Teacher, 48,* 354–356.

Ogle, D. M. (1986). K-W-L: A teaching model that develops active reading of expository text. *The Reading Teacher, 39,* 564–570.

Palincsar, A. S., & Brown, A. L. (1984). Reciprocal teaching of comprehension-fostering and comprehension-monitoring activities. *Cognition and Instruction, 1,* 117–175.

Palincsar, A. S., Brown, A. L., & Martin, S. M. (1987). Peer interaction in reading comprehension instruction. *Educational Psychologist, 22,* 231–253.

Pearson, P. D., & Camperell, K. (1994). Comprehension of text structures. In R. B. Ruddell, M. R. Ruddell, & H. Singer (Eds.) *Theoretical models and processes of reading* (pp. 448–467). Newark, DE: International Reading Association.

Pearson, P. D., & Fielding, L. (1996). Comprehension instruction. In R. Barr, M. Kamil, P. Mosenthal, & P. D. Pearson (Eds.), *Handbook of reading research,* Vol. II (pp. 815–860). Mahwah, NJ: Lawrence Erlbaum Associates.

Pearson, P. D., & Fielding, L. (1996). Comprehension Instruction. In R. Barr, M. L. Kamil, P. Mosenthal, & P. D. Pearson (Eds.) *Handbook of reading research,* Vol. II (pp. 815–861). Mahweh, NJ: Lawrence Erlbaum Associates.

Pearson, P. D., & Johnson, D. D. (1978). *Teaching reading comprehension.* New York: Holt, Rinehart and Winston.

Pressley, M. (1977). Imagery and children's learning: Putting the picture in developmental perspective, *Review of Educational Research, 47,* 585–622.

Pressley, M., Levin, J. R., & Delaney, H. D. (1982). The mnemonic keyword method. *Review of Educational Research, 52,* 61–92.

Raphael, T. E. (1982). Question-answering strategies for children. *The Reading Teacher, 36,* 188.

Raphael, T. E. (1984). Teaching learners about sources of information for answering comprehension questions. *Journal of Reading, 27,* 303–311.

Raphael, T. E. (1986). Teaching question-answer relationships revisited. *The Reading Teacher, 39,* 516–523.

Raphael, T. E., & Pearson, P. D. (1982). *The effect of metacognitive awareness training on children's question-answering behavior* (Tech Rep. No. 238). Urbana: University of Illinois, Center for Study of Reading.

Rashotte, C. A., & Torgesen, J. K. (1985). Repeated reading and reading fluency in learning disabled children. *Reading Research Quarterly, 20,* 180–188.

Roehler, L. R., & Duffy, G. G. (1996). Teachers' instructional actions. In R. Barr, M. Kamil, P. Mosenthal, & P. D. Pearson (Eds.) *Handbook of reading research* (Vol. II, pp. 861–883). Mahwah, NJ: Lawrence Erlbaum Associates.

Roller, C. M., & Beed, P. L. (1994). Sometimes the conversations were grand, and sometimes. . . . *Language Arts, 71,* 509–515.

Ruddell, M. R. (1994). Vocabulary knowledge and comprehension: A comprehension-process view of complex literacy relationships. In R. B. Ruddell, M. R. Ruddell, & H. Singer (Eds.), *Theoretical models and processes of reading* (pp. 414–447). Newark, DE: International Reading Association.

Samuels, S. J. (1979). The method of repeated readings. *The Reading Teacher, 32,* 403–408.

Samuels, S. J. (1997). The method of repeated readings. *The Reading Teacher, 50,* 376–381.

Scharer, P. L., & Peters, D. (1996). An exploration of literature discussions conducted by two teachers moving toward literature-based reading instruction. *Reading Research and Instruction, 36,* 33–50.

Sheehan, L., Feldman, R., Allen, V. (1976). Research on children tutoring children: A critical review. *Review of Educational Research, 46,* 355–382.

Simmons, D., Fuchs, L., Fuchs, D., Mathes, P., & Hodge, J. (1995). Effects of explicit teaching and peer tutoring on the reading achievement of learning disabled and low performing students in regular classrooms. *The Elementary School Journal, 95,* 387–407.

Singer, B. (1995). Written language development and disorders: Selected principles, patterns, and intervention possibilities. *Topics in Language Disorders, 16,* 83–98.

Speece, D. L., MacDonald, V., Kilsheimer, L., & Krist, J. (1997). Research to practice: Preservice teachers reflect on reciprocal teaching. *Learning Disabilities Research & Practice, 12,* 177–187.

Stahl, S. A. (1998). Teaching children with reading problems to decode: Phonics and "not-phonics" instruction. *Reading and Writing Quarterly: Overcoming Learning Difficulties, 14,* 165–188.

Stahl, S. A., & Fairbanks, M. M. (1986). The effects of vocabulary instruction: A model based meta-analysis. *Review of Educational Research, 56,* 72–110.

Stauffer, R. G. (1975). *Directing the reading-thinking process.* New York: Harper & Row.

Sternberg, R. J., & Powell, J. S. (1983). Comprehending verbal comprehension. *American Psychologist, 38,* 878–891.

Swanson, H. L. (1999). Reading research for students with LD: A meta-analysis of intervention outcomes. *Journal of Learning Disabilities, 32,* 504–532.

Swanson, H. L., & Berninger, V. (1995). The role of working memory in skilled and less skilled readers' comprehension. *Intelligence, 21,* 83–108.

Taylor, S. V., & Nesheim, D. W. (2000–2001). Making literacy real for "high-risk" adolescent emerging readers: An innovative application of readers' workshop. *Journal of Adolescent & Adult Literacy, 44,* 308–318.

Tompkins, G. E. (2000). *Teaching writing: Balancing process and product* (3rd ed.). Upper Saddle River, NJ: Merrill/Prentice Hall.

Topping, K. (1989). Peer tutoring and paired reading combining two powerful techniques. *The Reading Teacher, 40,* 608–614.

Troia, G. A., Graham, S., & Harris, K. R. (1999). Teaching students with learning disabilities to mindfully plan when writing. *Exceptional Children, 65,* 235–252.

Tully, M. (1996). *Helping students revise their writing: Practical strategies, models, and mini-lessons that motivate students to become better writers.* Jefferson City, MO: Scholastic Inc.

Wells, M. C. (1993). At the junction of reading and writing: How dialogue journals contribute to students' reading development. *Journal of Reading, 36,* 294–302.

White, T., Sowell, J., & Yanagihara, A. (1989). Teaching elementary students to use word-part clues. *The Reading Teacher, 42,* 302–308.

Wigfield, A., & Guthrie, J. (1997). Relations of children's motivation for reading to the amount and breadth of their reading. *Journal of Educational Psychology, 89,* 420–432.

Williams, J. P. (1998). Improving the comprehension of disabled readers. *Annals of Dyslexia, 68,* 213–238.

Wong, B. Y. L. (1997). Research on genre-specific strategies for enhancing writing in adolescents with learning disabilities. *Learning Disability Quarterly, 20,* 140–159.

Yuill, N. (1991). *Children's problems in text comprehension: An experimental investigation.* New York: Cambridge University Press.

Zhang, Y. (2000). Technology and the writing skills of students with learning disabilities. *Journal of Research on Computing in Education, 32,* 467–478.

Zutell, J., & Rasinski, T. (1991) Training teachers to attend to their students' oral fluency. *Theory Into Practice, 30,* 211–217.

CHAPTER 7
Advanced Literacy Skills

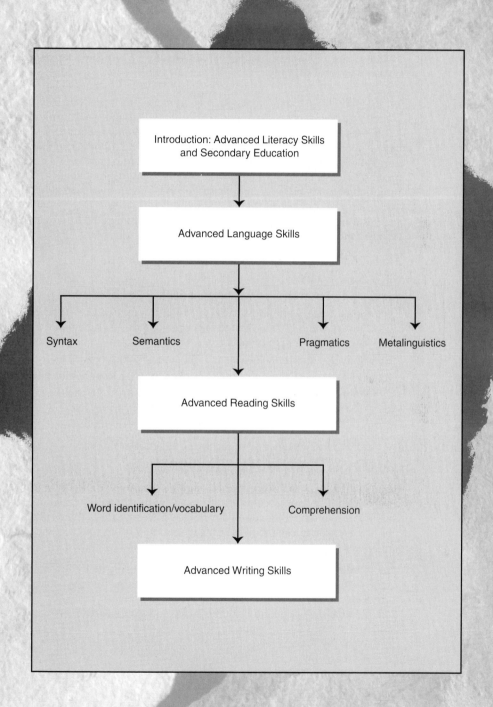

Introduction: Advanced Literacy Skills and Secondary Education

Advanced Language Skills

Syntax   Semantics   Pragmatics   Metalinguistics

Advanced Reading Skills

Word identification/vocabulary   Comprehension

Advanced Writing Skills

▪▪ STUDENTS' VOICES

Dr. Richard Vacca, a professor and past president of the International Reading Association tells this story about "Johnny," a student he taught in high school. Vacca had just told Johnny that he would be returning to college to get his doctoral degree. Johnny said, "Man, you read good already. F_____ reading. Reading robbed me of my manhood" (Vacca, 1998).

I really liked to read a lot when I was in 6th grade. For one thing, I didn't have anything else better to do. On average I probably read one book every two weeks. And I'd read these books just about anywhere. I carried them around everywhere I went. Books were just important to me then. But now that I'm in high school, I don't have time to read, or even an inclination to read. As a result, I don't read anywhere near what I used to read. I've got better things to do now, like playing sports, participating in clubs, doing homework, and working part-time jobs (11th grader quoted by Bintz, 1993).

Karen is a 13-year-old African-American female who attends a regular education classroom. She is being interviewed by a researcher:

R: Do you have to read very much in school?

K: No, not a lot.

R: Do you read as much as the other kids do in class?

K: Sometimes, sometimes she'll pick other people out of a whole day I don't read. Except she'll give us a page and we have to—each person has to do it on their own. And I'll read then.

R: Why do you think she doesn't always pick you to read?

K: Because she, she knows that I'm slow and, I guess she doesn't want the kids to make fun of me or anything.

▪▪ INTRODUCTION: ADVANCED LITERACY SKILLS AND SECONDARY EDUCATION

The students quoted in the vignettes in the beginning of this chapter illustrate some of the dilemmas of adolescents and literacy. By the time they reach adolescence, students are expected to have developed a range of literacy skills that will enable them to take on the increasing demands of middle school and high school and beyond. These demands include the ability to:

- Understand and use language in many contexts, including the ability to understand and interpret lectures and develop effective spoken language presentations
- Read and understand both narrative and expository texts in a variety of subject areas
- Write well-researched and clearly organized reports and other written assignments

These expectations require highly advanced literacy skills—skills that some students will have significant difficulty acquiring and some will not acquire at all. The

1998 National Assessment of Educational Progress report (U.S. Department of Education, 1999) indicated that, although reading scores have improved for 4th, 8th, and 12th graders, only 40% of 12th graders and 33% of 8th graders performed at a proficient or advanced level of reading.

Unfortunately, the increased academic expectations of secondary education come just at the time when students are dealing with the myriad of changes and challenges posed by adolescence itself. Clearly, adolescence is a time of great physical and emotional change, a time when students are seeking their identity and independence from their parents. Students typically struggle with a range of emotions including anxiety, anger, and shyness (Thornburg, 1982) as they seek their place in the ever-changing mosaic of social groups. For many middle and high school students, academic performance takes a backseat to concerns about physical, social, and emotional development.

Compounding the problem is the organization, curriculum, and expectations typically found in secondary education. Secondary schools tend to be large, impersonal settings in which students frequently change classes and teachers. Students must be able to switch from one subject to another and between varying sets of classroom procedures and expectations. Curricular emphases change from the development of students' skills that dominated elementary instruction to the content area focus predominant at the secondary level. For the most part, secondary teachers expect their students to come to class with the literacy skills needed to profit from the instruction that is presented (O'Brien, Stewert, & Moje, 1995).

For many students, the demands and expectations of secondary education, although challenging, are not insurmountable. However, a significant number of students struggle at the secondary level. Typically, these students lack the literacy skills that are needed for success at this level. Unfortunately, the emphasis on content knowledge makes it unlikely that they will get the help they need to be successful. As a result, they fall further and further behind their peers, often becoming "turned off" to school and dropping out, either literally or figuratively.

Vacca (1997) described the prevailing attitude toward adolescent literacy as one of "benign neglect." What he meant was that, despite the widely documented problems of literacy among adolescents in secondary school environments, schools rarely take on the challenge of addressing these problems. Moreover, these issues are often not an important part of textbooks in reading education or in teacher preparation programs.

There is good news, however. During the past two decades a small but persistent group of researchers and educators has focused on the challenges of developing advanced literacy skills. As a result of their work, a number of effective practices have been developed that can enhance the language, reading, and writing skills of all students. In this chapter we will examine both the challenges presented by secondary school environments and techniques that can be used to develop the advanced literacy skills that are needed for success at the secondary level.

ADVANCED LANGUAGE SKILLS

It may seem odd to talk about language "development" during adolescence. After all, by the time students reach middle school and certainly by the time they enter high school most children have thoroughly acquired their first language. For most children, the acquisition of the sound system of their language is completed early in elementary school. Most grammatical (syntactic) structures and even highly complex structures have been acquired and are used in conversation. Word learning has accelerated from a base of approximately 2,000 words at age five to 10,000 words by first grade to an astounding 40,000 words by the end of fifth grade (Anglin, 1993). What more is there to know? In fact, a great deal.

Although the language development norms of adolescents are not as clearly established as those for younger children (Nippold, 1995), there is increasing information about the continued language development that takes place during the adolescent years. By the time they reach adolescence, most typically developing children have completed their development in the areas of phonology (the sound system) and morphology (word formation). However, significant developments continue to occur in the areas of syntax (grammar), semantics (meaning), pragmatics (usage), and metalinguistics (knowledge of language) (see Table 7.1).

Syntax

Some researchers have reported that sentence length increases in students between grades 6 and 12 (e.g., Loban, 1976). Although sentence length is not always an accurate measure of language sophistication in older children, these researchers have described advanced language structures that are the cause of longer sentences. For example, during adolescence typically developing children learn to expand noun phrases by using structures such as *appositives* (e.g., Julia, *the doctor,* is at the office) and prepositional phrases as *postmodifiers* (e.g., She saw that the dog *with the collar* was running away). Other syntactic structures that mature during adolescence include the use of *modal verbs* (e.g., He *had been skiing* when he fell), the *passive voice* (e.g., The ball *was hit by* the girl), *subordinate clauses* (e.g., *When he saw the girl* he turned away) and *adverbials* such as "consequently," "furthermore," and "moreover" (Nippold, 1993). In many cases, these structures began to develop at an earlier age, but were used infrequently or inaccurately. As children mature, they are more likely to be able to understand and appropriately use these syntactic structures.

Semantics

During adolescence, there is a rapid expansion of vocabulary as students are exposed to new concepts in social studies and science. In addition, students typically learn to understand the subtle shades of meaning that enable them to accurately *interpret analogies* such as "EXPEDITE is to FASTER as OBFUSCATE is to CONFUSING," understand *multiple meaning words* [e.g., "table" can mean a piece of furniture or a table of elements or can be used as a verb (table the bill)], and *recognize homonyms and synonyms* (Norris, 1995).

One of the major semantic developments during the adolescent years is the increasing ability to understand and use *figurative* language. In middle and high school, students are expected to be able to read and understand text that includes the use of *metaphor* (an implied comparison such as "He has a heart of stone"), *simile* (an explicit comparison such as "The bird was as light as a feather), and *idioms* (e.g., "Don't put the cart before the horse."). Although skill in understanding and using figurative language begins to develop during the early school years, it matures during adolescence (Nippold & Martin, 1989). By the time they reach secondary school, students should not only be able to understand these linguistic devices but should also be able to incorporate them

TABLE 7.1	Language Development during Adolescence
Syntax:	Appositives
	Postmodifiers
	Modal verbs
	Passive voice
	Subordinate clauses
Semantics:	Interpret analogies
	Understand multiple meaning words
	Recognize homonyms and synonyms
	Understand and use figurative language including:
	Metaphor
	Simile
	Idioms
Pragmatics:	Knowing *what* to say, including:
	Being able to accurately give (and understand) directions
	The ability to use and interpret nonliteral language
	Metalinguistic knowledge
	Knowledge of content-area vocabulary
	Knowing *to whom* to say what, including:
	Being able to take the perspective of the speaker or listener (depending on the context)
	Being able to adjust to the varying norms and expectations of secondary classrooms and a variety of social situations
	Being able to effectively participate in classroom discussions
	Knowing *when* and *how much* to say, including:
	When to talk
	How much to say in response to an initiation
	How to successfully enter and exit from conversations
Metalinguistic knowledge:	Ability to state the rules for grammatical usage
	Ability to identify what makes figurative language different from literal language (Nippold, 1993)

into their own written output. Unfortunately, many students struggle to master the use of figurative language. They have difficulty with words that have abstract or multiple meanings (Wiig, 1982). As a result, they may have difficulty reading textbooks and producing the more sophisticated writing required at the secondary level.

Pragmatics

Socialization is an important part of adolescent life, and pragmatic competence, the ability to use language in social situations, is essential for successful socialization. Therefore, the continued development of pragmatic language skills is an important aspect of language growth during the adolescent years. Norris (1995) divides pragmatic development during adolescence into three elements:

- Knowing *what* to say: this includes being able to accurately give (and understand) directions, the ability to use and interpret nonliteral language, metalinguistic knowledge, and knowledge of content-area vocabulary. If students have difficulty understanding language, it is likely that they will experience difficulty using language for interaction.
- Knowing *to whom* to say what: this includes being able to take the perspective of the speaker or listener (depending on the context), being able to adjust to the varying norms and expectations of secondary classrooms and a variety of social situations, and being able to effectively participate in classroom discussions.
- Knowing *when* and *how much* to say: during adolescence, children are still learning skills that enable them to effectively participate in conversations. Among these skills are when to talk, how much to say in response to an initiation, and how to successfully enter and exit from conversations.

Adolescents who possess pragmatic skills such as those described are more likely to be successful in a variety of social situations, including the classroom. Conversely, students lacking these skills may experience problems with socialization and may have difficulty understanding and contributing to classroom discussions as well as understanding the structure of narratives (Nippold, 1993).

Metalinguistics

Metalinguistic knowledge enables the language user to think about and reflect on language. In the classroom, it is often demonstrated by the ability to state the rules that underlie a linguistic expression (e.g., "Tell what is wrong with the sentence": *The cat and dog is running.*). Metalinguistic knowledge has been found to be an important aspect of the development of reading and writing skills (Menyuk, 1995). By adolescence, most (though not all) children have developed metaphonological knowledge—the ability to identify and use the rules of the sound system. But in secondary schools, students are often required to learn and state the rules for grammatical usage and to identify what makes figurative language different from literal language. These are additional metalinguistic skills. In order to successfully develop metalinguistic knowledge, students must have both the cognitive skills to reflect on language and have fully developed the language skills themselves. Therefore, students who have difficulty reasoning and those with language disorders may have difficulty developing the metalinguistic skills demanded by the secondary curriculum.

Enhancing Advanced Language Skills

There are numerous opportunities to enhance language skills in secondary classrooms. For example, students can be offered multiple opportunities to talk, both in small-group and whole-class activities. Presentations, debates, and role playing all offer opportunities to develop and use spoken language skills. For some students, increased opportunities to participate may not be enough. They may need to observe models for interaction, be coached during discussions, and/or be monitored for participation. A number of methods can be used to enhance the participation of secondary-level students with limited communicative interaction, including:

- Pairing students with another student with more advanced language skills.
- Giving feedback that includes explicit pointers about what the student did well ("That's good, Jim. You remembered to tell us what the topic was at the beginning of your presentation"), as well as what they could improve on ("Next time, remember to use a summary of your main points at the end").
- Continual checking for participation with reminders that everyone is expected to contribute.

In addition, many literacy instruction techniques such as K-W-L (Chapter 6) include a spoken language component that gives students opportunities for interaction.

Another way that secondary-level teachers can enhance the spoken language development of their students is to establish a classroom atmosphere that encourages and supports interaction. Often classroom interactions take the form of the teacher asking a question and the student responding. Teachers can enhance classroom interaction by posing problems and asking the students to explain how they could be solved, by responding to students in ways that enhance further interaction (e.g., by saying, "What else can you tell me about that?" or "What do you think that means?"), and by asking students to lead classroom discussions in which the teacher's role is to listen and ask questions.

The methods described could be useful for any student. However, for students with language disorders additional help may be needed. Consultation with and support from a speech-language specialist may be needed in order to provide the extra support and instruction that will be needed by many of these students.

ADVANCED READING SKILLS

By the time they enter secondary school, students are expected to have acquired advanced reading skills. Among these advanced reading skills are the ability to:

- Use a variety of strategies for identifying and understanding unknown words
- Use a variety of strategies for comprehension of text
- Read for a variety of purposes at varying speeds appropriate to the text
- Understand the author's perspective and switch perspective as necessary

Students who have developed these advanced reading skills are better prepared to meet the challenges posed by reading at the secondary level.

One of the most formidable challenges in secondary education is reading content-area textbooks. Typically, these texts are concept rather than character based, use vocabulary that is unfamiliar and abstract, and contain fewer illustrations and other learning aids than texts at the elementary level (Carter & Klotz, 1991). In order to successfully learn from these books, students must learn to read in a very different way than they did at the elementary level. Specifically, they must learn to look for structure in the reading rather than being able to rely on a clear story structure provided by the author. They need to develop effective and efficient strategies for identifying new words. Most importantly, they need to develop reading strategies that will enable them to recall what they read.

Unfortunately, in many cases, both teachers and students view content-area reading as a boring, repetitive task. Lacking effective skills to read secondary content materials, students lose interest in reading. Studies have found that reading attitudes decline during the middle school years, and students read less frequently (Ley, Schaer, & Dismukes, 1994). Teachers often become frustrated by their students' reading behaviors. Look at these comments from teachers:

> "Students today just don't read. They read just enough to get by and that, of course, leads to poor reading habits and low reading test scores."

> "I just don't understand it. Here we are requiring more class reading than ever before, and student reading skills still seem to get worse and worse."

> (Blintz, 1993)

It seems apparent that there are some significant challenges for both students and teachers in regard to secondary-level literacy skills. Some students enter secondary schooling lacking one or more of the skills necessary to read at an advanced level. Some enter with those skills but become turned off to reading that they perceive as uninteresting. Although teachers recognize the importance of literacy skills, few of them are prepared or even willing to help their students acquire or enhance advanced reading skills. But there is good news. In the last 20 years a number of effective approaches have been developed to enhance reading at the secondary level. In the following section we will review some of these approaches.

Enhancing Word Identification and Vocabulary

One of the challenges of reading secondary-level, content-area textbooks is the amount and complexity of vocabulary present in these books. Secondary-level readers will need excellent word identification and vocabulary-learning strategies to be successful. Although many students can be expected to have these skills, some will need help applying what they have previously learned to the new challenges posed by content-area reading at the secondary level.

The traditional approach to vocabulary instruction has been to assign students a list of vocabulary words to study and memorize. Although this approach can help students prepare for reading content-area texts, it has not been found to be as effective as techniques that more actively involve students in learning (Bos & Anders, 1990). As a result, a number of learning strategy approaches have been developed to assist secondary-level learners with word identification and vocabulary acquisition. Learning strategies instruction helps students draw on their prior knowledge to develop strategies for word identification and/or vocabulary learning. For example, the DISSECT strategy was developed by Lenz and Hughes (1990) to help secondary students decode words. Students are taught to follow seven steps that require them to use context clues, break words into their constituents, and use additional resources when needed. The seven steps of the strategy are:

D—*discover* the context. Students are reminded to use the context as an aid to identifying the target word.

I—*isolate* the prefix: Students are instructed to find and separate the prefix and then try to say the word.

S—*separate* the suffix: Students are instructed to find and separate the suffix and then try to say the word.

S—*say* the stem: Once the prefix and suffix have been removed, what remains is the word stem. Students are told to now try to identify the stem.

E—*examine* the stem: Students are taught to use the "rule of twos and threes" to identify the stem. That is, if the stem begins with a vowel, students pronounce units of two letters. If the stem begins with a consonant, students separate and pronounce units of three letters.

C—*check* with someone: If students have followed the first five steps and still do not recognize the word, they can check with a peer, teacher, etc.

T—*try* the dictionary: Another (perhaps preferable) alternative is to check the dictionary.

In one study, DISSECT was found to significantly reduce the oral reading errors of eighth-grade students with learning disabilities after only 6 weeks of use (Lenz & Hughes, 1990).

IT FITS is a strategy designed to help students remember unfamiliar vocabulary words. This strategy uses a "keyword" (a word students already know) that will help them remember the word they need to learn (see Figure 7.1 for an example). The steps of the strategy are:

I—*identify* the term.

T—*tell* the definition of the term by writing it on an index card.

F—*find* a keyword that the student already knows that will help them remember the target word. The keyword should be related to the target word both by sound and meaning.

I—*imagine:* Students draw a picture that relates the keyword to the target word.

T—*think:* Students should think about the ways in which the keyword and target word are related.

S—*study:* Students continue studying until they know the target word.

In one study (King–Sears, Mercer, & Sindelar, 1992) students in sixth, seventh, and eighth grades were successfully taught to use the IT FITS strategy to learn science vocabulary.

Learning strategies such as DISSECT and IT FITS can be effectively used to help secondary-level students enhance their word identification and vocabulary skills. Although they may seem time consuming at first, once students become proficient at using these strategies, they can be more independent as well as more effective learners.

<u>I</u>dentify the term.

<u>T</u>ell the definition of the term.

<u>F</u>ind a keyword.

<u>I</u>magine the definition doing something with the keyword.

<u>T</u>hink about the definition doing something with the keyword.

<u>S</u>tudy what you imagined until you know the definition.

FIGURE 7.1

Example of the IT FITS Strategy
Source: King–Sears, M. E., Mercer, C. D., & Sindelar, P. T. (1992). Toward independence with keyword mnemonics: A strategy for science vocabulary instruction. *Remedial and Special Education, 13,* p. 27.

Enhancing Comprehension

Proficient readers use a variety of metacognitive strategies that enable them to understand what they read, to relate what they are reading to previously stored knowledge, and to apply what they have read in a variety of contexts (Swanson & De La Paz, 1998). Students who lack such strategies or who fail to use them to enhance their reading may experience significant difficulty in reading and recalling information from texts. Therefore, many students at the secondary level can benefit from instruction that teaches them to use metacognitive strategies to enhance their reading comprehension. These strategies may be used prior to reading, during reading, or following reading. In addition, there are strategies that guide the reader throughout the reading process. We will examine a few of these strategies that have been designed primarily for readers at the secondary level.

Strategies Prior to Reading

One of the most critical processes in reading at any level is the activation of prior knowledge for reading. Current models of reading emphasize the interactive nature of the reading process with the reader interpreting the text in reference to their own previously stored knowledge (Anderson & Pearson, 1984). A number of instructional techniques have been developed to help readers access their prior knowledge. For example, prereading discussions, story mapping, and vocabulary development have all been shown to be effective techniques to enhance prior knowledge (Dole, Brown, & Trathen, 1996). The most important factor is getting the student involved in the previewing activity. Completion of K-W-L charts or story maps are ways to involve reluctant readers. Students can work with a peer or a small group to preview the text and predict what it might be about. Ciborowski (1995) suggests that the following techniques have been found to be successful in enhancing comprehension prior to reading:

- Preteaching vocabulary
- Presenting graphic or advance organizers containing the main ideas prior to reading
- Finding answers to questions about the story prior to reading

Students share their own experiences and perceptions to broaden comprehension of a piece of literature.

Research studies on the effects of prereading activities have generally shown that these can be effective ways of enhancing comprehension. For example, two studies by Graves, Cooke, and Laberge (1983) showed that by asking questions and making statements (Box 7.1) that helped the student make a link between what they already know and the topic of the reading, low-achieving, inner-city eighth graders did much better on comprehension tasks than their peers who did not participate in previewing activities.

▌Box 7.1

EXAMPLE OF A "PREVIEWING" ACTIVITY

Graves, Cooke, and Laberge (1983) give the following example of a previewing discussion held prior to the reading of a story entitled "The Signalman," by Charles Dickens:

> It seems sometimes that life is full of dangers! Would you agree? Nearly every day an accident or a disaster of some kind happens somewhere. A plane crashes, an earthquake occurs, or cars pile up on the freeway. Can you think of some accidents or disasters that have happened lately?

> Many times before a disaster occurs a warning is given. For example, lights might blink on the instrument panel of an airplane, or instruments might pick up tremors in the earth that predict an earthquake is about to happen. Can you think of other types of warnings? Were warnings given for the disasters we just talked about?

> Some people believe that they are warned of dangers in supernatural ways. They believe in spirits or voices or maybe even ghosts guiding them to do—or not do—something. Have you ever heard of someone being warned like this? What did that person say?
>
> The story you will read today is about a man who often gets warnings. But, the warnings this man gets don't come from dreams or his mind. The man gets warnings of bad things about to happen from a ghost or specter. It seems that the ghost always appears before something terrible happens, as if he is trying to warn of danger.

The discussion continues as additional vocabulary is introduced and the setting and characters are reviewed.

Strategies During Reading

One of the most useful ways to help readers check for understanding as they read is through self-questioning strategies. Self-questioning has been found to be an effective way to enhance comprehension in many students, including those with learning disabilities (Mastroprieri, Scruggs, Bakken, & Whedon, 1996). For example, in a study by Wong and Jones (1982), learning-disabled eighth and ninth graders and nondisabled sixth graders were taught to use the following self-questioning technique:

- Ask yourself for what are you studying this passage.
- Find the main idea(s) in the paragraph and outline it (them).
- Think of a question about the main idea you have underlined and remember what a good question should be like.
- Learn the answer to your question.
- Always look back at your questions and answers to see how each successive question and answer provides you with more information.

The researchers found that the self-questioning training significantly enhanced the ability of the students with learning disabilities to ask questions about their reading as well as improving their overall reading comprehension. However, the training did not significantly improve the comprehension of the nondisabled students. The authors suggested that these students may have already acquired good strategies for understanding text materials.

Another example of a self-questioning approach is a strategy called ASK IT that was developed by Schumaker and her colleagues at the University of Kansas. This technique has been found to be effective for enhancing self-questioning skills (Schumaker, Deshler, Nolan, & Alley, 1994). The strategy steps are:

> A—*attend* to clues as you read.
> S—*say* a question about the clue and mark a symbol for the question. (For example, a "who" question is represented by a smiley face, a "what" question by a box.)
> K—*keep* a prediction in mind.
> I—*identify* the answers.
> T—*talk* about the answer to the question (compare their prediction to what they read in the text).

Another method to enhance comprehension during reading is to teach students to use a "look-back" strategy. Researchers have found that poor comprehenders tend to have a lot of difficulty with comprehension questions that require them to refer to earlier parts of their reading (i.e., look back). Students may feel that it is "cheating" to do so or may be so focused on completing their reading that they do not want to take the time to look back to check and locate information. Teachers can help students learn to look back as they read by modeling the process for them. An example of modeling was provided by Swanson and De La Paz (1998) (Box 7.2):

❚ Box 7.2

THE LOOK-BACK STRATEGY

The question is asking us which mountains separate France from Spain. I don't remember, so I'll look back in the chapter until I find it. First, I'll skim over the chapter until I come to the section where I think I'll find the answer. The first section of the chapter is about the history of France, so the answer won't be there. The second section talks about the people and culture, so the answer wouldn't be there. The next section is about the landscape. I think that the answer will be here somewhere, so I'll start to look a little more carefully. The first part talks about mountains. This is where the answer probably will be, so I will read this paragraph carefully. Here we go, it says that in the southwest, the Pyrenees separate France from Spain. So, my answer to the question is the Pyrenees.

Strategies to Enhance Recall

The goal of reading content-area texts is to get and retain information from those texts. Previewing strategies and strategies to enhance comprehension during reading can aid recall. In addition, specific techniques have been developed to help students summarize and recall what they have read.

Gist summaries are one type of text recall procedures. Using this technique, students are taught to use single sentences to summarize information found in a paragraph. In order to teach students to use gist summaries, the teacher can start with a single sentence for which the students must find the main idea. This can be followed with two or more sentences until the students are able to summarize an entire paragraph (Swanson & De La Paz, 1998). Researchers have found that this strategy can be effective in increasing the reading comprehension of middle school students (Bean & Steenwyk, 1984).

Hierarchical summaries are another technique that can be used to enhance recall of content-area texts. The basic idea behind hierarchical summaries is that students can be taught to recognize the structure within a text in order to enhance recall. Students are taught to develop an outline by skimming the passage, paying close attention to the headings, then reading each subsection to fill in the outline (Figure 7.2). For example, Taylor and Beach (1984) taught seventh-grade students to develop hierarchical summaries of social studies texts using the following procedure:

- Students made a "skeleton outline" for which they drew two lines at the top of a blank sheet of paper for the key idea or thesis statement.

	I. Johnson developed many programs to fight injustice and poverty.
	A. *Lyndon Johnson became President of the U.S. after Kennedy was assassinated.* hard worker, tried to carry out some of Kennedy's programs.
Civil Rights	B. *Johnson fought for civil-rights laws.* purpose: to protect blacks from discrimination in hotels and restaurants, blacks had not been allowed in some hotels and restaurants in the South
	C. *Johnson persuaded Congress to pass a law ensuring all people the right to vote.* protected black people's right to vote, literacy tests now illegal
	D. *Johnson started a "war on poverty."* job training, education for poor people, plans for a "Great Society"
Great Society Programs	E. *Johnson persuaded Congress to develop a medicare program.* for people at least 65 years old, hospital bills paid, doctor's bills paid in part.
	F. *Johnson persuaded Congress to pass a law giving money to schools.* purpose: to improve education of children from poor families, one billion dollars in aid to schools

FIGURE 7.2

An Example of a Hierarchical Summary
Source: Taylor, B. W., & Beach, R. W. (1984). The effects of text structure instruction on middle-grade students' comprehension and production of expository text. *Reading Research Quarterly, 19,* 134–146.

- Numbers were listed down the left side of the paper for every section in the passage designated by a subheading.
- Students read each section of the text and generated a main idea in their own words that they wrote by the appropriate number.
- Students listed two or three supporting details beneath each main idea statement.
- Students generated topic headings, which were entered in the left margin of their paper. These connect sections of the passage that are on the same topic.
- Students generated a key idea for the entire passage, which they wrote at the top of their paper.

Using the hierarchical summary technique, the students in the Taylor and Beach (1984) study significantly outperformed other students who used the more traditional method of textbook reading that involves reading and answering questions from a text. However, this difference was true only for unfamiliar material, suggesting that a time-consuming strategy such as hierarchical summarization may not be needed for familiar or less-challenging material.

Another effective approach to text recall is the use of a *rule-based strategy*. Students are taught a set of rules (or steps) to follow in order to summarize information from a text. The following rules have been found to be useful for enhancing recall:

- Delete trivial information.
- Delete important but redundant information.
- Compose a word to replace either a list or individual components of an action.
- Select or create a topic sentence.
- Relate the important supporting information (Swanson & De La Paz, 1998).

Clearly, many students will need instruction in each of these steps in order to use this strategy. They can begin with one paragraph and gradually increase the length of the passages that they are summarizing. In addition, teachers may have to help students identify what is "trivial" or "redundant" information in a text. In a study of the use of the rule-based summarization strategy just outlined, Rinehart, Stahl, and Erickson (1986) found that sixth-grade students were able to significantly increase their recall of major concepts from social studies texts after instruction in use of the summarization strategy.

Katims and Harris (1997) reported on the results of using a *paraphrasing strategy* called RAP with seventh-grade students in an ethnically diverse school. This simple strategy has three steps:

1. *Read* a paragraph.
2. *Ask* yourself, "What were the main idea and details in this paragraph?"
3. *Put* the main idea and details into your own words.

Half of the students were taught to use this strategy to aid their recall, and the remainder of the students continued to use the whole-language reading program that was already in place. The researchers found that the students who were taught to use the RAP strategy outperformed the other students on several measures of reading comprehension.

Collaborative Strategic Reading

The text comprehension strategies reviewed thus far are designed to help students enhance a single facet of their text comprehension. However, some cognitive strategy methods are designed to help students throughout the reading process. The *collaborative strategic reading* (Klingner, Vaughn, & Schumm, 1998) approach is an example of such a strategy.

The collaborative strategic reading approach consists of four major components that are used before, during, and after reading (Figure 7.3). The purpose of the "preview" strategy is to motivate students for their reading, activate background knowledge, and help students make predictions. Students are taught to look at headings, pictures, tables, and other text features in order to brainstorm about the topic of the reading and make predictions. Then students are taught to monitor themselves as they read using the "click and clunk" strategy. "Clicks" are those parts of the reading that can be easily understood—they can be read smoothly with good comprehension. "Clunks" are those places where comprehension breaks down, either because the student cannot read the word or cannot understand it. When the reader encounters "clunks," they are taught to use a series of steps (called "fix-up strategies") to identify the unknown word. During reading, students are also taught to "get the gist" by identifying the most important idea in a section of text. After reading, students learn to "wrap up" by formulating questions and answers about what they have learned.

In a study in which the collaborative strategic reading approach was used to enhance social studies reading, Klingner, Vaughn, and Schumm (1998) found that this procedure significantly increased the comprehension of those students who were taught to use the strategy. In addition, teachers have reported that they like to use this technique and find that it really helps students enhance their reading skills (Klingner & Vaughn, 1998).

Before Reading

1. Preview

   a. Brainstorm: What do we already know about the topic?

   b. Predict: What do we think we will learn about the topic when we read the passage? Find clues in the title, subheadings, or pictures about what you will learn. Skim the text for key words that might give you hints.

During Reading

2. Click and Clunk

   a. Were there any parts that were hard to understand (clunks)?

   b. How can we fix the clunks? Use fix-up strategies:

    • Reread the sentence and look for key ideas to help you understand the word.

    • Reread the sentence with the clunk and the sentences before or after the clunk looking for clues.

    • Look for a prefix or suffix in the word.

    • Break the word apart and look for smaller words.

3. Get the Gist

   a. What is the most important person, place, or thing?

   b. What is the most important idea about the person, place, or thing?

After Reading

4. Wrap Up

   a. Ask questions: What questions would show we understand the most important information? What are the answers to those questions?

   b. Review: What did we learn?

FIGURE 7.3

Collaborative Strategic Reading Approach

Source: Vaughn, S., & Klingner, J. K. (1999). Teaching reading comprehension through collaborative strategic reading. *Intervention in School and Clinic, 34,* 284–292, and Klingner, J. K., & Vaughn, S. (1998). Using collaborative strategic reading. *Teaching Exceptional Children, 30,* 32–43.

Graphic Organizers

Another widely used and often successful approach to enhancing comprehension of content-area texts is the use of graphic (or visual) organizers. Graphic organizers help students recognize the structure within expository text and use this structure to enhance recall. In addition, they provide students with a visual (as well as verbal) representation of text.

Graphic organizers come in many different forms (Figure 7.4), but four types that are commonly used with secondary-level, content-area texts are:

- Descriptive/thematic: main idea–subordinate ideas
- Sequential/episodic: use where sequence is important

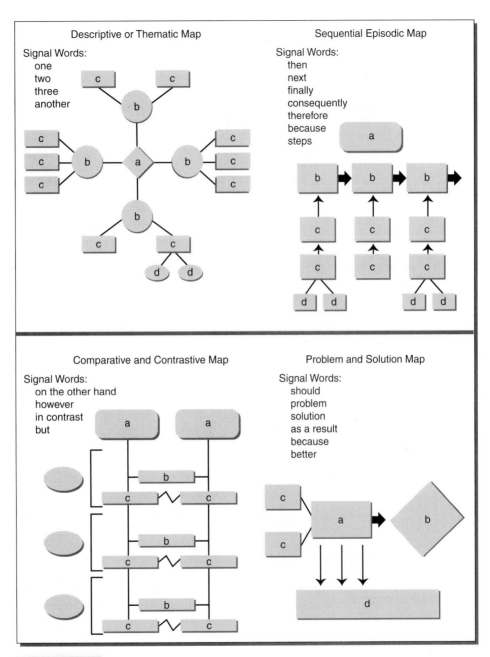

FIGURE 7.4

Four Types of Graphic Organizers

Source: Grossen, B., & Carnine, D. (1992). Translating research on text structure into classroom practice. *Teaching Exceptional Children, 24,* 48–53.

- Compare/contrast: look for similarities/differences
- Problem/solution: cause/effect, not sequential (Grossen & Carnine, 1992)

The selection of which graphic organizer to use should be based on the content of the text. In other words, for a text that presents a cause (for example, the causes of the Civil War in the United States) and effect (the war) a cause/effect organizer may be the most effective graphic organizer. Graphic organizers can be used prior to reading as a way of orienting the reader to the text, during reading as a means of monitoring comprehension during reading, or for recall after reading. Teachers can provide the graphic organizer or students can be taught to recognize the text structure and select the appropriate organizer.

Studies that have examined the use of graphic organizers have generally found that they can be an effective way of enhancing comprehension of content-area texts both for typically developing students and for students with reading and learning disabilities (Griffin & Tulbert, 1995). For example, one study found that when secondary-level, regular-education teachers used concept diagrams with their students, both students with learning disabilities and nondisabled students improved their performance on class tests (Bulgren, Schumaker, & Deshler, 1988). Similar findings were reported by Horton, Lovitt, and Bergerud (1990) when they studied the use of graphic organizers with middle and high school students. In their study, students with learning disabilities as well as remedial students and regular education students performed best on assessments of content knowledge when they used graphic organizers.

The research and practice with learning strategies and graphic organizers suggests that these techniques can be successfully used to enhance the reading of content-area texts with all secondary-level students. Although some of these methods do take additional time to implement, they may be well worth the outcome of improved performance.

Using Technology

As more and more books, both fiction and nonfiction, become available in digital formats, they open up new possibilities for the enhancement of literacy among secondary-age students. For many students, the novelty of reading from the computer may enhance their motivation and attention. In addition, as Anderson–Inman and Horney (1997) note, electronic books (e-books) have the advantage of being:

- **Searchable:** A key word or phrase can be located by entering the word into the program's "find" or "search" function. This feature is especially helpful when a student is researching a topic and looking for references to the topic.
- **Modifiable:** The book can be changed to meet the needs and abilities of the student. In many cases, the font size and appearance can be changed. In some programs, the text can be presented in another language.
- **Enhancable:** Features that enhance and support reading are often built into the software. Examples include definitions, pronunciation, and links to additional information.

Technology is a tool that can be used to enhance literacy experiences. It rarely solves all of the problems encountered with secondary-level reading. However, the emerging technologies of CD-ROM and web-based digital books provide the teacher with more options for modifying instruction for students. In addition, they increase the potential for participation for all students in the independent reading and research activities expected at the secondary level.

Advanced Writing Skills

Students at the secondary level are expected to have advanced writing skills that will enable them to meet the varied expectations for writing at that level. Among the writing activities that secondary-level students may be required to engage in are:

- *Descriptive writing:* writing that includes descriptions about the specific behavior of people, interesting behaviors, and the setting in which events occurred. Examples include journals, poems, and stories.
- *Persuasive writing:* writing in which students must build arguments by presenting a position that is supported by examples. Essays and editorials are examples of persuasive writing.
- *Expository writing:* writing that is intended to inform the reader about a topic. Research reports are an example of expository writing.
- *Narrative writing:* writing that involves the creation of a story. Students are expected to include characters and setting as well as a story structure (Cooter & Flynt, 1996).

In order to be able to successfully complete these and other writing activities, secondary-level students must have a range of writing skills, including the ability to:

- Use excellent mechanical skills for writing (handwriting, spelling, punctuation)
- Formulate an argument and construct sound reasoning to support the position
- Recognize and use story structure to guide the development of a story
- Write for a variety of audiences using a variety of styles
- Write quickly when necessary (e.g., during note taking and tests)
- Engage in independent research
- Use technology such as word-processing programs

How are secondary-level students doing in acquiring these skills? The 1998 National Assessment of Education Progress (NAEP) reported that, although 84% of 8th graders and 74% of 12th graders performed at or above the basic level of writing achievement, only 27 and 22% respectively performed at or above the proficient level. In other words, it appears that most secondary-level students have achieved enough writing skills to accomplish the basic tasks of secondary schooling, but a considerably smaller number have advanced skills. One of the challenges of secondary-level writing instruction is to help more students move to a proficient level of writing. And what about the students who have not even achieved the basic level of writing skills? What can be done to help them? This is another challenge for secondary-level education.

In recent years writing instruction has shifted from an emphasis on mechanical and structural aspects of writing to focusing on cognitive aspects of writing. The current approach emphasizes an understanding of the thought processes that writers use as they write and the development of these thought processes to enhance writing.

The "process" approach to writing instruction has generally been found to be an effective way of getting students to take more time in planning and editing their writing. However, it can be difficult to implement this approach at the secondary level due to the extensive time demands of this approach. One teacher put it this way:

> I felt success with the process approach almost immediately, but when I attempted to adapt it to writing in my 11th-grade English classroom, where literature, vocabulary, and grammar units had to be covered in addition to composition, I found that the constraints of time and curriculum made the change much more difficult (Carney, 1996, p. 28).

Despite the acknowledged difficulties of making the process approach to writing work at the secondary level, this teacher found ways to make it work. The first thing she did was to give students more ownership over their writing. Although certain types of writing were required by the curriculum (e.g., a character analysis), students could pick the character and the theme of their composition. A second compromise was to require that drafts be completed by certain dates. Although the process approach to writing emphasizes allowing individuals to work at their own pace, Carney realized that some students were not writing any draft other than the final one. Writing multiple drafts has been found to be one of the most important factors in improving writing (U.S. Department of Education, 1999). By developing some reasonable compromises, this teacher was able to use the process approach to writing despite the demands of the secondary-level curriculum.

One of the special challenges of writing at the secondary level is writing across the curriculum. There are opportunities in every subject area for students to apply and develop their writing skills. Obviously, classes such as English and social studies provide opportunities for many writing activities, but so do science and math classes. In fact, "mathematics as communication" is one of the curriculum standards recommended by the National Council of Teachers of Mathematics. Some of the ways that content-area teachers can enhance writing in their classes include:

- Using *journals* in which students reflect on their observations (e.g., in science) or write about their anxieties (e.g., math) (Borasi & Rose, 1989)
- Responding to *writing prompts* in which students respond to a question or problem posed by the teacher (Miller & England, 1989) (Box 7.3)
- Using *class summaries* in which students write a paragraph in which they describe what they have learned in class that day

▌Box 7.3

EXAMPLE OF A WRITING PROMPT AND RESPONSE

Prompt: Remember yesterday when you learned how to write a polynomial? Imagine that you are writing a note to your best friend to explain how to do that. Write your note, assuming that your friend really wants to know how to factor a polynomial and that he or she must rely on you for a complete explanation.

Response: One student responded: Factor $6^2b + 7b$. First find the number that could go into both the number 6 and 7. And there is no number that goes into 6 or 7 so now go to the letter. Second find the letter that is the lowest and the letter is "b" because b^2 is higher than b subtract b from b^2 and the letter is b because b^2 is higher than b subtract b from b^2 and the answer is b so put 6b next because $6b + b = 6^2b$. Then put 7 because $7 + b = 7b$ and work out to check the problem.

Source: Miller, L. D. (1991). Writing to learn mathematics. *Mathematics Teacher, 84,* 516–521.

Although writing across the curriculum presents many opportunities for secondary-level students to practice their writing skills, many teachers feel that they do not have the time to include writing in their already crowded curriculum. Miller (1991) suggests giving writing assignments to only one class at a time so as not to become overwhelmed with having to read hundreds of compositions, keeping writing time brief and focused (five minutes may be sufficient), and trying to make the writing assignment relate to the lesson.

All students, including those with significant writing difficulties, can benefit from the use of technology to enhance writing. There is an increasing variety of technological aids and approaches to assist students in writing. Of course, word processing can be useful in enhancing writing skills. However, research has found that word processing is most effective when the technology is combined with effective writing instruction (MacArthur, Graham, & Schwartz, 1993). Spellcheckers can also be useful aids in writing, although spellchecking programs vary in their ability to identify errors, and users must still be able to choose correctly spelled words from a list of options. Grammar and style checkers have similar advantages and limitations.

Two newer technologies that hold a lot of promise for enhancing writing are dictation programs and multimedia. Speech recognition programs such as *Naturally Speaking* from Dragon Systems and *ViaVoice* from IBM allow the user to speak rather than type. These can be a great help for students with physical disabilities as well as for students with milder eye–hand coordination difficulties. Multimedia programs can incorporate pictures, video, sound, and text into a full-featured presentation. For students with limited writing skills, the opportunity to support their writing with other media may significantly enhance their presentation.

▪▪ SUMMARY

Literacy development does not end in the elementary grades. Middle and high school students are continuing to develop both spoken and written language skills. In addition, the secondary-level curriculum provides numerous opportunities as well as high expectation for literacy. Students are expected to have the necessary written language skills to be successful at the secondary level. However, for those students who lack these skills there is a variety of strategies that can be used to enhance their performance.

▪▪ Linkages

1. What are some of the challenges faced by students in secondary schools in regard to literacy?
2. Describe developments in language skills in two domains of language that typically occur in the adolescent years.
3. Develop your own strategy for word identification that could be used by students at the secondary level.
4. What is self-questioning? Why could it be an effective strategy for enhancing the comprehension of students at the secondary level?
5. Describe the collaborative strategic reading approach to recall of text. How does it differ from gist recall?

6. Develop a graphic organizer for a section of this (or another) text book. Identify the type of organizer you used.
7. How could newer technologies be used to enhance the writing of secondary-level students?

On the Web

Dragon Systems
    www.dragonsys.com
Information about voice recognition software from Dragon Systems, Inc.

IBM
    www.ibm.com
Information about the *ViaVoice* voice recognition system

U.S. Office of Elementary and Secondary Education
    www.ed.gov/offices/OESE

National Council of Teachers of English
    www.ncte.org
Includes links to many useful sites for secondary literacy.

References

Anderson, R. C., & Pearson, P. D. (1984). A schema-theoretic view of basic processes in reading. In P. D. Pearson (Ed.), *Handbook of reading research* (pp. 255–292). New York: Longman.

Anderson–Inman, L., & Horney, M. (1997). Electronic books for secondary students. *Journal of Adolescent & Adult Literacy, 40*, 486–491.

Anglin, J. (1993). Vocabulary development: A morphological analysis. *Monographs of the Society for Research in Child Development*, 58 (10), Serial No. 238.

Bean, T. W., & Steenwyk, F. L. (1984). The effect of three forms of summarization instruction on sixth graders' summary writing and comprehension. *Journal of Reading Behavior, 16*, 297–306.

Bintz, W. P. (1993). Resistant readers in secondary education: Some insights and implications. *Journal of Reading, 36*, 604–615.

Borasi, R., & Rose, B. J. (1989). Journal writing and mathematics instruction. *Educational Studies in Mathematics, 20*, 347–365.

Bos, C. S., & Anders, P. L. (1990). Effects of interactive vocabulary instruction on the vocabulary learning and reading comprehension of junior high learning disabled students. *Learning Disability Quarterly, 13*, 31–42.

Bulgren, J., Schumaker, J. B., & Deshler, D. D. (1988). Effectiveness of a concept teaching routine in enhancing the performance of LD students in secondary-level mainstream classes. *Learning Disability Quarterly, 11*, 3–17.

Carney, B. (1996). Process writing and the secondary school, reality: A compromise. *The English Journal, 85*, 28–35.

Carter, C. J., & Klotz, J. (1991). What every principal should know about content area reading. *NASSP Bulletin, 75*, 97–105.

Ciborowski, J. (1995). Using textbooks with students who cannot read them. *Remedial and Special Education, 16*, 91–101.

Cooter, R. B., & Flynt, E. S. (1996). *Teaching reading in the content areas: Developing content literacy for all students.* Upper Saddle River, NJ: Merrill/Prentice Hall.

Dole, J. A., Brown, K. J., & Trathen, W. (1996). The effects of strategy instruction on the comprehension performance of at-risk students. *Reading Research Quarterly, 31*, 62–88.

Graves, M. F., Cooke, C. L., & Laberge, M. J. (1983). Effects of previewing difficult short stories on low ability junior high school students' comprehension, recall, and attitudes. *Reading Research Quarterly, 18,* 262–276.

Griffin, C. C., & Tulbert, B. L. (1995). The effect of graphic organizers on students' comprehension and recall of expository text: A review of the research and implications for practice. *Reading and Writing Quarterly, 11,* 73–88.

Grossen, B., & Carnine, D. (1992). Translating research on text structure into classroom practice. *Teaching Exceptional Children, 24,* 48–53.

Horton, S. V., Lovitt, T. C., & Bergerud, D. (1990). The effectiveness of graphic organizers for three classifications of secondary students in content area classes. *Journal of Learning Disabilities, 23,* 12–22.

Katims, D. S., & Harris, S. (1997). Improving the reading comprehension of middle school students in inclusive classrooms. *Journal of Adolescent and Adult Literacy, 41,* 116–123.

King-Sears, M. E., Mercer, C. D., & Sindelar, P. T. (1992). Toward independence with keyword mnemonics: A strategy for science vocabulary instruction. *Remedial and Special Education, 13,* 22–33.

Klingner, J. K., & Vaughn, S. (1998). Using collaborative strategic reading. *Teaching Exceptional Children, 30,* 32–43.

Klingner, J. K., Vaughn, S., & Schumm, J. S. (1998). Collaborative strategic reading during social studies in heterogeneous fourth grade classrooms. *The Elementary School Journal, 99,* 3–22.

Lenz, B. K., & Hughes, C. A. (1990). A word identification strategy for adolescents with learning disabilities. *Journal of Learning Disabilities, 23,* 149–158.

Ley, T. C., Schaer, B. B., & Dismukes, B. W. (1994). Longitudinal study of the reading attitudes and behaviors of middle school students. *Reading Psychology, 15,* 11–38.

Loban, W. (1976). *Language development: Kindergarten through grade twelve.* Urbana, IL: National Council of Teachers of English.

MacArthur, C. A., Graham, S., & Schwartz, S. S. (1993). Integrating word processing and strategy instruction into a process approach to writing. *School Psychology Review, 22,* 671–681.

Mastroprieri, M. A., Scruggs, T. E., Bakken, J. P., & Whedon, C. (1996). Reading comprehension: A synthesis of research in learning disabilities. In T. E. Scruggs & M. A. Mastroprieri (Eds.), *Advances in learning and behavioral disabilities* (Vol. 10, pp. 277–303). Greenwich, CT: JAI.

Menyuk, P. (1995). Language development and education. *Journal of Education, 177,* 39–62.

Miller, L. D. (1991). Writing to learn mathematics. *Mathematics Teacher, 84,* 516–521.

Miller, L. D., & England, D. A. (1989). Writing to learn algebra. *School Science and Mathematics, 89,* 299–312.

Nippold, M. A. (1993). Developmental markers in adolescent language: Syntax, semantics, and pragmatics. *Language, Speech, and Hearing Services in Schools, 24,* 21–28.

Nippold, M. A. (1995). Language norms in school-age children and adolescents: An introduction. *Language, Speech, and Hearing Services in Schools, 26,* 307–308.

Nippold, M. A., & Martin, S. T. (1989). Idiom interpretation in isolation versus context: A developmental study with adolescents. *Journal of Speech and Hearing Research, 32,* 59–66.

Norris, J. (1995). Expanding language norms for school-age children and adolescents: Is it pragmatic? *Language, Speech, and Hearing Services in Schools, 26,* 342–352.

O'Brien, D. G., Stewert, R. A., & Moje, E. B. (1995). Why content literacy is difficult to infuse into the secondary school: Complexities of curriculum, pedagogy, and school culture. *Reading Research Quarterly, 30,* 442–463.

Rinehart, S. D., Stahl, S. A., & Erickson, L. G. (1986). Some effects of summarization training on reading and studying. *Reading Research Quarterly, 21,* 422–436.

Schumaker, J. B., Deshler, D. D., Nolan, S. M., & Alley, G. R. (1994). *The self-questioning strategy.* Lawrence: University of Kansas.

Swanson, P. N., & De La Paz, S. (1998). Teaching effective comprehension strategies to students with learning and reading disabilities. *Intervention in School and Clinic, 33,* 209–218.

Taylor, B. W., & Beach, R. W. (1984). The effects of text structure instruction on middle-grade students' comprehension and production of expository text. *Reading Research Quarterly, 19,* 134–146.

Thornburg, H. D. (1982). *Development in adolescence* (2nd ed.). Monterey, CA: Brooks-Cole.

U.S. Department of Education. Office of Educational Research and Improvement. National Center for Educational Statistics. (1999). *The NAEP 1998 Reading Report Card for the Nation and the States,* NCES 1999–500, by P. L. Donahue, K. E. Voelkl, J. R. Campbell, & J. Mazzeo. Washington, DC.

Vacca, R. T. (1997). The benign neglect of adolescent literacy. *Reading Today, 14*(3), 3.

Vacca, R. T. (1998). Let's not marginalize adolescent literacy. *Journal of Adolescent and Adult Literacy, 41,* 604–609.

Vaughn, S., & Klingner, J. K. (1999). Teaching reading comprehension through collaborative strategic reading. *Intervention in School and Clinic, 34,* 284–292.

Wiig, E. H. (1982). Language disabilities in school-age children and youth. In G. H. Shames & E. H. Wiig (Eds.), *Human communication disorders: An introduction* (2nd ed., pp. 331–379). New York: Merrill/Macmillan.

Wong, B. Y. L., & Jones, W. (1982). Increasing metacomprehension in learning disabled and normally achieving students through self-questioning training. *Learning Disability Quarterly, 5,* 228–239.

CHAPTER 8

Specialized Approaches for Literacy Difficulties

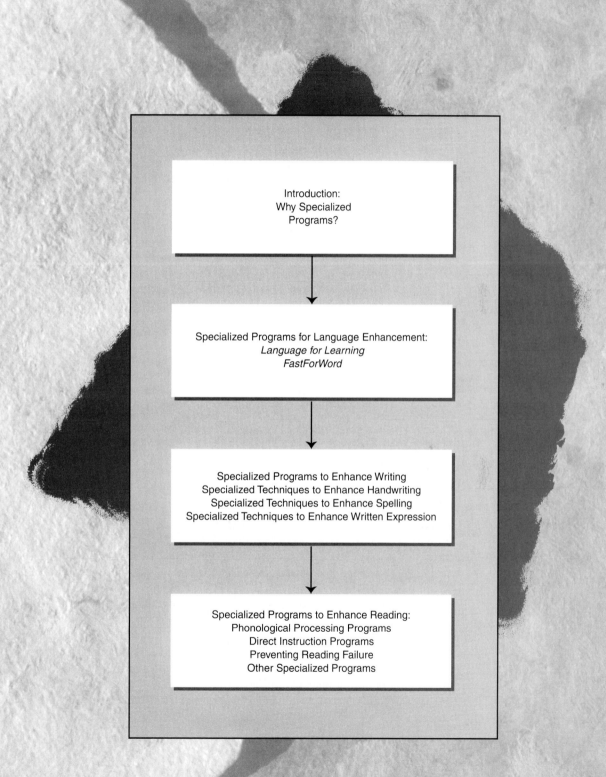

Introduction:
Why Specialized
Programs?

Specialized Programs for Language Enhancement:
Language for Learning
FastForWord

Specialized Programs to Enhance Writing
Specialized Techniques to Enhance Handwriting
Specialized Techniques to Enhance Spelling
Specialized Techniques to Enhance Written Expression

Specialized Programs to Enhance Reading:
Phonological Processing Programs
Direct Instruction Programs
Preventing Reading Failure
Other Specialized Programs

Case Studies

Tamika   Tamika is a 6-year-old, African-American female. Tamika has a history of language difficulties in schools. She is very quiet and rarely talks. When asked a direct question by her teacher, Tamika may lower her head and mumble a response or give no response at all. Tamika appears to withdraw from interaction both with adults and with her same-age peers. Assessment has revealed no significant disabilities that may be contributing to Tamika's difficulties. She appears to be intact in both motor and cognitive development. Tamika's mother says that her daughter has no problem talking to her at home. She acknowledges that Tamika is shy but does not think that she has a serious problem. Tamika has been receiving individual speech therapy once a week for a year. The speech therapist has been trying to help Tamika with vocal production and producing longer utterances. Recently Tamika has been placed in the *DISTAR Language Program* to enhance her language skills. Tamika receives instruction in a small group from a resource teacher.

Donald   Donald is an 8-year-old student in third grade. Donald's teachers have reported that he has significant difficulty with writing. Donald's written work tends to be short, with few ideas expressed. Donald actively expresses his dislike of writing, often refusing to write more than a few words. Donald writes slowly and appears to have trouble organizing his thoughts. Donald has been identified as having attention deficit disorder (ADD). His reading skills are on grade level, although comprehension appears to be ahead of word attack skills. Recently, Donald's class has been working with the *Writing-to-Read* program. Donald seems to like this program because it uses computers. His writing is longer with more ideas expressed and more complete sentences.

Sharon   Sharon is a 7-year-old student in first grade. Since entering kindergarten, Sharon has had difficulty acquiring reading skills. Her kindergarten teacher noticed that Sharon sometimes "seemed lost" during reading activities. She recognized fewer letters and words than other children and showed less interest in reading. These problems have continued in first grade. Sharon seems to have particular difficulty identifying sound-symbol relationships. That is, she has had a hard time learning to relate the sounds of English to the letters that represent them. As a result, she has a lot of difficulty reading individual words. Sharon has been selected to participate in the *Reading Recovery* program at her school. Sharon receives individualized, supplemental reading instruction for 30 minutes a day, 5 days a week from a certified "reading recovery" teacher. It is hoped that Sharon will develop sufficient reading skills so that she can remain in the regular classroom and catch up to her peers in reading.

▮▮ INTRODUCTION: WHY SPECIALIZED PROGRAMS?

Despite the best efforts of parents and teachers, some children experience significant difficultly acquiring literacy skills. Failure to develop adequate literacy, especially reading skills, is a cause for great concern. The number of children with significant reading difficulties has been estimated to range from approximately 40% (Grossen, 1997) to one in six (or somewhat less than 20%) of the school-age population (Kameenui, 1996). Putting aside, for the moment, the debate about what constitutes a reading disorder, it seems clear that a significant number of children experience substantial difficulty acquiring early literacy skills.

Fortunately, a number of specialized, intensive approaches to the improvement of literacy skills have been developed. Although most of these programs have focused on the enhancement of reading, we will also examine some programs designed to enhance language and writing skills. We will limit our review to programs that can be used with a broad range of children rather than to a specific population (e.g., students with severe disabilities). We will try to identify those programs that have been found to be successful and point out those for which there is little research support. Some of the features that characterize specialized programs are:

- Intensive instruction and practice on a specific skill or set of skills
- Designed for individuals or small groups rather than whole classes
- Require some preparation (sometimes extensive) for the teacher
- Usually not closely linked to regular education curriculum

▮▮ SPECIALIZED PROGRAMS FOR LANGUAGE ENHANCEMENT

Programs to enhance children's language learning take many forms. Some of these are discussed elsewhere in this book. "Incidental teaching" approaches (Chapter 9) utilize all of the individuals with whom the child comes in contact and the naturalistic opportunities that arise throughout the child's day as the basis for language instruction. Although usually used with children with significant language-learning difficulties, these programs can be useful for all children. On the other hand, a program such as the picture exchange communication system (PECS) has been designed for and used with children with significant developmental disabilities (e.g., autism).

In general, language enhancement programs are designed to pick up where normal language acquisition has left off. In other words, either because the natural language environment has failed to provide the child with sufficient opportunities to learn language or because the child has not been able to benefit from the opportunities that are available, something more has to be done. Language enhancement programs provide more structured activities to teach specific language skills. There are many programs available to enhance language skills (Table 8.1). We will review only a few of the most widely used programs.

TABLE 8.1 Commercial Programs for Language Enhancement

Program (Authors/Publishers)	Description
Auditory Memory for Language (language-delayed or disordered children) (K. Stefanakos & R. Prater, Austin, TX: Pro-Ed)	Sequenced tests and lesson plans to teach auditory memory
Auditory Perception Training (primary, intermediate) (R. Willette, I. Peckins, & B. Galofaro. Allen, TX: DLM Teaching Resources)	Audiocassettes and spirit masters to develop auditory memory, motor, figure-ground discrimination, and imagery skills
Auditory Processing in Action (APA)(K-6) (East Moline, IL: LinguiSystems)	Classroom and individual activities for teaching listening skills
Basic Concept Stories: Spatial Concepts, Comparatives and Opposites (regular and special ed., preschool to primary) (Allen, TX: DLM Teaching Resources)	Pictures accompanied by stories, photos, activities, and questions as basis for program
Clark Early Language Program (language and hearing impaired from CA 2 1/2 to adult) (C. R. Clark & D. F. Moores, Allen, TX: DLM Teaching Resources)	Teaches receptive and expressive language with rebuses, oral language, and an optional sign language component
CLAS: Classroom Listening and Speaking (K-2, 3-4) (L. Plourde, Tucson, AZ: Communication Skill Builders)	Activities for vocabulary, concepts, listening, giving, and following directions, memory, describing, etc.
Communication Training Program (CTP) Levels 1, 2, and 3 (preschool) (C. L. Waryas & K. Stremel-Campbell, Allen, TX: DLM Teaching Resources)	Oral communication from prelanguage through develement and redmediation of three- and four-word utterances
Communication Workshop (LD adolescents) (East Moline, IL: LinguiSystems)	Exercises in workbook and role-playing form
Communicative Competence: A Functional-Pragmatic Approach to Language Therapy (CA 6-adult) (C. S. Simon, Tucson, AZ: Communication Skill Builders)	Includes theoretical monograph, teaching manual, filmstrips, photo-diagram book, stimulus cards, and spinner boards for developing communication skills
Comprehensive Language Program (CLP) (MA 0 months-5 years, handicapped) (Bensenville, IL: Scholastic Testing Service)	Lesson plans for teaching low-functioning students attending, identifying, matching, following directions, etc.
Concepts for Communicatin (CFC) (elementary) (Allen, TX: DLM Teaching Resources)	Manuals, cassettes, picture books, games for teaching receptive and expressive language
Conversations: Language Intervention for Adolescents (adolescents) (B. Hoskins, Allen, TX: DLM Teaching Resources)	Utilizes natural conversation as a means of language remediation
Developing Understanding of Self and Others (DUSO): Play Kit and Manual (elementary) (D. Dinkmeyer, Circle Pines, MN: American Guidance Service)	Exercises for enhancing success in interpersonal communication; includes filmstrips, puppets, manual

Program (Authors/Publishers)	Description
Development of Functional Communication Competencies (K-6, 7-12) (B. S. Wood, Urbana, IL: Clearinghouse on Reading and Communication Skills)	Group-based regular classroom activities for elementary and secondary levels; designed to increase communicative options relative to different participants, settings, topics, and purposes
Developmental Communication Curriculum (DCC) (developmental ages 1-5) (San Antonio, TX: Psychological Corp.)	Activities for developing form, content, and function in prelinguistic, symbolic, and complex symbolic relationships
Developmental Syntax Program (Coughran-Liles Syntax Program) (CA 3-10) (L. Coughran & B.V. Liles. Allen, TX: DLM Teaching Resources)	Exercises for syntactic development and remediation
DISTAR I, II, III (K-8) (S. Engleman & J. Osborn. Chicago: Science Research Associates)	Presentation books, workbooks, behavioral objectives, mastery tests
Early Learning and Language Activities (ELLA) (birth-3 years) (M. B. Karnes. Benserville, IL: Scholastic Testing Service)	Activities for early language development in form, content, and use—preverbal, first words, and constructions
FILE (CA 9-16) (East Moline, IL: LinguiSystems)	600 cards of language exercises in semantics, syntax and morphology, pragmatics
Fokes Sentence Builder, Fokes Sentence Builder Expansion (elementary) (J. Fokes. Allen, TX: DLM Teaching Resouces)	Grammatical approach to sentence building; expansion permits building of additional sentences
Follow Me (K-3) (East Moline, IL: LinguiSystems)	Worksheets and lessons for teaching following directions and other listening skills
Following Directions Series (FDS) (grades 2-4) (Chatsworth, CA: Opportunities for Learning)	Spirit master activities for teaching listening skills
Functional Speech and Language Training for the Severely Handicapped (severely handicapped children and adults) (D. Guess, W. Sailor, & D. M. Baer. Austin, TX: Pro-Ed)	Behavioral management approach to language training for persons with autism, brain damage, severe impairment
Grammar for Teens (CA 10-18) (East Moline, IL: LinguiSystems)	Workbooks for teaching grammar, syntax
Great Beginnings for Early Language Learning (Language, speech, and developmentally delayed students) (L. Levine. Tucson, AZ: Communication Skill Builders)	Photographs, pictures, and manipulatives for teaching nouns, concept, verbs, prepositions, and associations
Helm Elicited Language Program for Syntax Stimulation (adolescents and adults) (N. Helm-Estabrooks. Austin, TX: Pro-Ed)	Practice provided on 11 sentence types sequenced in order of difficulty

TABLE 8.1   Continued

Program (Authors/Publishers)	Description
HELP 3 (CA 6-adult) (East Moline, IL: LinguiSystems)	Workbook of exercises for teaching pragmatic skills
Language Big Box (primary) (Allen, TX: DLM Teaching Resources)	Activities for teaching associations, categorizing, auditory discrimination, sequencing, etc.; includes cards, puppet, picture books
Language Facilitation: A Complete Cognitive Therapy Program (preschool, elementary) (J. M. Cimorell Strong. Austin, TX: Pro-Ed)	Plagetian-based language development program for language-impaired children; more than 400 activities to teach syntactic, semantic, and pragmatic aspects of language
Let's Talk for Children (CA 4-9) (E. H. Wiig & C. Bray. Columbus, OH: Charles E. Merrill Publishing)	Communication cards for modeling, role playing, activities with puppets, etc.
Let's Talk: Intermediate Level (CA 10–young adult, handicapped) (E. H. Wiig & C. Bray. Columbus, OH: Charles E. Merrill Publishing)	Communication activities to develop pragmatic functions for ritualizing, informing, controlling, and feeling
Listening to Go (CA 4-8) (East Moline, IL: LinguiSystems)	Worksheet activities for teaching listening skills
Listening to the World (K-2) (Circle Pines, MN: American Guidance Service)	Storybook, games, markers, cards, exercises, etc., to develop awareness of sounds of music, speech, and the environment
Magic of Sentence Sense: Activities of Syntax Practice (CA 7-12, language delayed, learning disabled). (E. B. Krassowski. Tucson, AZ: Communication Skill Builders)	Exercises for analyzing and changing language structures. From simple to complex
Monterey Language Program (Programmed Conditioning for Language) (elementary) (B. B. Gray & B. P. Ryan. Palo Alto, CA: Monterey Learning Systems)	Programmed approach to teaching expressive language
PALS: Pragmatic Activities in Language and Speech (adolescents) (B. X. Davis. Austin, TX: Pro-Ed)	Pragmatic language skills developed through pantomiming, role playing, memo writing, telephoning job interviewing, etc.
Peabody Language Development Kits—Levels P, 1, 2, 3 (CA 4-8) (L. M. Dunn, J. O. Smith, & K. B. Horton. Circle Pines, MN: American Guidance Service)	Lesson cards, teacher's manuals, posters, picture cards, puppets, audiocassettes, etc., for general language development stimulation
PEP: Spoken Language Enhancement Program, Volumes I-IV (elementary, language-delayed) (Austin, TX: Pro-Ed)	34 audiocassettes for teaching speech sound discrimination, following directions, improving listening skills, and chunking words, numbers, and phrases

PLA-ACT (CA 6-12, second-grade reading level) (San Antonio, TX: Psychological Corp.)	12 script adaptations of familiar stories and fairy tales for play acting
Program for the Acquisition of Language with the Severely Impaired (PALS) (all ages) (San Antonio, TX: Psychological Corp.)	Training activities for development of functional language with severely impaired persons at the presymbolic and symbolic levels
Question the Direction (K-6) (East Moline, IL: LinguiSystems)	Exercises for teaching careful listening and questioning of unclear or incomplete directions
Ready, Set, Grammar! (CA 4-10) (East Moline, IL: LinguiSystems)	Picture pages for early language structures
Resource of Activities for Peer Pragmatics (RAPP) (CA 9-18) (East Moline, IL: LinguiSystems)	Activities for developing social language, interpersonal communication, and communicative confidence
Semantic Fitness (CA 13-adult) (East Moline, IL: LinguiSystems)	Vocabulary worksheets
Semantics for Teens (CA 10-18) (East Moline, IL: LinguiSystems)	Workbooks for teaching semantics, vocabulary
Sourcebook Series: A Sourcebook of Pragmatic Activities (K-6); Sourcebook of Adolescent Pragmatic Activities (grades 7-12 and ESL); Sourcebook of Remediating Language (CA 2-14) (A. J. Glaser, E. B. Johnston, & B. D. Weinrich. Tucson, AZ: Communication Skill Builders)	Instructional objectives and activities for improving communication skills through a variety of age-appropriate pragmatic activities
Syntax Development: A Generative Grammar Approach to Language Development (M. S. Wilson. Cambridge, MA: Education Publishing Service)	Workbooks and grammar activities
Syntax Flip Books (nonreaders, preschoolers) (D. Phelps-Terasaki & T. Phelps-Gunn. Austin, TX: Pro-Ed)	Stimulus pictures representing basic sentence elements used to elicit key grammatic and semantic structures
Syntax of Kindergarten and Elementary School Children (elementary) (R. C. O'Donnell, W. J. Griffin, & R. C. Morris. Urbana, IL: National Council of Teachers of English)	Workbooks and activity sheets
TOTAL: Teacher Organized Training for the Acquisition of Language (6 months and up, handicapped) (B. Witt & J. Boose)	Games, lesson plans, songbook, art projects, storybooks, photographs, pictures, signed English illustrations, etc., for teaching language skills
WORD KIT (CA 7-12) (East Moline, IL: LinguiSystems)	Workbook, games, pictures for teaching vocabulary
Words, Expressions and Contexts (CA 9-adult) (San Antonio, TX: Psychological Corp.)	Activities for teaching figurative language to adolescents and young adults

Source: Hammill, D., & Bartel, N. (1990). *Teaching Students with Learning and Behavior Problems* (5th. ed., pp. 81–84). Boston: Allyn & Bacon.

Language for Learning Program

The *Language for Learning* program (Science Research Associates) is the latest version of the *DISTAR Language Program. Language for Learning* is a classroom-based, highly structured program of lessons designed to teach specific language skills to children who are experiencing delays in the acquisition of language skills. The publisher states that the program includes instruction in:

- Vocabulary
- Knowledge of "little" (but important) words such as first, next, between, who, what, where
- The use of sentence forms to ask and answer questions and to follow instructions
- The acquisition of important background information and world knowledge
- How to figure out the logical aspects of language, such as classification and "if–then" reasoning

Each lesson in the *Language for Learning* program is completely scripted so the teacher merely has to read and follow the directions (Figure 8.1). Teachers are encouraged to use hand signals to cue the children as to when to listen and when to respond. Reinforcement for correct responding and error correction procedures are also included.

The *Language for Learning* program is solidly based in principles of direct instruction. This instructional model has been frequently demonstrated to be an effective way of teaching. Therefore, there is reason to believe that the program can be effective. However, language is a highly complex process that is more than just the sum of a number of discrete steps. For this reason, it is unclear whether the *Language for Learning* program is effective in enhancing overall language use.

FastForWord

One of the newest, most innovative, and most controversial programs for the enhancement of language skills is the *FastForWord* program (distributed by Scientific Learning Corporation). *FastForWord* is a computer-based program designed to build language skills in individuals with language-learning difficulties. The program is designed for children between kindergarten age and 12 years old who have a wide range of language-learning difficulties (Veale, 1999). Scientific Learning Corporation claims that the program has been shown to "improve auditory processing speed, working memory, serial order processing, phonological awareness, listening comprehension, syntax, and morphology" (Scientific Learning Corporation, 2000).

The *FastForWord* program consists of seven computer games that are designed to teach specific language skills. Children play five computer games a day for a total of 100 minutes. The computer constantly monitors their success, adjusting the difficulty level upward or downward as necessary. Children progress through five levels on each of the seven games. According to Scientific Learning Corporation, children who use the program five days a week generally reach the criteria for program completion within six weeks, making one- to two-year gains in language skills (Scientific Learning Corporation, 2000).

One of the unique (and controversial) aspects of *FastForWord* is that at the first level of each game acoustic input is modified. That is, the sounds that the child hears are digitally manipulated to increase the duration and the intensity of the sound. It is

EXERCISE 1   Actions—Pronouns

1. I'm going to ask two children to do an action.

   a. (Ask two children to stand up.) Everybody, what are they doing? (Signal.) *Standing up.*
   Say the whole thing about what they are doing. (Signal.) *They are standing up.*

   b. (Ask the two children to sit down.) Everybody, what are they doing? (Signal.) *Sitting down.*
   Say the whole thing about what they are doing. (Signal.) *They are sitting down.*

   c. (Repeat steps a and b until all children's responses are firm.)

2. Now we're all going to do that.

   a. Everybody, let's all stand up. (Signal. Stand up with the children.)

   b. Everybody, what are you doing? (Signal.) *Standing up.*
   Say the whole thing. (Signal.) *I am standing up.*

   c. What are we doing? (Signal.) *Standing up.* Say the whole thing. (Signal.) *We are standing up.*

   d. What am I doing? (Signal.) *Standing up.* Say the whole thing. (Signal.) *You are standing up.*

3. (Point to a boy.) Look at him.

   a. What is he doing? (Signal.) *Standing up.*

   b. Say the whole thing. (Signal.) *He is standing up.*

4. (Point to a girl.) Look at her.

   a. What is she doing? (Signal.) *Standing up.*

   b. Say the whole thing. (Signal.) *She is standing up.*

5. (Point to two children.) Look at them.

   a. What are they doing? (Signal.) *Standing up.*

   b. Say the whole thing. (Signal.) *They are standing up.*

   c. (Repeat steps a and b until all children's responses are firm.)

EXERCISE 2   Information—Days of the Week

1. Let's do the days of the week.

   a. Everybody, how many days are there in a week? (Signal.) *Seven.*
   Say the whole thing. (Signal.) *There are seven days in a week.*

   b. Again. (Signal.) *There are seven days in a week.* (Repeat until all children's responses are firm.)

   c. Get ready to say the days of the week. (Signal. Do not respond with the children.) *Sunday, Monday, Tuesday, Wednesday, Thursday, Friday, Saturday.*

2. (Repeat part 1 until all children's responses are firm.)

Individual Turns

(Repeat the exercise, calling on different children for each step.)

EXERCISE 3   Concept Application

1. We're going to figure out which frog will jump. Only one frog will jump.

   a. Listen to the rule. The big frog will jump. Listen again. The big frog will jump. Everybody, say the rule about the big frog.
   (Signal.) *The big frog will jump.*

   b. Again. (Signal.) *The big frog will jump.* (Repeat step b until all children can say the rule.)
   Remember that rule.
   (Turn the page quickly.)

FIGURE 8.1

Example of *Language for Learning* Lesson
Source: www.SRA4kids.com

hypothesized that children with language-learning difficulties cannot process incoming auditory input as quickly as other children. Therefore, slowing down this input should enhance their language-learning abilities. As the children progress through the levels, these sound enhancements are reduced until the child is hearing normal auditory input. In this way, the developers claim that *FastForWord* can actually "retrain" the brain (Scientific Learning Corporation, 2000).

Research on *FastForWord* has generally been positive. An initial study by Paula Tallal and her colleagues (1996) found that children with speech and language difficulties who played computer games that utilized modified auditory input outperformed similar children who played games without modifications. Additional studies have been conducted with a large number of children who have participated in the *FastForWord* program (Scientific Learning Corporation, 2000). These studies have shown that up to 90% of the children completing the program make significant gains in skills such as auditory discrimination, the ability to follow directions, and listening and speaking fundamentals.

Although *FastForWord* is clearly an innovative program that shows great promise for enhancing the language skills of a wide range of children, there are some cautions that must be considered. First, there has been limited published research on the outcomes of this program. The field trial results reported by Scientific Learning Corporation are impressive, but it is important to keep in mind that there was no effort made in these studies to preselect participants using any standard criteria or to use a control group against which to compare results. Second, there continues to be a great deal of debate among researchers on whether children with speech and language difficulties actually have deficiencies in the rate of auditory processing. Therefore, there is a question as to whether it is really necessary to modify auditory input as in *FastForWord*. Finally, the developers of *FastForWord* claim that it leads to significant improvements in reading. However, they have not yet released any data on the results for reading.

This is not to say that *FastForWord* should not be used. On the contrary, there is a lot of evidence, both data based and anecdotal, that the program can successfully enhance language skills. But investigators such as Gillam (1999) suggest that teachers and clinicians should remain cautious about using *FastForWord* with a large number of children until there is more conclusive evidence for its effectiveness.

■■ SPECIALIZED PROGRAMS TO ENHANCE WRITING

Writing is a complex activity that involves the coordination of visual, motor, cognitive, and language systems to produce written text. Students who experience writing difficulties may have problems with one or more of the systems listed or in the coordination of those systems to produce written output. As a result, many children struggle with writing, producing short papers that contain little or no elaboration.

Until recently, much of the effort in enhancing writing skills was directed toward the improvement of handwriting and spelling skills. We will review some specialized approaches to enhance these skills. More recently, however, writing instruction has focused on enhancing written expression by focusing on skills such as organizing for writing, sequencing writing, editing, and writing for a variety of audiences. These skills are critical for writing success but are more difficult to teach. We will examine some specialized methods that have been developed to enhance written expression as well as programs designed to enhance writing in general.

Specialized Techinques to Enhance Handwriting

Handwriting is a challenge for many students, including some with specific disabilities. In some schools, a considerable amount of time is devoted to handwriting at the elementary level. Although questions have been raised about the amount of time devoted to handwriting instruction and whether this time might not be better spent learning word processing or general literacy skills, handwriting remains part of the elementary curriculum.

Manuscript Versus Cursive

Handwriting instruction usually begins with the teaching of manuscript (or block letter) writing. The assumption is that manuscript is easier to learn and that it most closely resembles the printed word. However, some have argued that cursive (script) writing instruction should precede (or replace) manuscript (Hagin, 1983). These advocates argue that cursive letters are more difficult to reverse and lead to whole-word learning. Certainly, for some students the transition from manuscript to cursive presents a considerable challenge. Unfortunately, research has not determined which approach is preferable. However, teachers may want to consider being flexible in allowing some students to move to cursive writing more quickly while some stay with manuscript writing exclusively.

Specialized Handwriting Approaches

Several alternatives to traditional handwriting instruction have been developed. Among the most popular is the *D'Nealian Handwriting Program*. This program blends manuscript and cursive writing by having the student produce manuscript letters with a continuous motion. This program can help children more easily make the transition to cursive writing.

Handwriting without Tears is a program that teaches both manuscript and cursive writing through the use of developmentally appropriate lessons that incorporate multisensory teaching aids and methods. The program provides a variety of materials and aids for both the teacher and student. Although there is no research available on the outcomes of this program, a number of teachers have reported success with it.

A number of aids are available to assist children in developing handwriting skills. These include:

- Large-diameter pencils and crayons
- "Stetro" grips that slip over a pencil to enhance grip
- Specialized paper that enables the child to feel the line
- Slant boards that help the child hold the paper

These and other adaptive devices are available from most educational supply companies.

Specialized Techniques to Enhance Spelling

Spelling is another writing skill that presents special challenges for students and teachers alike. Many students with reading difficulties struggle with spelling, but some good readers find spelling difficult as well. A wide variety of techniques and materials has been developed over the years to enhance spelling instruction. We will examine just a few of these approaches as a sample of what is available.

Some of the most popular specialized approaches to instruction utilize some form of multisensory (visual, auditory, and/or motor) input to enhance instruction. Although teachers often report success with these techniques, there is little research available on the effectiveness of these techniques.

One of the most widely used approaches is the Fernald method. As discussed in Chapter 5, this technique incorporates looking, saying, and writing in developing spelling skills. In brief, the steps are as follows:

1. The teacher writes the word and says the word as the student watches and listens.
2. The student traces the word, saying it several times.
3. The student writes the word while saying it.
4. The student writes the word from memory. If the word is incorrect, students repeat step 2. If the word is correct, it is placed in a file box.

The Fernald method is slow and tedious and requires a significant amount of direct teacher involvement. More recent multisensory techniques attempt to incorporate new knowledge about learning strategies into instruction. For example, Harris, Graham, and Freeman (1988) developed a simple but very effective *Five-Step Spelling Strategy*. Children are taught to use the following steps on their own as they attempt to learn new spelling words:

- Say the word.
- Write and say the word.
- Compare the written word to a model.
- Trace and say the word.
- Write the word from memory and check the model.

Specialized Techniques to Enhance Written Expression

Although many children experience difficulty acquiring handwriting and spelling skills, at least as many have difficulty expressing themselves adequately through writing. Their written products are short, poorly organized, and lack the more sophisticated use of language that is characteristic of more accomplished writing. The challenge has been how to enhance written expression.

One approach to this challenge is a program called *Cognitive Strategy Instruction in Writing* developed by Englert and Raphael and their colleagues at Michigan State University (Englert & Raphael, 1988). This approach uses teacher dialogues to model writing strategies for the student. The program combines instruction in specific skills such as brainstorming, grouping related ideas, and determining the appropriate structure, with instruction in metacognitive strategies. Two of the major elements of the *Cognitive Strategy Instruction in Writing* program are:

1. *Teacher modeling:* The teacher models text structures and modeling strategies by using a self-questioning technique. While reading a passage, the teacher might ask questions such as, "I wonder what the author meant when . . . ," or "What other questions can I ask?"
2. *Think sheets:* Students are given a series of "think sheets" that provide prompts to help them structure their writing. For example, the "plan think sheet" asks questions such as, "Who am I writing this for?" and "Why am I writing this?" Think sheets are also available for organizing and editing.

After students write a first draft, they use the "self-edit think sheet" to edit their text. As part of the editing process, they evaluate how well they addressed the planning and organization think sheets. This process is repeated with a peer editor. Finally, writers review the editorial suggestions and prepare a final draft.

Writing-to-Read Program

The *Writing-to-Read* program is a computer-based instructional system designed to develop the reading and writing skills of kindergarten and first-grade students. Developed by Dr. John Henry Martin, the program was supported and distributed by the IBM corporation for use with their computers. The program emphasizes a phonemic approach and uses writing as a skill to enhance reading.

In the Writing-to-Read program children rotate through five workstations as described next:

Station I: The Computer Station. Children sit at a computer and listen through headphones as a word is displayed on the screen and spoken by a digitized voice. Children are directed to listen to the word, say the word, and type the letters for each phoneme in the word.

Station II: The Work Journal Station. Children complete paper-and-pencil activities that reinforce the phonemes and words presented at the computer station.

Station III: The Writing/Typing Station. Students use a computer with word-processing software to type letters, words, and stories.

Station IV: The Tape Library. Children wear headphones and listen to stories that stress sound/symbol relationships.

Station V: The Make Words Station. Children play games that emphasize beginning consonant sounds, word families, and phonemes introduced at other stations.

The Writing-to-Read program has been implemented in many school districts throughout the United States. Some have found that the program can effectively enhance certain writing (Rogier, Owens, & Patty, 1999) and reading (Gilman, 1988) skills, but others have raised questions about the efficacy and cost of the program (Collins & Stevens, 1997). Rather than using the program as the sole or even primary literacy instruction program, the program may be best used as a supplement to other reading and writing approaches.

▌▌SPECIALIZED PROGRAMS TO ENHANCE READING

Reading plays a central role in the success of children in school as well as in overall quality of life. Unfortunately, many children experience significant difficulty acquiring reading skills. A large number of specialized programs have been developed to enhance or remediate reading skills. In this section we will review programs that emphasize the acquisition of phonological skills, programs that utilize some sort of tutoring as their primary method of instructional delivery, programs that utilize a direct instruction approach, and other programs that use a variety of techniques to enhance reading skills.

Programs to Enhance Phonological Processing

Research in the past 10 to 15 years has consistently demonstrated the crucial role that phonological awareness plays in the acquisition of beginning reading skills and as a factor in reading disorders (see Chapter 2 for a review). Therefore, it should not be surprising to find that a number of programs have been developed to enhance phonological processing. We will examine several of the programs.

Orton–Gillingham Method

The Orton–Gillingham method of reading instruction uses a systematic, multisensory approach to teach decoding skills. The method requires five lessons a week for a minimum of two years. Instruction progresses from learning individual sounds and letters,

Specialized programs often include the use of technology for advancing reading ability.

TABLE 8.2	Description of Instruction Using the Orton–Gillingham Approach

- A drill card with one letter is shown to the student.
- The teacher says the name of the letter and asks the student to repeat it.
- When this is mastered, the teacher says the sound of the letter and the student repeats the sound.
- Then the teacher shows the card and says, "What does this letter say?" The student is expected to give the sound.
- Then, without showing the card, the teacher makes the sound represented by the letter and says, "Tell me the name of the letter that has this sound."
- The teacher then writes the letter in cursive form and asks the student to trace the letter, copy it, and write it from memory.
- After mastering the first group of 10 letters (a, b, f, h, i, j, k, m, p, t), the student is taught to blend them into words.

through blending them into words, to spelling. The instructional procedure is described more completely in Table 8.2. Although the Orton–Gillingham method has been widely used for many years, there is limited research on its effectiveness. One of the few studies in the literature was described by Enfield (1988). She reported on the results of the use of a somewhat modified Orton–Gillingham approach with 45 children in a school in Minnesota. Compared to similar children in another school, the children who received the Orton-Gillingham instruction showed two to three times more progress on standardized reading tests. The Orton–Gillingham method has also been reported to be effective in enhancing the reading skills of children with learning disabilities who are also juvenile delinquents (Simpson, Swanson, & Kunkel, 1992) and with college-age students with reading difficulties (Guyer & Sabatino, 1989).

A number of variations of the basic Orton–Gillingham approach have been developed, including the Slingerland Method (1976), "Alphabetic Phonics" (Cox, 1980), and the "Dyslexia Training Program" (Beckham & Biddle, 1989). The latter program was evaluated in a well-designed study of 48 students with dyslexia (Oakland et al., 1998). Approximately half of the children received their primary reading instruction with the *Dyslexia Training Program* at the University of Texas' Learning Abilities Center. The other children continued to receive whatever reading program was used in their local school. The researchers found that the children in the Dyslexia Training Program made significantly more progress than the control group in reading during the two years of the study. Although the children in the experimental group outperformed the other students, their gains were relatively modest and there was little improvement in spelling performance.

Clinical experience and the limited published research base on the Orton–Gillingham method and its variants suggest that this technique can work in improving the phonological and reading skills of students with significant reading difficulties. However, the program requires intensive, one-on-one instruction for an extended period of time, and it may not be possible to implement in many cases.

Wilson Reading Program

The Wilson Reading Program (Wilson, 1996) is a multisensory approach to teaching reading and writing to children and adults with dyslexia. Based on the Orton–Gillingham model, the program utilizes a 12-step approach to help children master decoding and encoding skills. The program is designed to be used on a one-to-one basis with children experiencing significant difficulties with reading; however, the authors recently observed a first-grade classroom in which the program was being used as a supplementary reading program for the entire class (Box 8.1).

▌Box 8.1

A CLASSROOMWIDE APPLICATION OF THE WILSON READING PROGRAM

Mrs. C.'s first-grade class uses the Wilson Reading program as part of their regular literacy program. Last year Mrs. C. had several children who were pulled out of her class for extra help in reading using the Wilson program. Mrs. C. liked what it did for them and thought it might be beneficial for all of the children in her class. This year Mrs. C. has two classified children in her classroom and a third child whom she feels is at risk for classification.

A typical lesson begins with either Mrs. C. or her collaborating special education teacher, Mrs. B., reviewing previously taught content. For example, on one day Mrs. B. reviewed vowels, digraphs, nasals, and word groups. She used a felt board on which were placed letters that represented the various sounds and structures. Children were asked to repeat their "drill" for each sound and unit. For example, for the long o sound, the children said the letter (o), then a word that illustrated the sound (comb), then said the sound (o). As the children reviewed their drills, they were reminded to use the hand signals that stand for various sounds. For example, two fingers represent a digraph.

After spending some time reviewing their drills, the children were given numerous opportunities to build words using the structures they had already learned. The teacher modeled word building using the word, thank. She pointed out that their word consists of a digraph (th) and a "welded sound" (ank). As she said the type of unit, she illustrated it with the appropriate hand movement (two fingers for the digraph, a sweeping motion for a "welded" sound). Then children practiced their skills by creating their own words and sharing them with the class. At the end of the lesson the children completed a worksheet that asked them to identify digraphs, vowels (long and short), and welded sounds as well as the rules that govern their combination (e.g., the "vowel-consonant-e" rule that says that with this construction the first vowel is long).

All of the children in the class were very attentive throughout the lesson. They responded quickly to the teacher's prompts and seemed excited to participate. Mrs. B. (the special education teacher) said, "I really like Wilson. It has helped me improve my own spelling. I used to use SRA, then I used Wilson for some children. Now I use it for everyone. I find it really works." Mrs. C., the regular education teacher, feels that the Wilson approach can be helpful with all of the children in the class—even the proficient readers. She includes Wilson lessons about twice a week. She also uses a basal reader series and reading and writing workshops to enhance literacy skills.

Instruction in the Wilson Reading Program is based on six syllable types:

- Closed syllables (those with short vowels); for example, "cup"
- Syllables with vowels and silent "e"; for example, "bake"
- Open syllables (those with long vowels); for example, "he"
- Syllables ending in a consonant with "le"; for example, "tle"
- R-controlled syllables; for example, "pork"
- Diphthong syllables; for example, "bait"

Parts 1–5 of the program emphasize decoding skills. Parts 6–8 emphasize encoding, whereas parts 9 and 10 focus on comprehension skills.

Each lesson in the Wilson Reading Program consists of seven steps, as described next:

1. *Sound cards:* These cards are used to introduce new sounds and to drill old sounds. Each card contains a sound and a keyword (e.g., "m"—"man"). The teacher models the sound for the child, asks the child to repeat it (with the keyword) and, during phase one and two of instruction, the child learns finger movement to represent the sounds (e.g., the /m/ sound is said while tapping the index finger to the thumb).
2. *Word cards:* These are used to present and practice words made from sounds that have been taught previously. There are 390 words that are presented in a carefully controlled sequence.
3. *Word list reading:* Students read a list of words based on the skills acquired previously.
4. *Sentence reading:* Students read carefully controlled sentences.
5. *Preparation for written work:* Student(s) practice concepts using the sound and word cards in preparation for a spelling dictation task.
6. *Written work:* The teacher dictates sounds, words, and sentences. The student repeats, then writes, the target item in a workbook.
7. *Reading/listening:* The student reads independently from a program reader that carefully controls vocabulary.

Although the Wilson Reading Program appears to be gaining widespread acceptance in schools, there is a limited research base on its effectiveness. To date, there are two published studies, both of which indicate that the program can be successful. In one study (Banks, Guyer, & Guyer, 1993), 30 college students with dyslexia were assigned to one of three groups: those receiving Wilson training, those taught with a non-phonetic approach, and a third group that received no special intervention. The group that received the Wilson training significantly outperformed the other groups on spelling, the skill targeted in the study. Another study, by Barbara Wilson (the developer of the program) and Janet O'Connor (O'Connor & Wilson, 1995), looked at the results of the use of the Wilson Reading Program on 220 students with significant reading difficulties. According to the authors, these students had not shown progress in other reading programs. Teachers were trained in the Wilson method and students received an average of 62 lessons with the program. After completion of the program, students made significant gains in both word attack and comprehension.

Although there is clearly a need for more research on this program, including more carefully controlled studies that include control groups, there are indications that the Wilson Reading Program can be successfully used with students with significant reading difficulties. However, teachers will need to decide whether the significant time and expense involved in training for and implementing the program are worth the investment.

Lindamood Phoneme Sequencing Program for Reading, Spelling, and Speech (LiPS) (1998)

This program is an updated version of the *Auditory Discrimination in Depth* program that has been used for many years. The program provides intensive instruction in phonological and reading skills using a multisensory approach in which the student learns to use sensory information from the ear, eye, and mouth to identify, label, and classify sounds. The LiPS program comes in two versions—a classroom version for use with groups of five or more children and a clinical version for groups of four or fewer.

One of the unique features of the LiPS program is the labels that are assigned to each sound. For example, the /b/ and /p/ sounds are called "lip poppers," and the /t/ and /d/ sounds are labeled "tip tapper." These labels represent the lip and tongue placements associated with the target sound. As part of the program, children are taught to recognize the placement of the lips and tongue during sound production. Once children become proficient in awareness of sound production, they engage in a series of problem-solving exercises in which they learn to represent sequences of phonemes with either mouth-form pictures or colored blocks. Throughout the program, the teacher is expected to ask questions that will help the children discover the sounds in words and think about how those sounds are formed with their mouths. As children learn to label each phoneme, they are also taught to associate a letter with the sound. Then simple CVC spelling patterns are introduced. During this phase of instruction the children read short books in which the vocabulary is consistent with the decoding rules they have mastered. Later, trade books are introduced.

Although the *Auditory Discrimination in Depth* (LiPS) program has been used for many years, there is still limited research on the outcomes of the program. However, the results of current research suggest that this program can be an effective way of enhancing the phonological and reading skills of students with significant reading difficulties. For example, Alexander and associates (1991) reported significant increases in both phonological awareness and word attack skills for a group of 10 children with significant reading disorders following an average of 64 hours of training using the Lindamood system. In a major study designed to prevent significant reading problems in children by identifying children at risk for phonological processing difficulties, Torgesen, Wagner, and Rashotte (1997) compared three instructional approaches. From an initial group of 1,436 kindergarten children, 200 children were identified as having significant difficulty with phonological processing. These children were then assigned to one of four groups: (1) a group that received training in phonological awareness using the *Auditory Discrimination in Depth* program, (2) a group that received embedded phonological awareness instruction (training that was based on reading and writing activities), (3) a group that received instruction designed to supplement the regular classroom reading program, and (4) a group that received no special instruction. The researchers found that, by the end of first grade, all of the treatment groups were outperforming the control group on several measures of reading. Although each of the instructional approaches showed some success, children in the Lindamood program outperformed children in the other groups on several measures of reading and phonological awareness.

The results of research and clinical experience suggest that the Lindamood Phoneme Sequencing Program for Reading, Spelling, and Speech program can be effective both for children who have experienced reading difficulties and as a way of preventing serious reading problems in children with phonological processing difficulties. However, the program is intensive and requires a great deal of individualized instruction. Therefore, it may be most useful for children with significant phonological processing difficulties.

Other Programs to Enhance Phonological Processing

A large number of programs designed to enhance phonological processing have been developed recently. Some of the more popular include:

- *Earobics* (Cognitive Concepts). This program uses a series of computer-based activities to teach phonological awareness, auditory processing, and phonics skills. There are three versions of the program—one for children 4–7 years old, one for children ages 7–10, and a third program for adolescents and adults. In each program the participant moves through a series of levels while playing interactive games. The computer automatically adjusts the difficulty level in response to the participant's answers. The authors claim that children show "significant skill improvement" after using *Earobics* for 15 to 20 minutes a day, three times a week.
- *Phonemic Awareness in Young Children* (Adams, Foorman, Lundberg, & Beeler (1998). This program uses language "games" to teach basic phonological skills.
- *Phonological Awareness Training for Reading* (Torgesen & Bryant). This program consists of four sets of activities that are designed to help young children (kindergarten through grade 2) enhance their phonological processing skills. The activities include rhyming, sound blending, sound segmenting, and reading and spelling applications. The authors suggest that instruction take place in three to four short sessions a week for 12 to 14 weeks.

Direct Instruction Programs

The best-known and most widely used direct instruction program for the enhancement of reading skills is the *DISTAR* (direct instructional system for teaching arithmetic and reading) reading program. The program now consists of two elements: *Reading Mastery* (McGraw-Hill) for students in preschool through grade 3 and the *Corrective Reading* (Science Research Associates) program for students in grades 4–12. The *DISTAR* reading program is a highly structured program that follows a strict hierarchy of skill development. The program is based on the direct instruction model of learning, which has the following basic principles (Gersten, Woodward, & Darch, 1986):

- An explicit step-by-step strategy
- Development of mastery at each step of the process
- Strategy (or process corrections) for student errors
- Gradual fading from teacher-directed activities toward independent work
- Use of adequate, systematic practice with a range of examples
- Cumulative review of newly learned concepts

The *Reading Mastery* program emphasizes the acquisition of basic phonics skills through the use of a synthetic phonics approach. That is, students are taught that letters represent specific sounds, then learn to blend those sounds to form words. The program includes games to teach sequencing skills, blending tasks, and rhyming activities. Basal readers are included in the program. The readers use a marking system that indicates how vowels should be pronounced. In Level I of the program students learn how to read words, sentences, and stories both aloud and silently and to answer literal comprehension questions. In Level II, students learn to decode more difficult words and answer inferential comprehension questions.

A typical *Reading Mastery* lesson begins with the teacher calling together a group of students (usually five) to sit around her in a semicircle. The teacher reads the lesson from the teacher's manual. Lessons typically begin with a review of a previously learned skill, then introduce a new skill. The teacher models the skill for the students then directs the students to practice the skill. If students make an error, the teacher uses a correction procedure to correct and review the skill. Students receive verbal and concrete (e.g., marks on the board) reinforcement for correct responding. The lesson continues with the application of the skill in a sentence, paragraph, or story and concludes with a review of the target skill. Throughout the lesson, the teacher uses hand signals to indicate when it is her turn to speak and when it is the students' turn to respond.

The *Corrective Reading Program* is divided into two components: decoding and comprehension. Each component includes 315 lessons lasting 35 to 45 minutes. The decoding component includes word-attack skills, decoding strategies, and skill applications. The comprehension component includes thinking basics, comprehension skills, and concept applications. Like *Reading Mastery, Corrective Reading* provides the teacher with completely scripted lessons that include built-in error correction and reinforcement procedures.

There is a great deal of research evidence that the *DISTAR* reading program is effective for many types of children. The program was originally developed for low-income children and has been used extensively with that population with success (Meyer, Gersten, & Gutkin, 1983). The program has also been successfully used with children with a variety of disabilities, including children with autism and hearing impairments (Becker & Carnine, 1980). Although the program has been used widely with children with learning disabilities, the results are less clear cut for this population. There are several research studies that have found that the *Corrective Reading* program can be effective for older students with significant reading difficulties (e.g., Polloway, Epstein, Polloway, Patton, & Ball, 1986) but the results for the *Reading Mastery* program have been less clear cut (Kuder, 1990).

The *DISTAR Reading Program* (*Reading Mastery* and *Corrective Reading*) represent another approach to the remediation of reading difficulties in children. The programs have been found to be effective for a variety of children. However, their very strength (tightly structured, hierarchical lessons) may be seen as a disadvantage to those who view reading as a more creative process.

Preventing Reading Failure

Recently, several specialized reading programs have been developed that are designed to prevent reading failure rather than to intervene after reading difficulties emerge. The most prominent of these programs are *Reading Recovery* and *Success for All*.

Reading Recovery

Reading Recovery is an intensive, highly structured program of instruction for children at high risk for reading difficulties. First developed by Marie Clay in New Zealand, *Reading Recovery* was brought to the United States in 1984 by researchers from Ohio State University. Since its introduction, *Reading Recovery* has spread rapidly to hundreds of school districts throughout the United States.

The basic premise of the *Reading Recovery* program is that all children can learn to read if given sufficient opportunity to do so. Rather than intervening after reading failure, the goal of the *Reading Recovery* program is to identify children who may be at risk for reading difficulties (defined as children in the lowest 20% of reading achievement) and helping them develop better reading skills through intensive, short-term instruction.

Reading Recovery lessons are provided on an individual basis for 30 minutes a day for 12 to 14 weeks. Children may be discontinued from the program earlier than this if they demonstrate the ability to read independently at or above grade level or if they are not making sufficient progress in the program.

Although there is an overall structure to the *Reading Recovery* program as a whole and to the lessons that comprise the program, *Reading Recovery* teachers are encouraged to individualize the program for each child. Teachers typically spend up to 10 days in exploratory activities with the child, discovering how the child reads, and establishing rapport with the child. When actual lessons begin, they follow the following format:

1. *Reading familiar stories:* The child begins by rereading familiar stories. The teacher's role is to point out the strategies the child is using rather than to correct mistakes. Pinnell, Fried, and Estice (1990) provide an example of this approach in the following interaction: As Dante read from the book, *Three Little Ducks*, he said, "Came and his, said Mother Duck." He then stopped and repeated the sentence, this time reading it accurately as,"Come and hide, said Mother Duck." Dante's teacher says, "That's right. What you read first didn't make sense. I like the way you fixed that up yourself. Going back really helped you."
2. *Taking a running record of text reading:* As the child reads a book that was read once the previous day, the teacher listens for and records behaviors such as substitutions, omissions, and insertions. After the lesson, the teacher reviews the running record to make inferences about the child's use of reading strategies and to direct the next day's lesson.
3. *Working with letters:* For children having little knowledge of letters, the teacher may introduce letters using plastic letters and a magnetic board. Other opportunities for letter work occur during reading.
4. *Writing a message or story:* The child composes a brief (one to two sentences) message each day. After the message is written, the teacher writes it on a sentence strip and cuts it apart for the child to reassemble. Sometimes messages are extended over several days to create a story.
5. *Reading a new book:* Every day the child reads a new book. The teacher introduces the book by looking through it with the child and discussing the pictures. The teacher adjusts the amount of introduction to the level of the child, providing more information for children who need more assistance.

Reading Recovery teachers receive extensive training in the intricacies of the program. Teachers begin their training by attending a 30-hour workshop at which they learn about the philosophy of *Reading Recovery* and how to administer the diagnostic test that accompanies the program. This is followed by a full year of training during which teachers learn how to conduct lessons. An important component of this training is "behind-the-glass" sessions at which teachers observe actual *Reading Recovery* lessons with children.

There is an extensive research base on *Reading Recovery* beginning with studies in New Zealand and continuing through the present. With few exceptions, researchers have found the program to be very successful. For example, early studies in several school districts in Ohio found that approximately two-thirds of the children who were discontinued from (i.e., completed) the *Reading Recovery* program performed within the average range of their class in reading. Moreover, these gains continued several years later (Pinnell, 1989). Similarly, Pinnell and her colleagues (1994) found that low-achieving readers taught in *Reading Recovery* outperformed children in other individualized tutorial programs as well as a comparison group who received no specialized training (Pinnell et al., 1994).

Although there is a great deal of research and clinical evidence that *Reading Recovery* can be successful, there are some concerns that have been raised about the program. One of the concerns involves the children who do not successfully complete the program. Shanahan and Barr (1995) note that large-scale studies on the effectiveness of the *Reading Recovery* program have found that anywhere from one-quarter to one-third of children fail to complete the program. Sometimes these children are not included in reports of program effectiveness, thus overstating the effectiveness of the program. A more significant concern involves the cost of the program. *Reading Recovery* teachers must be trained extensively. Following their training, they are allowed to work with a proscribed number of children. This makes the program very expensive to operate. On the other hand, providing remedial and special education programs to children who experience significant reading difficulties is also expensive.

It seems clear that the *Reading Recovery* program can be a successful method of intervening early with children who are at risk for reading difficulties. Although the program may not help everyone, it appears to work for a significant number of children. The question that school districts will have to continue to confront is whether the costs of early, intensive intervention are worthwhile.

Success for All

Success for All is a comprehensive schoolwide restructuring program developed by researchers at Johns Hopkins University. Designed primarily for schools in low-income communities, Success for All has been successfully implemented in a number of communities. Currently, *Success for All* is being used in some 600 schools in 48 states across the United States as well as in several other countries. The program consists of a number of elements, including regrouping of students in grades 1–3 from heterogeneous, age-grouped classes to homogeneous groups based on ability rather than age; reduced class sizes in language arts; a family support team to help those experiencing health and/or personal problems; and a reading program that includes extensive assessment and one-on-one tutoring.

The reading program that is included as part of the *Success for All* program is designed to prevent reading problems before they become a significant problem. Students in grades 1–3 are regrouped into homogeneous groups based on their reading levels for a 90-minute reading period. This regrouping is destined to make it easier for the teacher to work with the class as a whole and to reduce the need for multiple reading groups within the class. In kindergarten and grade 1 the program uses phonetically regular storybooks (*Reading Roots*) to support instruction that focuses on phonemic awareness, auditory discrimination, and sound blending as well as comprehension skills and self-monitoring strategies. Kindergarten classes also use the Peabody Language Development Kits to enhance vocabulary skills. In grades 2–5, students use district-selected reading materials in a program that emphasizes cooperative learning and the development of reading strategies.

An important component of the *Success for All* reading program is the use of reading tutors. The tutors must be certified teachers with previous experience with remedial reading programs. Tutors serve as additional reading teachers during the 90-minute reading lessons. They also conduct one-on-one tutoring for students who are experiencing difficulty with reading. These sessions are held during an hour-long social studies period so that students are not taken from their language arts class. The tutoring sessions are intended to reinforce and support the regular instruction that takes place during the regular reading session rather than to replace that instruction.

A typical 90-minute reading lesson begins with the teacher reading a story to the class and engaging the group in a discussion of the story. In kindergarten and grade 1 the program emphasizes the use of a technique called, "Story Telling and Retelling," with which children learn to listen, retell, and dramatize stories. In the K–1 reading program, instruction continues with an emphasis on sounds and sound-symbol relationships. Repeated reading and partner reading are used in order to engage all of the children in reading. At the higher grade levels, a technique called, "Cooperative Integrated Reading and Writing (CIRC)" is used to enhance vocabulary acquisition and comprehension skills (Table 8.3).

TABLE 8.3 Cooperative Integrated Reading and Composition (Slavin, Madden, & Stevens, 1990)

- Teacher introduces and discusses a story from the students' reading book.
- Students work in dyads, reading the story silently, then reading the story aloud, alternating readers after each paragraph.
- Students respond to various story-structure tasks, such as identifying main characters, describing the setting, and making predictions about the story.
- After reading the story, students work as a team to produce a written product on a topic related to the story.
- Students work in dyads or in larger teams to read and define a list of new or difficult words from the story.
- Students retell the main points of the story and are checked by partners who have a list of the story elements.
- Students test each other on spelling words until all words are spelled correctly.
- Partners sign an assignment sheet to indicate that their partner has successfully completed all activities.
- Students take tests to assess mastery of reading material.
- Teams are rewarded based on the performance of the team.

Beginning in the second year of the program, *Success for All* classrooms begin to implement programs that integrate writing with the other language arts.

Success for All has been extensively researched. In several instances schools that have implemented the program have been compared to similar schools in their community. The results are encouraging. In one study (Madden et al., 1993) five *Success for All* schools in Baltimore were compared to similar schools in the district. In almost every case children in the *Success for All* schools outperformed children from the comparison schools on measures of reading and school attendance. The differences were especially true for the lowest-performing children in each of the schools. Another study of the program, conducted not by the Johns Hopkins researchers but by an independent team of investigators, found similar, though less-dramatic results (Smith, Ross, & Casey, 1996). These authors note that the program's outcomes can be influenced by factors such as teacher training, school conditions, and the type of student included in the program.

Given the success of programs such as *Reading Recovery* and *Success for All*, one might wonder which is the best program. Although this is a very complex question that is not easily answered, a study by Ross, Smith, Casey, and Slavin (1995) examined the outcomes of the implementation of the programs in three schools within one school district. The researchers found that students who were tutored in the *Reading Recovery* program outperformed those tutored in *Success for All*, but that nontutored students did better in the *Success for All* program. Students in the *Success for All* program outperformed *Reading Recovery* students on word attack tests but did not do as well on passage comprehension tests. The researchers also examined the performance of students with special needs. In the *Success for All* schools these children are included in the regular classroom, whereas in the *Reading Recovery* school they remained in a self-contained special education classroom. The special education students in the *Success for All* school significantly outperformed their peers in the *Reading Recovery* school. The researchers concluded that each program has particular strengths. *Reading Recovery* can have a profound effect on a small number of students who are having difficulty with initial reading. *Success for All* can improve the performance of both nontutored as well as tutored students. The authors suggest that some merging of these two programs might be desirable.

Other Specialized Reading Programs

Edmark Reading Program

The Edmark Reading Program was originally developed as an ungraded, criterion-referenced set of materials designed to teach sight words and certain word endings to students with mental retardation. In its current form, the Edmark program (IEP Resources) consists of two levels. Level I teaches 150 words from the Dolch word list. There are 227 highly structured lessons that teach these words plus basic reading skills such as reading from left to right and reading simple sentences. Level II introduces 200 new words while reviewing the 150 words previously taught. There are 345 lessons that use short stories to teach comprehension as well as word identification skills. After completion of both levels, children should be reading at approximately a second-grade level.

Most of the research on the Edmark Reading Program was carried out in the 1970s and 1980s. In general, this research found that the program can be very effective in helping students with mental retardation acquire a sight word vocabulary (e.g., Vandever & Stubbs, 1977). For example, Walsh and Lamberts (1979) compared the Edmark program to a fading approach to learning sight words in which children are taught to match a word with a picture that is gradually faded out. The authors found that the Edmark program was much more effective in teaching sight words to students with moderate mental retardation than the picture fading approach.

The *Edmark Reading Program* can be a useful tool for helping students with significant learning difficulties acquire initial skills in reading. However, its emphasis on sight word acquisition and memorization suggests that students will not gain the word-attack skills that would enable them to identify new words or the comprehension skills needed for successful reading. Therefore, the program should probably be used in conjunction with other instructional methods that emphasize word-attack and text-level reading skills.

Benchmark Reading Program

In the *Benchmark Word Identification Program*, students are taught a set of high-frequency words that serve as anchors for learning new words. Based on extensive study and program evaluation (Gaskins et al., 1997), the original program was revised in 1996. The extended program consists of several elements:

- Clarifying goals and rationale: Teachers share knowledge of phases of word learning and provide examples to show why students should analyze all the sounds in a word.
- Teaching and modeling how to self-talk: The teacher pronounces the word, the students analyze the sounds, and the word is written on the board. The teacher fully models the steps in the analysis. First the teacher stretches out the word so that all the sounds in the word can be heard. As the teacher stretches out each sound, she holds up a finger to count the number of sounds. Next, the teacher looks at the word and counts the letters and asks: "Do we have the same number of letters as sounds, or will it take more than one letter to represent some of the sounds?" Next, the teacher demonstrates how to figure out what letters go with what sounds. (Gaskins et al., 1997, p. 320).
- Providing guided practice: Students stretch out sounds, analyze and self-talk, and summarize clues they have discovered. They state what the spelling pattern is and give further examples of words with the same spelling pattern. They compare the words with words previously placed on the words wall, and practice creating new words by changing one letter.
- Applying word-learning procedures: Students read texts that contain the spelling pattern. The texts may be specifically written to provide the practice or may be easy trade books. Predictable rhymes of the week are sent home with the children to practice with their families.
- Reviewing features of our language: Students share their language learning with their classmates, their families, and in their journals.

Program evaluations have indicated that the revised program has led to greater gains than the original one (Gaskins et al., 1997) and has helped children with learning disabilities learn about the structure of words (Gaskins, Ehri, & Cress, 1997).

Reading ASSIST Institute

Reading ASSIST (Alphabetic Sound Symbol Instruction Systematically Taught) *Institute* (formerly known as Project ASSIST) is another variation of the Orton–Gillingham approach to reading instruction. Developed by Virginia Biasoto, *Reading Assist* is a highly structured program of intense multisensory phonics instruction. Using flashcards, games, and controlled vocabulary stories, the program systematically introduces children to the sounds of English and their orthographic representation (letters).

Although the instructional model of *Reading Assist* appears to be well grounded in research on phonological acquisition and instruction, there is, to date, no independent research on the effectiveness of this program.

▌▌SUMMARY

For some learners, modification of instruction is not sufficient to address their special literacy learning difficulties and needs. Students such as these may benefit from specialized programs that provide more intensive instruction in literacy skills. Although these programs require a significant investment in time and, in some cases, money, they may prevent or reduce later literacy difficulties. However, the decision to use a specialized program must be carefully weighed, as their use sometimes separates the children with learning difficulties from their peers and reduces their access to the regular education curriculum.

Linkages

1. What are the possible advantages and disadvantages of using a specialized program?
2. List and briefly describe three of the unique features of the *FastForWord* program.
3. Go to the *FastForWord* website (www.scilearn.com) and check out the latest research posted there. Summarize what the research says about the effectiveness of this program.
4. What are the similarities and differences between the following reading programs?
   – Orton–Gillingham
   – Wilson
   – Lindamood
5. Describe a typical *Reading Mastery* lesson.
6. There is considerable evidence that programs designed to prevent reading failure, such as *Reading Recovery* and *Success for All* are successful. Analyze these programs and suggest why these programs are successful.

On the Web

Scientific Learning—information on *Fastforward* and other programs.
     www.scilearn.com
SRA—information on SRA language arts programs including *Language for Learning* and *Corrective Reading*
     www.SRA4kids.com
Handwriting without Tears—program website
     www.hwtears.com

References

Adams, M. J., Foorman, B. R., Lundberg, I., & Beeler, T. (1998). *Phonemic awareness in young children.* Baltimore: Paul H. Brookes.

Alexander, A. W., Andersen, H. G., Heilman, P. C., Voeller, K. K. S., & Torgesen, J. K. (1991). Phonological awareness training and remediation of analytic decoding deficits in a group of severe dyslexics. *Annals of Dyslexia, 41,* 193–206.

Anderson–Inman, L., & Horney, M. (1997). Electronic books for secondary students. *Journal of Adolescent & Adult Literacy, 40,* 486–491.

Banks, S. R., Guyer, B. P., & Guyer, K. E. (1993). Spelling improvement by college students who are dyslexic. *Annals of Dyslexia, 43,* 186–193.

Becker, W. C., & Carnine, D. W. (1980). Direct instruction: An effective approach to educational intervention with the disadvantaged and low performers. In B. Lahey & A. Kazdin (Eds.), *Advances in clinical child psychology* (Vol. 3, pp. 429–473). New York: Plenum.

Beckham, P. B., & Biddle, M. C. (1989). *Dyslexia Training Program Books.* Cambridge, MA: Educators Publishing Service.

Collins, J. D., & Stevens, L. M. (1997). Does Reading Recovery work? *The American School Board Journal, 184,* 38–39.

Cox, A. (1980). *Alphabetic Phonics: Structures and Techniques: Multi-sensory Teaching of Basic Language Skills.* Cambridge, MA: Educators Publishing Service.

Enfield, M. L. (1988). The quest for literacy. *Annals of Dyslexia, 38,* 8–21.

Englert, C. S. & Raphael, T. E. (1988). Constructing well-formed prose: Process, structure, and metacognitive knowledge. *Exceptional Children, 54*(6), 513–520.

Gaskins, I., Ehri, L., & Cress, C. (1997). Analyzing words and making discoveries about the alphabetic system: Activities for beginning readers. *Language Arts, 74,* 172–184.

Gaskins I., Ehri, L., Cress, C, O'Hara, C., & Donnelly, K. (1997). Procedures for word learning: Making discoveries about words. *Reading Teacher, 50*(4), 312–327.

Gersten, R., Woodward, J., & Darch, C. (1986). Direct instruction: A research-based approach to curriculum design and teaching. *Exceptional Children, 53,* 17–31.

Gillam, R. B. (1999). Treatment for temporal processing deficits: Computer-assisted language intervention using FastForWord®. *Language, Speech, & Hearing Services in Schools, 30*(4), 363–370.

Grossen, B. (1997). *Thirty years of research: What we know about how children learn to read: A synthesis of research on reading from the National Institute of Child Health and Human Development.* Santa Cruz, CA: The Center for the Future of Teaching and Learning.

Guyer, B. P., & Sabatino, D. (1989). The effectiveness of a multisensory alphabetic approach with college students who are learning disabled. *Journal of Learning Disabilities, 22,* 430–434.

Hagin, R. A. (1983). Write right- or left: A practical approach to handwriting. *Journal of Learning Disabilities, 16,* 266–271.

Harris, K. R., Graham, S., & Freeman, S. (1988). Self-instructional strategy training. *Teaching Exceptional Children, 20,* 35–37.

Kameenui, E. J. (1996). *Learning to read/reading to learn: Helping children with learning disabilities to succeed information kit.* (Technical Report). Eugene, OR: National Center to Improve the Tools of Educators.

Kuder, S. J. (1990). Effectiveness of the DISTAR reading program for children with learning disabilities. *Journal of Learning Disabilities, 23,* 69–71.

Lindamood, P., & Lindamood, P. (1998). *The Lindamood Phoneme Sequencing Program for Reading, Spelling, and Speech.* Austin, TX: Pro-Ed.

Madden, N. A., Slavin, R. E., Karweit, N. L., Dolan, L., & Wasik, B. A. (1993). Success for all: Longitudinal effects of a restructuring program for inner city elementary schools. *American Educational Research Journal, 30,* 123–138.

Meyer, L. A., Gersten, R. M., & Gutkin, J. (1983). Direct instruction: A project follow through success story in an inner-city school. *Elementary School Journal, 84,* 241–252.

Oakland, T., Black, J. L., Stanford, G., Nussbaum, N. L., and Balise, R. R. (1998). An evaluation of the dyslexia training program: A multisensory method for promoting reading in students with reading disabilities. *Journal of Learning Disabilities, 31,* 140–147.

O'Connor, J., & Wilson, B. (1995). Effectiveness of the Wilson reading system used in public school training. In C. McIntyre & J. Pickering (Eds.), *Clinical studies of multisensory structured language education* (pp. 247–254). Salem, OR: International Multisensory Structured Language Education Council.

Pinnell, G. S. (1989). Reading Recovery: Helping at-risk children learn to read. *The Elementary School Journal, 90,* 161–183.

Pinnell, G. S., Fried, M. D., and Estice, R. M. (1990). Reading recovery: Learning how to make a difference. *The Reading Teacher, 43,* 282–295.

Pinnell, G. S., Lyons, C. A., DeFord, D. E., Bryk, A. S., & Seltzer, M. (1994). Comparing instructional models for the literacy education of high-risk first graders. *Reading Research Quarterly, 29,* 9–37.

Polloway, E. A., Epstein, M. H., Polloway, C. H., Patton, J. R., & Ball, D. W. (1986). Corrective reading program: An analysis of effectiveness with learning disabled and mentally retarded students. *Remedial and Special Education, 7,* 41–47.

Rogier, L. L., Owens, J. L., & Patty, D. L. (1999). Writing to read: A valuable program for first grade? *Reading Improvement, 36*(1), 24–34.

Ross, S. M, Smith, L. J., Casey, J., & Slavin, R. E. (1995). Increasing the academic success of disadvantaged children: An examination of alternative early intervention programs. *American Educational Research Journal, 32,* 773–800.

Scientific Learning Corporation (2000). Results. Retrieved from http://www.scilearn.com.

Shanahan, T., & Barr, R. (1995). Reading recovery: An independent evaluation of the effects of an early instructional intervention for at-risk learners. *Reading Research Quarterly, 30,* 958–995.

Simpson, S. B., Swanson, J. M., & Kunkel, K. (1992). The impact of an intensive multisensory reading program on a population of learning-disabled delinquents. *Annals of Dyslexia, 42,* 54–66.

Slavin, R. E., Madden, N. A., & Stevens, R. J. (1990). Cooperative learning models for the 3Rs. *Educational Leadership, 47,* 22–28.

Slingerland, B. H. (1976). *A multi-sensory approach to language arts for specific language disability children: A guide for primary readers.* Cambridge, MA: Educators Publishing Service.

Smith, L. J., Ross, S. M., & Casey, J. (1996). Multi-site comparison of the effects of Success for All on reading achievement. *Journal of Literacy Research, 28,* 329–353.

Torgesen, J. K., Wagner, R. K., & Rashotte, C. A. (1997). Approaches to the prevention and remediation of phonologically based reading disabilities. In B. Blachman (Ed.), *Foundations of reading acquisition and dyslexia* (pp. 287–304). Mahwah, NJ: Lawrence Erlbaum.

Vandever, T. R., & Stubbs, J. C. (1977). Reading retention and transfer in TMR students. *American Journal of Mental Deficiency, 82,* 233–237.

Veale, Tina K. (1999). Targeting temporal processing deficits through FastForWord: Language therapy with a new twist. *Language, Speech, and Hearing Services in Schools, 30*(4), 353–362.

Walsh, B. F., & Lamberts, F. L. (1979). Errorless discrimination and picture fading as techniques for teaching sight words to TMR students. *American Journal of Mental Deficiency,* 83, 473–479.

Wilson, B. A. (1996). *Wilson Reading System: Instructor manual.* Millbury, MA: Wilson Language Training Corporation.

Enhancing Literacy with Students with Moderate and Severe Disabilities

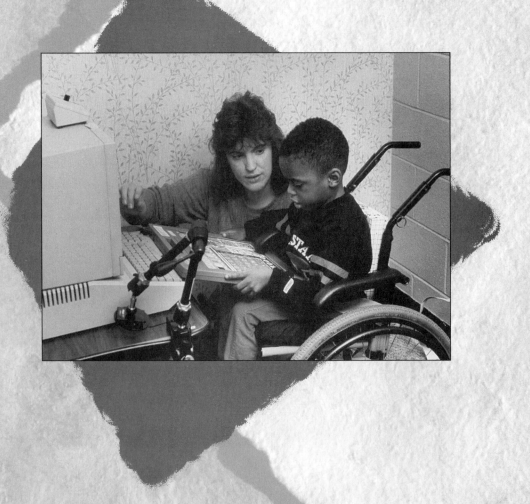

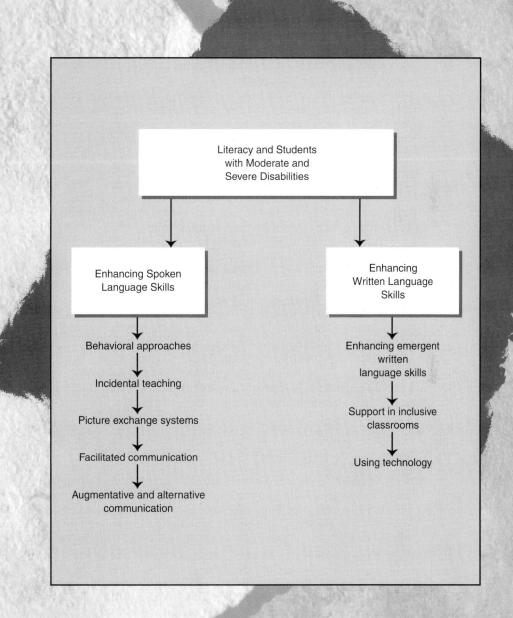

▌▌▌INTRODUCTION

In 1967 Nigel Hunt, a young man with Down syndrome (Trisomy 21), published an extraordinary book entitled, *The World of Nigel Hunt*. The book was extraordinary not so much for its content (mostly descriptions of Nigel's fairly mundane experiences) but for the fact that it was written at all. After all, the prevailing opinion among experts was that people with mental retardation could not read, let alone write.

How did Nigel do it? In the foreword to the book, Douglas Hunt, Nigel's father, described how Nigel's mother began teaching Nigel sound–symbol relationships at a very early age. As Nigel accompanied his mother around the house, she labeled objects and sounded them out for him. Eventually Nigel began to spontaneously sound out words and match letters to the sounds. Later, his father taught him how to type.

Clearly, the combination of his parents' high expectations for their son, their willingness to devote many hours to his instruction, and Nigel's own determination to succeed led to his success. Although Nigel's achievement is certainly unusual, there have been other examples of people with mental retardation and other significant disabilities who have succeeded in developing "unexpected" literacy skills. According to Kliewer (1998), what all of these cases had in common was that someone valued these individuals as symbolic beings and that there was recognition that they needed a tool to connect symbolically with the wider community.

Unfortunately, the history of literacy development in persons with moderate to severe disabilities (including students with mental retardation, autism, severe hearing and vision impairment, significant motor disabilities, and brain injury) includes few instances of high expectations and interest in providing these individuals with effective symbolic communication systems. As Erickson and Koppenhaver (1995) point out, it is not easy to learn to read and write if you are a child with severe disabilities in a public school setting. Teachers are unlikely to be aware of the research on emergent literacy and may, therefore, deny their students access to literacy experiences because they lack "readiness" skills. Many teachers do not believe that people with moderate to severe disabilities can learn to read and write. Even if they do include literacy instruction in the curriculum, it is likely to focus on learning specific "survival" words that are taught in a drill-and-practice format.

▌▌▌RATIONALE FOR LITERACY DEVELOPMENT

Developments in several domains are making it increasingly important that teachers and other professionals who work with students with moderate and severe disabilities develop higher expectations for their students and use effective literacy instruction practices. For example, with the inclusion of an increasing number of students with moderate and severe disabilities in the regular education classroom, expectations for these students are rising. Recent changes to the Individuals with Disabilities Education Act (IDEA) have put greater emphasis on participation in the regular education curriculum for all students. In addition, the new regulations require that students with disabilities participate in state and districtwide assessments. Although students with disabilities can have modifications in instruction and assessment, and in some cases, can participate in an alternative program, there is a clear expectation that most students will participate in the regular education program. Therefore, it is more important than ever that all students, including those with moderate and severe disabilities, be helped to acquire the literacy skills that will enable them to participate in, and benefit from, placement in the regular education classroom.

In addition to changes in educational requirements and legal requirements, there are other reasons to reconsider the development of literacy skills in people with moderate and severe disabilities. First, literacy skills are essential for full participation in society. Reading is not only important for successful employment, it also can be an important part of leisure-time activities.

Second, there is increasing evidence that people with significant disabilities can acquire literacy skills. For example, in their review of the research on reading instruction for people with mental retardation, Singh and Singh (1986) found evidence that people with mental retardation at all levels could learn to read. Similarly, Fowler, Doherty, and Boynton (1995) report on research that has found that approximately 40% of individuals with Down syndrome acquire at least some reading skills. In the past there was an assumption that students with moderate and severe disabilities could not acquire reading, writing, and language skills, but there is reason for greater optimism today.

The rationale for teaching literacy skills to students with moderate to severe disabilities seems clear. As mentioned earlier, more often these children are being included in the regular education classroom where reading, writing, and language skills are both highly valued and essential for success. Literacy skills are also an important part of success in life after school.

Finally, there is reason to believe that most, if not all, individuals with moderate and severe disabilities can acquire some literacy skills. In the sections following we will examine methods that have been successfully used to enhance the literacy skills of persons with moderate and severe disabilities.

ENHANCING SPOKEN LANGUAGE SKILLS

Individuals with moderate and severe disabilities frequently have significant delays in the development of spoken language. In some cases, they use little or no spoken language. Researchers have found that speech and language disorders have been found to be the most frequent secondary disability among children with mental retardation (Epstein, Polloway, Patton, & Foley, 1989). Significant language disabilities are one of the primary characteristics of autism. Individuals with serious hearing impairments usually have great difficulty developing spoken language, although they may develop a gestural language system.

Language impairments can have a significant impact on individuals with moderate and severe disabilities. These impairments limit participation in the classroom, interfere with the development of social relationships, and limit employment options and recreational opportunities (Aram & Nation, 1980). Therefore, it is important that teachers and other professionals who work with these students become aware of effective approaches to enhance language skills and then use these techniques with their students.

A number of approaches for the remediation of language and communication disorders of students with moderate and severe disabilities have been developed, including some that are very controversial.

Behavioral Approaches

Behavioral approaches to language instruction for children with moderate and severe disabilities have focused on teaching specific, often discrete, language skills using behavioral principles. These include prompting and reinforcement in order to guide instruction. Typically, behavioral approaches feature a therapist working one on one with a child for a concentrated period of time (Box 9.1).

▌ Box 9.1

A BEHAVIORAL LANGUAGE LESSON

Paula is a 5-year-old child who has been identified as autistic. She is currently placed in a self-contained classroom with other children who have severe disabilities.

During language instruction, Paula is seated away from her peers in a small area that is blocked off from the rest of the room. Paula sits across from her teacher at a table.

Mrs. Wells, Paula's teacher arranges the stimulus materials (a pencil and a book) and the reinforcers (orange slices) in front of her, just beyond Paula's reach.

Mrs. Wells begins the session by saying to Paula:
   "Look at me, Paula."
When she has Paula's attention, she says:
   "Paula, what's this?" (holding up the pencil).
Paula looks away.
Mrs. Wells raises her voice and says:
   "Paula, what's this?"
Paula makes an utterance that sounds like, "Uhn."
Mrs. Wells says:
   "Good Paula. That's right. It's a pencil. Here." (She hands Paula an orange slice.)
Mrs. Wells continues by holding up the book and saying:
   "Paula, what's this?"

The session continues like this for about 20 minutes. From time to time Paula is distracted by noises from outside her cubicle and turns toward them. Each time, Mrs. Wells calls Paula back to attention.

When behavioral approaches are used consistently and are implemented appropriately, they can work for many students with severe disabilities (Connell & Stone, 1992). An example of a successful program is that developed by Lovaas and his colleagues (Lovaas, 1987; McEachlin, Smith, & Lovaas, 1993). In this approach, the therapist uses a stimulus (verbal prompt) to elicit a response (verbalization) that is reinforced. Gradually, responses are shaped toward the adult model. Lovaas (1987, p. 53) gives the following example of a child being trained with this approach. In this example, "E" is the trainer and "B" is Billy, a child with autism. There is a breakfast tray (stimulus) between them.

E: What do you want?

B: Egg.

E: No, what do you want? I . . . .

B: I want . . . .

E: Egg (pause). O.K., what do you want?

B: (no response)

E: No, what do you want? I . . . .

B: I want egg.

E: Good boy (feeds Billy).

Lovaas has reported that autistic children who received early, intensive behavioral intervention (including language intervention) scored higher on tests of intelligence and were more successful in school than similar children who received less-intensive intervention (Lovaas, 1987). A follow-up study several years later found that these differences continued to exist (McEachlin, Smith, & Lovaas, 1993).

Although behavioral intervention approaches to language instruction can work, they have been criticized on several grounds. The most significant criticism centers on the issue of generalizability. Individuals with moderate and severe disabilities often have significant difficulty applying what they learn to new situations. Therefore, when they learn a new skill they must be helped to learn how and when to apply that skill. Language training methods that teach discrete skills in clinical, rather than in natural conversational, settings have been criticized for their lack of attention to generalization (Hunt & Goetz, 1997).

Look at the example in Box 9.1. Even if the teacher is successful in teaching Paula to say the word *pencil,* what is the likelihood that Paula will spontaneously use this word when she needs a pencil? In fact, she has not been taught to request a pencil at all—she has only learned to label the object. Furthermore, Paula may only learn to say the word *pencil* when presented with the specific pencil used during instruction. Concerns about generalization as well as other concerns about the effectiveness of behavioral approaches to language training for persons with moderate and severe disabilities have led researchers and practitioners to look for other methods for teaching language skills.

Incidental Teaching

"Incidental teaching" is a technique that has been used with both typically developing children as well as children with moderate and severe disabilities. Incidental teaching approaches utilize the opportunities that occur in the child's natural environments (home, school, and community) as the basis for instruction. Incidental teaching, and approaches similar to it (e.g., milieu training, naturalistic training), differ from behavioral approaches to language intervention in many ways (Table 9.1). On the other hand, incidental teaching approaches use some of the same techniques (e.g., reinforcement and shaping) as do behavioral approaches; however, they use them in more naturalistic ways.

Incidental teaching techniques rely on the child taking the lead in an interaction. However, many students with moderate and severe disabilities rarely, if ever, initiate a verbal interaction. In these cases, the teacher can initiate the interaction by noticing

TABLE 9.1	A Comparison of Incidental and Behavioral Approaches to Language Instruction for Individuals with Moderate and Severe Disabilities

Characteristic of Teaching	Behavioral Approaches	Incidental
Location of environment for instruction	Isolated environment	Natural
Targets for the instruction language	Discrete language skills	Language skills in context of use
Length of interactions instructional session	Lengthy sessions	Brief
	Massed practice	Distributed practice
Nature of reinforcers	Determined by therapist	Determined by child's response
	Reinforcement for correct response	Reinforcement for participation

the child's interest and asking a question (e.g., "Do you want the crayons?"). Additionally, in some cases, these children also may initiate interactions in ways that are difficult to interpret. For example, the child may jump up and down, grab an adult's hand, bang his or her head, or perform in other ways that may be interpreted as behavior problems. In many cases these actions may actually represent attempts to communicate (Table 9.2). Unfortunately, teachers and other professionals may misinterpret these behaviors as "resistant" or "aggressive." Instead, teachers should make an effort to try to understand what such behaviors may mean and to help the child substitute a more readily understandable behavior (a verbalization or a sign) so people in the child's environments can respond appropriately. For example, a student can be taught to make the sign for "bathroom" rather than walking up to the teacher and grabbing his or her hand.

TABLE 9.2	Examples of Communicative Attempts by Individuals with Moderate and Severe Disabilities

Behavior	Communicative Function
Shawn drops the dishcloth as he is doing the dishes.	Shawn is saying that he does not want to do the dishes.
Brianna grabs her mother's hand and leads her to the door.	Brianna is asking to play on the swings.
Shawn pushes boxes away.	Shawn is saying that he is tired of stacking boxes.
Brianna pulls on her teacher's sleeve and leads her to a cupboard containing the bubbles.	Brianna is saying she wants to play.

Source: Ostrosky, M. M., Drasgow, E., & Halle, J. (1999). How can I help you get what you want? *Teaching Exceptional Children, 31,* 56–61.

Incidental teaching approaches have been found to be effective ways of teaching language skills to children with a wide range of abilities, including children with moderate and severe disabilities (Warren & Kaiser, 1986). Indeed, some researchers have found that naturalistic approaches such as milieu training can be more effective than behavioral approaches for children with the most severe disabilities (Yoder, Kaiser, & Alpert, 1991). Most importantly, these methods not only teach specific language skills but also have been shown to lead to generalization of language to a variety of environments. That is, children who are taught to use language in natural situations are better able to use their newly acquired skills in a variety of settings.

Picture Exchange Systems

Picture exchange programs such as the *Picture Exchange Communication System* (PECS) (Bondy & Frost, 1994) use pictures as the means of fostering meaningful communicative exchanges (Box 9.2). The PECS program utilizes a combination of behavioral methodology and incidental teaching principles to enhance social communication in children with significant disabilities, especially children with autism. The program progresses through six phases in which the child is taught to communicate with a variety of people using increasingly complex language.

▌ Box 9.2

A PECS Case Study

Billy, a child with autism, was 3 years old when he began to use the *Picture Exchange Communication System* (PECS). At that time Billy showed little interest in people and preferred to play with objects rather than interact with people. Billy displayed no speech or communication skills. He made only occasional eye contact. It was also observed that Billy liked snack foods such as pretzels and potato chips.

Using Billy's preference for pretzels, he was taught to place a picture of a pretzel in his teacher's hand when he wanted one. It took only 10 trials to get Billy to do this. Gradually, staff moved away from Billy when he picked up the picture, forcing him to approach them. Over the next few weeks, pictures of additional snack foods were added to Billy's repertoire. Each time Billy gave a staff member a picture of a desired item, the staff person said, "Oh, you want a _____" and gave it to him.

During the third week of teaching, the staff began to require that Billy make a choice between two pictures. Billy began to learn to use a picture card that showed, "I want" in response to the prompt, "What do you want?" By the end of the fourth month of training, Billy was beginning to use speech while manipulating pictures, although his speech was not very clear. Over the next few months, Billy's picture repertoire exceeded 100 items and the intelligibility of his speech improved. After 11 months, Billy used only speech to communicate.

Source: Bondy, A. S., & Frost, L. A. (1994). The picture exchange communication system. *Focus on Autistic Behavior, 9,* 10 & 11.

A typical PECS Phase I training session might proceed as follows:

- The trainer places an object in front of the child that the trainer has previously observed the child wants.
- When the child reaches for the object, the trainer places a picture into the child's hand.
- The trainer then guides the child into handing the picture to the trainer.
- When the child exchanges the picture, the trainer makes a verbal response and offers a reinforcer.

In later phases of the program, the child is helped to develop more spontaneous interactions, the ability to discriminate between pictured items, the use of sentence strings, and a broader repertoire of communicative functions and language concepts.

Bondy and Frost (1994) report that of 66 children without functional speech who were taught to use PECS, 76% either developed speech as their means of communication or used a combination of speech and the picture system. In addition, the same authors report significant improvements in behavior for children using the PECS program. These results suggest that PECS may be a useful program for helping children with little or no functional language begin to develop communication skills.

Facilitated Communication

Facilitated communication (FC) is another technique that has been developed to help nonspeaking individuals with moderate and severe disabilities, including those with autism, mental retardation, and physical disabilities, to develop communication skills. Ever since its introduction, facilitated communication has been a very controversial technique.

The methodology of facilitated communication appears to be simple. The student types messages using a handheld device such as a Canon Communicator.[TM] A "facilitator" holds the hand, arm, or shoulder of the individual being facilitated while he or she types. The facilitator is told to provide "resistance" to movement, rather than guiding the movement of the individual with whom she or he is working.

At first, proponents of facilitated communication claimed that all (or nearly all) children who were exposed to the program were able to produce written communication. In one study (Biklen & Schubert, 1991) it was reported that 20 of 21 subjects were able to type words following the implementation of FC. Even more surprising, many of the children demonstrated unexpected literacy skills. Students were typing complete sentences that expressed profound thoughts and used advanced vocabulary. Students who had previously been in special schools were now attending regular high school classes and excelling. Some were going to college.

Despite the warnings of proponents of facilitated communication that the phenomenon could not be tested, a number of researchers began to investigate facilitated communication shortly after its introduction to the United States. Most of the studies have found that, under clinical conditions, when the facilitator was "blind" to the stimulus item, the subject was unable to produce independent communication (e.g., Eberlin, McConnachie, Ibel, & Volpe, 1993; Regal, Rooney, & Wandas, 1994; Wheeler, Jacobson, Paglieri, & Schwartz, 1993). That is, when the facilitator knew what the student was looking at, the student typed the correct word. However, when the facilitator saw a different item from the student, the student rarely, if ever, typed the correct item. Apparently, the students using facilitated communication were being influenced, apparently unintentionally, by the facilitator.

Because of concerns about the efficacy of facilitated communication, organizations such as the American Speech-Language-Hearing Association and the American Association on Mental Retardation have issued warnings to their members about the use of this method. However, there are still some clinicians who use facilitated communication and claim that it works. Such claims should be carefully examined.

Augmentative and Alternative Communication

Some individuals with moderate and severe disabilities may benefit from procedures and devices that either augment existing speech and language skills or provide an alternative to spoken language. Augmentative and alternative communication (AAC) procedures range from low-technology approaches that use signs or pictures to high-tech devices that use digitized speech outputs. Examples of AAC systems and procedures include:

- *Communication boards:* Utilize pictures or a symbol system to represent concepts and communicative needs of the individual in his or her various environments. Individual with disability points to picture or symbol as means of communication.
- *Sign language:* For persons with moderate and severe disabilities, sign language systems (such as American Sign Language) have sometimes been used to augment or replace spoken language. Although individuals with disabilities can often acquire a number of useful signs, concerns have been raised about limited communication opportunities (Bryen, Goldman, & Quinlisk–Gill, 1988).
- *Voice output devices:* A growing number of digital communication devices are available. Devices range widely in cost and complexity. They can be programmed with words and phrases that are needed by the individual with disabilities.

The selection of an AAC system should be based on two factors: the abilities of the individual who will use the system and the demands of the environments in which the individual functions. Mirenda and Iacono (1990) have suggested that the following factors be considered when selecting an AAC procedure:

- *Mobility:* including the individual's positioning and ability to walk
- *Manipulation:* the individual's fine motor skills
- *Communication:* existing communication skills
- *Cognitive/linguistic factors:* ability to understand and use symbols
- *Sensory/perceptual:* vision and hearing abilities

In addition, all of the environments in which the individual may use the AAC system should be assessed to determine words that are commonly used in these settings, communicative opportunities, and potential communicative partners who need to be trained.

There are several significant issues related to the use of AAC systems. One of these is the issue of accessibility. Although many children with disabilities use some sort of AAC device or procedure, it is estimated that many more could benefit from the use of

AAC systems (Zangari, Lloyd, & Vicker, 1994). Recent changes to the Individuals with Disabilities Education Act now require that the use of assistive devices, including AAC systems, be considered for all students with disabilities. However, some practitioners still believe that persons with disabilities should demonstrate certain prerequisite skills before an AAC system is provided. Yet, research has failed to find that there is any absolute level of cognitive or language skills that individuals with disabilities need in order to benefit from the use of AAC systems. As a result, McGregor and associates (1992) recommend that practitioners spend their time trying out AAC procedures in order to find the best one for each individual, rather than waiting for the person to reach some prerequisite skill level.

Another important issue related to the use of AAC systems involves the functional use of these systems. It is not unusual to go into a classroom that includes individuals with disabilities who use AAC systems and find them not using their device. When asked, teachers may report that the individual does not like to use the system or it no longer works. In fact, what often happens is that the student has not been helped to enhance his or her communication skills. Simply providing the individual with a device or other means of communication does not ensure that the person will use it. Teachers must help the student learn essential communication skills, such as initiation of a conversation and taking turns during conversation. Researchers have found that students with moderate and severe disabilities who use AAC systems communicate much more effectively when they use their AAC systems (Romski, Sevcik, & Adamson, 1999).

▪▪ Enhancing Written Language Skills

Until recently, the prevailing assumption among many professionals who study people with disabilities has been that these individuals are capable of acquiring few, if any, written language skills. Although there may be the rare individual (such as Nigel Hunt) who acquires significant written language skills, these were thought to be isolated cases. However, changes in beliefs about the development of literacy skills have brought about a reexamination of assumptions about the interest in the reading and writing skills of individuals with moderate and severe disabilities.

Research on Written Language and Disability

There is a long history of research on reading instruction for individuals with moderate and severe disabilities, especially those with mental retardation. Much of that research has focused on the acquisition of sight words. This research has generally found that students with moderate and severe disabilities, especially those with mental retardation, can acquire a significant number of sight words (Browder & Xin, 1998). At the same time, Browder and Xin caution that there is little research evidence on the functional use of these skills. In other words, research studies have shown that people with moderate and severe disabilities can acquire sight words, but may not be able to use their knowledge when they need to do so.

There is also research evidence that indicates that students with moderate and severe disabilities can acquire word analysis (phonics) skills. For example, when

Children with moderate to severe disabilities can develop their writing skills through the use of special keyboards.

Singh and Singh (1985) asked students with moderate mental retardation to read short passages, they found that the students made the fewest errors when they were helped to sound out words as compared to just being given the word and repeating it. Although this study was done with only two students, Conners' (1992) review of a number of research studies led her to conclude that individuals with moderate mental retardation can learn phonics skills. The significance of this finding is that it suggests that individuals with moderate and severe disabilities may be able to read new words that they have not previously been taught and may be able to more fully participate in literacy activities.

The research on written language skills of people with moderate and severe disabilities suggests that many can learn to read and, in some cases, to write. Although the prevailing assumption has been that they can only acquire a limited set of "functional" words, there is evidence that at least some students can acquire word analysis (phonics) skills. Unfortunately, educational programs for these students have traditionally given little, if any, emphasis to the development of written language skills. These students are provided with limited reading instruction—less than their nondisabled peers. They seldom read or write more than a paragraph. They spend a great deal of time completing worksheets that focus on surface features of language arts such as punctuation and spelling (Koppenhaver & Yoder, 1993). If instruction in written language skills is included, it usually focuses largely on teaching functional sight-word skills. Students spend many tedious hours memorizing long lists of "survival" words—often the same words every year. The result of these instructional practices has been the creation of a self-fulfilling prophecy that students with moderate and severe disabilities cannot acquire written language literacy skills (Cousin, Weekley, & Gerard, 1993).

Enhancing Emergent Written Language Skills

Recently, a number of effective approaches to the development of literacy skills in students with moderate and severe disabilities have been developed. These include programs that incorporate the "whole language" approach, programs that emphasize the acquisition of phonics skills, and approaches that teach sight-word identification skills.

"Whole Language" Approaches

Recently, one of the authors had the opportunity to spend an extended amount of time observing a classroom for young children with significant disabilities. This class was housed in a regular, public school. The students had a variety of disabilities, including moderate mental retardation, autism, and behavior disorders. All of the children had significant language delays.

The instructional day began just like that in many preschool and kindergarten classrooms—with a circle time. During circle time, the children were encouraged to both communicate with the teacher and with each other. At some point during circle time, the teacher introduced (or reviewed) the "sound of the week." She asked the children to repeat the sound with her. She then introduced a letter that represents the sound (for example, the "buh" sound and the letter *B*).

Following circle time, the students moved to the "story corner" where they listened to an age-appropriate book read by the teacher (for example, *Stellaluna* by Jannell and Jewell Cannon). The teacher showed the children pictures from the book and led a brief discussion about what the story might be about. She also reminded the students to listen for the "buh" sound as she read. Because *Stellaluna* is about bats, there were numerous opportunities to hear the "buh" sound. After reading, she asked the students to tell what they remembered about the story. As students responded, the teacher wrote down their comments.

Students were then dismissed to the "writer's workshop" table to write about the story they just heard. Three words from the story that begin with the "buh" sound were written on the board. The students were encouraged to incorporate one or more of these words into their writing. Most of the students scribbled, with few lines that could be called letters. However, when asked to share their writing, most could "read" what they had written. Finally, the students were given the opportunity to illustrate their story. Sometimes, there were additional activities that followed a theme that was introduced by the story. For example, following a story about fall, students went on a short walk to find signs of fall. When they returned to the classroom, they discussed what they had found and created a class display.

These activities probably sound familiar to most teachers of young children. They are not unlike the "whole language" lessons that go on in many regular education classrooms. What may be surprising is that most of these children with significant disabilities were able to participate in this lesson. Some needed assistance and prompting from the teacher. Some needed adaptive equipment, such as special pencil grips. Some of the children made few contributions to the discussion, but some had to be asked to give others a chance. There was no doubt in the mind of the observer that all of the children had participated in a rich, lively, and meaningful literacy lesson.

These techniques can be successfully implemented in regular education classrooms as well. Cousin, Weekley, and Gerard (1993) found that the following activities were useful in including students with disabilities in their classrooms:

- Immerse students in a print-filled environment.
- Read to students several times each day.
- Purposely talk about books and information gleaned from books.
- Establish multiple opportunities for students to observe teachers and more proficient peers reading and writing.
- Support students as they construct a personal understanding of print and make connections between themselves and the content of books.
- Support the functions of oral and written language that make the most sense to each child.
- Combine the academic and functional curriculum through the use of theme cycles.

Although there is, as yet, little research on the outcomes of the use of "whole language" type procedures with students with moderate and severe disabilities, observations such as those reported above and by researchers such as Erickson and Koppenhaver (1995) and Hodges and Shedden (1997) suggest that these techniques can help all children develop literacy skills.

Phonics Instruction

Earlier in this book we reviewed the substantial research base on phonological processing and reading. This research has established that phonological skills are essential for beginning reading, that poor readers often lack phonological skills, and that instruction in phonological processing can lead to improvements in reading.

Most of this research, however, has been conducted with students labeled learning disabled. But, what about the phonological skills of students with mental retardation and other moderate and severe disabilities? Although there is a limited amount of research, the studies suggest that enhancing phonological skills in these students can be successful (Gottardo & Rubin, 1991). For example, Nietupski, Williams, and York (1979) reported a study in which six students with moderate mental retardation (IQs ranged from 42–54) participated in a phonics skills instructional program. The students were taught four sets of consonant sounds, followed by short vowel sounds, vowel-consonant (VC) combinations (e.g., *at, on*), and consonant-vowel-consonant (CVC) combinations (e.g., *sat, beg*). The students participated in a variety of activities, including group instruction, individual tutoring, and phonics games (Box 9.3). The authors reported significant progress in learning phonics skills for five of the six participants.

Working with a similar group of students, Hoogeveen, Smeets, and van der Houven (1987) used a picture-sound matching activity to teach phonics skills (Figure 9.1). Students were taught to say the sound associated with an action in the picture (e.g., the hissing sound *s* of a snake). Later, in instruction, the picture was faded out but the letter remained so that students could begin to make the phoneme-grapheme match. These researchers found that all seven of the moderately mentally retarded students in their study (IQs ranged from 27–43) were able to learn the letter-sound matches presented in the training program.

FIGURE 9.1

"Action Mnemonic" Pictures
Source: Hoogeveen, F. R., Smeets, P. M., & van der Houven, J. E. (1987). Establishing letter-sound correspondences in children classified as trainable mentally retarded. *Education and Training in Mental Retardation, 22,* 80, 82.

▌Box 9.3

PHONICS GAME

Phonics Bingo Game

When a card is drawn, players must say the VC or CVC combination and place a marker on the appropriate word or pseudoword.

	Bingo		
cat	bid	man	juz
lox	nek	fig	web

Phonics Concentration Game

The object of the game is for students to locate and label pairs of consonants, vowels, VC, or CVC combinations. One student picks up a card, labels the sound or sounds out the word and directs the second student to find the same word in the array. If the second student's card matches the first, the students keep the pair. If they do not match, both return their cards to the array.

1	2	3	4
5	6	7	8
9	10	11	12

Source: Nieputski, J., Williams, W., & York, R. (1979). Teaching selected phonic word analysis reading skills to TMS labeled students. *Teaching Exceptional Children, 11,* 142.

The results of research on phonics-based approaches for enhancing the written language skills of students with moderate and severe disabilities suggest that this can be a useful approach for these students. However, there is still much we do not know about phonics and phonological skills in children with significant disabilities. For example, there is little if any research on populations other than children with mental retardation. There is also little research on the effect of phonological training on the subsequent reading achievement of students with moderate and severe disabilities. Despite these limitations, instruction in phonics and phonological skills should be a part of the literacy program for students with moderate and severe disabilities.

Sight-Word Approaches

As we noted earlier in this chapter, there has been a great deal of research on methods for teaching sight-word acquisition to students with moderate and severe disabilities. In general, this research has found that, through effective teaching practices, it is possible to teach sight-word skills to many students with significant disabilities. Among the practices that have been used successfully are:

- Time-delay techniques, in which the teacher shows the student a word and waits for the student to respond
- Providing the word after a specified period of time
- Picture fading, in which pictures are paired with written words then faded until all that is left is the word
- The Edmark Reading Program, which requires the student to find a word read by the teacher from among several distracter words (Conners, 1992)

According to Browder and Xin (1998), the most effective sight-word teaching programs use real materials activities that lead not only to word acquisition but also to the functional use of these words.

McGee, Krantz, and McClannahan (1986) have described a sight-word reading approach that utilized incidental teaching procedures to teach reading to children with autism. The two children in the program were first given the opportunity to select objects for play. Then word cards for the objects were prepared. During play time, if a child indicated that he or she wanted one of the objects, the teacher placed a word card between the child and the object and said, "Give me the word _____." If the child answered incorrectly, the teacher pointed to the correct word, mixed up the cards, and asked the child to try again. If the child still did not respond or responded incorrectly, the teacher physically guided the child's hand to the card. Using this system, the child learned the target words at a rapid pace and was able to use the words in other contexts.

As noted earlier, sight-word instruction programs for students with moderate and severe disabilities have been criticized on two grounds: First, they do not always translate into functional use, and second, they may limit students to a restricted range of literacy skills. Although these concerns are important, sight-word instruction should be included in a literacy program for these students, but it should be only one component of the program.

Parent's Role

The research on emergent literacy in typically developing children (see Chapter 4) tells us that parents play an important role in setting the stage for literacy acquisition. Through activities such as shared reading, parents teach their children about books, about words, and about the importance of written language.

Children with moderate and severe disabilities also benefit from growing up in a literate environment. Recall the experience of Nigel Hunt, described in the beginning of this chapter. Nigel's parents provided him with direct instruction on word learning and on writing as well as a supportive environment. However, research by Light, Binger, and Smith (1994) suggests that parents may not always be making the most of their opportunities to develop literacy. They observed parents reading books to their young (2- to 5-year-old) children who were physically disabled, had severe speech impairments, and were using an augmentative and alternative communication system. They found that parents tended to dominate the interaction, failing to give their child opportunities to participate in the interaction. Moreover, most of the children did not have access to their communication system during the reading session.

The reading instruction techniques that Kimberly Voss, the parent of Ashley, a child with Down syndrome and acquired brain injury, developed (Box 9.4) provide an extraordinary example of what a dedicated and persistent parent can accomplish. Not all parents are as able as Mrs. Voss to develop and carry out a reading instruction program with their child, nor should they be expected to do so. However, all parents have opportunities to help their children develop literacy skills.

▌ Box 9.4

DEVELOPING READING SKILLS IN A CHILD WITH SEVERE DISABILITIES

Kimberly Voss, the mother of Ashley Voss, a child with Down syndrome and acquired brain injury, worked intensively to help her daughter develop literacy skills. Not satisfied with simply teaching her daughter sight words, she searched for other ways of expanding her daughter's literacy skills. It was suggested to her that she should help her daughter learn "word families."

Although Mrs. Voss thought this was an excellent idea, she wondered how she was going to teach word analysis skills to a child who could not speak, had serious vision difficulties, could not write, and was not able to use a keyboard.

Mrs. Voss began by considering the strengths that Ashley brought to literacy learning. She was able to match objects, understood that an icon could represent a concept, could recognize the letters of the alphabet, and learned best through motor activities. She also recognized that some of Ashley's limitations could be overcome by adapting the size of items, providing a higher contrast, and by positioning.

Mrs. Voss began by teaching Ashley to match large plastic letters to printed text. However, she noticed that Ashley seemed to be bothered by the difference in size, shape, and color between the plastic letters and the printed text. So Mrs. Voss developed her own computer-generated font to match the plastic letters. She also designed fonts with dashed lines to help Ashley learn to trace letters. Mrs. Voss designed materials for 58 different two- ("at", "op") and three-letter ("ick," "ate") word families. She matched these to icons selected from Mayer–Johnson's *Boardmaker*™ software. The text of each target word was typed in the special font next to the icon. The beginning of the word was typed in blue, and the root was typed in black. The color prompt was faded out as Ashley learned to say the words.

Not only did Mrs. Voss use this approach with Ashley at home, but both Ashley's resource room and regular education teacher used the technique with success.

Adapted from: Voss, K. S. (1997). *Designing computer-generated multi-sensory materials for teaching reading and writing through word families.* Presentation at the 6th Annual Symposium on Literacy and Disabilities, Raleigh, NC.

There is ample evidence that students with moderate and severe disabilities can acquire written language skills if they are taught in effective ways. What are some of the principles of effective literacy instruction for these students?

- Provide opportunities for students to participate in literacy activities: These might include listening to stories, watching videos, and sharing stories.
- Provide sight-word instruction and practice: Students can benefit from learning essential vocabulary words, especially if they are taught in a way that encourages their functional use.
- Provide instruction in phonological (word analysis) skills: Research indicates that many students with significant disabilities can benefit from phonological instruction.
- Help students apply reading and writing skills: Students need to do more than learn words and isolated phonics skills. They need to apply these immediately to real reading and writing activities.
- Provide opportunities for communicative interaction: Language, reading, and writing support each other. Students benefit from opportunities to communicate with each other as well as with the teacher.

If students with moderate and severe disabilities are to be included in regular education environments in a meaningful way, they must have reading and writing skills. Some may need more time to develop these skills. Some may develop a limited repertoire of written language skills. All will require support and high expectations from parents and teachers.

■■ SUPPORT IN INCLUSIVE CLASSROOMS

For many students with moderate and severe disabilities, inclusion in regular education classrooms has become a reality. For others, it is a goal. Unfortunately, some students with significant disabilities are physically included in classrooms without truly becoming part of the class. Our goal in this section is to present methods that teachers and other professionals can use to enhance the literacy skills of all students in classrooms that include both typically developing children as well as children with moderate and severe disabilities.

The primary challenge in fully including students with significant disabilities is how to make it possible for them to participate in the regular education curriculum while providing them with the opportunity to develop the functional skills that they need (and that their IEP may require). Jorgensen (1994) provides eight suggestions that may be helpful in addressing this challenge:

1. Supplement instructions: This can be done by repeating or clarifying instructions for those students who need this or by breaking instructions down into smaller steps or changing terminology. This could be done by the classroom teacher, an instructional aide, or a peer. For example: The teacher says, "Open your workbooks to page 97, complete the first five problems, then check your work with a partner. When you agree on your answers, complete the next five items." The instructional aide opens the workbook to page 97 and says, "Point to the first problem on the page."

2. Change how instructions or information are presented: For example, provide written or pictorial instructions, provide a demonstration for the student, or provide a completed model so the student can see how the finished product should appear.

3. Change the type of output required: For example, instead of requiring written reports, allow the student to develop a computer-based presentation, a photo album, a song, or a picture.

4. Change amount or quality of output required: Require the student to complete fewer problems, provide the student with more time, or use a "value-added" approach that grades the student on the amount of improvement rather than on an absolute standard.

5. Involve students in "process steps" of the lesson: Most lessons contain opportunities for students to become actively involved. For example, students might hand out materials, change slides, or help set up learning centers.

6. Make an adaptation to the environment or provide an assistive device: For example, using larger print or better contrasting colors can help students with vision disabilities. Using computers and augmentative communication devices may help some students.

7. Provide physical assistance: Some students may need physical prompting to help them type or hand-over-hand guidance to turn a page.

8. Help the student do part of the task: In some cases, the student may be able to complete part of the activity, but may need assistance with part of the lesson.

How can these principles be applied to classroom literacy activities? Let's look at several examples. King–Debaun (1995) suggests that one way that children with significant disabilities can be included in literacy activities is for the teacher to select books that promote language learning. She suggests that appropriate books should have:

- Simple, repeated text or predictable text or rhyme and rhythm
- Contexts that are familiar to the child
- Large and simple text
- Simple graphics that clearly depict concepts
- Opportunities to include props (objects that support the text)
- Opportunities for generating related literacy activities (e.g., art, songs, plays)

Another example of adaptations to literacy instruction is presented in Box 9.5. In this scenario Johanna is a second grader with multiple disabilities. Note how Johanna's expected output was changed. Rather than saying the name of an animal or even pointing to it (which may be very difficult for her to do), Johanna's peers helped her select an animal by observing her eye gaze. Then the other students helped create an adaptation (the vocabulary overlays) that make it possible for Johanna to make a choice of words to use in her report. While the instructional aide puts the words into a narrative format, Johanna participates by making the cover.

▌Box 9.5

ADAPTING INSTRUCTION: A CASE STUDY OF JOHANNA

Johanna is a second-grader with multiple disabilities. She has a long attention span and loves watching other children act out plays or tell stories. Each child in Johanna's class must do a report on an endangered animal. Johanna's friends help her narrow down her choices by asking her to pick her "favorite animal" by gazing at pictures of animals on the covers of nature magazines. She chooses the panda. Johanna's assistant asks a small group of Johanna's peers to name "words that Johanna will need to use if she writes a story about pandas." The assistant then makes a series of overlays using panda-related vocabulary words—black, white, big, bamboo, China, cubs. Responding to "yes and no" questions and gazing to indicate her choice of words, Johanna communicates what she wants to write about. Her assistant turns Johanna's one-word responses into narrative, reads it back to Johanna for confirmation, and has Johanna illustrate a cover for the report using an ink pad and stamp set. A classmate might read Johanna's story aloud during sharing time or Johanna could activate a tape-recorded version of a classmate reading her story.

Source: Jorgensen, C. M. (1994). Modifying the curriculum and short-term objectives to foster inclusion. In S. Calculator & C. Jorgensen (Eds.), *Including students with severe disabilities in schools.* San Diego: Singular, 100.

Musselwhite (1997) has provided some examples of techniques that can be used to help students with significant disabilities participate in poetry activities—an essential element in the development of phonological skills. Color coding is one technique that can be used to help students participate in poetry reading. Each line of the poem can be written on a chart or on the board with a color next to it. The student is given a card with a color. The student is taught to respond when the teacher reaches the line with the color that is held by the student. Another technique to involve students with significant disabilities in poetry activities is the use of poems with repeated lines. Students can be prompted to repeat the line after hearing it said by a teacher or peer. There are

TABLE 9.3	Levels of Poetry Participation

Level I: Repeated Line as Refrain (Final Position)

Poem	Author	Prompt	Refrain (#)
Little Orphant Annie	James W. Riley	"An the Gobble-uns 'll git you"	"If you Don't Watch Out" (4)
The Voice That Beautifies	Navaho trad.	"Again and again it sounds"	"The voice that beautifies the land" (3)
Times-Square-Shoeshine	Maya Angelou		"pow pow" (18)

Level 2: Repeated Line within a Poem

Poem	Author	Repeated Line (#)
Song of the Settlers	Jessamyn West	"Freedom is a hard-bought thing" (4) (initial)
The Rum Tum Tugger	T. S. Eliot	"Yes, the Rum Tum Tugger is a Curious Cat" (3)

Level 3: Insert One Line Only

Poem	Author	Single Line—Final Position
Mommy Slept Late ...	John Ciardi	"I'd sooner eat the plate!"
Stopping by Woods ...	Robert Frost	"And miles to go before I sleep" (2)

Level 4: Repeated Phrases or Words

Poem	Author	Words or Phrases/Position (#)
Arithmetic	Carl Sandburg	"Arithmetic is ..." (initial) (5)
Give Me The Splendid Silent Sun	Walt Whitman	"Give me ..." (initial) (7)
We Real Cool	Gwendolyn Brooks	"we" (embedded) (8)

Level 5: Insert Two Different Lines/Phrases

Poem	Author	Repeated Lines/Phrases (#)
Father William	Lewis Carroll	"You are old" (4), "In my youth" (3)
Conversation	David McCord	"No dear" (8), "Oh dear" (3)

Level 6: Insert Several Different Lines/Phrases

Poem	Author	Repeated Lines/Phrases (#)
Mr. Mistoffelees	T. S. Eliot	"And we all say: OH" (3), "Well I never!" (3)
		"Was there ever" (2), "A cat so clever" (3)
		"As Magical Mr. Mistoffelees" (3)

Poem	Author	# of Lines
Autumn, I'm Nobody, I Never Saw a Moor, etc.	Emily Dickinson	8, 8, 8
Fog, Paper I, Paper II, Doors, Phizzog, Primer Lesson	Carl Sandburg	6, 5, 5, 6, 8, 4
The Panther, The Termite, The Kitten, The Lama, Celery	Ogden Nash	6, 4, 4, 8, 4

Source: Musselwhite, C. (1997). Reading, writing, rhyming, and reciting: Using poetry to support emergent literacy. Presentation at the 6th Annual Symposium on Literacy and Disabilities, Raleigh, NC.

many poems that contain repeated lines. For example, the well-known poem "Stopping by Woods on a Snowy Evening" by Robert Frost contains the repeated lines, "And miles to go before I sleep. And miles to go before I sleep." For additional poems that contain repeated lines see Table 9.3.

Students with moderate and severe disabilities face a number of challenges that make it difficult for them to achieve success in literacy. However, in many cases it is possible to modify the curriculum or adapt instruction to make it possible for these students to fully participate in the regular education classroom. Blischak (1995) has identified several skills that are essential for literacy development. She describes some of the difficulties that students with visual impairments and physical impairments may face in achieving these skills as well as providing suggestions for addressing these impairments (Table 9.4).

Although curriculum modifications and instructional modifications are essential for the success of students with moderate and severe disabilities in regular education classrooms, they are not enough to ensure success. Other elements that are needed are:

- *Administrative support:* Administrators play a crucial role in setting the tone for inclusion. If they truly believe that inclusive education can work and back this up with appropriate support and training for their staff, the likelihood of success increases significantly.
- *Collaboration:* Many different professionals may be assigned to work with students with significant disabilities. When these individuals work together toward mutually defined goals rather than pursuing narrow, discipline-specific goals, the outcomes for students with disabilities improves considerably.
- *Involvement of parents:* Involvement means more than informing parents about what is going on in the classroom. Parents should be partners in instruction; they should be asked to help define their child's instructional program and guided to support that program at home.

USING TECHNOLOGY

For many students with moderate and severe disabilities, literacy instruction can be enhanced by the use of appropriate technology. We have already discussed the important role that augmentative and alternative communication systems can play in the literacy development of many individuals with moderate and severe disabilities. If a child uses an AAC system, it is essential that the child use the system in all environments, including all school environments. Unfortunately, there are cases where teachers do not permit the child to use their system in class because of a misguided belief that it will prevent the child from developing language skills. In other cases, the child may use the system during their academic classes but not take it to other classes, such as art or physical education, because the system is not easily portable or because there is concern that a device could be damaged. The unfortunate result is that the child may not be able to fully participate in these classes.

In addition to AAC systems, computers and related technologies hold a great deal of promise for students with moderate and severe disabilities. Although they are certainly not a panacea for all of the challenges faced by these students, they can be

TABLE 9.4 Constraints in the Development of Language and Literacy and Suggested Intervention Strategies

Components of Literacy Development	Constraints from Visual Impairment	Constraints from Physical Impairment	Suggested Intervention Strategies
Broad experiences (Stratton & Wright, 1991)	• Difficulty matching language input to event • Difficulty reaching and feeling objects	• Difficulty ambulating • Difficulty reaching and feeling objects; limited sensorimotor interaction (Carlson, 1987; Hogg & Sebba, 1987) • Difficulty moving independently to bring objects, persons, experiences closer and making compensatory postural adjustments	• Involve in everyday routines (Kekelis & Anderson, 1984) • Describe and bring experiences to him (Kekelis & Anderson, 1984; Landau & Gleitman, 1985) • Imaginative play (Rogow, 1988) • Adapted toys (Carlson, 1987) • Positioning to facilitate participation (Foley, 1990; McEwen & Lloyd, 1990)
Language experiences (Stratton & Wright, 1991)	• Tendency of others to give directives, labels, child-centered topics (Kekelis & Anderson, 1984) • Difficulty matching language input to objects, persons, experiences (Landau & Gleitman, 1985) • Limited access to graphic means of communication	• Severe speech impairment (Carlson, 1987) • Severely restricted use of direct selection, slow rate, altered communication patterns (Fried-Oken, 1988)	• Respond to natural signals (Mills, 1983; Rogow, 1988) • Early, multimodal AAC intervention (Carlson, 1987) • Social language play in routines (e.g., rhymes) (Rogow, 1983, 1988, 1993) • Encourage to ask questions (Erin, 1986) • Stress social nature of language and literacy (Koppenhaver, Evans, & Yoder, 1991)
Reading aloud (Stratton & Wright, 1991)	• Cannot see print or follow text with eyes • Cannot choose his own books independently • Cannot ask questions about print (Hiebert, 1986)	• Cannot choose his own books independently (Light & Kelford-Smith, 1993) • Difficulty retelling, asking questions about stories (Katims, 1993)	• Provide means to request books, encourage active participation (Foley, 1990; Teale, 1986) • Make up stories (Beringer & Gans, (1986) • Predictable books, poetry, rhymes, music (Koppenhaver & Coleman, 1991; Rogow, 1988)

Book handling; understanding purposes of print (Hiebert, 1986; Stratton & Wright, 1991)	• Cannot see print	• Cannot handle books independently (Light & Kelford-Smith, 1993)	• Bring close, enlarge, describe (Landau & Gleitman, 1985; Stratton & Wright, 1991) • Tactile supplements (Miller, 1985; Stratton & Wright, 1991)
Scribbling/writing/composing (Light & Kelford-Smith, 1993; Stratton & Wright, 1991)	• Cannot see detail • Little direct experience with writing	• Cannot scribble/write independently • Single switch user • Little direct experience with writing	• Hand-over-hand or adapted writing device (Doherty, 1987) • Story and journal dictation (Beringer & Gans, 1986; Katims, 1993) • Text-to-Speech potential of VOCA (Beevers & Hallinan, 1990) • Encourage phonemic analysis and blending, sound-letter correspondence, spelling and invented spellings (Catts, 1991; Hiebert, 1986; Foley & Eule, 1992; Katims, 1993)
Observe others reading (Light & Kelford-Smith, 1993; Teale, 1986)	• Cannot incidentally observe others reading	• Cannot independently move or bring print closer	• Describe, involve in reading for pleasure, church, and work (Light & Kelford-Smith, 1993; Teale, 1986) • SQUIRT—super quiet uninterrupted reading time (Foley, 1990) • Expose to reading experiences (e.g., library trips) (Koppenhaver et al., 1991)

Source: Blischak, D. M. (1995). Thomas the writer: Case study of a child with severe physical, speech, and visual impairments. *Language, Speech, and Hearing Services in Schools, 26,* 16.

an important part of the instructional program. Research, though limited, has generally found that the use of computers and related software can enhance the literacy skills of students with significant disabilities (Schery & O'Connor, 1992).

Many types of computer applications can be used to enhance the reading and writing skills of students with moderate and severe disabilities. A few examples of literacy software that are designed for students with disabilities are provided in Table 9.5. Steelman, Pierce, and Koppenhaver (1993) have suggested that when considering computer software, the software should:

- Be flexible, allowing for modification to suit individual learner needs
- Support the educational strategies that the teacher wishes to use
- Present skill development in the context of student experiences
- Be easily integrated into the curriculum
- Be interesting to the user and appropriate for the student's cognitive abilities and age
- Include record-keeping capabilities to allow the teacher to monitor progress
- Use multimedia to tap into various learning styles
- Be easy to use, with clear documentation

TABLE 9.5   Examples of Software for Literacy Development

Reading

Words Around Me (Edmark)	Teaches 275 words plus plurals through a variety of activities. Includes built-in scanning.
Start-to-Finish Books (Don Johnston)	High interest, age-approriate stories for students with reading difficulties.
The Reading Lesson (Attainment Co.)	Combines phonics and whole language to teach 270 of the most common English words.
Readable Stories (Laureate)	Stories designed to enhance reading comprehension. Option for computer to "read" story to child.
Simon Sounds It Out (Don Johnston)	Phonics activities to teach letter-sound relationships. Automatically increases difficulty level.

Writing

IntelliTalk (IntelliTools)	Speaks as person types. Can be used for word processing and/or alternative communication.
EasyBook (Sunburst)	Creates books from children's stories. Includes clip art and drawing tools.
Kid's Media Magic (Humanities Software)	Easy-to-use word processing program that includes text-to-speech feature.
Storybook Weaver (Learning Company)	Students can write and illustrate a book using a simple word processor.

When used appropriately and consistently, technology can be an important part of the literacy program for students with literacy disabilities. Consider the case of Thomas, a 9-year-old boy with quadriplegic cerebral palsy who is included in a second-grade whole-language classroom (Blischak, 1995). Thomas does not have functional use of his hands, arms, or legs. He uses a head switch to operate both a power wheelchair and an assistive communication device. Thomas also has a vision impairment that significantly limits his functional vision. Thomas has a full-time paraprofessional who assists him in the classroom as well as peer helpers who change from day to day.

Although Thomas can talk, his speech is difficult to understand and he can produce only short utterances. Therefore, Thomas uses his head switch to operate *Talking Screen*™ software (Words +) that is loaded on a laptop computer mounted to his wheelchair. When Thomas wishes to initiate an interaction or respond to an initiation, he activates his device, which presents him with selections in both graphic and auditory forms. When he wants to choose a word or phrase, he activates a second switch that selects the item, and a voice output is generated.

Thomas has made significant progress in his second-grade class. He has studied for and passed grade-level spelling tests and can dictate stories and journal entries. Because Thomas expressed an interest in doing homework, questions are tape-recorded for him along with multiple-choice questions. Thomas uses his AAC device to select and print answers. Thomas is now a full-time student in a regular third-grade classroom.

SUMMARY

There is renewed interest in the development of literacy skills in persons with moderate and severe disabilities. There are many reasons for this reexamination of assumptions about the abilities of this population. The emergent literacy model has helped reduce the emphasis on prerequisite skills while shifting the focus to the importance of early literacy experiences. The movement to include students with disabilities, including those with significant disabilities, into the regular education environment challenges educators to find the best way to help all students develop their skills. The results of research studies and practitioner reports indicate that many students with significant disabilities can develop language, reading, and writing skills. Finally, the rapid advances of technology have provided some individuals with moderate and severe disabilities with a voice. For others, it has increased the number and quality of instructional options.

However, rising expectations and dazzling technologies are not enough to ensure the success of students with moderate and severe disabilities. They need teachers and other education professionals as well as parents who all believe that these students can learn and who have knowledge of effective instructional methods to support that learning.

Linkages

1. Describe some of the developments in the education of students with disabilities that make literacy development an increasingly important goal.
2. Contrast the goals and methods used in behavioral approaches to incidental teaching approaches to language instruction.
3. What are the advantages and disadvantages of using an augmentative and alternative communication system for individuals with disabilities?

4. What evidence supports the claim that individuals with mental retardation can develop written language skills?
5. Describe how a "whole language" approach to literacy instruction could be modified so that individuals with significant disabilities can participate.
6. Review the case of Johanna (Box 9.5). What did her teacher do to make it possible for Johanna to more completely participate in classroom activities? What additional methods could help Johanna?

On the Web

Check out these World Wide Web sites for more information about students with moderate and severe disabilities:

American Association on Mental Retardation
    aamr.org

Autism Society of America
    autism-society.org

Brain Injury Association
    biausa.org

Closing the Gap (technology for disabled)
    closingthegap.com

International Society for Augmentative and Alternative Communication
    isaac-online.org

National Down Syndrome Congress
    members.carol.net/~ndsc

The Association for the Severely Handicapped
    tash.org

United Cerebral Palsy Association
    ucpa.org

References

Aram, D., & Nation, J. (1980). Preschool language disorders and subsequent language and academic difficulties. *Journal of Communication Disorders, 13*, 159–170.

Biklen, D., & Schubert, A. (1991). New words: The communication of students with autism. *Remedial and Special Education, 12*, 46–57.

Blischak, D. M. (1994). Phonologic awareness: Implications for individuals with little or no functional speech. *Augmentative and Alternative Communication, 10*, 245–254.

Blischak, D. M. (1995). Thomas the writer: Case study of a child with severe physical, speech, and visual impairments. *Language, Speech, and Hearing Services in Schools, 26*, 11–20.

Bondy, A. S., & Frost, L. A. (1994). The picture exchange communication system. *Focus on Autistic Behavior, 9*, 1–19.

Browder, D.M., & Xin, Y.P. (1998). A meta-analysis and review of sight word research and its implications for teaching functional reading skills to individuals with moderate and severe disabilities. *Journal of Special Education, 32*, 130–153.

Bryen, D. N., Goldman, A. S., & Quinlisk-Gill, S. (1988). Sign language with severe/profound mental retardation: How effective is it? *Education and Training in Mental Retardation, 23*, 129–137.

Connell, P. J., & Stone, C. (1992). Morpheme learning of children with specific language impairments under controlled conditions. *Journal of Speech and Hearing Research, 35,* 844–852.

Conners, F. A. (1992). Reading instruction for students with moderate mental retardation: review and analysis of research. *American Journal on Mental Retardation, 96,* 577–597.

Cousin, P. T., Weekley, T., & Gerard, J. (1993). The functional uses of language and literacy by students with severe language and learning problems. *Language Arts, 70,* 548–556.

Eberlin, M., McConnachie, G., Ibel, S., & Volpe, L. (1993). Facilitated communication: A failure to replicate the phenomenon. *Journal of Autism and Developmental Disorders, 23,* 507–530.

Epstein, M., Polloway, E., Patton, J., & Foley, R. (1989). Mild retardation: Student characteristics and services. *Education and Training in Mental Retardation, 24,* 7–16.

Erickson, K. A., & Koppenhaver, D.A. (1995). Developing a literacy program for children with severe disabilities. *The Reading Teacher, 48,* 676–684.

Fowler, A. E., Doherty, B. J., & Boynton, L. (1995). The basis of reading skill in young adults with Down syndrome. In L. Nadel and D. Rosenthal (Eds.), *Down Syndrome: Living and Learning in the Community* (pp. 182–196). New York, Wiley-Liss.

Gottardo, A., & Rubin, H. (1991). Language analysis skills of children with mental retardation. *Mental Retardation, 29,* 269–274.

Hodges, A., & Shedden, B. B. (1997). *Exploiting natural acquisition of literacy skills: A case example.* Presentation at the 6th Annual Symposium on Literacy and Disabilities, Raleigh, NC.

Hoogeveen, F. R., Smeets, P. M., & van der Houven, J. E. (1987). Establishing letter-sound correspondences in children classified as trainable mentally retarded. *Education and Training in Mental Retardation, 22,* 77–84.

Hunt, N. (1967). *The World of Nigel Hunt.* New York: Garrett.

Hunt, P., & Goetz, L. (1997). Research on inclusive educational programs, practices, and outcomes for students with severe disabilities. *Journal of Special Education, 31,* 3–29.

Jorgensen, C. M. (1994). Modifying the curriculum and short-term objectives to foster inclusion. In S. Calculator and C. Jorgensen (Eds.), in *including students with severe disabilities in schools* (pp. 75–112). San Diego, Singular.

King–Debaun, P. (1995). *Merging whole language and technology: Strategies for children with severe disabilities.* Presentation at the 73rd Annual International Convention of the Council for Exceptional Children, Indianapolis, IN.

Kliewer, C. (1998). Citizenship in the literate community: An ethnography of children with Down syndrome and the written word. *Exceptional Children, 64,* 167–180.

Koppenhaver, D. A., & Yoder, D. E. (1993). Classroom literacy instruction for children with severe speech and physical impairments (SSPI): What is and what might be. *Topics in Language Disorders, 13,* 1–15.

Light, J., Binger, C., & Smith, A. K. (1994). Story reading interactions between preschoolers who use AAC and their mothers. *Augmentative and Alternative Communication, 10,* 255–267.

Lovaas, O. (1977). *The autistic child.* New York: Irvington Publishers.

Lovaas, O. (1987). Behavioral treatment and normal educational and intellectual functioning in young autistic children. *Journal of Consulting and Clinical Psychology, 55,* 3–9.

McEachlin, J., Smith, T., & Lovaas, O. (1993). Long-term outcome for children with autism who received early intensive behavioral treatment. *American Journal on Mental Retardation, 97,* 359–372.

McGee, G. G., Krantz, P. J., & McClannahan, L. E. (1986). An extension of incidental teaching procedures to reading instruction for autistic children. *Journal of Applied Behavior Analysis, 19,* 147–157.

McGregor, G., Young, J., Gerak, J., Thomas, B., & Vogelsberg, R. T. (1992). Increasing functional use of an assistive communication device by a student with severe disabilities. *Augmentative and Alternative Communication, 8,* 243–250.

Mirenda, P., & Iacono, T. (1990). Communication options for persons with severe and profound disabilities: State of the art and future directions. *Journal of the Association for the Severely Handicapped, 15*, 3–21.

Musselwhite, C. R. (1997). *Reading, writing, rhyming, and reciting: Using poetry to support emergent literacy.* Presentation at the 6th Annual Symposium on Literacy and Disabilities, Raliegh, NC.

Nietupski, J., Williams, W., & York, R. (1979). Teaching selected phonic word analysis reading skills to TMS labeled students. *Teaching Exceptional Children, 11*, 140–143.

Ostrosky, M. M., Drasgow, E., & Halle, J. W. (1999). How can I help you get what you want? *Teaching Exceptional Children, 31*, 56–61.

Regal, R., Rooney, J., & Wandas, T. (1994). Facilitated communication: An experimental evaluation. *Journal of Autism and Developmental Disorders, 24*, 345–355.

Romski, M. A., Sevcik, R. A., & Adamson, L. B. (1999). Communication patterns of youth with mental retardation with and without their communication speech-output devices. *American Journal on Mental Retardation, 104*, 249–259.

Schery, T. K., & O'Connor, L. C. (1992). The effectiveness of school-based computer language intervention with severely handicapped children. *Language, Speech, and Hearing Services in Schools, 33*, 43–47.

Singh, J., & Singh, N. N. (1986). Reading acquisition and remediation in the mentally retarded. In N. Ellis (Ed.), *International Review of Research in Mental Retardation* (Vol. 14, pp. 165–199). New York: Academic Press.

Steelman, J. D., Pierce, P. L., & Koppenhaver, D. A. (1993). The role of computers in promoting literacy in children with severe speech and physical impairments. *Topics in Language disorders, 13*, 76–91.

Voss, K. S. (1997). *Designing computer generated/multi-sensory materials for teaching reading and writing through word families.* Presentation at the 6th Annual Symposium on Literacy and Disabilities, Raleigh, NC.

Warren, S. F., & Kaiser, A. P. (1986). Incidental language teaching: A critical review. *Journal of Speech and Hearing Disorders, 51*, 291–299.

Wheeler, D., Jacobson, J., Paglieri, R., & Schwartz, A. (1993). An experimental assessment of facilitated communication. *Mental Retardation, 31*, 49–60.

Yoder, P. J., Kaiser, A. P., & Alpert, C. L. (1991). An exploratory study of the interaction between language teaching methods and child characteristics. *Journal of Speech and Hearing Research, 34*, 155–167.

Zangari, C., Lloyd, L. L., & Vicker, B. (1994). Augmentative and alternative communication: An historic perspective. *Augmentative and Alternative Communication, 10*, 27–59.

Literacy and Diversity

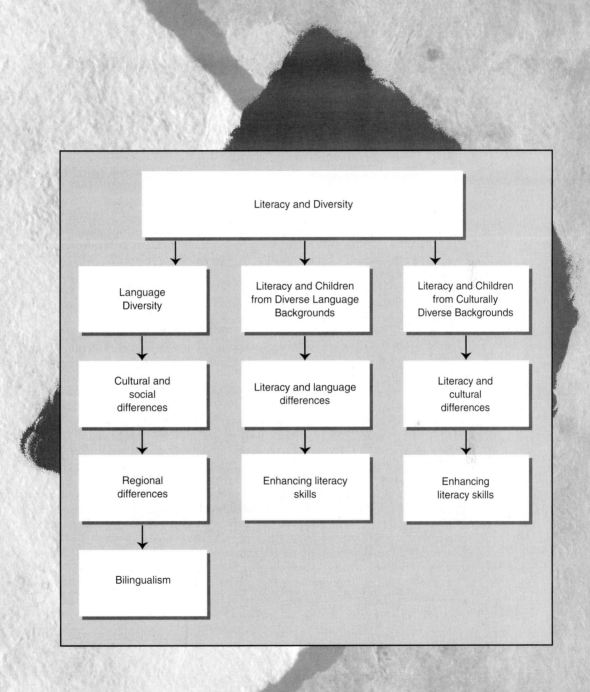

Literacy and Diversity

Language Diversity

Literacy and Children from Diverse Language Backgrounds

Literacy and Children from Culturally Diverse Backgrounds

Cultural and social differences

Literacy and language differences

Literacy and cultural differences

Regional differences

Enhancing literacy skills

Enhancing literacy skills

Bilingualism

▌▌▌INTRODUCTION

It has almost become a cliche to state that schools in the United States are becoming increasingly diverse. But, cliche or not, it seems undeniably true. In some areas, ethnic "minorities" have become the majority. In many urban areas, neighborhoods that were traditionally European American or African American have become peopled with persons from Asian and Latino cultures. Even many suburban areas have experienced increasing diversity. For example, in one suburban area outside Philadelphia a recent survey conducted by the school system found more than 100 languages spoken by families in the district.

As a result of this trend toward increasing diversity, teachers in the 21st century can expect to teach students from a wide variety of ethnic, cultural, racial, religious, and language backgrounds. In many cases, these children will come to school with cultural norms and traditions that differ from that of the prevailing school culture. This often presents a challenge to schools, which must decide thorny issues such as what to include in the traditional "Christmas" concert, how (or whether) to celebrate Halloween, and how to reach out to parents who may have different language skills and differing views of school authorities.

The increasing diversity of the school population also presents profound challenges for literacy education. Many children will enter school speaking a language other than English as their first language. Others speak dialects of English that may be rejected by some educators as "inappropriate" or even deficient. Some children may come from a cultural background where an oral tradition of storytelling is more important than a written tradition. In all cases, schools are being challenged to enhance the literacy of all their students while providing high-quality reading materials that reflect the diversity in society. How schools respond to these challenges will, in large measure, determine whether the United States can remain both a pluralistic and a democratic society.

In this chapter we will examine some of the challenges to enhancing literacy in children who come from a variety of ethnic and cultural backgrounds. We will discuss how teachers should respond to children who use nonstandard dialects [a dialect is a systematic variation of a language that is spoken by a large number of people (Warren & McCloskey, 1997)] of English or who speak languages other than English as their first language. We will discuss methods to enhance the reading and writing of children from diverse cultures, and we will consider the special problems posed by children with special needs who also come from diverse cultural backgrounds. As you read this chapter, you will no doubt notice the very sensitive nature of issues of culture, race, and language. You may even feel uncomfortable yourself with some of these issues. There is nothing wrong with having strong feelings about some of these issues as long as these feelings do not interfere with your ability to teach children from a variety of cultural backgrounds.

▌▌▌LANGUAGE DIVERSITY

Cultural and Social Differences

A few years ago the Oakland, California, school board enacted a resolution directing teachers to recognize and appreciate the language used by their students (called "Ebonics") and to use this language to help students make the transition to standard

American English (SAE) (Applebome, 1996). This action ignited a firestorm of reaction throughout the United States and, indeed, around the world. In making their resolution, the Oakland board indicated their belief that Ebonics (also known as "Black English" or "Black English Vernacular") is not a dialect of English but a separate language. Furthermore, they claimed that it was not only learned through interaction with others who spoke the language but was genetically based—though they later retracted this portion of their statement (Golden, 1997). Numerous researchers, educators, and leaders within the African-American community spoke out against this resolution. Their concerns ranged from the academic (Is Ebonics actually a language?) to the sociopolitical (Are African-American children being denied the opportunity to become full members of the dominant culture?).

The Ebonics controversy raised a number of significant issues regarding language, culture, and power—many of which have not been and are not likely to be completely resolved. One question is whether Ebonics, or Black English Vernacular, is a language in its own right or a dialect of English. In general, speakers of different languages are unable to understand each other whereas those who speak different dialects of a language can understand each other. However, this is not always true (for example, speakers of Mandarin and Cantonese dialects of Chinese are unable to understand each other). In fact, the distinction between what comprises a language and what is a dialect is not always clear.

Although linguists continue to debate the distinctions between languages and dialects, there are several facts about Ebonics that cannot be disputed. First, Ebonics is used by a large number of poor, inner-city African Americans. It shares some characteristics with Standard American English while differing in many ways (Table 10.1). The Linguistic Society of America (1997) recognized that Ebonics is a systematic and rule-governed language system that should not be called "slang" or "ungrammatical." In fact, this learned society applauded the Oakland School Board's recommendation that teachers use Ebonics to teach Standard American English.

Whether we call it a dialect or a language, it is clear that many, though not all, African-American children use language that differs from the standard expected in schools. What should teachers do? Should they discourage African-American children from using Ebonics or incorporate Ebonics into instruction? The answers to these questions are often based more on considerations of race, class, and power than on educational efficacy. Experts often disagree on the extent to which teachers should incorporate Ebonics into instruction, but most agree that it is important that teachers show respect for children who speak differently from others. This means that children should not be "corrected" in front of their peers or told that they cannot use this "dirty" or "gutter" language in school. Instead, teachers should try to understand the language differences of the children in their class and help them make the transition to Standard American English so they can be successful in all aspects of literacy (Taylor, 1998).

Whether Ebonics is considered to be a dialect of English or a language in itself, it is an example of a language difference that is the result of social and cultural factors. The relative isolation of inner-city African Americans from white, middle-class society has influenced the development and persistence of Ebonics.

Regional Differences

Despite the influences of media and transportation, regional differences persist in the United States and in many other countries. For example, some residents of New

TABLE 10.1 Some Differences between Ebonics and Standard American English

Ebonics Grammatical Structure	SAE Grammatical Structure
• Possessive "'s"	
Nonobligatory where word position expresses possession.	Obligatory regardless of position.
"Get *mother* coat."	"Get *mother's* coat."
"It *be* mother's."	"It's mother's."
• Plural "s"	
Nonobligatory with numerical quantifier.	Obligatory regardless of numerical quantifier.
"He got ten *dollar*."	"He has ten *dollars*."
"Look at the *cats*."	"Look at the *cats*."
• Regular past "ed"	
Nonobligatory; reduced as consonant cluster.	Obligatory
"Yesterday I *walk* to school."	"Yesterday I *walked* to school."
• Indefinite "an"	
Use of indefinite "a."	Use of "an" before nouns beginning with a vowel.
"He ride in *a* airplane."	"He rode in *an* airplane."
• Future tense	
More frequent use of	More frequent use of "will"
"be going to" (gonna).	"I *will* dance tonight."
"I *be going to* dance tonight."	
• Negation	
Triple negative	Absence of triple negative
"*Nobody don't never* like me."	"No one ever likes me."
Use of "ain't"	"Ain't" is unacceptable
"I *ain't* going."	"I'm not going."

Source: Owens (1995), pp. 496–497.

England drop the final *r* sound in words such as pronouncing "chowdah" for "chowder." In the Philadelphia, Pennsylvania, area, a soft drink is usually called a "soda," whereas just a few hundred miles away in Pittsburgh it is called "pop." Significant dialect differences exist in the Appalachian mountain region, in the islands off the southeast coast of the United States, in the Cajun regions of Louisiana, and in many other parts of the United States.

Language differences such as those described can be amusing, charming, and occasionally embarrassing. Sometimes, however, they have more serious consequences. Individuals whose languages differ from the "standard" may be perceived as less intelligent, deficient, even disabled. This is the result of a widespread belief that there is one "right" way to speak. In fact, this is not true. What is "right" is the language of the dominant social group within a language group (Warren & McCloskey, 1997). For example, Standard American English is the language spoken by a majority of white, European Americans primarily residing in the northern half of the United States. Linguists claim that there is nothing inherently superior in the linguistic structure of this dialect of English, any more than the Oxbridge dialect of British English is superior to a Yorkshire or Cornish dialect. These dialects are "superior" only in the sense that they are used by those in power. Unfortunately, individuals who speak a dialect other than the "standard" one may feel inferior intellectually and socially (Luhman, 1990).

It is important that educators understand what is and is not true about dialects and dialect differences. First, no dialect is linguistically superior to another. All dialects have a system of rules, although the rules certainly differ from one to another. Although at one time some scholars (e.g., Bernstein, 1970) claimed that individuals who spoke with a working-class dialect were linguistically inferior, most researchers today believe that there is no inherent superiority of one dialect over another. Second, although there are no inherently superior dialects, there may be a preferred dialect in the community. Children who speak a dialect other than the preferred one should be helped to learn the preferred dialect while being allowed to use their own dialect without correction or scorn. Third, a dialect difference is not a disability. Children who pronounce words in ways that differ from the community norm, have different meanings for words, or have different communicative characteristics (such as avoiding eye contact during interaction) should not automatically be assumed to be language disordered. Instead, a careful investigation of their social, cultural, and language history should be undertaken in order to discover the source of these language differences. On the other hand, a child with a language difference may also have a language disorder. Only a careful and comprehensive assessment can differentiate language differences from language disorders.

Bilingualism

In the United States, many children enter school speaking a language other than English as a first language. According to the 1990 census, approximately 6.3 million children between the ages of 5 and 17 speak a language other than English at home. Some of these children have already learned English as a second language and come to school already bilingual. Others have had either limited or no exposure to English and must acquire their second language while in school. This latter group is sometimes called "limited English proficient" (LEP) because of their limited English skills.

It is important to understand that there is more than one type of "bilingualism" and that, in fact, there is a great deal of heterogeneity among the population of children who may be called "bilingual." Some children acquire two (or more) languages simultaneously. Despite some occasional mixing of the two languages, there are generally no negative consequences for simultaneous bilingualism. On the contrary, children who learn multiple languages at an early age may actually be at an advantage in language and literacy development (Wallace & Goodman, 1989). Other children begin to acquire a second language after the usual time for first-language acquisition (about age 3). A number of factors may influence their acquisition of this second language, including the amount of interaction they have had with speakers of this language, their motivation to learn the second language, and the social and cultural desirability of learning this language. Although some second-language learners may enter school with what seems to be competence in speaking a second language, Cummins (1984) cautions that there are two levels of language proficiency. Students may have what he calls "basic interpersonal communicative skill," but lack "cognitive/academic language proficiency." In other words, some students may be able to carry on a conversation but be limited in the application of their language skills to reading, writing, and problem solving.

There continues to be a heated debate in the United States about how to teach children who are second-language learners. In brief, the debate centers on when and to what degree these children should be taught in English. Although there are many variations, three types of instructional approaches have emerged:

- *Submersion (or immersion) programs:* Children with limited English proficiency are placed in regular classrooms where English is the only language spoken. The second-language learners receive little or no special help with English.
- *English as a second language (ESL) programs:* As with the submersion approach, English is the sole means of instruction, but children with limited skills in English receive some support for learning English, often in a pullout or supplemental program.
- *Bilingual education:* Academic instruction is conducted in both the native language of the child and in English. Baca (1998) has identified several types of bilingual programs, including:
  - Transitional: The child's native language and culture are preserved only to the extent necessary for the child to acquire English. Reading and writing in the child's native language are not generally taught.
  - Maintenance: Children are encouraged to become literate in their native language while English language acquisition is promoted.
  - Restoration: Children are helped to recover the language and culture of their ancestors. Such a program might be used with Native American children.
  - Enrichment: A new language and culture is added to a group of monolingual children.

Recently, the debate over bilingual education in the United States has heated up because of the passage of Proposition 227 in California, which reduced and, in some cases, eliminated funding for bilingual programs. This action was prompted by claims from some proponents that bilingual programs were actually preventing children from learning English and were a waste of time and money. However, research on bilingual education programs has shown that such programs can be beneficial for children. Benefits have been found in cognitive development, the development of reading and writing skills, and the development of more positive attitudes (Baca, 1989). Therefore, educators should be advised to examine the research on bilingual education before abandoning this approach.

LITERACY AND CHILDREN FROM CULTURALLY DIVERSE BACKGROUNDS

Literacy and Cultural Differences

The 1998 National Assessment of Educational Progress indicated that African-American, along with Hispanic and Native American, children continue to lag behind

Literacy instruction should reflect an understanding of the different purposes and forms of literacy for students from diverse cultural backgrounds.

their white and Asian peers in the development of reading skills at all of the grade levels (4th, 8th, and 12th) measured by the assessment (U.S. Department of Education, 1999). Although African-American 4th- and 8th-graders did make significant improvements in reading from the 1994 results, they still lag far behind the average scores for white children. In fact, almost two-thirds (64%) of African-American children in grade four scored below what is considered to be the basic level of reading performance compared to 27% of white children. Although it is certainly not true that all African-American or other children from minority groups have poor literacy skills (18% of African-American 12th graders scored at or above the proficient level in reading), there is a significant overrepresentation of children from minority cultures in the lower-performing groups.

What accounts for the poor reading performance of African-American children? The answers to this question are certainly complex and not completely clear. Without a doubt, they are rooted in the historical racism and poverty to which many African-Americans have been subjected. But, sometimes, the causes are more subtle. For example, Dr. Arlette Willis, an African-American scholar, described this conversation with her 9-year-old:

> "Jake, what's wrong? Why are you so unhappy?" I ask.
> "We have the Young Authors [writing] Contest today, and I don't have anything to write about."
> "Sure you do. There are lots of things you can write about," I encourage him. "Why don't you write about baseball or soccer?"

"No," he replies. "A kid at our school wrote about cancer last year and the story went all the way to the next state [regionals]."

"Well," I answer, "maybe you should write about something funny—like when you go to the barbershop. You and your brothers are always talking about your trips there."

"Oh no, Mom, they wouldn't understand. When I just get my hair cut, they always ask me, 'Why do you have that line in your hair?' 'It's not a line, it's a part,' I try to tell them. I can't write about the barbershop. They won't understand."

"Well," I say, trying to clarify what I really mean, "I don't mean write about getting a haircut. I mean write about all the funny people that come in and the things that happen while you are at the barbershop. You and your brothers always come home tellin' a funny story and laugh about it for the rest of the week. That's what I mean about writing about the barbershop."

"No, Mom. They won't understand," he insists.

"What do you mean, 'they won't understand?' Who is the 'they'?" I ask.

"The people in my class," he replies, somewhat frustrated.

Jake continues, "You should read this story that M. wrote. It is a mystery story and it's really good. I can't beat that story. I'll bring you a copy of it if I can. I know it will win."

Wanting him to participate in the contest, I ask, "How do you know M.'s story is good?"

"She read it in class. Everybody said it's really good," he responds.

"Well, I still think you should try. You are a really good writer. Look at all the 'good stuff' you wrote in Mrs. S.'s room. You could rewrite some of it and turn it in."

Finally, he answers, "I'll think about it," and we go off to school. (Willis, 1995)

Jake seems to be a bright and articulate child from a caring and supportive family. Yet, this conversation suggests that he has developed some negative attitudes about his literacy skills. Jake's mother believes that he is reluctant to write about his life and culture because he does not believe that they will be understood by his classmates and teacher. He is, according to her, trying to figure out how he can express his true self while trying to please his teacher and classmates, who may not understand his culture.

Willis has described what some researchers have called, "home-school-discontinuity" or "cultural mismatch" (Thompson, Mixon, & Serpell, 1996). The claim is that some children come to school with cultural norms and expectations that differ from those of the prevailing school culture. In Jake's case, his classmates' lack of knowledge about African-American haircuts caused him embarrassment and a reluctance to write about what could have been an interesting topic. Other examples of discontinuity between the home and school culture abound. You may recall from Chapter 1 Shirley Heath's pioneering ethnographic studies of children from Trackton, an African-American working-class community, found that many of these children struggled with the questions asked in class. From the children's perspective, it seemed strange for teachers to ask questions to which they already knew the answer. At home, Heath found that these children had few opportunities to answer questions. Instead, parents and other adults tended to primarily use directive statements. When questions were used, they sought information unknown to the adults (Heath, 1983). As a result of these differences between home and school, children from Trackton and similar African-American communities may find that they do not "fit in" to the classroom. If they are to succeed in school, they must change or suffer the consequences.

Another example of cultural mismatch is in narrative styles. Narrative style (or storytelling) is an important component of both spoken and written language. In school, children are expected to tell and retell stories, to comprehend story structure, and to use a sequential style of storytelling in their writing. However, some African-American students have a narrative style that is less linear than that of white children and more characterized by a series of personal associations (Michaels, 1981). Contrast the two stories in Box 10.1. Note how Evan, the white child, gets right to the point and keeps the story focused on a single event, whereas Renee's story meanders back and forth over several incidents and time periods. There is nothing intrinsically "wrong" with either narrative style. However, Evan's style is more consistent with what is generally expected in the classroom—a clear, concise, linear retelling with few, if any, digressions.

▌Box 10.1

EXAMPLE OF NARRATIVE STORYTELLING BY TWO CHILDREN

Child 1 (White):

Evan: Last Christmas, my mom she I was telling my mom that I want a stamp pad and so on Christmas I mean on my birthday she got a stamp pad and a stamp pad for me.

Child 2 (African American):

Renee: Um, . . . at Thanksgiving when I went to my grandma and grandpa um . . . . we were, we had all-all this food . . . and I was at the table right? And I was saying and I said . . . . and I ss it was the day before Thanksgiving, and I said to my I was really really stuffed because we were um 'cuz we had finished eating and I said, "I'm so full I could eat a Thanksgiving turkey." And she said, "well you could eat the stuffing too." And I said, I said "why don't you and daddy put the stuffing in bed," . . . and, and . . . my daddy my father looked at me and he said, "Huh? Huh?" That's what that's what he always does when um I say something like he should be chicken or something, he goes "Huh? Huh?" [laughs] he goes like that . . . Then un, and in midnight . . . ac-actually it was like two o'clock in the morning I heard a scratch again and I went to the same room and it was just a little, little baby rabbit with his mo- with one mother and he was so cute and I fed them some milk, and some leftover turkey and um then I an um, then I let them out . . . [the conversation continues for several hundred more words]

Source: Foster, M. (1992). Sociolinguistics and the African-American community: Implications for literacy. *Theory into Practice, 31,* 395.

Recently, some researchers (e.g., Hester, 1996; Hyter & Westby, 1996) have begun to question whether African-American children really do have a narrative style that differs from white children. They have claimed that African-American children produce a range of narrative structures, depending on the task. When the task calls for more structured, topic-centered narratives, they can produce them. These findings suggest that teachers should make all students aware of the expectations for storytelling and retelling and help those whose style differs from what is required to use the required style.

Cultural mismatch is one of several possible factors that Thompson and associates (1996) believe may contribute to the underperformance of African-American children in reading and writing. The other factors are:

- Cultural deprivation
- Discriminatory educational provisions and practices
- Oppositional counterculture among students

We shall consider each of these in turn.

Cultural Deprivation

Though largely discredited as a cause of literacy and learning difficulties among African-American children, cultural deprivation theory remains an influential factor in American society. The roots of this theory lie in the work of those such as Bernstein (1970) and others who equated cultural and linguistic differences with deficits. The theory claimed that children from poor and minority families had been "deprived" of the opportunity to develop the language, social, and cognitive skills that they would need in order to be successful in school because of their "deficient" language and lack of enriching experiences. As was noted earlier in this chapter, most researchers today believe that there is nothing inherently deficient about dialect differences and, by extension, cultural differences. Although some children may, indeed, come to school with experiences that differ from what is expected by the school, these differences in no way represent deficiencies.

One of the cultural differences that is sometimes cited as a cause of the poor literacy performance of African-American children is attitudes toward literacy. Many people believe that African-American families do not value or even discourage literacy skills. However, researchers who have actually examined attitudes toward literacy and family practices have found that, on the whole, African-American families hold education in general and literacy in particular in high regard (Baumann & Thomas, 1997; Gadsen, 1992).

Discriminatory Policies and Practices

Some have claimed that a significant factor in the poor literacy performance of many African-American children is discriminatory policies and practices followed by some educators. Researchers have found that teachers tend to hold more negative views of minority children and that these can influence instructional decisions (Hilliard, 1989). African-American children are overrepresented in low-achieving groups and in special education placements. As a result, they may be called on less often in class, given less feedback, and criticized more frequently (Irvine, 1990). All of these factors may contribute to the continuing underperformance in all areas of school performance, including literacy.

Oppositional Counterculture

Another factor that may contribute to the poor literacy performance of some African-American children is their attitude toward school. In a study of several inner-city schools, Ogbu (1987) found that many students frowned on academic success as a sign of conforming to the dominant school culture. In addition, some students may be discouraged by what they see as racist policies and practices that may prevent them from succeeding. Why try, they ask, if I have no chance for success?

Enhancing the Literacy Skills of Culturally Diverse Students

Although we may not have all of the answers about the causes, there can be little doubt that many African-American students have poor literacy skills. What can teachers and other education professionals do to enhance the performance of African-American and other culturally different students in their classroom?

Successful teachers of children from diverse cultural and ethnic backgrounds have high achievement expectations for all of their students. They resist cultural stereotypes that claim that African-American and other groups do not value literacy and are unwilling to work hard to achieve. Successful teachers also try to inform themselves about the cultural background of their students. Strickland (1994) suggests that teachers should learn about the community in which they teach, read literature by and about the cultural group(s) they are teaching, and meet and talk to people from the community in order to gain a deeper understanding of the experiences their students bring to school.

In addition to bringing appropriate attitudes and expectations into the classroom, teachers also need to implement effective instructional practices for all of their students. Strickland (1994) reviewed the research on effective literacy instruction and identified five major approaches that she believes could significantly enhance the literacy skills of children from a variety of cultural and socioeconomic backgrounds.

Principle I. Literacy learning starts early and continues throughout life. Like all children, African-American children enter school eager to learn. Despite some reports to the contrary, all children have been exposed to print in a variety of forms, although their experience with books may vary. Rather than identifying "deficiencies" in children, schools should build on what the children already know to enhance emergent literacy. Specific suggestions include:

- Create learning environments that give children the confidence they need to learn.
- Start coordinated school and social service intervention programs early and make them ongoing.
- Treat instruction in phonics as an important part of beginning reading and writing, but not a precursor to it.
- Initiate family literacy programs in which adults and children approach literacy learning as a cooperative social experience.

An example of a family literacy program is one described by Edwards (1992). Edwards began by recruiting an unlikely group of community leaders to help spread the word about her program. Her group included a bar owner who insisted that his patrons spend at least as much time reading to their children as they spent in his establishment, a bus driver who offered to drive parents to the literacy program, and people out on the streets who encouraged parents to attend the literacy meetings. Recognizing that some of the parents in her program had poor reading skills themselves, Edwards gave them a lot of experience with simple books and told them that it was all right to use repeated readings. The literacy program taught parents how to read to their children by modeling these techniques with participants and giving them opportunities to practice their new skills. Over time, the literacy program became a sort of extended family for the participants in which they could share their frustrations and successes with their children and with their schools.

Principle II. Literacy learning is used to make meanings out of our world. Strickland (1994) suggests students should be assigned tasks that make sense to them. Assignments that require reasoning and reflective thought are preferable to low-level, rote tasks. Meaningless drills on isolated skills should be avoided. Instructional materials should be literature-based, including both fiction and nonfiction. Literacy instruction should be integrated so that reading, writing, and speaking are seen as related tasks. In addition, an inquiry-based curriculum, in which children are encouraged to pose and respond to questions, should be developed. If these suggestions are followed, children should find reading and writing to be meaningful activities rather than just the accumulation of isolated facts and skills.

Principle III. Literacy learning takes place through active involvement and use. This goal can be accomplished through activities such as the use of collaborative groups and peer teaching, both of which promote active learning. Other suggestions include postreading activities that use student-generated questions rather than those provided by a teacher or a textbook and the modeling of strategies to accomplish a task (such as learning new vocabulary or editing written work). Classrooms in which there is active student involvement tend to be busy, noisy places in which there is much purposeful movement.

Principle IV. Literacy learning is influenced by one's language and cultural background. Ladson-Billings (1992) describes what she calls a "culturally relevant" approach to teaching. She defines the culturally relevant classroom as one in which classroom teachers:

- Do not shy away from issues of race and culture; instead, they try to appreciate and celebrate students as individuals as well as members of a culture
- Speak and instruct in Standard American English while incorporating students' home languages into conversations without correction
- Are in constant physical contact with their students, giving hugs and kisses as signs of approval
- Build an atmosphere of academic achievement, support, and trust
- Create a literate environment in which their classrooms are filled with books and other reading matter as well as student work (Box 10.2)
- Design curriculum that makes their students and their students' heritage the focus

▌ Box 10.2

Examples of Culturally Diverse Books

African-American Literature

The Dream Keeper	Langston Hughes
Roll of Thunder, Hear My Cry	Mildred Taylor
Let the Circle Be Unbroken	Mildred Taylor

Road to Memphis	Mildred Taylor
Stevie	John Steptoe
Black Snowman	Phil Mendez
Fat Up, Gemma	Sarah Hayes
Jamaica's Find	Juanita Havill
Tell Me a Story, Mama	Angela Johnson

Latino Literature

Arroz Con Leche: Popular Songs and Rhymes from Latin America	LuLu Delacre
Tortillas Para Mama and Other Nursery Rhymes	LuLu Delacre
Baseball in April and Other Stories	Gary Soto
Local News	Gary Soto
Going Home	Nicholasa Mohr
Miguel y el Pastel (Miguel and the Cake)	Maribel Suarez

Principle V. Literacy learning is influenced by social context. Teachers should attempt to develop classroom communities in which each child feels valued and supported by their teacher and by their peers. Schools can enhance a sense of community by avoiding grouping and tracking students based on only their ability levels and replacing that with flexible grouping and cooperative learning. In addition, schools can create uninterrupted blocks of time for literacy instruction that encourage interaction and reflection. One inner-city school forbids announcements and visitors during a two-hour literacy block at the beginning of each day.

Thompson and associates (1996) identified five specific instructional strategies that they believe can be particularly useful for cultural minority learners in urban schools because of their emphasis on student motivation, social interaction, and literacy modeling. These programs are:

- *ALERT* (Allen, Wright, & Laminack, 1988): ALERT combines the language experience approach with the use of advertisements to develop critical thinking skills. Children are taught to listen and read advertisements critically. Components of the program include: advance organizer, listen and learn, examine/explain, restate/read, think/test/talk. According to Thompson and associates (1996), this approach is useful for cultural minority students because it ensures their participation in critical reading activities, which are sometimes denied them. Also, children in urban communities may be particularly vulnerable to advertising that portrays an attractive world that is just beyond their reach. This program helps them become more critical and informed consumers.
- *Story retellings:* Story retellings are postreading activities in which the reader (or listener) is asked to tell what they remember orally or in writing. Retelling requires reconstruction and integration of the text by the student. Story retellings can be used to help children from cultural minority groups learn a narrative style with which they may be less familiar. At the same time, retellings give the child the opportunity to personalize the story from their own previous experiences.
- *Interactive reading guides:* In this approach, students work in cooperative learning groups to complete a study guide. Students engage in discussions that help them

to make predictions, develop associations, and engage in a variety of critical reading activities. For students from cultural minority groups, the opportunity to work in cooperative learning groups can enhance the sense of belonging and support from peers.

- *Transactional strategies instruction* (Pressley et al., 1992): Students are taught to use strategies that incorporate the students' personal understanding of the text in order to construct meaning from text. In encouraging students to use their own experiences, this approach can be useful for children who come from diverse cultural backgrounds.
- *Question–answer relationships* (QARs) (Raphael, 1982): QAR questions require students to look for information that is explicitly presented in the text, integrate information from several parts of the text, apply previous experience to what they have read, or rely on previous experience alone. The opportunities to engage in discussion, use their personal experiences, and engage in higher-order thinking are especially useful for children from cultural minority groups.

Most of the techniques for enhancing the literacy skills of children from diverse cultural and socioeconomic backgrounds are not unique to this population. They are methods that can be useful for any child in any classroom. However, when these methods are used by teachers who are aware of and respectful to the diverse experiences of their students, they can be effective in enhancing the literacy skills of all children.

LITERACY AND CHILDREN FROM DIVERSE LANGUAGE BACKGROUNDS

Literacy and Language Differences

In the beginning of this chapter we reviewed results from the National Assessment of Educational Progress (NAEP) that indicated that African-American students lag behind their white peers in literacy development. Similar results can be found for Hispanic students. Despite some increase in reading scores for 12th grade between 1994 and 1998, the test results indicate that Hispanic students lag significantly behind their white peers at all of the grade levels sampled by the test (grades 4, 8, and 12). How can we account for these results and, more importantly, what can be done to improve the results for Hispanic and other students from language and cultural minority groups?

Many factors may contribute to the poor literacy development of children with limited proficiency in English. Aside from the obvious difficulties inherent in learning to read—as well as speak—a second language, many students with limited English proficiency also live in poor, inner-city communities that are beset by a variety of problems, including violence, poor nutrition, and limited access to health care. The schools they attend may be ill equipped, with large class sizes and teachers who may feel that they lack adequate support to provide effective instruction. Some children may move frequently from community to community within the United States or back and forth from another country. Although all of these factors may have some impact on the literacy development of children with limited English proficiency, we will focus our attention on language and metacognitive factors, as these are more amenable to the instructional programs generally offered by schools.

One of the prevailing assumptions about the literacy development of students with limited English proficiency is that reading proficiency in English is closely linked to spoken language proficiency. As a result, there has been a push to immerse non-English speakers in the English language as quickly as possible. However, as Reyes (1992) points out, most of the research on the academic achievement of second-language learners has found that they attain higher achievement levels when allowed to begin literacy instruction in their primary language before switching to English. In fact, the relationship between reading ability and oral language proficiency in English is far from clear. A review of the research conducted by Fitzgerald (1995) found that the relationship depended on three factors:

- *Native language:* Some researchers have found that skill in English is important for Hispanic students but less important for other second-language learners, such as students who speak Cantonese as their first language.
- *Age or grade level:* English language proficiency has generally been found to be more important for older students.
- *Type of English language proficiency measured:* Correlations between English language skill and reading ability were generally lower when naturalistic measures of conversational skill were used in contrast to more structured tests of language ability.

Some researchers have claimed that, rather than being an impediment to learning, bilingualism may actually be a potential strength (Jimenez, Garcia, & Pearson, 1996). They cite research that has found that bilingual children may have greater awareness of the metacognitive aspects of reading.

The implications of the research on spoken language skill and reading proficiency in a second language are that schools should help children develop literacy skills in their native language first while helping them to develop English language skills that will assist them in making the transition to literacy in English. However, there is no reason to wait for a certain level of proficiency in English before beginning literacy instruction. In fact, some researchers have suggested that second-language learners may be able to learn oral and written language skills at the same time. They claim that reading comprehension actually enhances language development (Anderson & Roit, 1996).

In addition to obvious differences in spoken language proficiency, some have claimed that second-language learners differ in the cognitive processes they bring to reading and writing. However, Fitzgerald's (1995) review of the research on the reading processes of second-language learners suggests that any differences are more quantitative than qualitative. In other words, Fitzgerald found more similarities than differences in the processes that native and nonnative speakers of English used in reading. Both groups use metacognitive strategies during reading and monitor their comprehension as they read. On the other hand, second-language learners tended to use fewer metacognitive strategies and use them less often.

Jimenez, Garcia, and Pearson (1996) took a somewhat different approach to understanding the reading processes of bilingual readers by observing the strategies used by successful readers whose first language was Spanish. They found that they focused a considerable amount of their attention on unknown vocabulary, carefully monitored their comprehension, connected their prior knowledge to the text, and made a large number of inferences about what they were reading. For example, one student indicated that he uses the following strategy to monitor his comprehension:

Student: Oh! OK . . . I sometimes read the sentence out loud, then it makes more sense than when I read it to myself.

Enhancing the Literacy Skills of Students with Diverse Language Backgrounds

The research on literacy development and cognitive and language skills in children who are learning English as a second language has many implications for effective instructional practice. The research suggests that students might benefit from instruction that teaches strategies for making the connection between what they know in their first language and unknown words and concepts in their second language. Additionally, instruction should include strategies for monitoring comprehension and making inferences about text, as successful bilingual readers seem to use these strategies. Gertsen (1996) suggested the following instructional strategies based on several years of observation in classrooms for students with limited proficiency in English:

1. Structures, frameworks, scaffolds, and strategies
   - Provide support to students by "thinking aloud," building on, and clarifying input of students.
   - Use visual organizers, story maps, or other aids to help students organize and relate information.
2. Relevant background knowledge and key vocabulary concepts
   - Provide adequate background knowledge to students and informally assess whether students have background knowledge.
   - Focus on key vocabulary words.
   - Use consistent language.
   - Incorporate students' primary language meaningfully.
3. Mediation/feedback
   - Provide feedback that focuses on meaning, not grammar, syntax, or pronunciation.
   - Provide activities and tasks that students can complete.
   - Indicate to students when they are successful.
   - Assign activities that are reasonable, avoiding undue frustration.
   - Allow use of native language responses (when context is appropriate).

Drawing on several years of careful observations of instructional practices in classrooms that included high percentages of language-minority students, Anderson and Roit (1996) suggested using the following instructional strategies to enhance the oral-language proficiency and reading comprehension of second-language learners:

- *Shared reading:* Shared reading involves a teacher reading and sharing a book with students. Students with limited English proficiency can be helped to gain more from shared reading by listening to the story before it is read to the whole class, by being encouraged to participate, and by asking questions about unknown words so they can more fully participate in discussions of the meaning of the text.

- *Vocabulary networking:* This instructional approach utilizes semantic mapping strategies in which a graphic representation is used to support vocabulary learning. Anderson and Roit (1996) suggest that networking can be used effectively with language minority students by adding new words to the networks as necessary, by placing difficult words at the top of the page for inclusion in the web, and by color coding crucial words.
- *Expanding contexts:* Students may benefit from paying attention to the context for words. Teachers can encourage students to discuss how a particular word fits into a selection and how they can use the word in their writing. The goal is to move away from learning words in isolation.
- *Predicting:* Predicting can reveal a great deal about what the students understand prior to a story. It is also important to review predictions after reading as a further check for understanding.
- *Imagery:* The use of visual images can be helpful in enhancing comprehension of text. One way to encourage the use of imagery is to discuss illustrations that accompany the text. Students can also be encouraged to develop their own illustrations for the text.
- *Text structures:* Anderson and Roit point to research that shows that some language-minority students can improve their comprehension by learning to recognize the structure of the text. Students can be taught to recognize various structures (e.g., cause/effect or problem/solution) and then use a metacognitive strategy and/or graphic organizer to identify the text elements (Figure 10.1).

In reading a passage in a social studies text about the causes of the Civil War in the United States, a student might use the following strategy:

Step 1: What is the text structure (in this case, problem/solution)?

Step 2: Apply the appropriate comprehension strategy:

For a problem/solution text the strategy might include questions such as:

• What is the problem? (secession by the South)

• What is the cause of the problem? (slavery and economic differences)

• What will happen if the problem continues? (war)

• How can the problem be solved? (legislation; compromise)

• How else can the problem be solved? (states' rights)

Step 3: Develop a graphic organizer:

Problem	Solutions	Outcomes
Slavery and Economic Differences	1. Legislation 2. Compromise 3. States' Rights	Settlement Secession War

FIGURE 10.1

Application of a Text Structure Approach to Comprehension

- *Questioning, identifying problems, and sharing strategies:* Students can be encouraged to think out loud about the strategies to solve reading problems. Teachers can model these strategies for students who can then utilize these strategies in small group discussions.
- *Explaining text:* Rather than simply retelling a story, students can be guided to explain the meaning of the text and to discuss and compare their understanding with that of other students. This discussion could be conducted in the students' native language.
- *Culturally familiar informational texts:* Reading materials that reflect the variety of cultures represented in the community can be utilized (Box 10.2). In addition to books, encyclopedia passages and magazines can be useful sources of text materials.
- *Conversational opportunities:* Discussions should be more conversational and less structured to enable the students to feel comfortable asking questions and seeking clarification. The teacher's role should be to encourage natural conversations rather than constraining the discussion to a set of structured, limited question–response sequences.

Students with limited English language skills face special challenges in secondary school. Not only do the vocabulary and language sophistication of texts become more challenging but, typically, students receive less support and are expected to read and write more independently. Therefore, it is important to consider instructional techniques that may enhance the success of language-minority students at the secondary level.

While acknowledging the limited research base on effective strategies for improving content-area learning for second-language learners, Reyes and Molner (1991) identified several successful approaches in three general categories: background-building strategies, writing-to-learn activities, and cooperative learning. Their suggestions include:

1. *Background-Building Strategies:* These are techniques that help the students link their background knowledge to new concepts from the text. They include:
   - Semantic mapping: Students are helped to generate ideas and arrange them in a visual map that is used to guide recall.
   - Prereading plan (PReP): Students are guided through a three-step process that asks them to:
     - Generate associations with a key concept
     - Refine and elaborate on these associations
     - Reorganize and synthesize their statements
   - *Experience-text-relationship method (ETR):* Following an initial discussion period, students read short segments from the text. The teacher then asks questions, clarifies misconceptions, and assists students in linking their background knowledge to the text.
2. *Writing-to-Learn Activities:* Reyes and Molner (1991) note that many ESL writing programs consist largely of highly structured grammar exercises. They suggest that students participate in writing activities that help them learn how to construct meaning and synthesize their thinking. Examples of this type of activity include:
   - Guided writing procedure (GWP): This method uses oral language as a tool for integrating reading and writing instruction in the content areas. Steps include:
     - Brainstorming
     - Outlining: Students create an outline and write a short piece.

- Editing: The teacher edits using a checklist.
- Rewriting (I): Students rewrite the piece using the teacher's comments and the checklist.
- Researching: Students research the topic in greater depth.
- Rewriting (II): Students incorporate their research in this draft.
- Conferencing: The teacher provides feedback to the students on this draft.
- Connecting school writing with the community: This approach links expository writing to community concerns.
- In one application (Trueba, Moll, & Diz, 1982), students conducted interviews on a topic then, with teacher guidance, created papers based on their research. Both students' attitudes and writing quality improved.
3. *Cooperative Learning Activities:* Reyes and Molner (1991) note that research demonstrated that linguistically diverse learners benefit from cooperative learning. Several factors are cited as explanations for the utility of cooperative learning including:
   - "Cultural congruence": Cooperative learning utilizes activities such as cooperation and group interaction that some cultures (e.g., Mexican American and Asian) value.
   - Opportunity to learn: With cooperative learning activities all students receive equal teacher attention and have equal opportunities to learn.
   - Rewards: Students may be motivated by group and peer rewards.

As with the suggestions provided earlier in this chapter for enhancing the literacy of African-American students, most of the recommendations for students with language differences are really just good teaching. However, it is important that teachers use these strategies consistently, incorporate culturally diverse texts whenever possible, and give students opportunities to discuss what they have read both in their first language as well as in English.

▌▌ STUDENTS WITH LANGUAGE AND CULTURAL DIFFERENCES AND SPECIAL NEEDS

According to some estimates, more than one million students who speak English as a second language also exhibit significant learning difficulties (Baca & Cervantes, 1989). Called by some "triple threat" students, they face the multiple challenges of speaking a language other than English as their first language, having a disability, and experiencing discrimination for both their language and cultural and learning differences (Rueda & Chan, 1979).

One of the challenges that teachers face is identifying those students who have both a language difference and a language disability. This is no easy task. One of the authors encountered a student in a class for students with cognitive disabilities in an upper-middle class school district. This student spoke Haitian Creole as her first language and had recently moved to the United States. The author noticed that this student seemed to be significantly different from other students in the class. She appeared to have good social skills, was attentive, and could learn quickly. In fact, she was spending a significant portion of her day working with other students. A discussion with the classroom teacher revealed that the child had been placed in this classroom after initial testing in English only. This assessment indicated that the child had intelligence scores in the mentally retarded range. Although the teacher knew the child had been misplaced in her classroom she reported that nothing would be done until the next school year because the team did not want to reevaluate the student.

Unfortunately, this sort of tragic scenario is repeated all too often in schools where appropriate assessment in the child's native language is not available. At the same time, some students who really need additional support are denied this because the focus is entirely on their language difference—ignoring an apparent significant learning difficulty. Roseberry–McKibbin (1995) suggests that there are four types of linguistically and culturally diverse students:

1. *Normal language ability/adequate background:* These students have a normal underlying ability to learn language and come from backgrounds rich in stimulation and experiences. Their needs can often be met in bilingual education programs. Given some assistance, these students can usually succeed in school.
2. *Normal language ability/limited background:* These students have a normal underlying ability to learn language but come from backgrounds where they received limited stimulation and experiences. Usually these children come from very impoverished families. In addition to needing bilingual education programs, these students also need tutoring and enrichment programs. These students are often inappropriately placed in programs for students with special needs.
3. *Language-learning disability/adequate background:* Despite coming from family and community backgrounds where they have had stimulating experiences, these students struggle in school. Often, they could benefit from special educational services that would address their learning difficulty. However, they may not receive such services because there is an assumption that their language difference is the cause of their learning difficulty.
4. *Language-learning disability/limited background:* These students represent the most difficult to assess and identify because they have all three problems: language and cultural differences, limited background experiences, and a learning difficulty. Any one of these problems may prevent consideration of the other difficulties. Ideally, these children would benefit from bilingual special education programs. However, because programs like these are rare, they are often taught in English special education classrooms with some support in their first language.

Roseberry–McKibbin (1995) has also provided some guidelines that teachers can use to distinguish linguistically and culturally diverse (LCD) students from those with language disorders (Box 10.3).

▌**Box 10.3**

DISTINGUISHING LANGUAGE DIFFERENCES FROM LANGUAGE DISORDERS

Teachers can tell when an LCD student might need special education services for a language-learning disability when some of the following behaviors are manifested in comparison to similar peers:

 1. Nonverbal aspects of language are culturally inappropriate.
 2. Student does not express basic needs adequately.
 3. Student rarely initiates verbal interaction with peers.
 4. When peers initiate interaction, student responds sporadically/inappropriately.
 5. Student replaces speech with gestures, communicates nonverbally when talking would be appropriate and expected.
 6. Peers give indications that they have difficulty understanding the student.
 7. Student often gives inappropriate responses.
 8. Student has difficulty conveying thoughts in an organized, sequential manner that is understandable to listeners.
 9. Student shows poor topic maintenance ("skips around").
10. Student has word-finding difficulties that go beyond normal second language acquisition patterns.
11. Student fails to provide significant information to the listener, leaving the listener confused.
12. Student has difficulty with conversational turn-taking skills (may be too passive, or may interrupt inappropriately).
13. Student perseverates (remains too long) on a topic even after the topic has changed.
14. Student fails to ask and answer questions appropriately.
15. Student needs to hear things repeated, even when they are stated simply and comprehensibly.
16. Student often echoes what she or he hears.

If an LCD student manifests a number of the above behaviors, even in comparison to similar peers, then there is a good chance that the student has an underlying language-learning disability and will need a referral to special education.

Source: Roseberry–McKibbin, C. (1995). Distinguishing language differences from language disorders in linguistically and culturally diverse students. *Multicultural Education, 3,* 79.

Enhancing the Literacy Skills of Students with Language and Cultural Differences and Special Needs

Only recently have researchers begun to investigate instructional methods that might be useful in helping students with language and cultural differences and special needs enhance their literacy skills. In one study (Rousseau, Tam, & Ramnarain, 1993), two methods to increase oral reading and comprehension—discussion of key words and listening previewing—were used with Hispanic students in a class for students with speech and language impairments. For the *keyword procedure,* the teacher preselected 10–12 words from the story, which she wrote on the chalkboard. The teacher then read the words to the students, who repeated them chorally. The teacher then explained the meaning of each word. Following the keyword procedure, the students read the story orally and answered comprehension questions. In *listening previewing* the teacher read aloud the story while the students read silently. The researchers found that students learned best when both of these methods were used together.

Klingner and Vaughn (1995) reported the results of a study that used reciprocal teaching of reading comprehension with seventh and eighth graders with learning disabilities who used English as a second language. The teacher modeled a reading strategy that included the following steps:

1. *Prediction:* of what the test might be about
2. *Brainstorming:* what they already know about the topic
3. *Clarifying:* unknown words or phrases
4. *Highlighting:* the main idea in a paragraph
5. *Summarizing:* the main idea
6. *Asking and answering questions:* about a passage

Following the teacher modeling sessions, students took turns leading the discussions and playing the role of "teacher." The researchers reported significant improvements in reading comprehension for the students in their study and continued to do so even after the intervention itself stopped.

The studies reviewed previously provide two examples of the many techniques that could be used to enhance the literacy skills of students with language and cultural differences and special needs. Clearly, these students have a number of challenges that make school success more difficult, but it is also apparent that caring teachers who are knowledgeable about effective instructional methods can make a difference in the lives of these students.

▌▌SUMMARY

Students with diverse language and cultural backgrounds represent a large and growing proportion of the student population in most parts of the United States and in many other countries. It is important that teachers and other education professionals make the distinction between a language difference and a language disorder. Linguists have determined that no language or dialect is linguistically "superior" to another. However, some are more desirable because of political and cultural factors. Schools face the challenge of being sensitive to and respectful of language and cultural differences while helping students acquire the literacy skills that will enable them to become full participants in society.

Many students whose language and culture differ from that of the dominant group experience difficulty in school. Research has established that there are a number of methods that can be successfully used to enhance the literacy skills of these students. The key, however, is teachers and other education professionals who are sensitive to the special challenges faced by students with language and cultural diversity and who have the repertoire of skills to teach them successfully. In addition, for those students who have both language and cultural differences and a disability, additional supports and supportive instruction may be necessary.

▌▌▌ Linkages

1. Give arguments for and against the claim that Ebonics is a dialect of English or a separate language. What are the implications for schools of each position?
2. Give some additional examples of regional dialect differences.

3. Is there a "right" way to talk? What should schools do about children whose language differs from the norm?
4. Briefly describe three types of language education programs for students with limited English proficiency.
5. What accounts for the poor reading performance of African-American children?
6. In what ways are students with dialect differences similar to students with limited English language skills? In what ways are they different?
7. Describe three specific classroom-based suggestions that could be used to enhance the literacy skills of students from diverse cultural backgrounds.
8. Why have students who speak English as a second language and who also exhibit significant learning difficulties sometimes been called "triple threat" students?

On the Web

Center for Applied Linguistics (information on Ebonics)
www.cal.org/ebonics

National Association for Bilingual Education
www.nabe.org

National Center for Bilingual Education
www.ncbe.gwu.edu

Urban Education Web (information for families)
www.eric-web.tc.columbia.edu/families

References

Allen, E. G., Wright, J. P., & Laminack, L. L. (1988). Using language experience to ALERT pupils' critical thinking skills. *The Reading Teacher, 41,* 904–910.

Anderson, V., & Roit, M. (1996). Linking reading comprehension instruction to language development for language-minority students. *The Elementary School Journal, 96,* 295–309.

Appelbome, P. (1996, December 20). School district elevates status of black English. *New York Times,* p. 18.

Baca, L. M. (1989). Bilingualism and bilingual education. In L. Baca & H. Cervantes (Eds.), *The bilingual special education interface.* Upper Saddle River, NJ: Merrill/Prentice Hall.

Baca, L. M., & Cervantes, H. T. (1989). *The bilingual special education interface.* Upper Saddle River, NJ: Merrill/Prentice Hall.

Baumann, J. T., & Thomas, D. (1997). "If you can pass Momma's tests, then she knows you're getting your education": A case study of support for literacy learning within an African American family. *Reading Teacher, 51,* 108–120.

Bernstein, B. (1970). A sociolinguistic approach to socialization: With some reference to educability. In F. Williams (Ed.), *Language and poverty.* Chicago: Markham Publishing.

Cummins, J. (1984). *Bilingualism and special education: Issues in assessment and pedagogy.* Clevedon Avon, England: Multilingual Matters.

Edwards, P. A. (1992). Involving parents in building reading instruction of African-American children. *Theory into Practice, 31,* 350–359.

Fitzgerald, J. (1995). English-as-a-second-language learners' cognitive reading processes: a review of research in the United States. *Review of Educational Research, 65,* 145–190.

Foster, M. (1992). Sociolinguistics and the African-American community: Implications for literacy. *Theory into Practice, 31,* 303–311.

Fox, S. (1997). The controversy over Ebonics. *Phi Delta Kappan, 79,* 237–240.

Gadsen, V. L. (1992). Giving meaning to literacy: Intergenerational beliefs about access. *Theory into Practice, 31,* 328–336.

Gertsen, R. (1996). Language instruction for language-minority students: The transition years. *The Elementary School Journal, 96,* 226–244.

Golden, T. (1997, January 14). Oakland scratches plan to teach black English. *New York Times,* p. 10.

Heath, S. B. (1983). Questioning at home and at school: A comparative study. In G. Spindler (Ed.), *Doing ethnography: Education anthropology in action.* New York: Holt, Rinehart, & Winston.

Hester, E. (1996). Narratives of young African American children. In A. Kamhi, K. Pollock, & J. Harris (Eds.), *Communication development and disorders in African American children: research, assessment, and intervention.* Baltimore, MD: Paul H. Brookes.

Hilliard, A. G. (1989). Teachers and cultural styles in a pluralistic society. *NEA Today, 7,* 65–69.

Hyter, Y., & Westby, C. (1996). Using oral narratives to assess communicative competence. In A. Kamhi, K. Pollock, & J. Harris (Eds.), *Communication development and disorders in African American children: research, assessment, and intervention.* Baltimore, MD: Paul H. Brookes.

Irvine, J. J. (1990). *Black students and school failure: Policies, practices, and prescriptions.* New York: Greenwood.

Jimenez, R. T., Garcia, G. E., & Pearson, P. D. (1996). The reading strategies of bilingual Latina/o students who are successful English readers: opportunities and obstacles. *Reading Research Quarterly, 31,* 90–112.

Klingner, J. K., & Vaughn, S. (1996). Reciprocal teaching of reading comprehension strategies for students with learning disabilities who use English as a second language. *The Elementary School Journal, 96,* 275–291.

Ladson-Billings, G. (1992). Reading between the lines and beyond the pages: A culturally relevant approach to literacy teaching. *Theory into Practice, 31,* 312–319.

Linguistic Society of America (1997). LSA resolution on the Oakland "Ebonics" issue [On-line]. Available: http://www.lsadc.org/web2/ebonicsfr.htm.

Luhman, R. (1990). Appalachian English stereotypes: Language attitudes in Kentucky. *Language in Society, 19,* 331–348.

Michaels, S. (1981). "Sharing time": Children's narrative styles and differential access to literacy. *Language in Society, 10,* 423–442.

Ogbu, J. (1987). Variability in minority school performance: A problem in search of an explanation. *Anthropology and Education Quarterly, 12,* 290–307.

Owens, R. (1995). Language disorders: A functional approach to assessment and intervention. Boston: Allyn & Bacon.

Pressley, M., El-Dinary, P. B., Gaskins, I., Schuder, T., Bergman, J. L., Almasi, J., & Brown, R. (1992). Beyond direct explanation: Transactional instruction of reading comprehension strategies. *The Elementary School Journal, 92,* 513–535.

Raphael, T. E. (1982). Question-answering strategies for children. *The Reading Teacher, 36,* 186–190.

Reyes, M. de la Luz. (1992). Challenging venerable assumptions: Literacy instruction for linguistically different students. *Harvard Educational Review, 62,* 427–447.

Reyes, M. de la Luz, & Molner, L. A. (1991). Instructional strategies for second-language learners in the content areas. *Journal of Reading, 35,* 96–103.

Roseberry–McKibbin, C. (1995). Distinguishing language differences from language disorders in linguistically and culturally diverse students. *Multicultural Education, 3,* 12–16.

Rousseau, M. K., Tam, B. K. Y., & Ramnarain, R. (1993). Increasing reading proficiency of language-minority students with speech and language impairments. *Education and Treatment of Children, 16,* 254–271.

Rueda, R., & Chan, K. (1979). Poverty and culture in special education: separate but equal. *Exceptional Children, 45,* 422–431.

Strickland, D. S. (1994). Educating African American learners at risk: Finding a better way. *Language Arts, 71,* 328–336.

Taylor, O. L. (1998). Ebonics and educational policy: Some issues for the next millennium. *Journal of Negro Education, 67,* 35–41.

Thompson, R., Mixon, G., & Serpell, R. (1996). Engaging minority students in reading: Focus on the urban learner. In L. Baker, P. Afflerbach, & D. Reinking (Eds.), *Developing engaged readers in school and home communities.* Mahwah, NJ: Lawrence Erlbaum.

Trueba, H. T., Moll, L. C., & Diaz, S. (1982). *Improving the functional writing of bilingual secondary school students* (Contract No. 400-81-0023). Washington, DC: National Institute of Education.

U.S. Department of Education. Office of Educational Research and Improvement. National Center for Educational Statistics. (1999). *The NAEP 1998 Reading Report Card for the Nation and the States,* NCES 1999-500, by P. L. Donahue, K. E. Voelkl, J. R. Campbell, & J. Mazzeo. Washington, DC: Author.

Wallace, C., & Goodman, Y. (1989). Research currents: Language and literacy development of multilingual learners. *Language Arts, 66,* 542–550.

Warren, A. R., & McCloskey, L. A. (1997). Language in social contexts. In J. Gleason, (Ed.), *The development of language.* Needham Heights, MA: Allyn & Bacon.

Willis, A. I. (1995). Reading the world of school literacy: Contextualizing the experience of a young African American male. *Harvard Educational Review, 65,* 30–49.

Working with Families to Enhance Literacy Skills

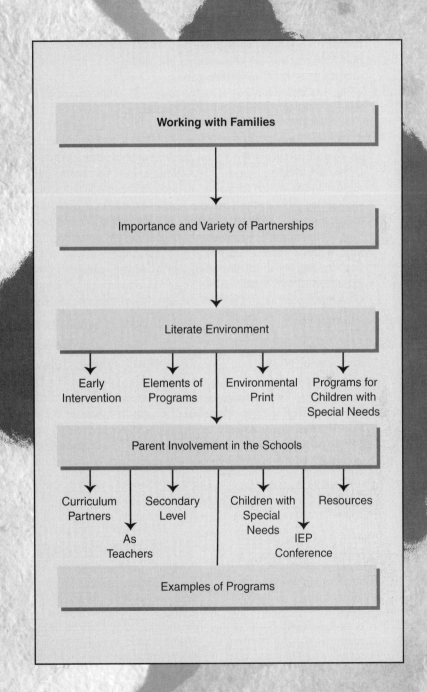

Scenario 1: In their writing center the children in Mrs. P.'s kindergarten class have been writing books. For each book, the children have an author's page with pictures of themselves and information about themselves. Every other week, three children are chosen as author of the week. Their pictures are displayed outside the room, and their parents are invited on Friday for an authors' tea. At the tea, each author reads his or her book and then takes a bow in response to the audience's enthusiastic applause. Parents beam proudly. In addition to inviting parents to the tea, Mrs. P. has a core of parent volunteers come into the room regularly to work with small groups in their centers and help the teacher with special projects when necessary.

Scenario 2: Janine is a fourth-grade student with learning disabilities in a school that has an inclusion program. The parents and the school have engaged in ongoing communication. In May the child study team meets with Janine's parents to discuss her instructional plan for fifth grade and to formalize the individualized education plan (IEP). The case manager, the special education teacher, the regular education teacher, the speech and language specialist, and both parents are present at the meeting. The teachers describe the current educational program for Janine and provide current data about Janine's performance in the academic and social areas. The parents ask questions for clarification about current services and inquire about the possibility of adding additional services. Decisions are made about appropriate modifications in Janine's educational program and the responsibilities of the school, parents, and Janine to ensure her success. At the conclusion of the meeting all parties present sign the IEP.

Scenario 3: Mrs. H. advertises a parent-child reading night. She involves community leaders, religious leaders, business owners, school personnel, and community groups in planning a program for increasing the children's at-home reading. The program consists of six sessions from September to February in which parents are taught how to select books and read with their children. Modeling of appropriate reading behaviors occurs at every session. Through the community support parents are provided with various books. At the end of the six sessions a celebration is held and all participants receive a gift. The celebration is covered by the local newspaper and radio station.

▌▌ACTIVATING SCHEMA

As you can see from the preceding scenarios, parent involvement can take many different forms and involve parents to very different degrees. Many schools are now trying to forge home–school partnerships. In your own experiences with school, what was the relationship between parents and the school? Were they an integral part? As you read this chapter think of the different ways in which parents could be involved in a school. Consider the ways in which you would feel comfortable involving parents in your classroom.

There is much talk of school–home or school–community partnerships. On January 25, 1994, Congress passed H.R. 1804, *Goals 2000: Educate America Act,* whose purpose was to "improve learning and teaching by providing a national framework for education reform; to promote the research, consensus building, and systemic changes needed to ensure equitable educational opportunities and high levels of achievement for all students. . . ." Goals 2000 provided resources to local school districts for efforts to raise academic achievement in relationship to the National Education Goals established at the 1989 Charlottesville Education Summit. An emphasis was placed on building *partnerships among schools, parents, colleges, and communities* to improve education for all students. The complexity of education and the diversity of the educational community necessitates the broadening of educational responsibility to include the home and the community.

■■ THE IMPORTANCE OF FAMILY–SCHOOL PARTNERSHIPS

When families and schools work together, education is enhanced. In the discussion that follows, the term *parents* is used throughout. It should be interpreted in its broadest sense to include the variety of caregivers present in our society today. Programs that teach parents about the teaching of reading and encourage their active participation in schools lead to greater literacy achievement. There is evidence that schools that are more successful with at-risk children tend to have higher levels of parent involvement (Cunningham & Allington, 1999; Ollila & Mayfield, 1992). Partnerships with parents do not begin with the child's entrance to formal education; parents can enhance their child's education by providing an appropriate environment before the child enters school as well as giving support during the school year.

Despite the documented benefits of parent involvement in literacy efforts, however, schools often do not encourage parent involvement or provide parents with the necessary tools to be successful. In a study of school practices to help parents become more involved, Hannon and Cuckle (1984) reported that actual participation was often restricted. Their research indicated that the main focus for parent involvement was requesting that parents read to their children and help their children learn key words. Yet, few schools encouraged children to take books home. The parent involvement efforts were limited by the books that were presently accessible to the parents. Schools are also not always clear about their definition of parent involvement and objectives for parents (Bauch, Vietze, & Morris, 1973). For some, parental involvement is limited to communication and parental support of school efforts. In studying parent participation in the development of the IEP, Scanlon, Arick, and Phelps (1981) found that most schools' implementation of PL-142 (the precursor to IDEA, establishing the rights of children with disabilities to an appropriate education in the least restricted environment) was not in compliance with the intended practice set forth in the law. Parents did not work in conjunction with the schools in developing the IEP, but were mainly recipients of information about the plan. In fact, greater involvement of the parents often led to more strained relations between the home and the school.

The disagreement on definiton, lack of focus and clarity of goals, and limited materials are inhibiting factors in partnership efforts. Time demands for planning and implementing true partnership efforts also tend to deter many schools. We feel, however, that the benefits are worth the time invested.

▌▌▌THE VARIETY OF PARTNERSHIPS

The term *partnership* implies a two-way process. Parents cannot only help the school and support school activities, but should also provide input into their child's education and provide learning environments that meld the characteristics of the school and the home culture. The nature of partnerships include developing programs that help parents support the school program, ongoing communication between parents and schools, and involving parents in decisions regarding their children's education. Berger (1991) describes five levels of parent involvement: (1) parent as active partner and educational leader, (2) parent as decision maker, (3) parent as school volunteer or paid employer, (4) parent as liaison to support homework, and (5) parent as supporter of educational goals of the school. The different levels require varying amounts of parent participation and decision making. There is no one model for family–school partnerships. They vary with the characteristics of the school, the community, and the goals of the programs. Effective models are those that meet the needs of all the participants, the students, family, and school.

▌▌▌THE LITERATE ENVIRONMENT

As we discussed in Chapters 1 and 4, children who come from literate environments already have many of the skills necessary for becoming successful readers. The presence of books in the home, the amount of reading done with the child, the parents as literacy role models, guidance and encouragement, and the responsiveness of the parent to the efforts of the child to explore his or her world have all had positive relationships with children's reading ability (Durkin, 1966; Glazer & Burke, 1994; Hansen, 1969; McBride–Chang et. al., 1991; Miller, 1969; Morrow & Paratore, 1993). Symons, Szuskiewicz, and Bonnell (1996) found that access to print had a significant effect on children's phonological awareness. They studied 39 children in their first year of school and found that parental print exposure—the amount of reading that parents engaged in—correlated with the children's phonemic awareness and vocabulary development.

Although most parents have the desire to provide their children with the necessary support for success in school, not all parents have the necessary knowledge to provide a literate environment for their children. Further, economics may have an effect on some of the characteristics of the literate environment; for example, economics may impact how many books are available in the home. Low-income parents may have the desire to provide their children with a good foundation for reading achievement, but lack the resources necessary to do so. Schools need to reach out to these parents to give them access to appropriate materials in order for them to provide the necessary support for their children. The issue becomes more complex for parents of children with special-needs. These children may require specialized interventions to help them reach their potential. Parents may not be knowledgeable about special needs and effective intervention strategies. Without training they may not know how to help their children. In all of these cases the challenge for the schools is to increase the likelihood that the children will be exposed to literacy prior to entering school by providing parents with necessary training and resources.

Early Intervention Programs

Early intervention programs can be instituted for parents or other caregivers of preschool children. In general, these programs are designed to provide parents with the tools necessary to create a literate environment in their homes that will support the child's literacy development prior to entering school. Successful programs have centered on helping parents provide verbally stimulating environments and enhanced language development in at-risk and communications-disordered children (Levenstein, 1970; Lombardino & Mangan, 1983) and teaching parents how to instruct their children (Karnes, Teska, Hodgind, & Badger, 1970). Ongoing sessions in which instructors visited homes weekly to model appropriate behaviors (Weikart, 1975) further enhanced these programs.

Family Literacy Programs

Family literacy programs have taken a holistic approach to helping parents provide support for their children. Their focus is on families as a system and developing programs that help parents better their own lives as well as teach them strategies to aid in their children's literacy development. Programs have focused on improving the parents' literacy skills in addition to improving their ability to help their children with early reading and writing (Brooks, 1998). These programs may provide help in managing family life, supporting parents with their concerns about themselves and their children, helping to build the parents' self-esteem, and providing the parents with the necessary literacy skills to better their economic conditions.

The goals of the school and the expectations of the parents for a family literacy program may not be completely parallel. An example is the "Even Start Family Literacy Program," which was established in 1989 to integrate early childhood and adult education for parents. The school had two major goals for the program: improving the literacy of the parents, and helping parents better prepare their children for school through improved parenting skills and implementation of literacy activities. The program was comprised of an adult basic literacy education (ABLE) class, which focused on helping participants pass the General Education Development (GED—high school equivalency) test, improving their academic skills, and participating in a parenting program, and for those who desired it, an early childhood program. The early childhood caregiver engaged children in age-appropriate literacy activities. The program impacted on the presence of reading materials in the home, parental expectations of school success, and school readiness skills (National Research Council, 1998).

In evaluating a local Even Start program, Yaffe and Williams (1998) found that the parents' goals for enrolling in the program centered on improving their own lives. Passing the GED, which could lead to a better job, increasing self-esteem, establishing economic and personal independence, strengthening and developing job skills and serving as role models for their children, were the major expectations of the parents. In examining the components leading to the mother's satisfaction, they found that parents mainly cited the trusting, supportive environment by women for women and the lack of competition as well as a focus on individual needs. They also believed that the program was relevant to their own lives. Parents did not, however, cite family literacy components. Only one parent read to and wrote with her children, and in the segment of the program where the parents and children were together (PACT) the parents generally avoided interacting with their children. The activities expected of parents in that part of the program may not have been congruent with the parents' cultural expectations of parenting.

Yaffe and Williams concluded that for family literacy programs to be most effective, parents need to understand that children growing up in a literate environment learn a great deal about literacy in family-based interactions and that parents are children's first teachers. They further concluded that "family literacy providers need to examine the interactional patterns that exist within families and build on those patterns. Further, the literacy activities we share with parents should be culturally consistent with current family functioning" (p. 27). Rather than imposing the schools' values on the homes, many researchers believe that family literacy programs should focus on ways in which schools and families can learn from one another (Morrow & Paratore, 1993).

Characteristics of Successful Programs   Planning and collaboration are critical elements in successful family literacy programs (Box 11.1). Goals should be clearly articulated and should be a result of cooperative efforts of all participants. Effort must be placed on obtaining quality staff whose teaching depicts excellent instructional procedures and reflection. Sessions should be devoted to building group solidarity in which all members feel ownership of the program. Each meeting should provide parents with a sense of accomplishment for their own learning and their contribution to the learning of their children.

▮ **Box 11.1**

CHARACTERISTICS OF SUCCESSFUL FAMILY LITERACY PROGRAMS

- Clearly articulated goals—programs should have clear goals that are carefully articulated to all participants. The goals should be attainable in a finite period of time.
- Careful selection of teachers—teachers should have strong instructional and reflective skills. They should be willing to adapt curriculum to meet the needs of the participants.
- Collaborative planning—the programs should be developed collaboratively by educational and community groups. There should be ongoing assessment and modification.
- Motivated participants—participants in the program should believe that the goals are attainable and be willing to contribute to the success of the program.
- Clear message given to parents of the benefits to the parent and the child—parents should be made aware of the contributions they can make to their children's literacy development. They should see a clear relationship between their behaviors and the increased literacy of the child.
- Ongoing reflective teaching—all participants should engage in ongoing reflection about the success of the program in meeting its goals. Participants should seek continued betterment of the program.

Major Elements of Early Literacy Programs
Selecting Appropriate Books

As mentioned in previous chapters, there are a number of research studies that show a correlation between the children's access to print and their readiness for formal reading instruction. Children who have been surrounded by books from very early ages come to school with a great deal of print knowledge before they begin their formal instruction. Choosing appropriate books for the different ages can be difficult, however. Libraries and bookstores often place all the "early readers" in one section with no differentiation for the different ages. Many parents want to buy or borrow books for their children, but they are often unclear about the appropriateness of books for children of different ages. Familiarizing parents with characteristics and examples of books for different-aged children is, thus, an important element of a literacy program.

Infants and Toddlers   In order to engage the child in reading, books must be visually appealing, with brightly colored objects and, for the early ages, with few words on a page. Very young children learn mostly through taste; thus, fabric or soft plastic books are good choices for their own library. Interactive books, in which the child moves an object or touches various textures, such as *Pat the Bunny* (Kunhardt, 1984), have great appeal.

Older Toddlers and Preschool-Aged Children   As children become older, they become attracted to books with repetitive refrains, patterns, and rhymes. Some books become favorites and are requested over and over again. Children can learn much from these repeated readings.

Early intervention programs can focus on helping parents obtain books and select appropriate books. Parents should have guidelines for selecting appropriate books for their children. Characteristics of books at different developmental levels should be discussed to assist parents in selecting their own books. Lists that describe popular children's books and their approximate levels can be very helpful. In addition, programs should increase parents' access to books by providing them with books as rewards for participating in the program.

Reading to Children

The benefits of reading aloud to children are well documented. Numerous research studies indicate that children who are read to develop a greater facility with print, knowledge about books and "book talk," and a greater sense of the way stories develop (story grammar) (Cohen, 1968; Feitelson & Goldstein, 1986). Many adults who enjoy reading fondly remember the experience of being read to when young. For many, this practice set the foundation for a lifelong love of reading. Not all parents, however, know how to read to children for maximum benefit. Presenting guidelines for reading to children and modeling will enhance the experience for both adult and child (Box 11.2). These guidelines extend the ones presented in Chapter 4.

When working with parents, it should be stressed that the experience should be pleasurable for both parent and child if it is to be successful. Paul, an adult student in a reading foundations course, once related that his father used to sit them down on the couch at the same time each day to be read to. Often they preferred to be outside playing at the time, but they needed to abide by the routine. The father meant well, but instead of creating an enjoyable opportunity for his children, he created resentment toward reading. Choosing an appropriate time for reading is essential. It should be a time when both parent and child are relaxed and when there are no other outside distractions, such as playing with friends or a favorite television program. Many parents find that bedtime and naptime are the most enjoyable times. They are not the only times for reading, however. For 1-year-old Eric, lunchtime was the best time to read to him, as it was the only time that he was willing to sit still! Parents should be aware of their needs and the needs of their children in finding an optimal time for reading.

The amount of time spent reading with the child should also vary with the child's age and ability to attend to the task. A guideline to strive for is 30 minutes a day every day. This will also vary with the needs of the child, however. In order for this to remain a positive experience, parents must be attuned to the child's desires and capabilities and discontinue reading when it is no longer productive. For very young children, 5 or 10 minutes a session might be sufficient. As children mature, though, if they have been read to consistently, they will begin to enjoy it for longer and longer periods of time.

❚ Box 11.2

READING ALOUD TO CHILDREN

- **Select age-appropriate books:** Books should be colorful and easy for a child to manipulate. Number of words on a page should vary with the age of the child.
- **Choose the setting:** Have a regular reading time. This should be a special time between parent and child when both participants are relaxed and anxious to engage in the activity. Find a quiet place to read.
- **Have the child sit near you:** The child should be close to the reader and to the text. The child should be able to see the text clearly and play with it as desired.
- **Read in an animated fashion:** Use feeling when you read. Exaggerate the emotions of the characters, slow down or speed up your reading to build suspense. Change your voice for different characters.
- **Allow the child to interact with the text:** Let the child assume the role of a character by reciting that character's part. Have the child join in for a repetitive refrain or add a rhyming word when he or she can. After becoming more familiar with the text, the child can read various parts of the story.
- **Engage in conversation and response:** Let the child ask questions throughout the text. Ask the child questions for prediction-making and relationship to the child's experiences. Keep questions low risk. Share your reactions to the text.

ENJOY THE EXPERIENCE

Interaction between parent and child as they are reading is also very important. The parent and child should be sitting close to one another so that the child can see the book as it is being read. The child should be able to touch the book and turn the pages. When reading, the parent should try to read as expressively as possible. Changes in tone for characters, different inflections, and emphases on different words add to the enjoyment for the children and also provide important modeling of fluent reading. The reading should be interactive throughout, at first allowing children to name the objects in the text, then joining in the reading when they can. Children love to read common refrains from well-loved books or insert the rhyming words. In the book *Good Night Moon,* the character says good night to the different objects in the room. After hearing the book a number of times, children learn the rhyming pattern and can participate in the reading. For example, while reading the page "Good night, kittens and good night *mittens,*" the parent can stop and allow the child to say the word *mittens.* In this way the child becomes an active participant in the reading and begins to focus on different word and sound patterns. Refrains such as "I wish I can, I wish I can" from *The Little Engine That Could* (Piper, 1979), or "Koala Lou, I DO love you!" from *Koala Lou* (Fox, 1988) are often recited by children as they are read to.

Children learn much from natural conversation about text. Parents should stop at various points in the text to discuss it with the child. Relating the text to the child's own experiences, questioning the child about reactions, and repeating some of the language of the text all help the child extend the reading experience. Parents may want to question the child to make sure the story is understood, but it is important that the questions not become a test of comprehension. Reading aloud should always remain informal and pleasurable.

When schools develop programs that assist parents with methods for enhancing oral reading, an important element of these programs should be working *with* parents, not just presenting information to them. An example of a successful program in which the norms of the community were addressed is the "Parents as Partners in Reading" program (Edwards, 1995). In this program, parents in a rural Louisiana district met with their children to learn how to read with them. The university facilitator trained parent leaders who were members of the community to model effective reading practices. There were three phases to the program: instruction, which involved discussion and modeling; peer modeling in which parents practiced with their children; and discussion and feedback. In assessing the program, the parents felt that having community members as leaders was a very positive aspect. It helped the parents feel that they, too, could be successful in this endeavor. It allowed the community to personalize the experience, modifying it in ways that made sense within their value system and empowered the participants. As a result of the experience, participants continued to further their own education and felt a greater part of their children's educational experience. They felt successful with a school program in a way they may not have if the program had been merely imposed on them.

Environmental Print

Books are not the sole source of print for the child. Newspapers, signs, notes, and shopping lists are examples of other types of print that can be available in the environment. Theorists who view literacy from a social perspective believe that few homes are completely void of a literate environment, and that educators need to look at the naturally occurring examples of literacy events and literacy products and help parents use them successfully in developing children's awareness of print (Heath, 1983; Taylor, 1983).

Early Intervention Programs for Children with Special Needs

Children with special needs benefit from the same elements of a literate environment as other children. In an article about the role of parents of exceptional children in literacy development, Dudley-Marling (1989) describes four general strategies for encouraging literacy development: (1) reading aloud to children, (2) modeling reading behavior, (3) writing to and with children, and (4) responding to children's reading and writing—the same strategies found to be critical for children without special needs.

In addition to general literacy strategies, school personnel also need to address specific concerns of families of children with special needs (deBettencourt, 1987; Polloway & Patton, 1993; Smith, Polloway, Patton & Dowdy, 1995; Turnbull, Turnbull, Shank, & Leal, 1999). Emotional needs may be stronger. Parents are often not prepared in advance and have suffered a loss—of expectation. Their grief at this loss may be complicated by guilt. At first, the child's disabilities can be the center of the parent's thoughts. They can be assisted in focusing on the child's abilities, rather than disabilities, and providing congruence between the demands placed on the child and an ability to meet them (Creekmore, 1988). In working with parents, schools must be sensitive to, and sensitize families to, the effect that the presence of a special-needs child has on the entire family dynamic. Schools also need to expand their knowledge of the handicapping condition to help parents' facilitation of the social, emotional, and academic goals for the child (Brantlinger, 1991).

Parents can engage their children in specific cognitive and academic activities. Lombardino and Mangan (1983) describe a program in which parents were trained as language facilitators with developmentally delayed children. They examined behavior change in the course of an intensive communication/language training program. Parents were taught to plan and implement structured teaching sessions as well as to stimulate language through free play. Parents used the following language stimulation techniques when playing with their children: (1) referencing (direct the child's attention to an object), (2) imitating, (3) expanding, (4) naming, (5) parallel talk in which the parent described an action as it was occurring, (6) questioning, (7) replying, and (8) demanding. Five of the techniques (referencing, parallel talk, questioning, replying, and demanding) were found to significantly enhance the language of the children in the study. The authors concluded that the importance of training parent–child dyads in the context of naturally occurring activities should be emphasized. The authors focused their study on language achievement. Given the nature of the reading process as a language-based activity, it would be interesting to extend this study to see the impact on later reading achievement.

▌▐ PARENT INVOLVEMENT IN THE SCHOOLS

Parents are necessary partners in their children's literacy development. Their roles do not diminish, but evolve as the child enters formal education (Rasinski & Padak, 1996; Rudman, 1956). Reread the introductory scenarios in this chapter. In each of them the parent is involved with the child's education. As you can see, involvement may take many forms, and schools with active parent involvement programs collaborate with parents in different ways (Meyer & Blacher, 1987). They encourage different levels of participation, involving parents as curriculum leaders and decision makers, as volunteers in the classroom, and as supporters for school projects, such as fund-raising for necessary equipment or organizing a book fair. Parents may be asked to support the child's literacy development at home by engaging in various literacy activities with the child such as spending a specific amount of time together each evening and reading. Parents may also be asked to engage in general participation by attending key events (Berger, 1991; Comer & Haynes, 1991; Flood, Lapp, Tinajero, & Nagel, 1995).

As you read the following sections, reflect on the introductory scenarios. Consider what roles the parents are playing in each example and what elements should be present to maximize the success of the situation.

Parents as Curriculum Partners

Parents may serve as members of planning or curriculum committees to help develop better literacy programs in the school. Parent representatives serve as a voice for the community. By doing so, they assist educators in forming programs that are in congruence with the parents' values and goals for their children. They also inform educators about the parents' conceptions about literacy and may help the schools see where better communication is necessary. An example of this can be found in the Jamesville, New York, school district, which formed a language arts committee to completely revamp the literacy program.

Along with school representatives, two parents sat on the committee. While discussing the changes in the primary program, the issue of spelling arose. Many teachers were using a developmental spelling approach, which allowed for "invented spellings" in the primary grades. The parents expressed concern that teachers accepted what they

Community members can be very valuable resources in the school by providing individual assistance to students with literacy difficulties.

clearly saw as "misspellings." It was evident from the conversation that the school had not communicated well the reasons for using the spelling approach, leaving parents only partially informed and often distressed by a new approach. It was important for the district to address these parents' concerns and, in addition, ensure that a system be implemented to communicate other changes to the parents. By serving on committees, parents can also be invaluable for disseminating information about the program and providing community feedback to the school.

The Community as Resources in the Classroom

Community members may be excellent resources in the classroom. They may provide sustained assistance, volunteering to help in the classroom at a regular time each week. They can help prepare materials, work with small groups of children, or provide extra assistance for certain literacy projects. For example, community members may serve as a scribe for process writing assignments, either writing a preliterate child's words or helping students with typing or word processing. Knowing that there is another adult in the room can very positively change the teacher's assignments for the class. Some of the more complex computer programs, for example, may require more monitoring, at least in the beginning, than a teacher is capable of providing alone. Community members may also provide the critical difference in an inclusive classroom. Their support and presence may provide the special-needs student with just the necessary amount of assistance for the student to succeed on an assignment.

Many community members do not have the ability to provide ongoing support in a classroom, but they may still be involved in the literacy of the class. Community members may be guest readers in the classroom, sharing their personally favorite stories with the children or stories that reflect their culture. Such readings give the students another model of an adult reading and also expose children to the literature of diverse cultures. Study of the literature of different ethnic groups can be enhanced by involving community members as storytellers, sharing stories from their oral tradition, sometimes dressed in traditional garb, and incorporating appropriate language and inflection.

Community members' expertise may be used in a variety of ways in the classroom. They may provide resources and information to children as part of thematic units. They often have particular interests and abilities that can be used very successfully to support instruction. By bringing their own expertise, training, and interests, they may present information to children in a very effective manner, thus having a greater impact on the children.

As an example, Binkard (1985) described an exceptionality awareness program implemented by parents of special-needs children. In this program, the parents, using puppets, dramatized scripts that provided information on exceptionalities and adaptive devices and the emotional and social concerns of special-needs children. Through lively dialogue, the program emphasized the commonality of all children, encouraging the nondisabled child to look beyond the disability and relate to a special-needs peer as a whole person with many similar thoughts and feelings. In evaluating the program, Binkard found that there were consistently positive, substantial, and sustained attitudinal changes on the part of the students and that teachers increased their ability to address the social and emotional effects of inclusion.

Parents as Teachers at Home

To reiterate a point that has been made many times before in this text, the more children practice actual reading and writing, the more their literacy abilities will improve. By engaging their children in reading and writing activities at home, parents can greatly impact on their children's continued literacy development. In planning activities that involve parents as teachers, schools should consider the following:

Goals of the Program   Goals should be achievable and clearly articulated. Parents should be apprised of the expected benefits to the children from participating in the program. Activities should be selected for maximum effectiveness in improving literacy.

Resources   Schools should ask themselves what resources are needed to participate in the program and how parents can obtain resources that they currently do not have. Many programs ask parents to read with a child at night. Schools must determine whether parents have the appropriate reading materials. Many of the new reading programs now have provisions for take-home books. These are short, black-and-white books that may be reproduced or bought inexpensively for children to read at home. Reading materials from the classroom can also be lent on a daily basis.

Requisite Competencies   Schools should determine what skills are being asked of the parents. Many parents are not professionally trained teachers and should not be asked to provide sophisticated instruction for their children. Activities should be simple, clear, and engaging. The primary purpose of the activities should be to involve parents and children in literacy activities in a low-risk, positive environment. Both parent and child should enjoy the activity.

Time Commitment   Programs should not be very time consuming. After fulfilling their other family obligations, many parents do not have a lot of extra time, despite good intent. Consistent programs of short, daily duration will be more effective in encouraging participation.

Training   Parents sometimes require training to appropriately implement a program. Training sessions might be held in which the program is modeled and the parents have the opportunity to practice under the guidance of a facilitator. Training is particularly necessary when parents are placed in an instructional role.

Guidelines for Implementation   Instructions should be clear and well sequenced. They should provide simple procedures for working with a child and include information about praise, error correction, and recording data (Thurston, 1989). Simple guidelines for selecting materials, such as a "fistful of words," should also be included (Box 11.3).

PROCEDURES FOR A "FISTFUL OF WORDS"

1. Choose a page from the beginning of the book, or for shorter books a few pages (enough for 50 words).
2. Have the child spread out the fingers on one hand.
3. Have the child begin reading. For every miscue or unknown word the child should put down one finger.
4. If the child makes a fist before completing the selection, then you know the book is too difficult.

Know the Community   Educators need to know the community and be willing to modify projects to meet community needs. In a 4-year study of a Southern California school district's parent involvement activities, Delgado-Gaitan (1991) found that conventional means for involving parents were not successful because specific cultural knowledge was needed to participate. The author concluded that culturally responsive communication and nonconventional activities were more successful.

Working with Parents at the Secondary Level

Most parent involvement programs focus on the primary level. Parents tend to be less directly involved with their children's education at the secondary level, both in regular and special education (Cone, Delawyer, & Wolfe, 1985). Cairney (1995) postulates, however, that secondary parents can be engaged in a partnership that meets their specific needs. Participants in a program that focused on secondary literacy needs gained new strategies to assist their children, increased their understanding of literacy and learning, and felt empowered. Cairney concludes that truly collaborative programs can affect the literacy learning of at-risk adolescents.

▮▮ COMMUNICATING WITH PARENTS

Communicating About Literacy

Schools need to communicate effectively with parents and the community. Teachers should provide continuous communication with parents about the nature of the literacy program being used, the benefits of the program, and the goals and expectations for the students. Communiques should solicit feedback from parents. Parents should feel that their questions and concerns are valued. Many teachers believe that they are too busy with teaching to communicate regularly. One often hears, "I'm too busy doing it to talk about it." However, consistent communication is imperative. Schools should be particularly diligent about communication when changing instructional practices or materials. When schools do not communicate well with parents, parents obtain information from other sources, namely politicians, the media, and advertisements (McQuillan, 1999). The information may be often filled with half-truths and sensational charges. There may be little research or theoretical support for the statements (Routman, 1996), but if it is the only information parents receive, then it has great impact on their notions of literacy learning.

Teachers can keep parents informed through frequent letters (Box 11.4), educational newsletters, telephone calls, and conferences. Newsletters written by children not only provide information about the program, but also allow parents to see the products of student learning (Box 11.5).

▌Box 11.4

SAMPLE SCHOOL LETTER

August 3, 2001

Dear Parents of Jamie White:

All of us at Johns Elementary School are excited about the new school year! We have a brand-new language arts and inclusion program, three new teachers, and a bunch of great students.

We believe it is very important for parents to understand the programs their children are involved in at Johns Elementary School. We want you to join us as partners in these programs to ensure the best education for your children.

You are invited to a special parents' orientation to meet with your child's teacher, Mrs. Abbott, and to learn about the language arts and inclusion program at Johns Elementary School. Three evenings have been set aside for the parents of children in grade 2. Choose the date that is most convenient for you, then call or fax us by August 20 so we can reserve a space for you.

    Sept. 9, 2001
    Sept. 10, 2001
    Sept. 18, 2001

Here is the agenda for each parents' orientation meeting:

Time	Program	Discussion Content
6:00-6:20	Reading	Philosophy of Program-Text-Supplement
6:25-6:45	Writing	Process Writing-Developmental Spelling
6:50-7:10	Phonics	Philosophy-Demonstration
7:15-7:35	Inclusion	Structure of Classroom-Collaboration
7:40-8:00	Questions	Open Forum for Parents' Questions
8:00-9:00	Conferences	Individual Parent/Teacher Meetings

I know we're going to have a great year at Johns Elementary School. I look forward to seeing you soon.

Sincerely,

Louise Johnson
Principal

SAMPLE SCHOOL NEWSLETTER

The following two pages contain a sample school newsletter.

How To Make Mud Pies

By Ron P.

Make the bottom nice and flat as you can. Then make the sides nice and round. Then put a little dot if you want to make it a birthday or pumpkin pie. Then you put mud inside the round part and get a top for it and get plastic and push it down on top. Then you have your pie. If you want to make two pies you do the whole thing over again you want to throw it. I wouldn't if I were you!

Sports

Two Baseball Greats

By Ken G.

Babe Ruth was on the New York Yankees. He was the pitcher for the Yankees. He was known for his home runs. The story took place in Chicago. He called the shot and hit the ball exactly where he pointed with his bat. It was over the fence!

Carlos May was on the White Sox He was the left fielder. The story took place in Chicago.

He was missing part of his thumb because a shell exploded in his hand during training with the U.S. Marines. With a lot of practice, he was able to play again.

BEAVERS

By Elissa P.

When beavers are hungry in the

winter they go to their pile of sticks and they eat. They stay in their lodge until spring.

Soon the mother has babies. When the babies are older they help repair the lodge.

He cuts the sticks then he puts them in mud then he builds his lodge.

Because he puts dry grass in his house, the beavers stay warm in the winter.

Book Review

By Laura K.

Freckle Juice

By: Judy Blume

Once there was a boy named Andrew who wanted freckles, just like Nicky. Nicky sat in front of him in class. One day in school, one of Andrew's classmates named Sharon, said, "I know how you can get freckles." "How?" said Andrew. If you pay me 50 cents I will tell you. So he payed her 50 cents, for a special recipe. After he created it, he started to turn GREEN!!!!!!!!!! How would you feel if you drank a glass of: grape juice, vinegar, mustard, mayonnaise, juice from one lemon, pepper, salt, ketchup, olive oil, and one speck of onion. So he didn't go to school the next day.

It was exciting! Now you have to find out what happens to Andrew when you read the book.

Clifford
By Robin W.

Clifford likes to play and make a mess. He likes to give rides to Emily Elizabeth. He likes to chase cars. He likes to chase cats. He likes to eat a lot. Clifford is big and red.

The Tree That Gave So Much

By Matt K.

There is a book called the *Giving Tree* by Shel Silverstein. We asked one of the main characters, the tree, some questions about her relationship with the little boy, the other main character. Here is our interview with the tree:

Q: How do you feel about the boy?

A: I love the boy with all my heart because he is my best friend. He would come to see me and he cared about me.

Q: Where is the boy now and when was the last time you saw him?

A: I do not know, he might be at home or he may have passed away. The last time I saw him was 30 years ago when our story was published and he came to see me.

Q: Why are you only a stump now?

A: I cared about the boy so much that I gave him all I had.

The Internet is a powerful communications tool. Districts, schools, or classes can create websites to provide information in critical areas. Conferencing with parents and providing information sessions allow for open dialogue and discussion. Inviting parents to student literacy events at the school is a vivid means of including parents in their children's literacy learning.

Communicating with Parents of Children with Special Needs

Communicating with parents of children with special needs is not only advantageous, it's the law! Under the 1997 amendments to the Individuals with Disabilities Education Act (IDEA), parents are now considered to be part of the decision-making team for their child. Parents must be included in every step of the process, from initial evaluation through development of the child's individual educational plan (Box 11.6). Therefore, it is more important than ever to establish good relationships between parents and the schools. The purpose of involving parents on the IEP team is to effect shared decision making.

▌Box 11.6

PARENTS' RIGHTS UNDER IDEA

Provide Consent

- Before conducting an initial evaluation to determine if a child qualifies as a child with a disability, the agency must obtain informed consent from the parent. Parental consent does not imply consent for placement.
- The parent must give consent for conducting a reevaluation, although the school may conduct the reevaluation if the parent fails to respond.

Receive Information about the Child and His or Her Placement

- The local education agency (LEA) must provide a description of the evaluation procedures to the parent.
- The parent must be given a copy of the evaluation report and documentation for determination of eligibility.
- The LEA must state how the parent will be regularly informed of the child's progress toward the IEP goals and the extent to which the progress is sufficient to enable the child to meet the goals.
- The LEA must provide prior written notice to the parents whenever the agency proposes to initiate or change, or refuses to change, the identification, evaluation, or educational placement of the child.
- Parents must have access to all of the child's records.
- Information must be written in the parents' native language unless it is clearly not feasible.

Participate in Decision Making

- The LEA must provide a reevaluation on parental request.
- In conducting the evaluation, the LEA must include information provided by the parent that may assist in determination of disability and the content of the instructional program.
- The parent is included in the team that determines eligibility.
- Input from the parent is needed to identify what additional data is needed for eligibility, present level of performance, need of services, and appropriate modifications.
- The parent is a member of the Individualized Education Program Team (IEP Team).
- The parents may determine that additional people with knowledge or expertise be included on the team.

Procedural Safeguards

- Parents must receive notice of procedural safeguards, including opportunity to present complaints, due process hearings, mediation, and civil actions.

However, research indicates that schools sometimes follow the letter of the law, rather than the spirit of the law. They communicate, mainly by written notice, but often do not collaborate with the parents in actual planning for the child's educational needs (Scanlon et al., 1981; Yanok & DeRuberto, 1989). In studying parents' and teachers' perspectives on inclusion, Bennett, DeLuca, and Bruno (1997) found that as parents' advocacy efforts increased, positive relations with the teachers decreased. They concluded that teachers appeared willing to communicate, but were less accepting of parental input on their teaching.

The IEP Conference

As members of the IEP team, parents should be active participants in the educational decisions for their child. In reality, however, the district often creates the plan and uses the conference to present it to the parents and gain their acquiescence. School personnel need to recognize that although parents may not have the same technical expertise for instruction, they bring a lot of knowledge about the child that will be of great benefit in developing a program.

Teachers can prepare for and organize the IEP conference to maximize parent decision making and satisfaction with the process. In addition to notification of the meeting, the school should send questions to parents and solicit questions from them. The physical environment of the meeting place should be addressed. The room should be an appropriate size and free of distractions. If possible, loudspeakers should be turned off so as not to interrupt the meeting. The chairs should be arranged so that all participants can comfortably face one another.

The purpose of the meeting should be articulated at the beginning of the session. Information should be presented in a direct, understandable manner during the meeting. Technical terms should be explained and the information presented should furnish a complete picture of the child's performance. Although test scores provide information about a child, they should not be used as the sole source of information. Samples of student work and results of observation should be included as well.

Teachers need to demonstrate active listening at the conference. Turnbull and Turnbull (2001) assert that teachers should (a) reinforce parental comments, (b) paraphrase statements (c) respond appropriately to affect and feelings, (d) question effectively, and (e) summarize major points. The meeting should end with positive comments about the student.

The case manager should organize notes immediately after the meeting, initiate action, and communicate with all professional staff members who work with the child. All teachers should understand their obligations under the IEP and the agreed-upon modifications. By adhering to these guidelines and engaging parents in participatory efforts to develop appropriate educational plans, schools will reduce the possibility of adversarial relationships with parents.

SPECIFIC SCHOOL PROGRAMS FOR INVOLVING FAMILIES

As you read the descriptions of the following programs, consider the guidelines for involving families in school literacy programs. Look at the ways they were addressed, and think of other guidelines that should be considered.

Backpack Programs

In backpack programs, teachers gather all the materials necessary to complete the task and place them in a little "backpack" for the child to take home. Many teachers use plastic food storage bags with locking tops. The bag might have the instructions, the book or other reading material, and a page for recording the time spent and for providing feedback. In the Johnson School, the third-grade teachers sent home books that supported their thematic unit and asked parents and children to practice reading the selection every night for a week. They found that the students' fluency, comprehension, writing, and motivation all improved with the practice. In addition, the parents felt more invested in their child's learning as a result of participation.

Family Writing Programs

In family writing programs, parents and children agree to write together each night or are engaged in a specific writing project together. An example can be an oral history project. Children can interview parents and other relatives to discover aspects of their family history. Together, the parent and child create a presentation for the child to share. The parent gains the benefit of sharing the information with the child in an enjoyable way. This also validates the family's culture and provides an authentic reason for parent and child to write.

Reading Incentive Programs

In reading incentive programs, parents and children agree to read together for a specific amount of time each night. There are usually rewards, such as pizza certificates or recognition, for participating in the program. In the Bama Bookworm program (Brown

& Moore, 1992) the authors describe a reading incentive program used in a summer reading clinic. The goals of the program were to motivate reluctant readers to read at home with their parents, encourage the participants to maintain or increase the number of pages read, and help the readers improve their ability to answer comprehension questions. A token economy was used, with stickers leading to prizes. At the end of the summer the participants felt that they had met their goals. On the average, the students read 20 books each during the duration of the program.

Paired Reading Workshop

Paired reading, described in detail in Chapter 5, is an instructional technique in which a proficient and a less-proficient reader read a text together. It is similar to the neurological impress method, which is one of the techniques described for building fluency, and has been used in tutoring. In paired reading the two readers read together at the less-proficient reader's pace. They continue to read together until the less-proficient reader signals that he or she wishes to read alone. He or she continues to read alone until an error is made. At that point, the more-proficient reader says the word correctly; it is repeated by the other student, and then the pair continues reading together. Paired reading is an effective technique for increasing readers' fluency (Topping, 1987, 1989).

In the paired reading workshop, the teachers adapted the program to use with parents. First, they identified children who needed additional reading practice to develop their fluency. They then very actively recruited the parents to attend the paired reading workshops. The workshops consisted of a series of five sessions over a school year. Parents and children signed a contract agreeing to read together daily for 10 minutes. This time was devoted to the parent and child working together without any distractions. The first workshop consisted of discussing the purpose of the workshops and the paired reading procedure, modeling, and guided practice. In subsequent workshops the teachers reviewed the technique, discussed the progress with the parents, provided extension activities, and introduced parents to different narrative and expository books to read with their children. Motivation was a central part of all of the workshops. The sessions ended with a culminating activity and celebration. Feedback from the parents and test scores indicated that the program was personally rewarding to the parent and child and that students' reading did improve (Hopson & Donovan, 1996).

Families That Read Succeed!

Come and Fredericks (1995) described a schoolwide parent involvement program for the families of at-risk children in Savannah, Georgia. Five critical criteria of the program were: (1) the program was built on the expressed needs and wishes of the parents; (2) there was a willingness of both parents and teachers to promote shared responsibility; (3) parents were actively involved in decision making and implementation; (4) there was open communication throughout the year, and (5) there was a long-term commitment to continuous involvement. Specific objectives included increasing students' reading achievement and parents' and students' attitudes toward reading, creating lifelong readers, and increasing parent involvement in the school and fostering home–school connections.

The project spread to the larger community with support coming from business leaders, politicians, and book publishers. The program consisted of a series of parent workshops centered on topics such as reading to children, storytelling, the importance of talking about the story and relating it to the children's life, motivation, and a collaborative bookmaking project. At the same time in-school activities were designed to increase children's reading, bring parents into the classroom to support the literacy activities, and reinforce literacy instruction through at-home activities. The authors believed that the key to the success of the program was the involvement of the parents in the planning and the commitment of the teachers, parents, and staff to various tasks to promote the project.

▮▮▮SUMMARY

Families have a large role to play in children's literacy development. They build the foundation for literacy through the environment that is provided during the preschool years. By reading to children and exposing them to print they contribute to the child's growing literacy awareness. Early intervention programs, which include family involvement, have a positive impact. Successful programs are planned well and include collaboration with parents on goals and methods.

Families and the community can also be valuable resources for children of school age. They can provide extra assistance for children with reading needs as well as resources for classrooms, and they can help children learn about their unique needs and abilities. Communication between school and home is critical in helping schools receive necessary support and ensuring that children receive an appropriate education.

The positive effects of working with families are well documented. When families are involved with the school, they develop a greater stake in their children's education and become invaluable resources for the teachers. Developing true partnerships requires much time and commitment from both teachers and families. The benefits, however, are great—to the teachers, the families, and the students.

▮▮▮▮ Linkages

In the text:
1. You wish to increase parent participation in your classroom, but your principal thinks it involves too much effort. Write a memo to the principal explaining the benefits of including parents in your educational effort.
2. You have convinced your principal! Now write a proposal delineating the steps you will take to increase parent involvement.

Outside the text:
1. Interview a member of a child study team in a school district about the IEP meeting. Evaluate the school district's procedures according to the most recent IDEA guidelines.
2. Interview a teacher about parent participation. What types of programs exist for parent involvement in the school? What percentage of parents are involved? What suggestions does the teacher have for improving parent participation?

On the Web

U.S. Department of Education Even Start Literacy Program
  www.evenstart.org
Gives links for parents and teachers.

Family Literacy Foundation
  www.read2kids.org
Provides suggestions for parents and teachers for improving early literacy.

Ohio Literacy Resource Center
  literacy.kent.edu/oasis/resc/educ/kidresc.html
University-based website with many resources on family literacy.

Reading is Fundamental Organization
  www.rif.org
Has resources for parents and teachers.

Macomb Projects
  www.mprojects.wiu.edu
University-based website with literacy and other projects for families of children with disabilities.

References

Bauch, J., Vietze, P., & Morris, V. (1973). What makes the difference in parental participation? *Childhood Education, 50,* 47–51

Bennett, T., DeLuca, D., & Bruno, D. (1997). Putting inclusion into practice: Perspectives of teachers and parents. *Exceptional Children, 63,* 115–131.

Berger, E. (1991). Parent involvement: Yesterday and today. *Elementary School Journal, 91,* 209–219.

Binkard, B. (1985). A successful handicap awareness program - run by special parents. *Teaching Exceptional Children, 18,* 12–20.

Brantlinger, E. (1991). Home-school partnershipss that benefit children with special needs. *Elementary School Journal, 91,* 249–259.

Brooks, G. (1998). The effectiveness of family literacy programmes in England and Wales for parents. *Journal of Adolescent and Adult Literacy, 42,* 130–132.

Brown, D., & Moore, L. (1992). The Bama bookworm program: Motivating remedial readers to read at home with their parents. *Teaching Exceptional Children, 24,* 17–21.

Brzeinski, J. (1964). Beginning reading in Denver. *Reading Teacher, 18,* 16–22.

Cairney, T. H. (1995). Developing parent partnerships in secondary literacy learning. *Journal of Reading, 38,* 520–526.

Cohen, D. (1968). The effects of literature on vocabulary and reading achievement. *Elementary English, 45,* 209–213, 217.

Come, B., & Fredericks, A. (1995). Family literacy in urban schools: Meeting the needs of at-risk children. *Reading Teacher, 48,* 566–571.

Comer, J., & Haynes, N. I. (1991). Parent involvement in schools: An ecological approach. *Elementary School Journal, 91,* 271–277.

Cone, J.D., Delawyer, D., & Wolfe, V. (1985). Assessing parent participation: The parent/family involvement index. *Exceptional Children, 51,* 417–422.

Creekmore, W.N. (1988). Family-classroom: A critical balance. *Academic Therapy, 24,* 207–222.

Cunningham, P., & Allington, R. (1999). *Classrooms that work: They can all read and write.* New York: Addison Wesley Longman.

deBettencourt, L. (1987). How to develop parent relationships. *Teaching Exceptional Children, 19,* 26–27.

Delgado- Gaitan, C. (1991). Involving parents in the schools: a process of empowerment. *Americal Journal of Education, 100,* 20–45.

Dudley-Marling, C. (1989). Role of parents in children's literacy development: Collaborating with parents of exceptional children. *The Pointer, 33,* 16–19.

Durkin, D. (1986). *Children who read early.* New York: Teachers College Press.

Edwards, P. (1995). Empowering low-income mothers and fathers to share books with young children. *Reading Teacher, 48,* 558–563.

Feitelson, D., & Goldstein, Z. (1986). Patterns of book ownership and reading to young children in Israeli school-oriented and nonschool-oriented families. *Reading Teacher, 39,* 924–930.

Flood, J., Lapp, D., Tinajero, J., & Nagel, G. (1995). I never knew I was needed until you called!: Promoting parent involvement in schools. *Reading Teacher, 48,* 614–617.

Fox, M. (1988). *Koala Lou.* San Diego, CA: Harcourt Brace Jovanovich.

Fuqua, R. W., Hegland, S. M., & Karas, S. C. (1985). Processes influencing linkages between preschool handicap classrooms and home. *Exceptional Child, 51,* 307–314.

Glazer, S., & Burke, E. (1994). *An integrated approach to early literacy.* Needham, MA: Allyn & Bacon.

Hannon, P. W. & Cuckle, P. (1984). Involving parents in the teaching of reading: A study of current school practice. *Educational Research, 26,* 7–19.

Hansen, H. (1969). The impact of the home literary environment on reading attitude. *Elementary English, 46,* 17–24.

Heath, S. B. (1983). *Ways with words: Language, life and work in community and classrooms.* Cambridge, UK: Cambridge University Press.

Hopson, S., & Donovan, H. (1996, March). *Paired Reading Workshop.* Paper presented at the meeting of the New Jersey Reading Association, New Brunswick, NJ.

Karnes, M., Teska, J., Hodgind, A., & Badger, E. (1970). Educational intervention at home by mothers of disadvantaged infants. *Child Development, 41,* 925–935.

Kunhardt, D. (1984). *Pat the Bunny.* Racine, WI: Western Publishing Co.

Levenstein, P. (1970). Cognitive growth in preschoolers through verbal interaction with mothers. *American Journal of Orthopsychiatry, 40,* 426–432.

Lombardino, L., & Mangan, N. (1983). Parents as language trainers: Language programming with developmentally delayed children. *Exceptional Children, 49,* 358–361.

McBride-Chang, C., Manis, F. R., Seidenberg, M. S., Custodio, R. G., & Doi, L. M. (1991). Print exposure as a predictor of word reading and reading comprehension in disabled and nondisabled readers. *Journal of Educational Psychology, 85,* 230–238.

McQuillan, J. (1999). *The Literacy crisis: False claims, real solutions.* Portsmouth, NH: Heinemann.

Meyer, C.E., & Blacher, J. (1987). Parents' perceptions of schooling for severely handicapped children: home and family variables. *Exceptional Children, 53,* 441–450.

Miller, W. (1969). Home pre-reading experiences. *Reading Teacher 22,* 641–646.

Morrow, L. (1993). *Literacy development in the early years.* Needham, MA: Allyn & Bacon.

Morrow, L.M., & Paratore, J. (1993). Family literacy: Perspectives and practices. *The Reading Teacher, 47,* 194–201.

National Research Council (1998). *Preventing reading difficulties in young children.* Washington, DC: National Academy Press.

Ollila, L., & Mayfield, M. (1992). Home and school together: Helping beginning readers succeed. In S. J. Samuels and A. E. Farstrup (Eds.), *What research has to say about reading instruction* (2nd ed.). Newark, De: International Reading Association.

Piper, W. (1979). *The little engine that could.* New York: Scholastic.

Polloway, E. A., & Patton, J. R. (1993). *Strategies for teaching learners with special needs.* New York: Macmillan.

Rasinski, T., & Padak, N. (1996). *Holistic reading strategies: Teaching children who find reading difficult.* Upper Saddle River, NJ: Prentice-Hall.

Routman, RT. (1996). *Literacy at the crossroads: Crucial talk about reading, writing, and other teaching dilemmas.* Portmouth, NH: Heinemann.

Rudman, H. (1956). Parents and their children's reading interests. *Reading Teacher, 10,* 26–32.

Scanlon, C., Arick, J., & Phelps, N. (1981). Participation in the development of IEP: Parents's perspective. *Exceptional Children, 47,* 373–375.

Smith, T. E. C., Polloway, E. A., Patton, J. R., & Dowdy, C. A. (1995). *Teaching students with special needs in inclusive settings.* Needham Heights, MA: Allyn & Bacon.

Symons, S., Szuszkiewicz, T., & Bonnell, C. (1996). Parental print exposure and young childrens's language and literacy skills. *Alberta Journal of Educational Research, 42,* 49–58.

Taylor, D. (1983). *Family Literacy: Young children learning to read and write.* Portsmouth, NH: Heinemann.

Topping, K. (1987). Paired reading: A powerful technique for parent use. *The Reading Teacher, 40,* 608–614.

Topping, K. (1989). Peer tutoring and paired reading: Combining two powerful techniques. *The Reading Teacher, 42,* 488–494.

Thurston, L. (1989). Helping parents tutor their children: A success story. *Academic Therapy: 24,* 579–587.

Turnbull, A., & Turnbull, R., Shank, M., & Leal, D. (1999). *Exceptional lives: Special education in today's schools.* Upper Saddle River, NJ: Merrill/Prentice Hall.

Turnbull, A., Turnbull, H. R. (1986). *Families, professionals, and exceptionality: A special partnership* (4th ed.). Upper Saddle River, NJ: Merrill/Prentice Hall.

Weikart, D. (1975, April). *Parent involvement: progress and result of the High/Scope Foundations' projects.* April '75. Paper presented at the meeting of the Society for Research in Child Development, Denver, CO.

Yaffe, D., & Williams, C. L. (1998). Why women chose to participate in a family literacy program and factors that contributed to the program's success. *Journal of Adolescent & Adult Literacy, 42,* 8–19.

Yanok, J., & DeRubertis, D. (1989). Comparative study of parental participation in regular and special education programs. *Exceptional Children, 56,* 195–199.

Index